MOBILE SUIT GUNDAM
THUNDERBOLT 8

VIZ Signature Edition

STORY AND ART **YASUO OHTAGAKI**
Original Concept by **HAJIME YATATE** and **YOSHIYUKI TOMINO**

Translation **JOE YAMAZAKI**
English Adaptation **STAN!**
Touch-up Art & Lettering **EVAN WALDINGER**
Cover & Design **SHAWN CARRICO**
Editor **MIKE MONTESA**

MOBILE SUIT GUNDAM THUNDERBOLT Vol. 8 by Yasuo OHTAGAKI
Original Concept by Hajime YATATE, Yoshiyuki TOMINO
© 2012 Yasuo OHTAGAKI
© SOTSU·SUNRISE
All rights reserved.
Original Japanese edition published by SHOGAKUKAN.
English translation rights in the United States of America,
Canada, the United Kingdom, Ireland, Australia and New Zealand
arranged with SHOGAKUKAN.

ORIGINAL COVER DESIGN / Yoshiyuki SEKI for VOLARE inc.

EDITORIAL COOPERATION / Shinsuke Hiraishi

Printed in the U.S.A.

Published by VIZ Media, LLC
P.O. Box 77010
San Francisco, CA 94107

10 9 8 7 6 5 4 3 2 1
First printing, August 2018

viz.com   **VIZ SIGNATURE**
vizsignature.com

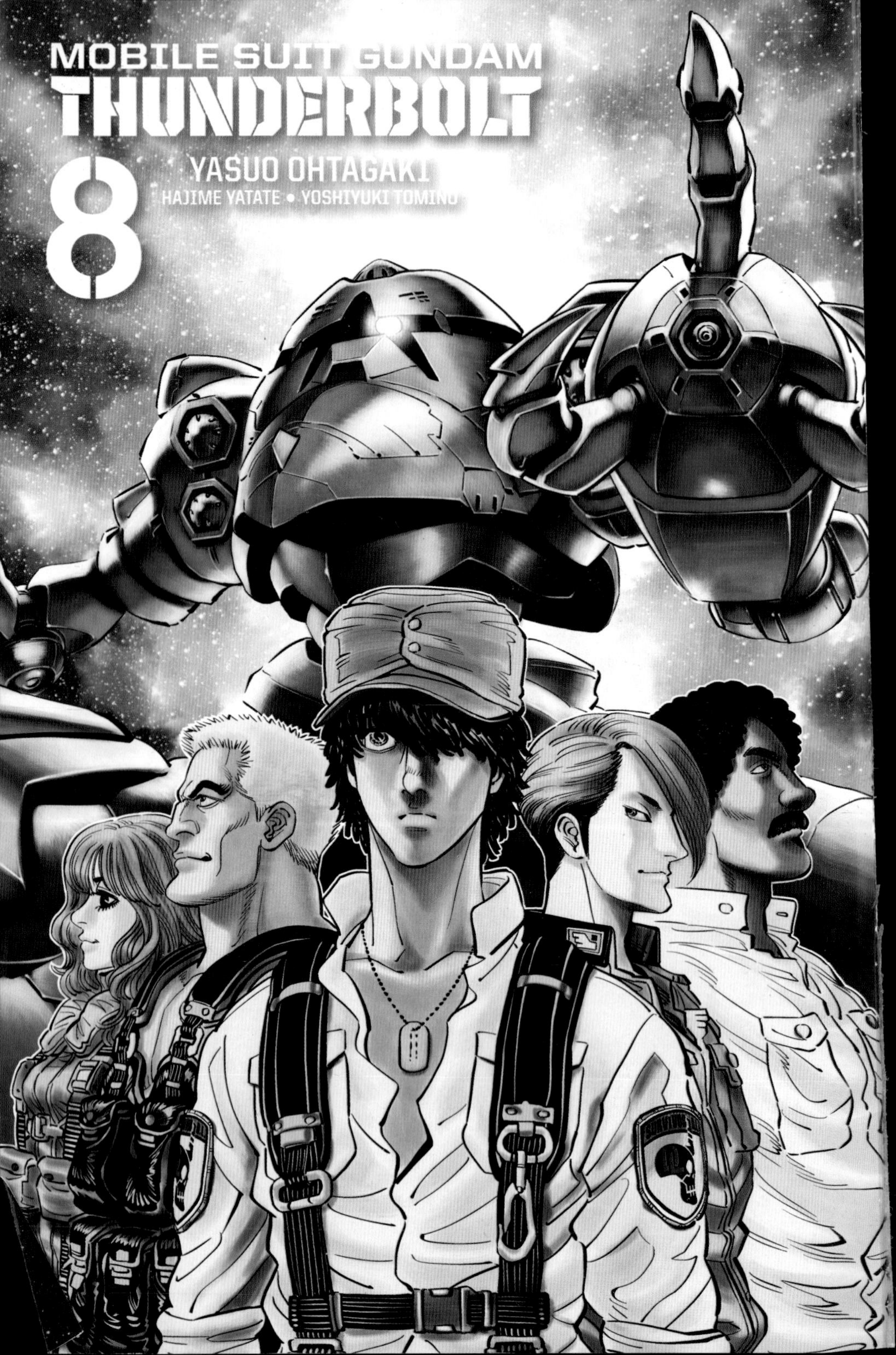
MOBILE SUIT GUNDAM
THUNDERBOLT
8
YASUO OHTAGAKI
HAJIME YATATE • YOSHIYUKI TOMINO

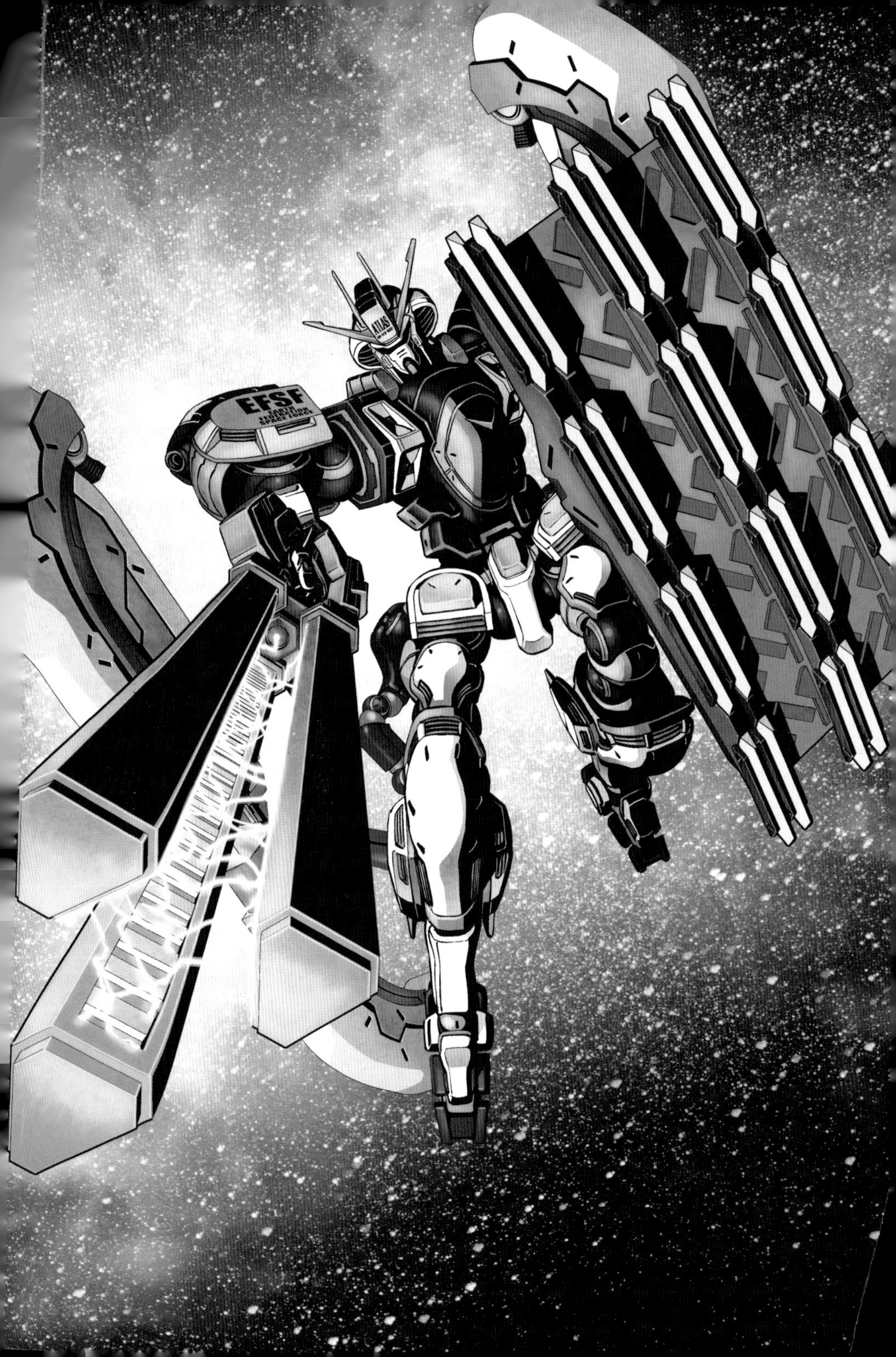
ATLAS
EFSF
EARTH FEDERATION SPACE FORCE

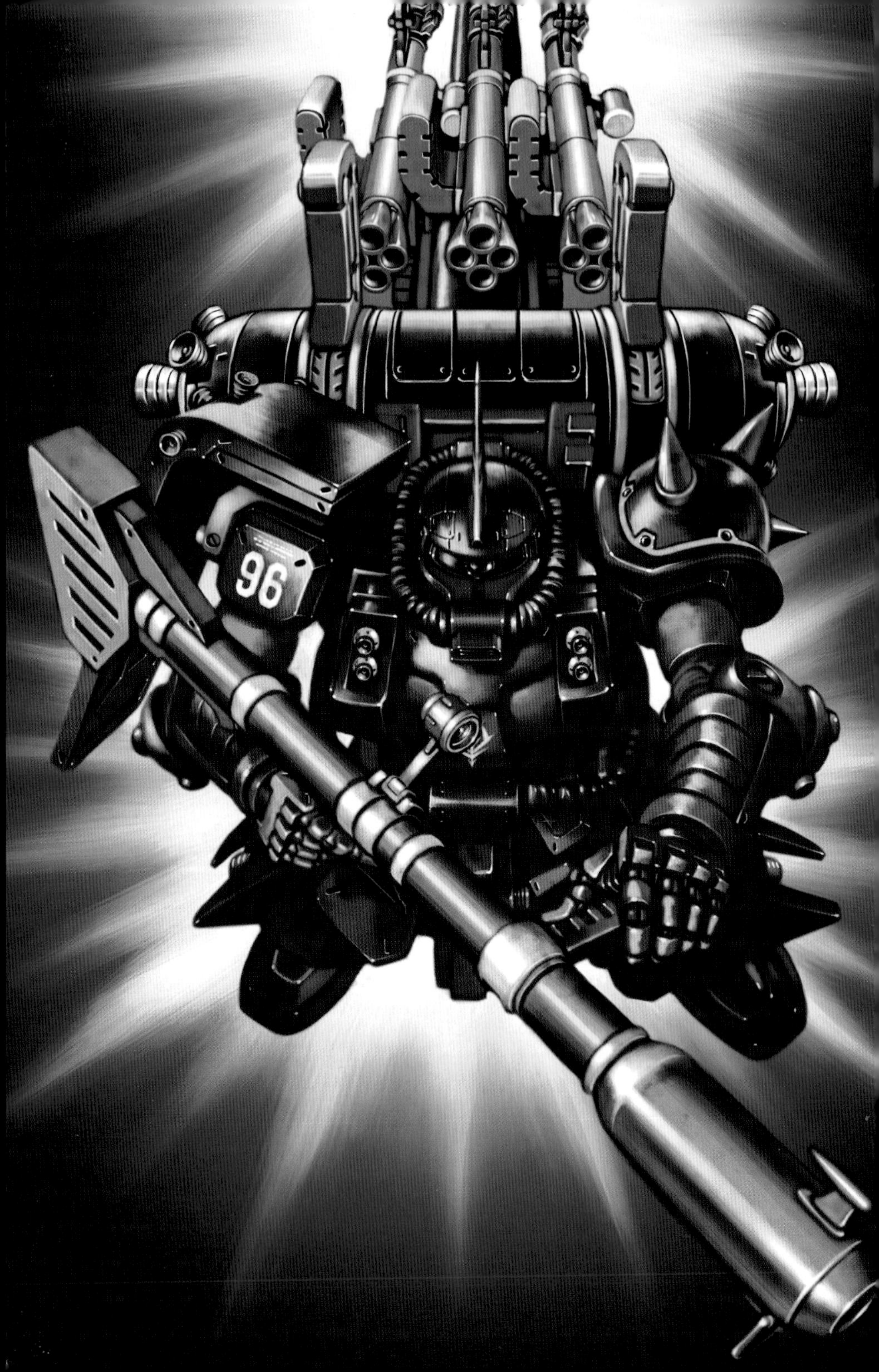
96

MOBILE SUIT GUNDAM
THUNDERBOLT

8

CHAPTER 62
...005...

CHAPTER 63
...029...

CHAPTER 64
...053...

CHAPTER 65
...077...

CHAPTER 66
...101...

CHAPTER 67
...129...

CHAPTER 68
...153...

CHAPTER 69
...177...

CHAPTER 70
...201...

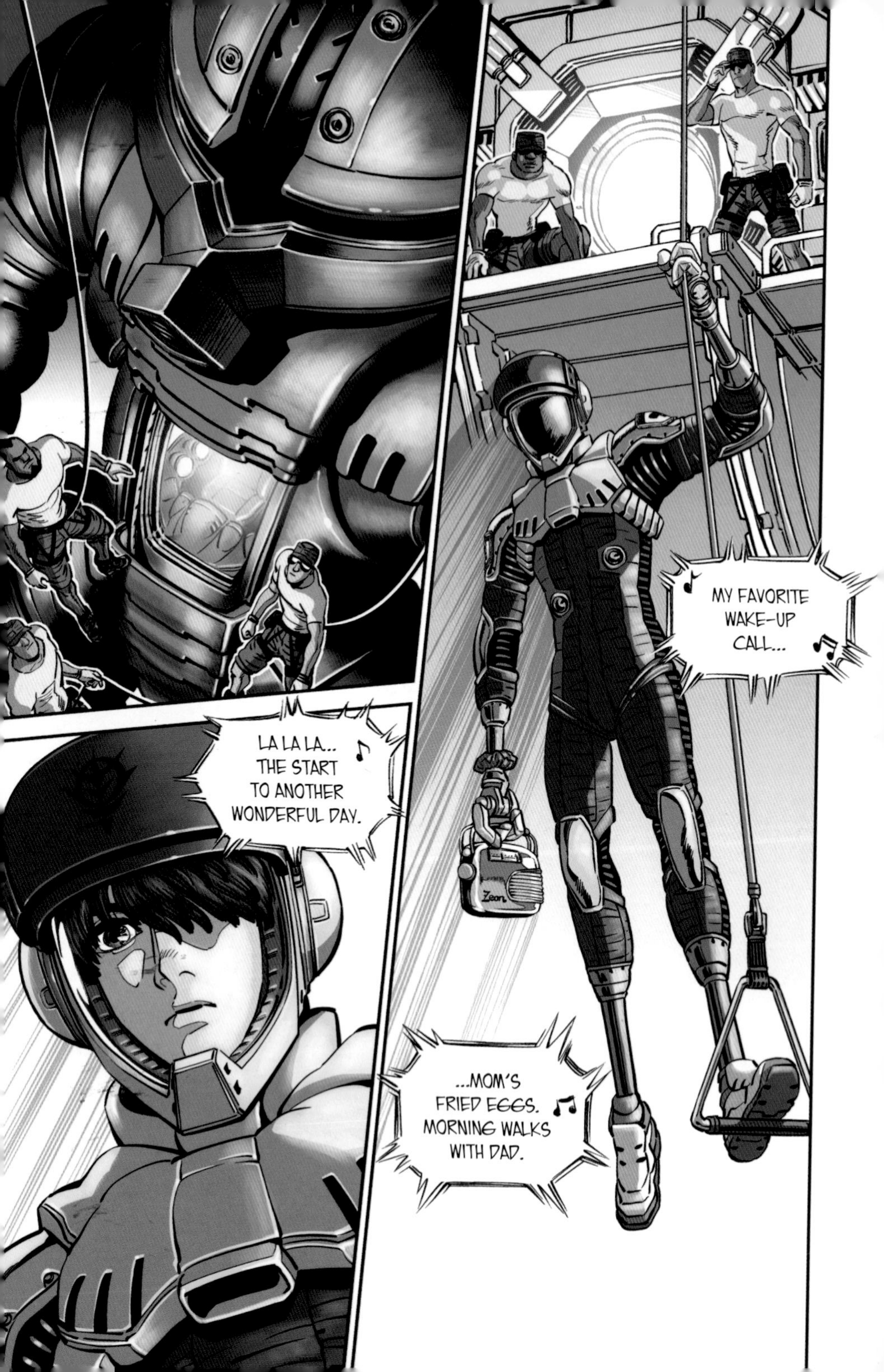
MY FAVORITE WAKE-UP CALL...
Zeon
...MOM'S FRIED EGGS. MORNING WALKS WITH DAD.
LA LA LA... THE START TO ANOTHER WONDERFUL DAY.

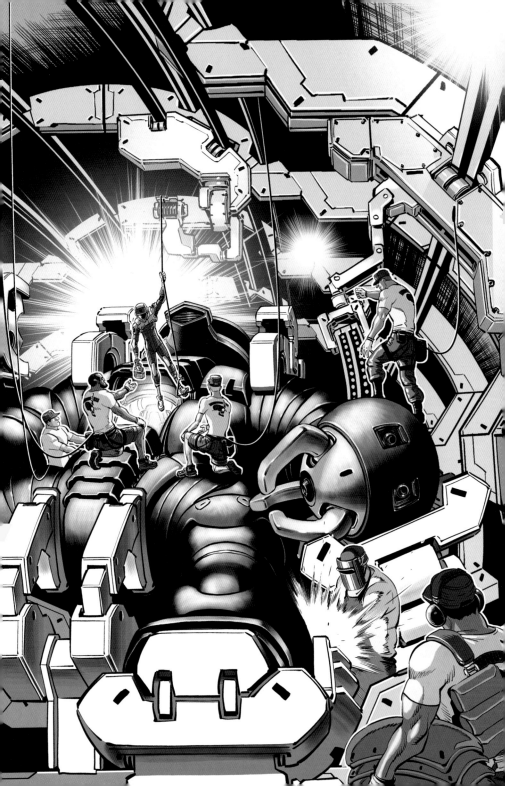

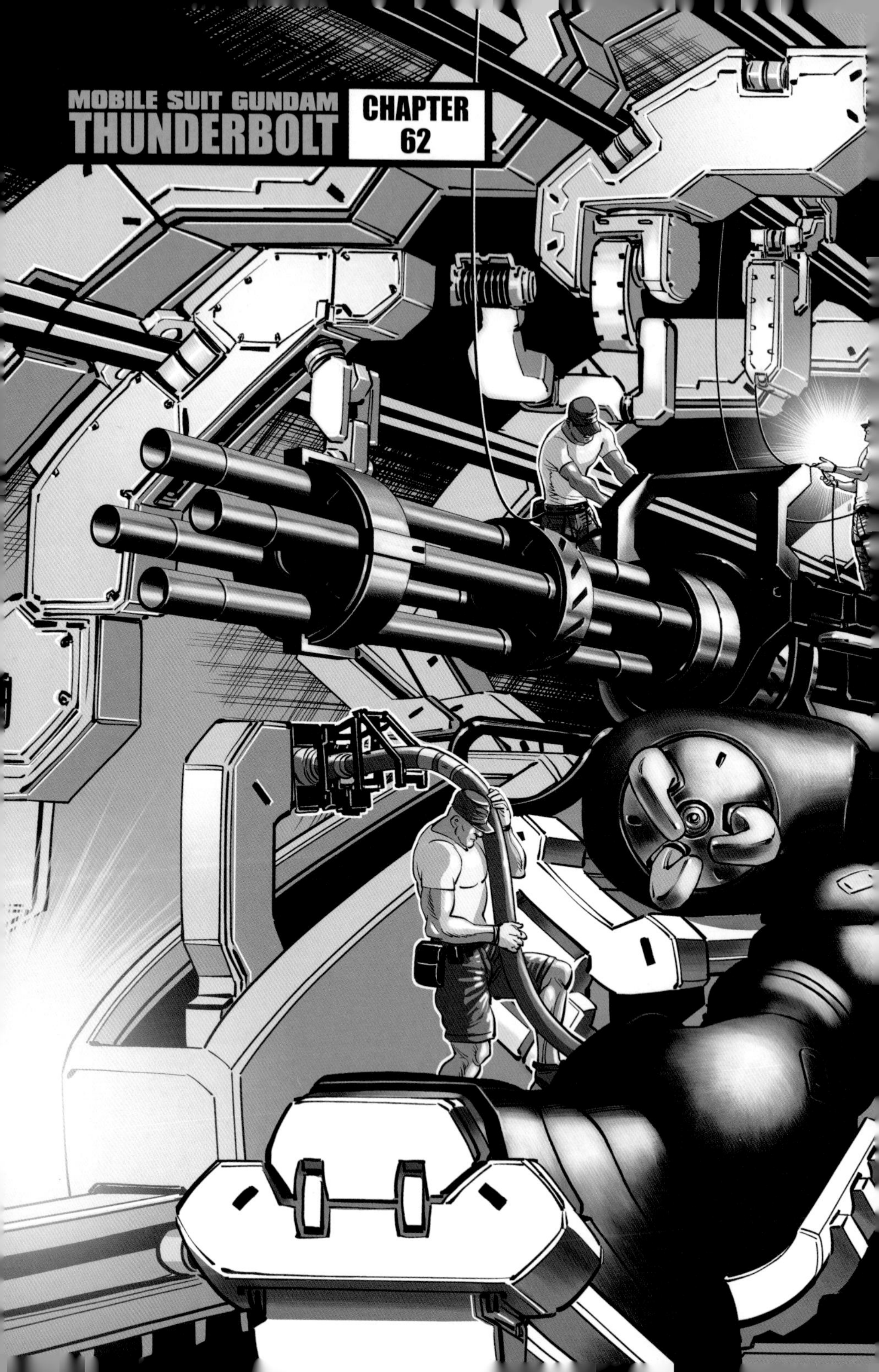
MOBILE SUIT GUNDAM
THUNDERBOLT
CHAPTER
62

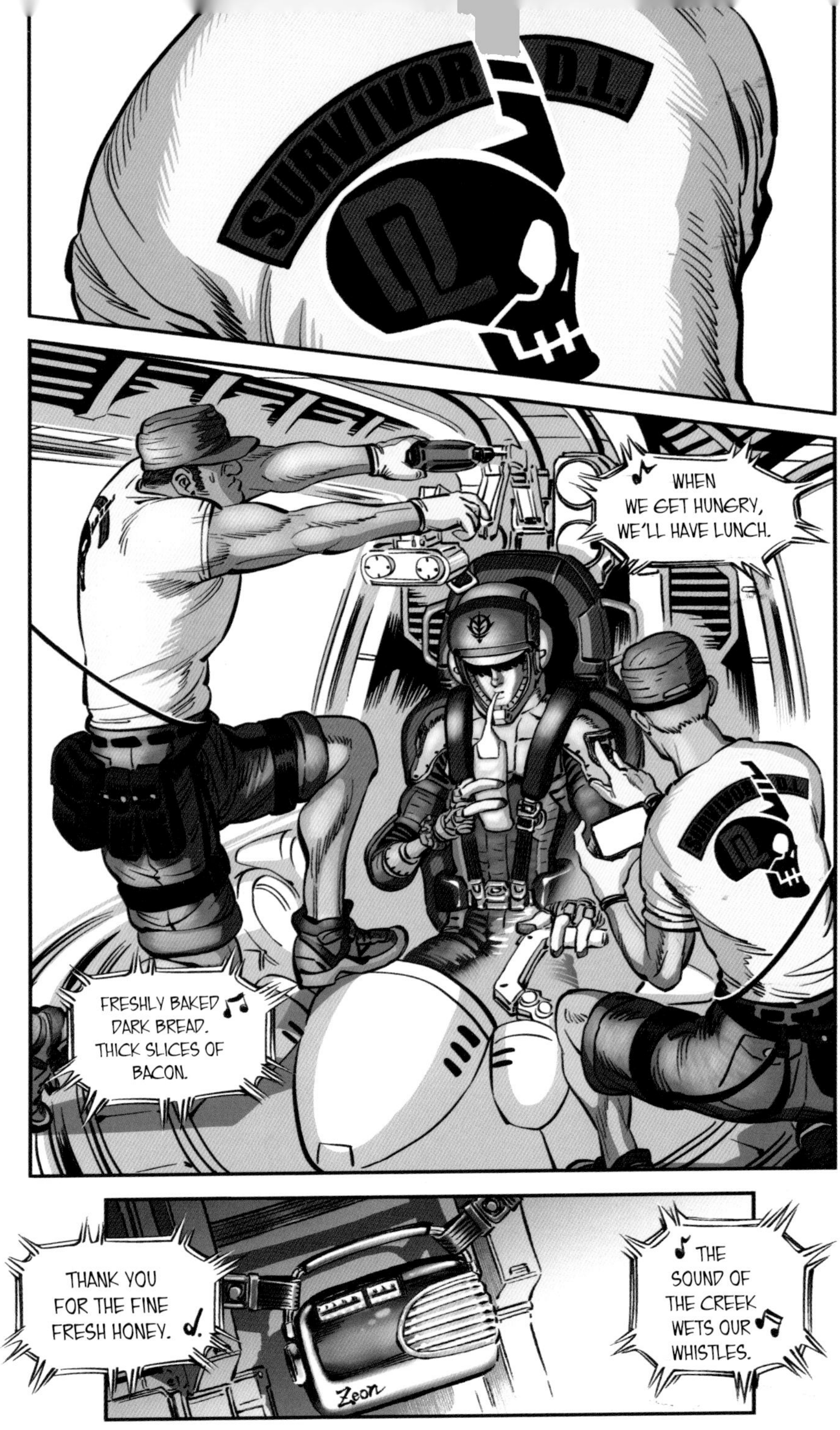
SURVIVOR D.L.
WHEN WE GET HUNGRY, WE'LL HAVE LUNCH.
FRESHLY BAKED DARK BREAD. THICK SLICES OF BACON.
THE SOUND OF THE CREEK WETS OUR WHISTLES.
THANK YOU FOR THE FINE FRESH HONEY.
Zeon

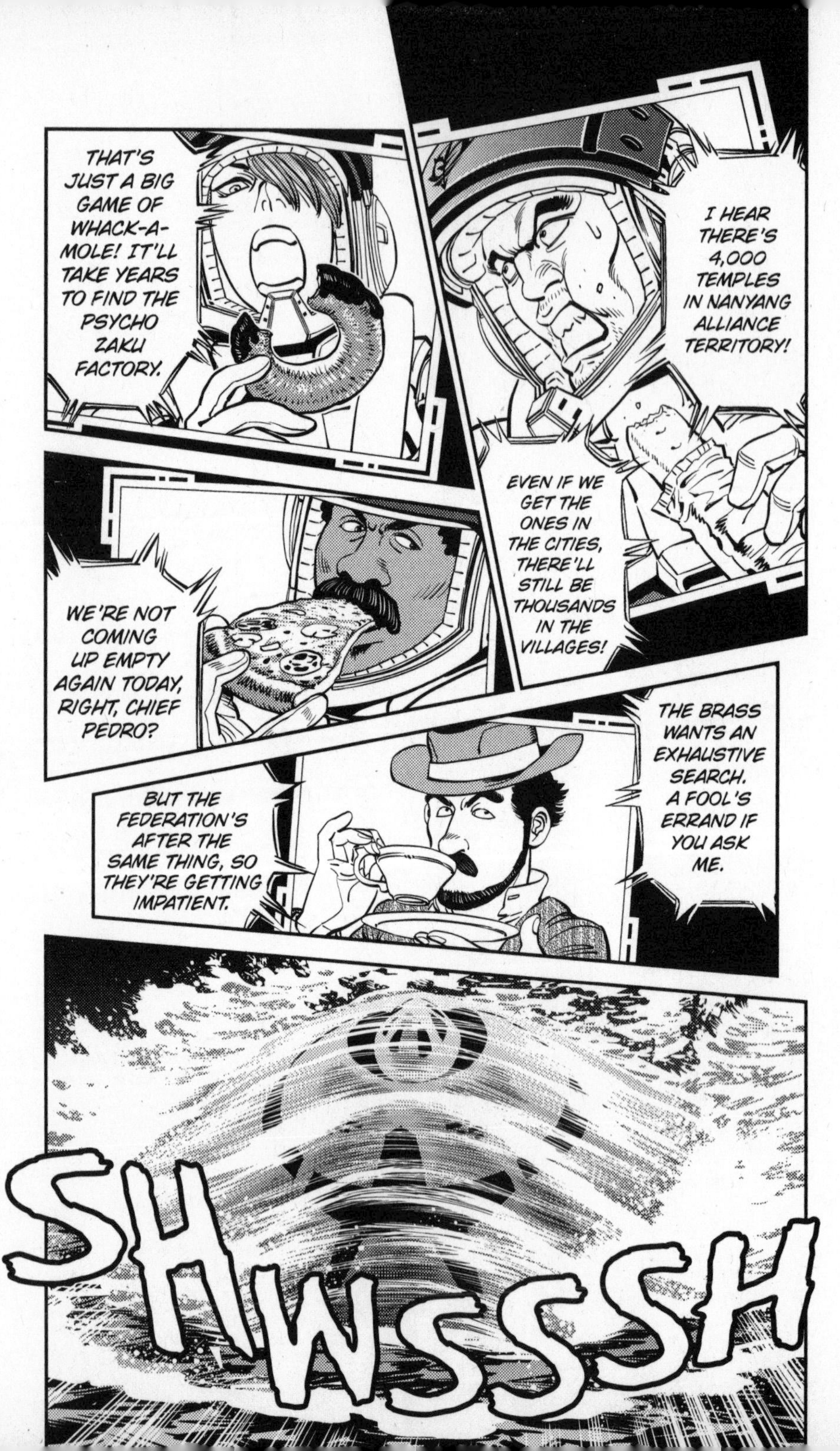
I HEAR THERE'S 4,000 TEMPLES IN NANYANG ALLIANCE TERRITORY!
EVEN IF WE GET THE ONES IN THE CITIES, THERE'LL STILL BE THOUSANDS IN THE VILLAGES!
THAT'S JUST A BIG GAME OF WHACK-A-MOLE! IT'LL TAKE YEARS TO FIND THE PSYCHO ZAKU FACTORY.
WE'RE NOT COMING UP EMPTY AGAIN TODAY, RIGHT, CHIEF PEDRO?
THE BRASS WANTS AN EXHAUSTIVE SEARCH. A FOOL'S ERRAND IF YOU ASK ME.
BUT THE FEDERATION'S AFTER THE SAME THING, SO THEY'RE GETTING IMPATIENT.
SHWSSSH

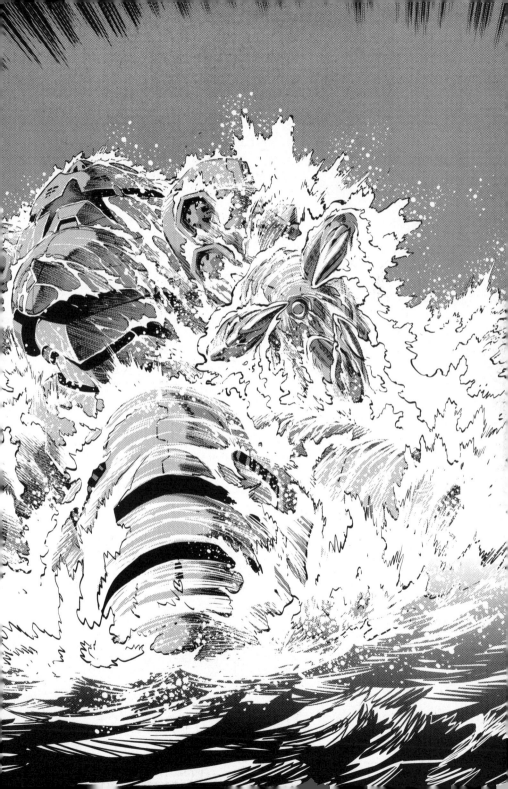

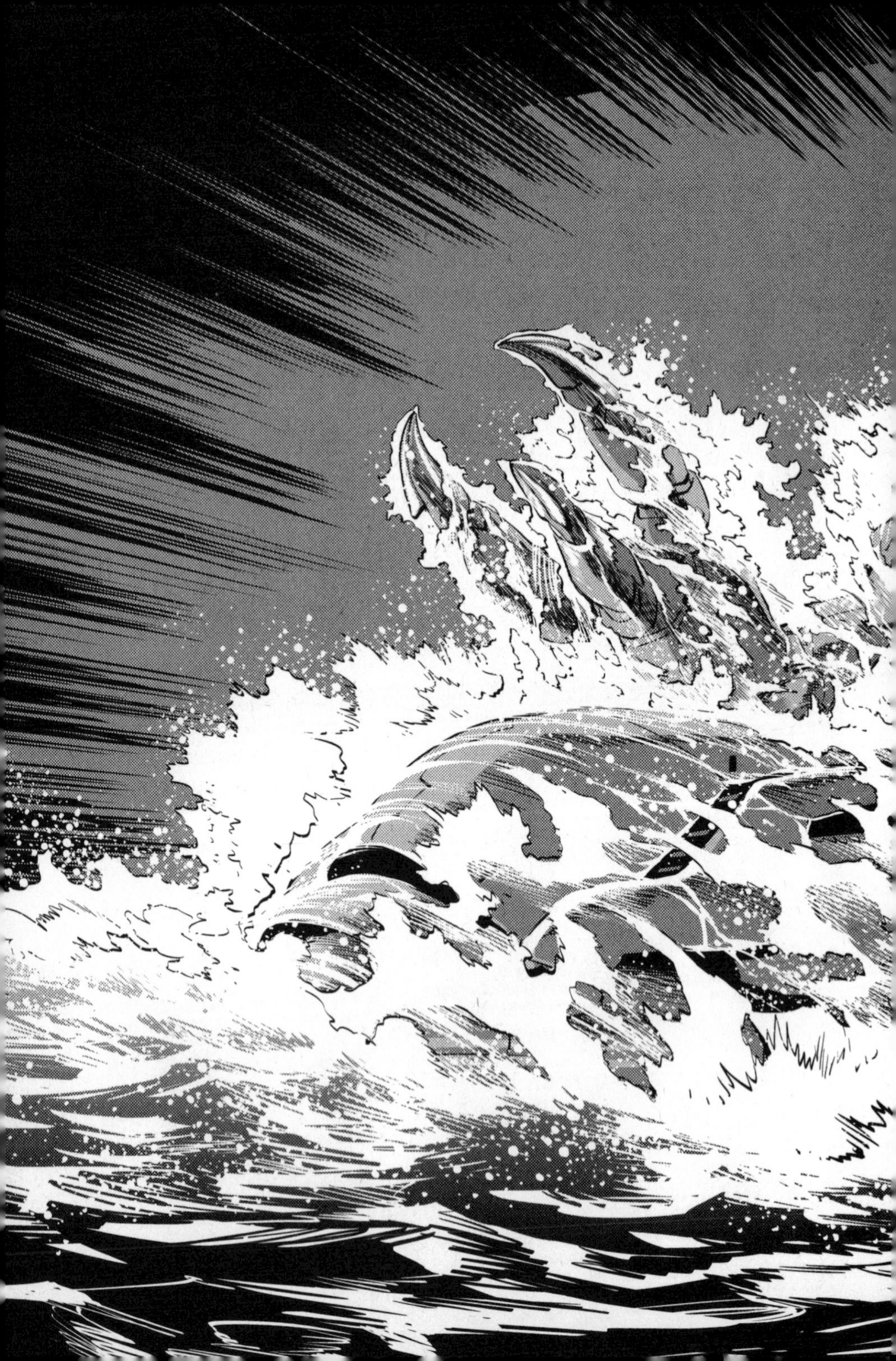

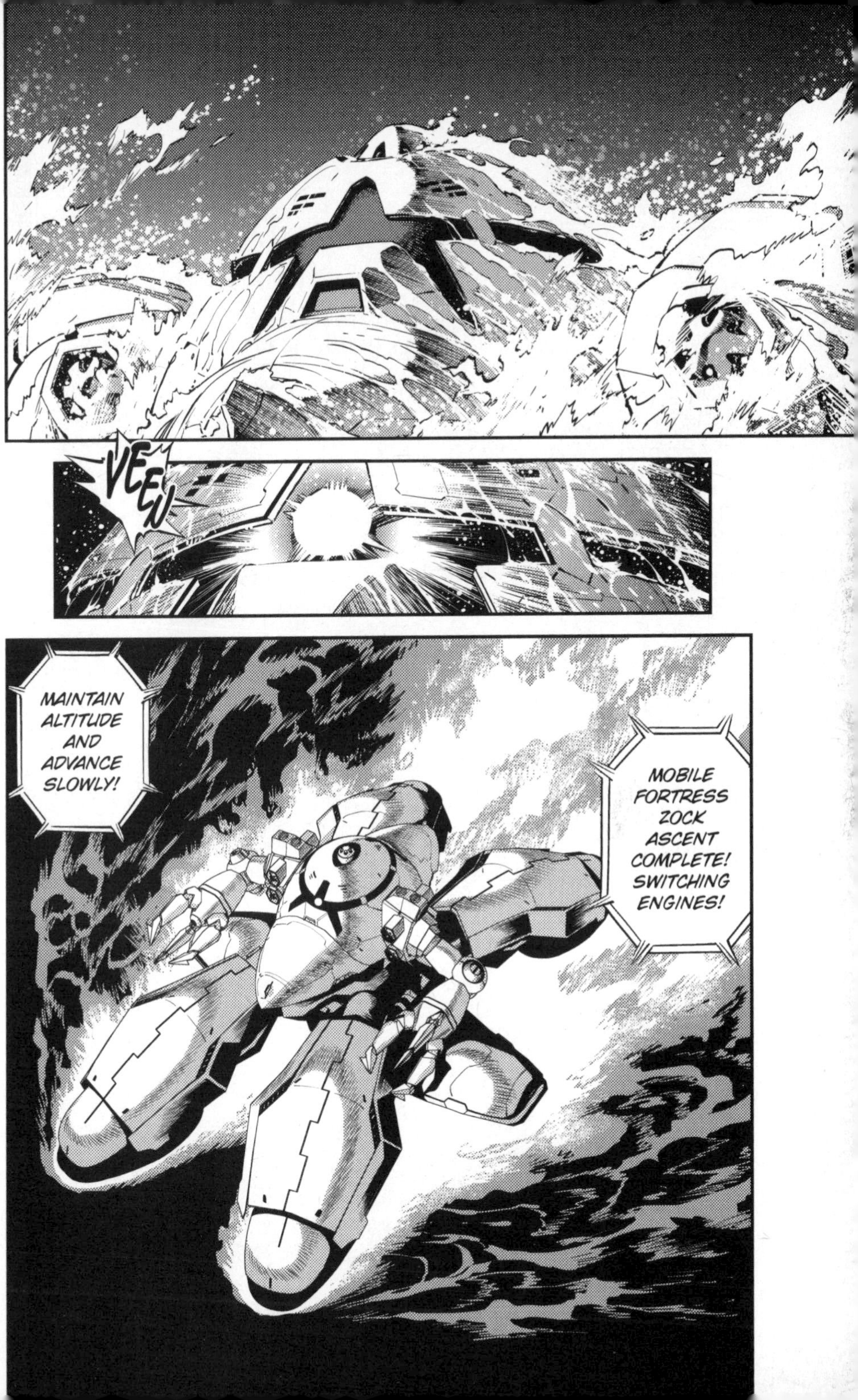
VEEW
MOBILE FORTRESS ZOCK ASCENT COMPLETE! SWITCHING ENGINES!
MAINTAIN ALTITUDE AND ADVANCE SLOWLY!

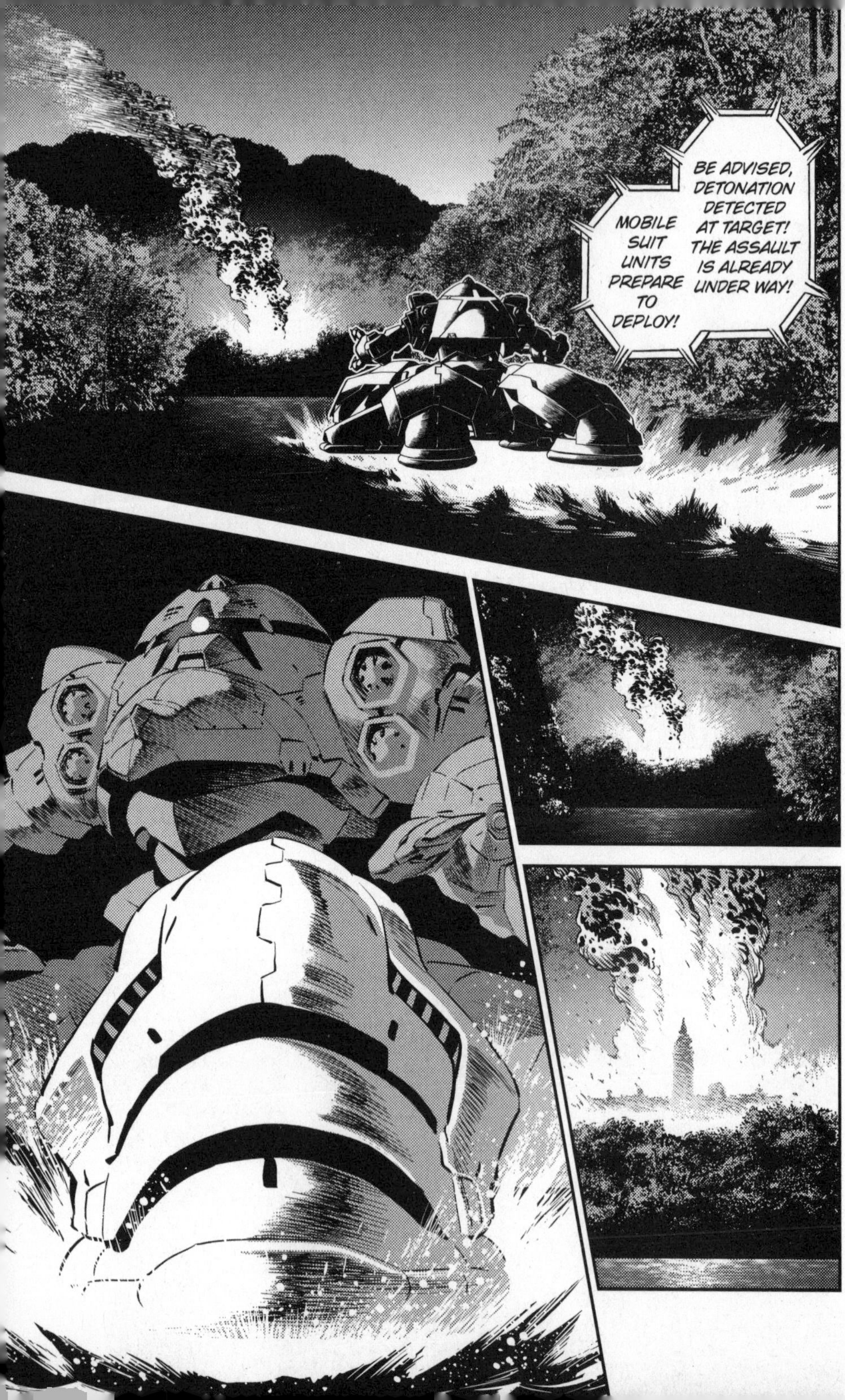
BE ADVISED, DETONATION DETECTED AT TARGET! THE ASSAULT IS ALREADY UNDER WAY!
MOBILE SUIT UNITS PREPARE TO DEPLOY!

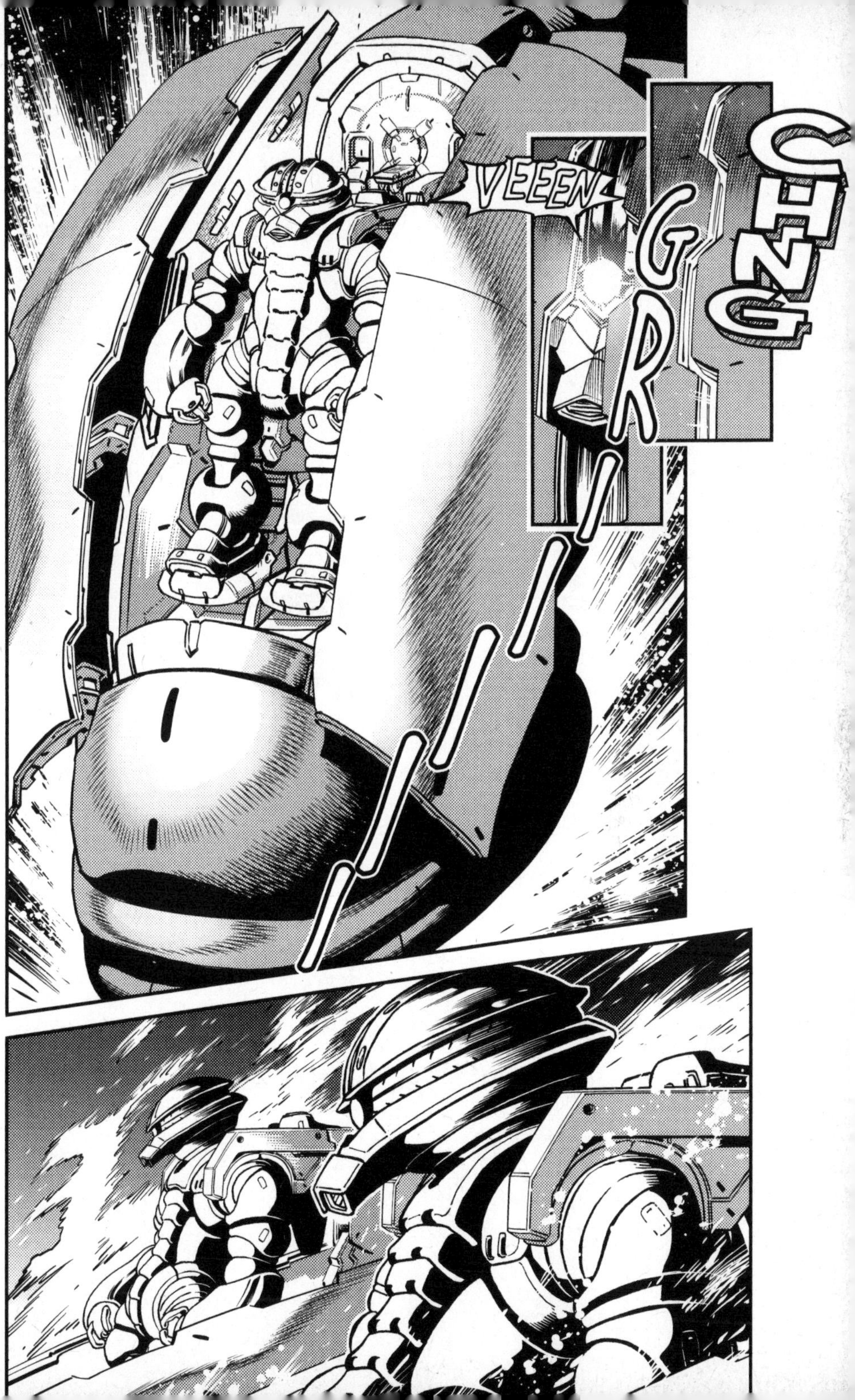
CHNG
GRR
VEEEN

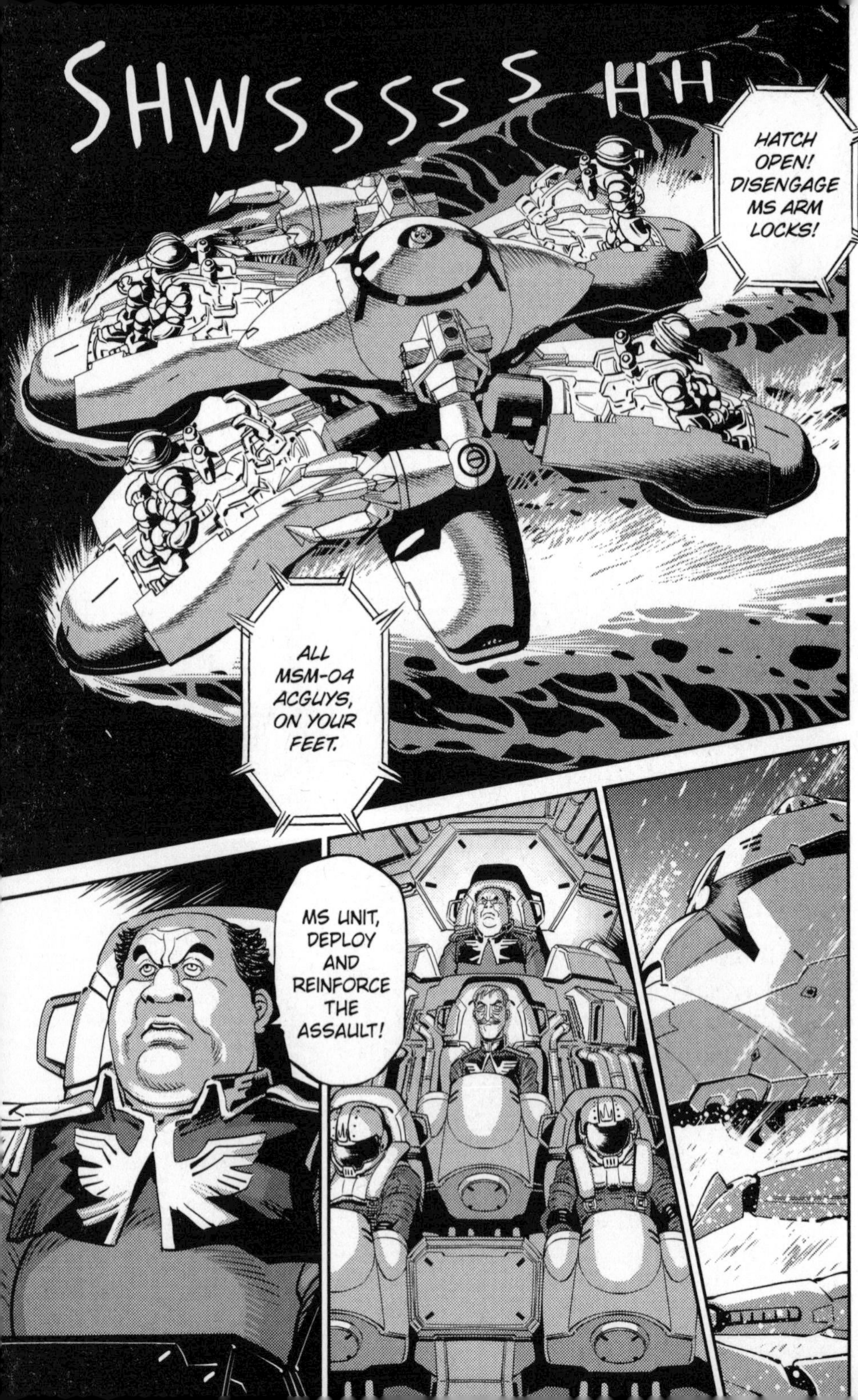
SHWSSSSS HH
HATCH OPEN! DISENGAGE MS ARM LOCKS!
ALL MSM-04 ACGUYS, ON YOUR FEET.
MS UNIT, DEPLOY AND REINFORCE THE ASSAULT!

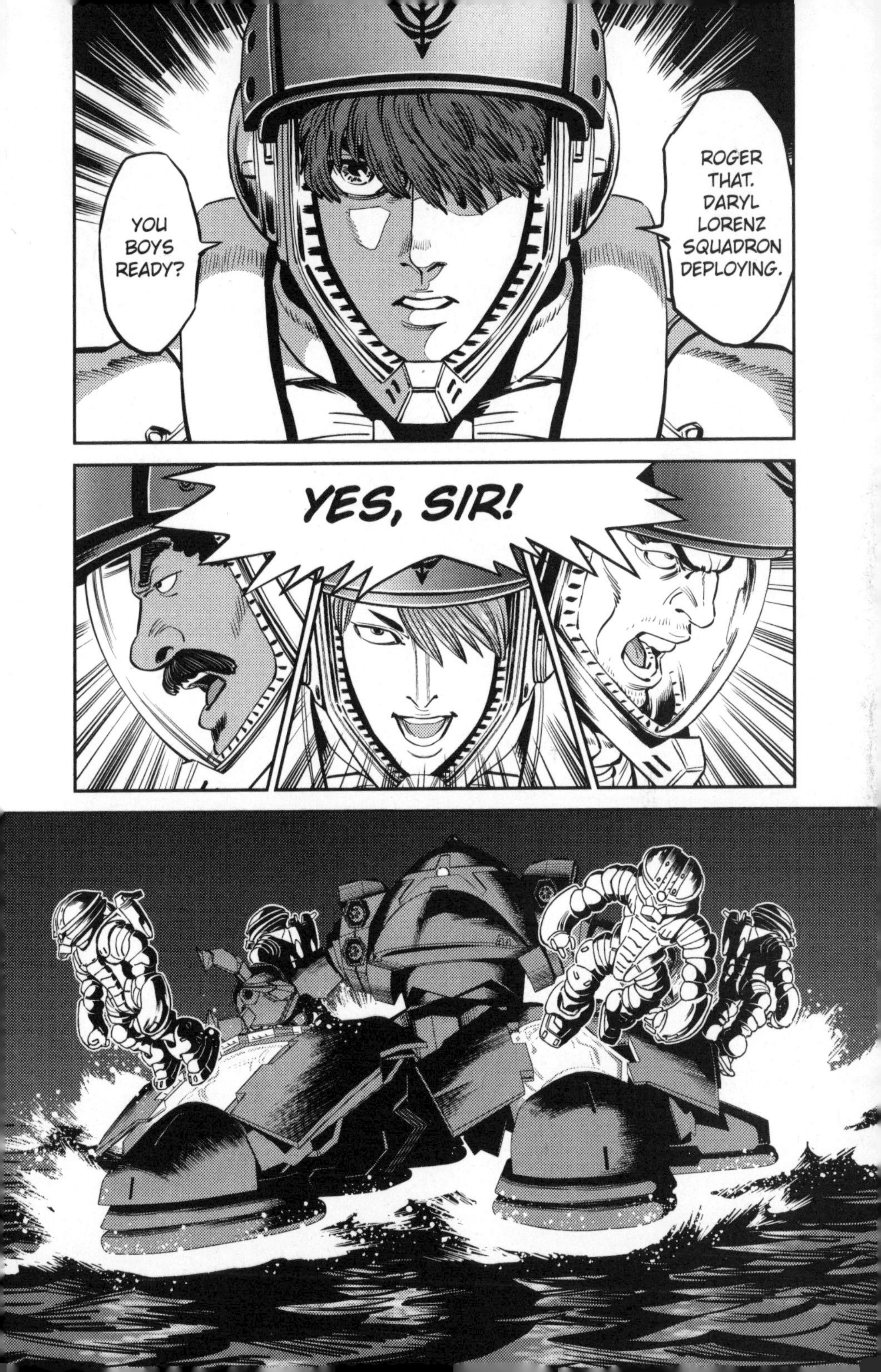
ROGER THAT. DARYL LORENZ SQUADRON DEPLOYING.
YOU BOYS READY?
YES, SIR!

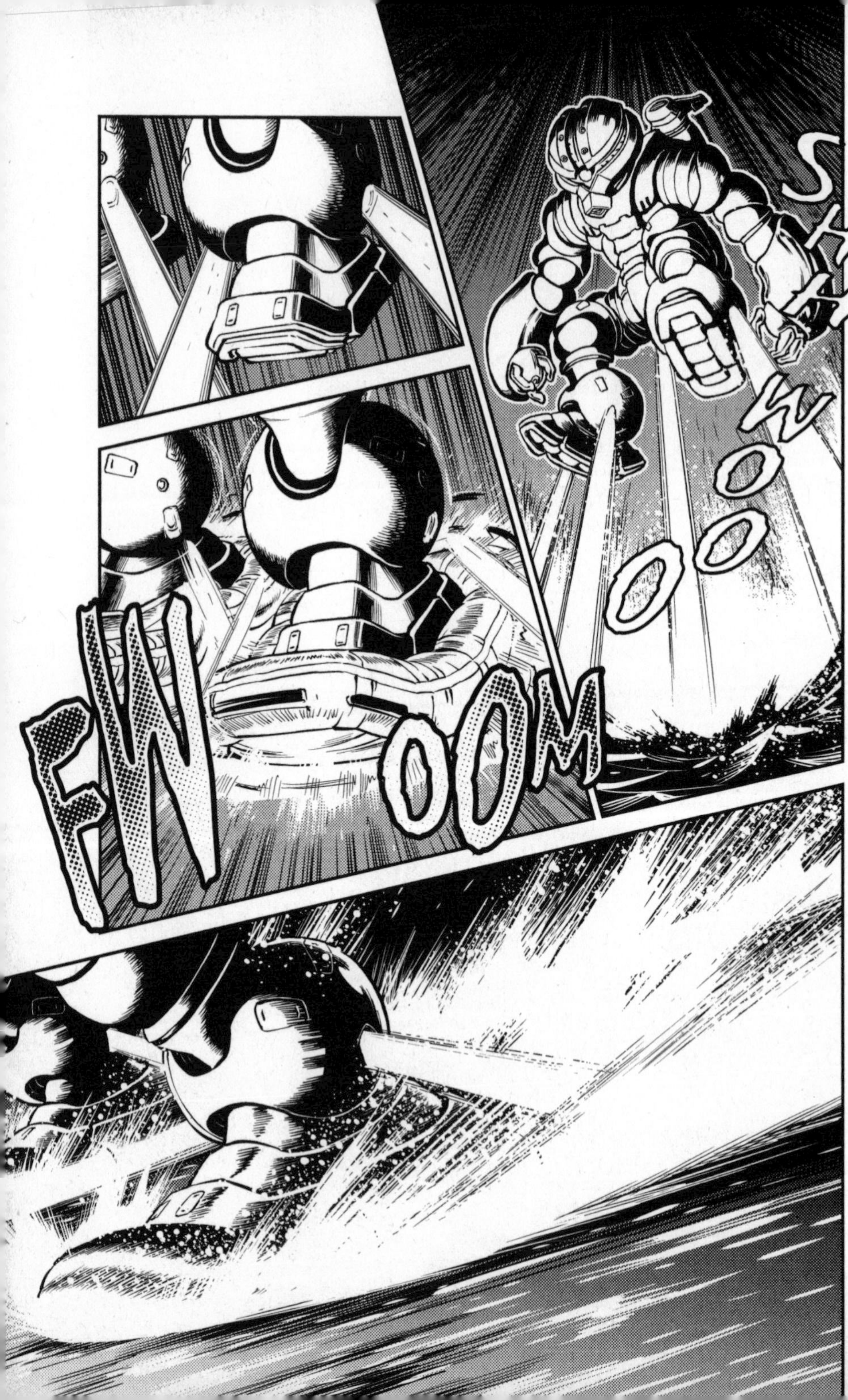
SHHWOOO
FWOOM

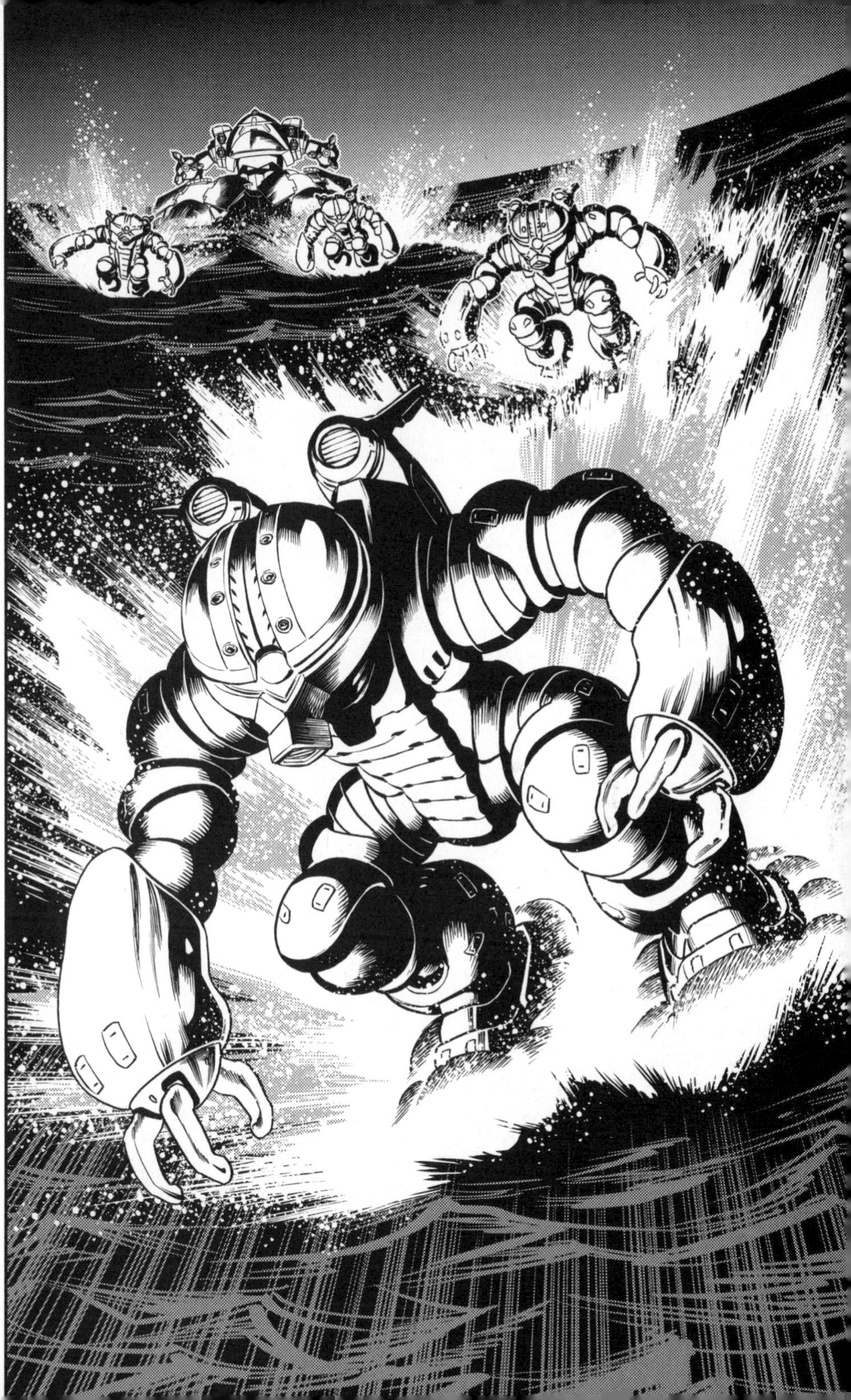

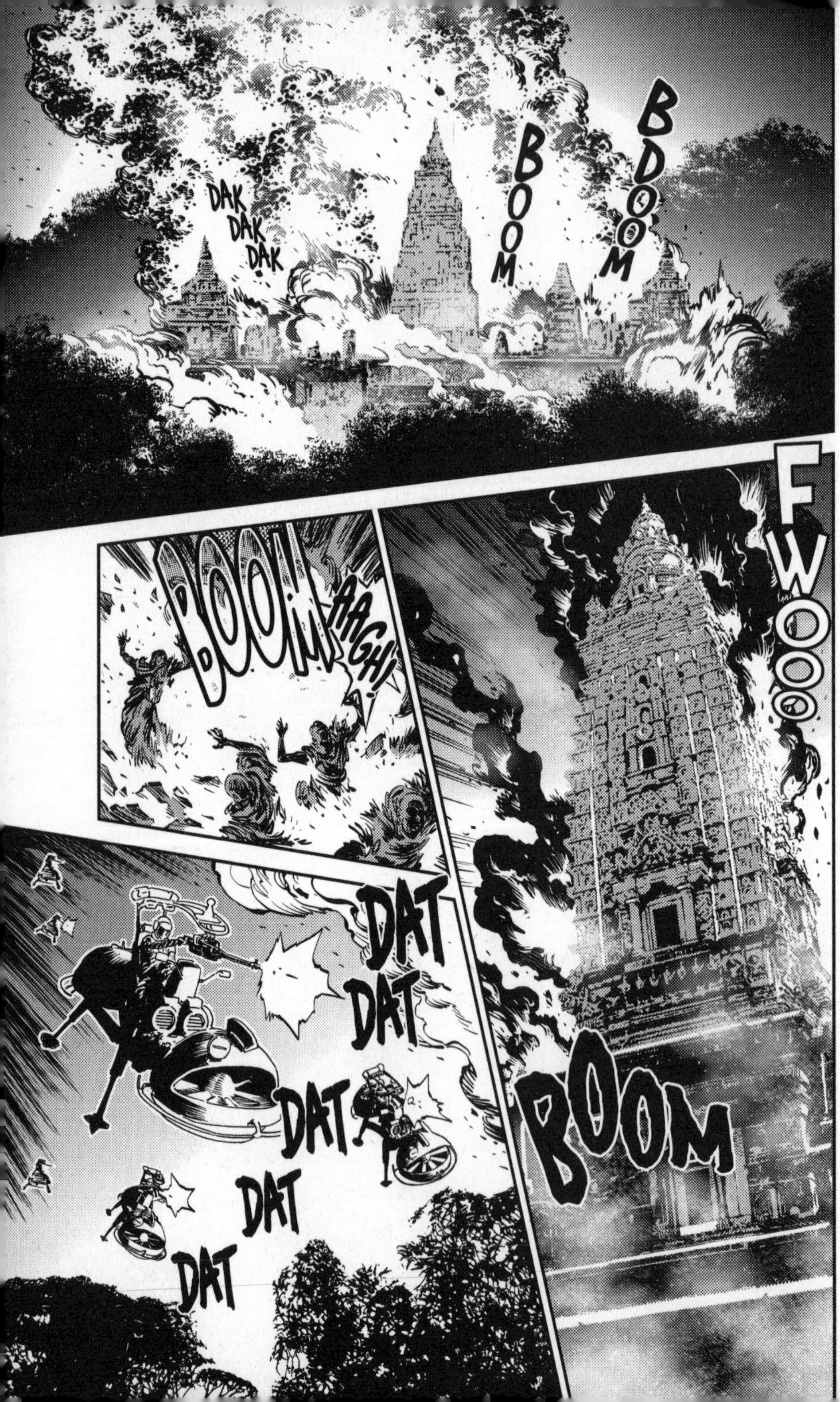
BDOOM
BOOM
DAK DAK DAK
FWOOO
BOOM
BOOM
AAGH!
DAT DAT DAT DAT DAT

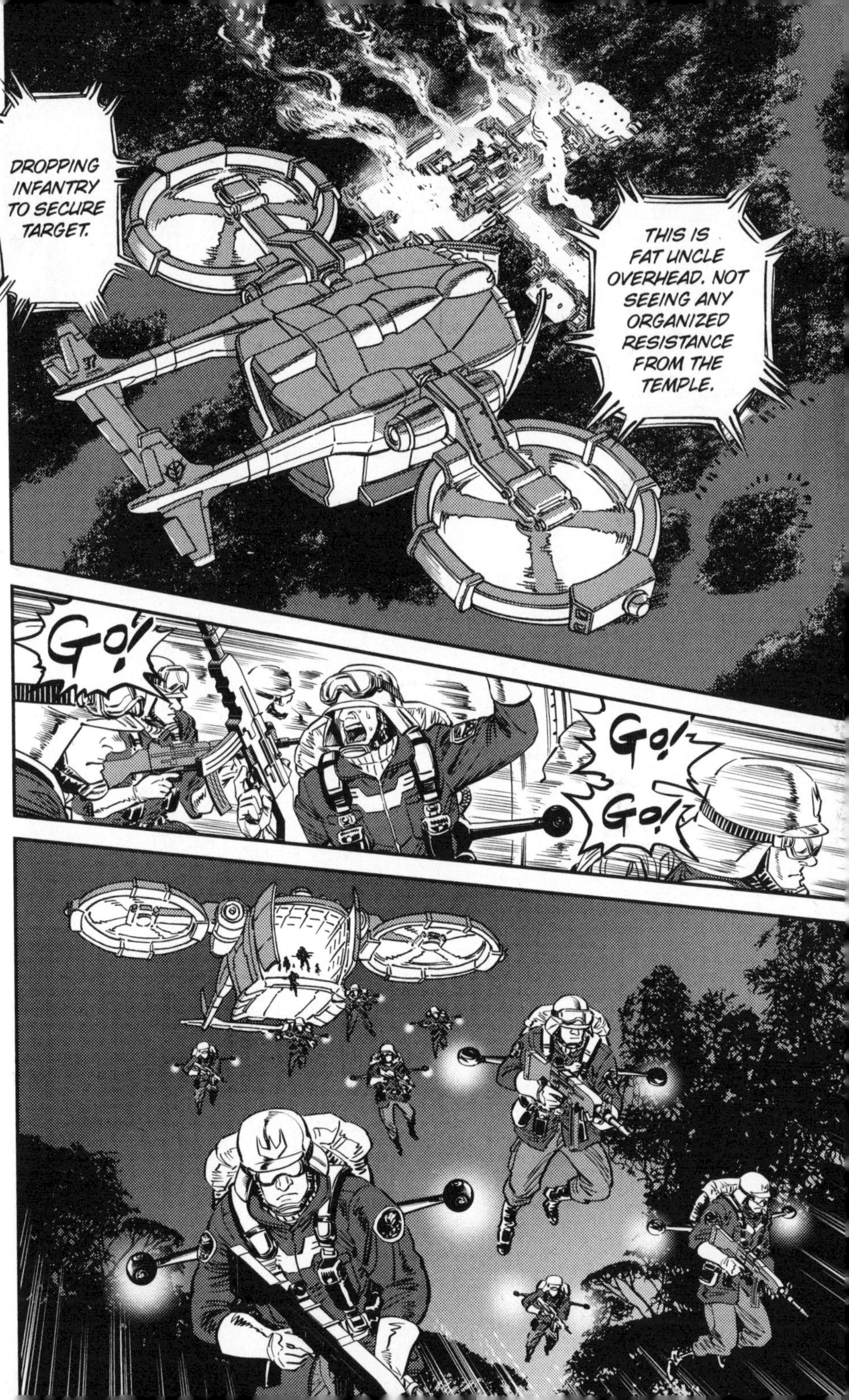
THIS IS FAT UNCLE OVERHEAD. NOT SEEING ANY ORGANIZED RESISTANCE FROM THE TEMPLE.
DROPPING INFANTRY TO SECURE TARGET.
GO!
GO!
GO!

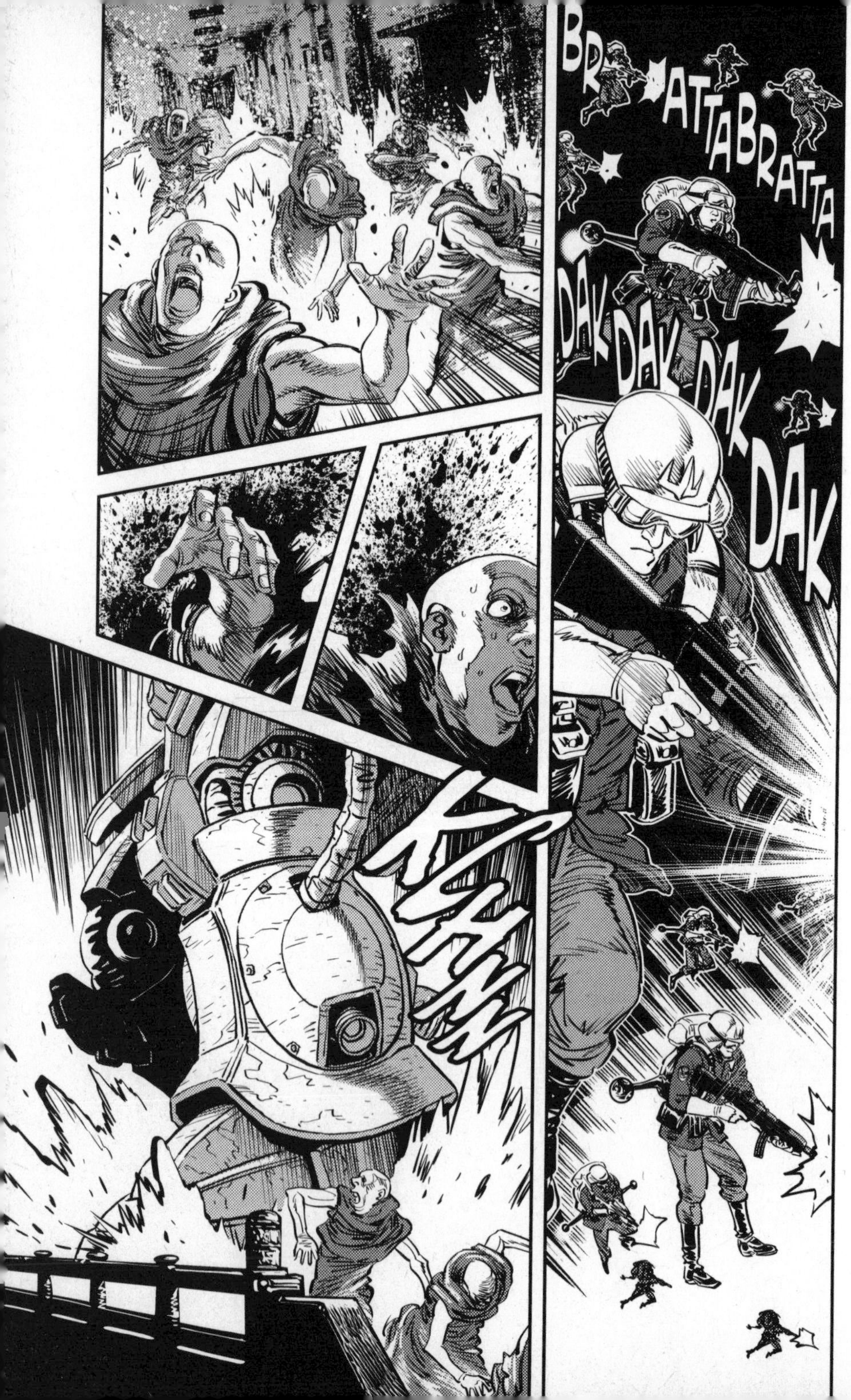
BR
ATTABRATTA
DAK DAK DAK DAK DAK

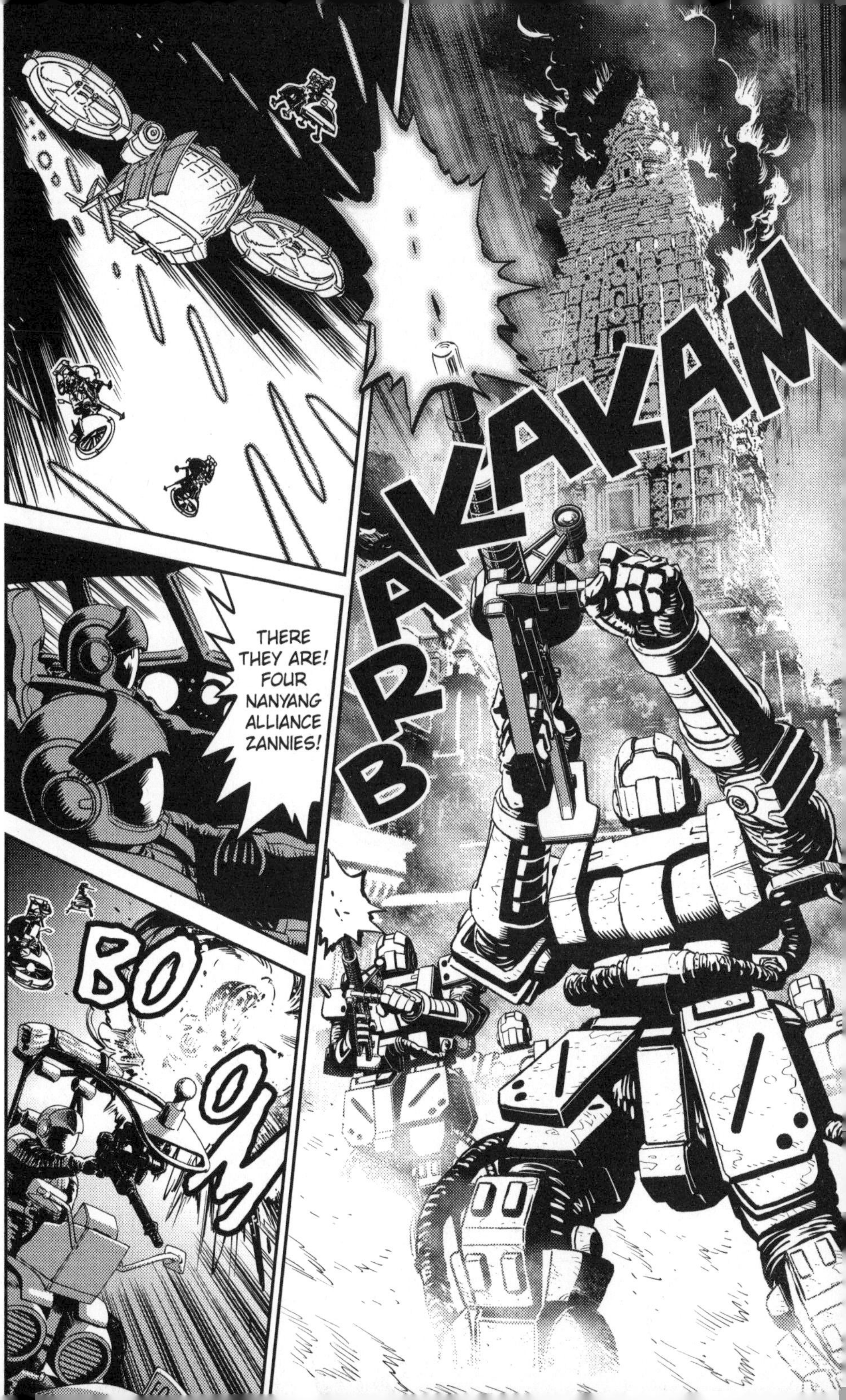
BRAKAKAM
THERE THEY ARE! FOUR NANYANG ALLIANCE ZANNIES!
BOOM

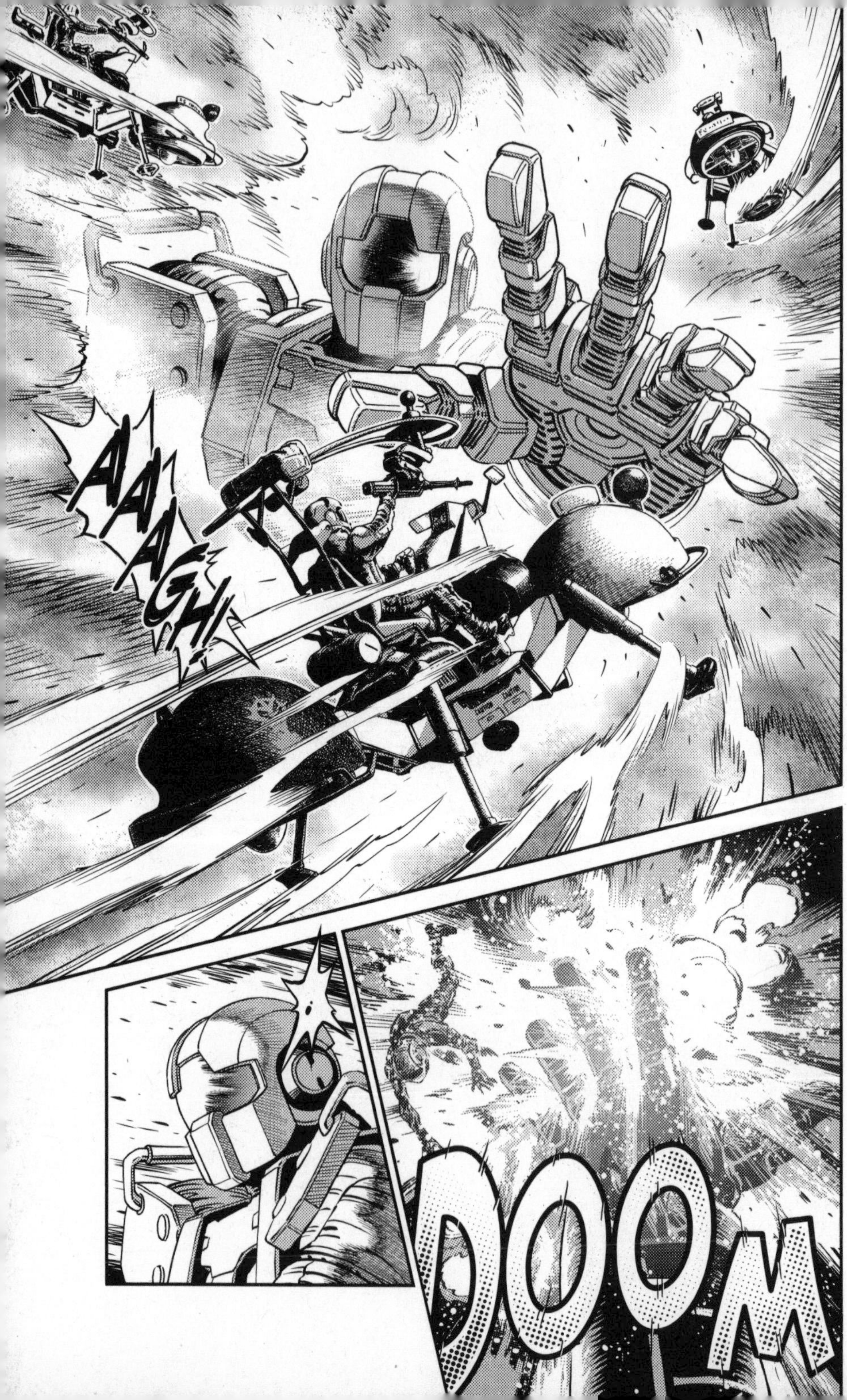
AAAAGH!
DOOM

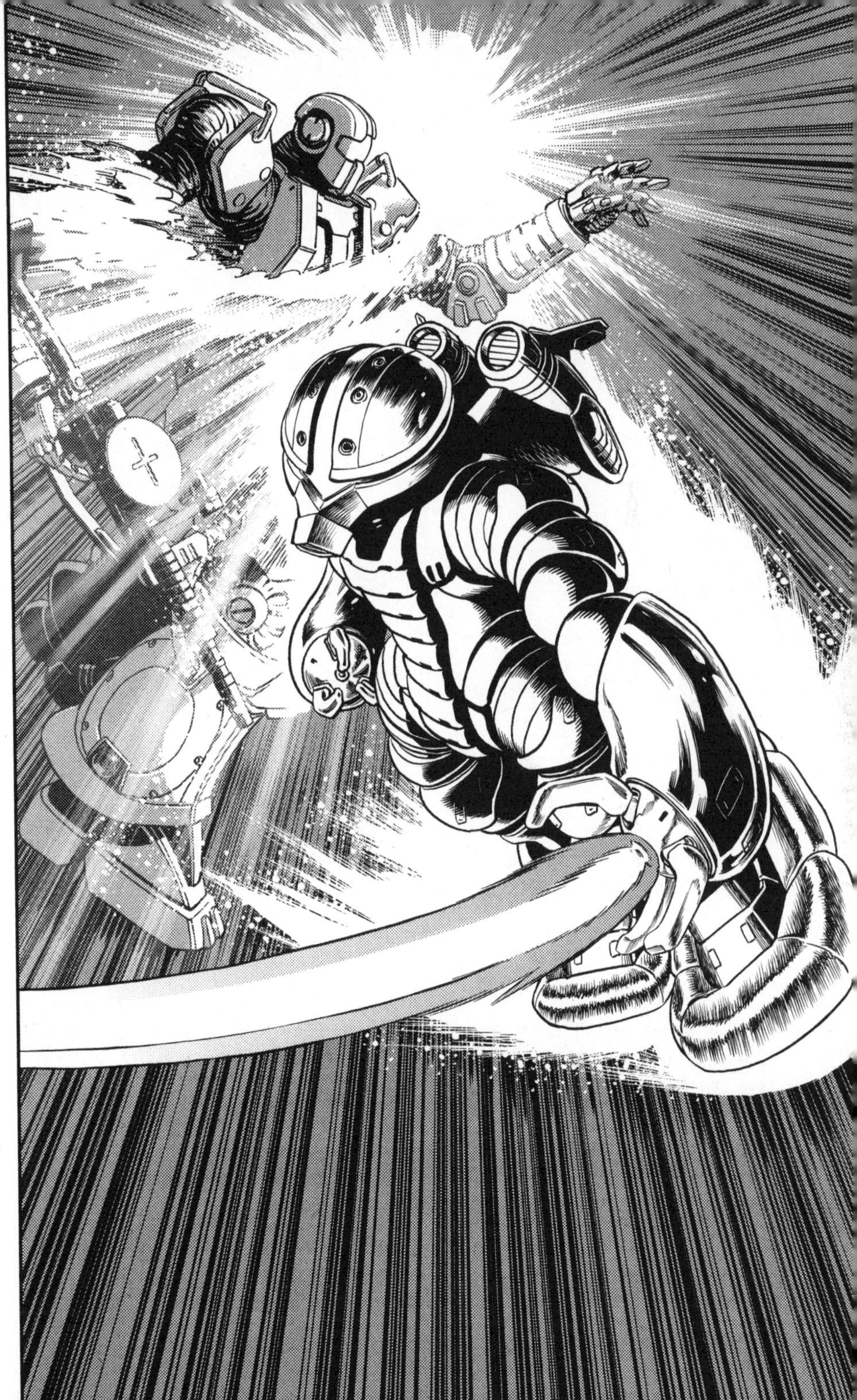

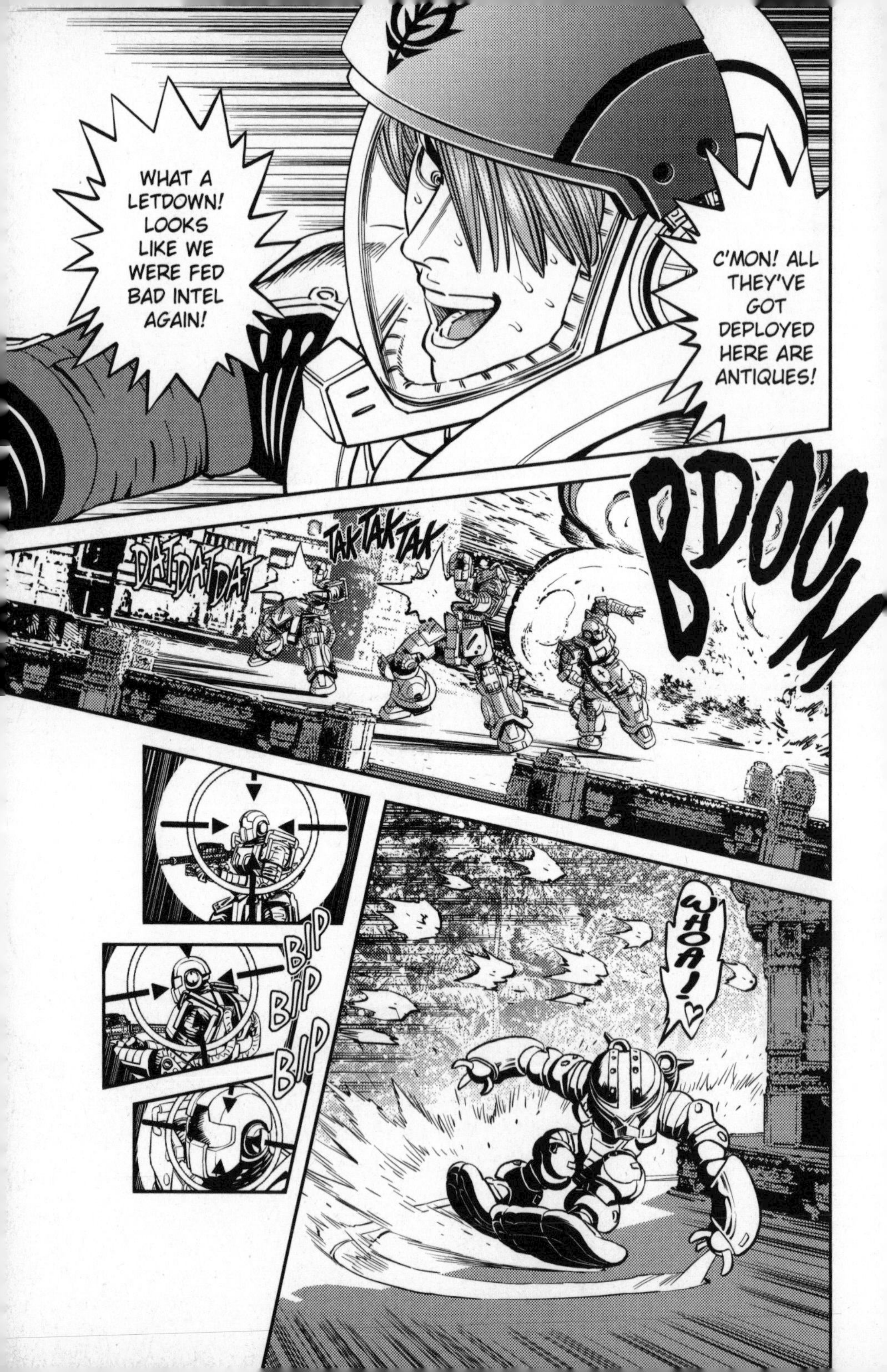
WHAT A LETDOWN! LOOKS LIKE WE WERE FED BAD INTEL AGAIN!
C'MON! ALL THEY'VE GOT DEPLOYED HERE ARE ANTIQUES!
BDOOM
TAK TAK TAK
DAT DAT DAT
WHOA!♥
BIP BIP BIP

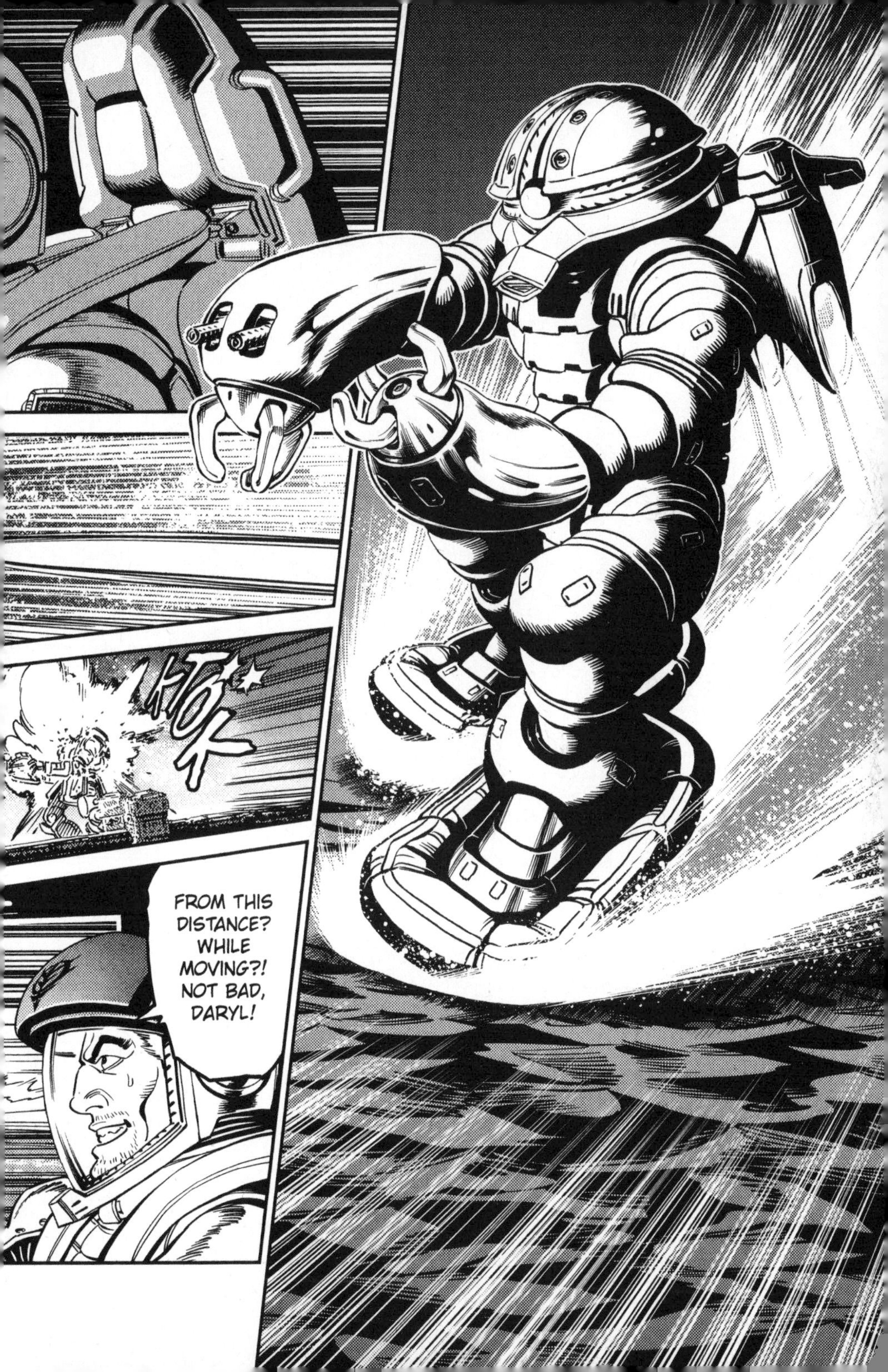
KTOK
FROM THIS DISTANCE? WHILE MOVING?! NOT BAD, DARYL!

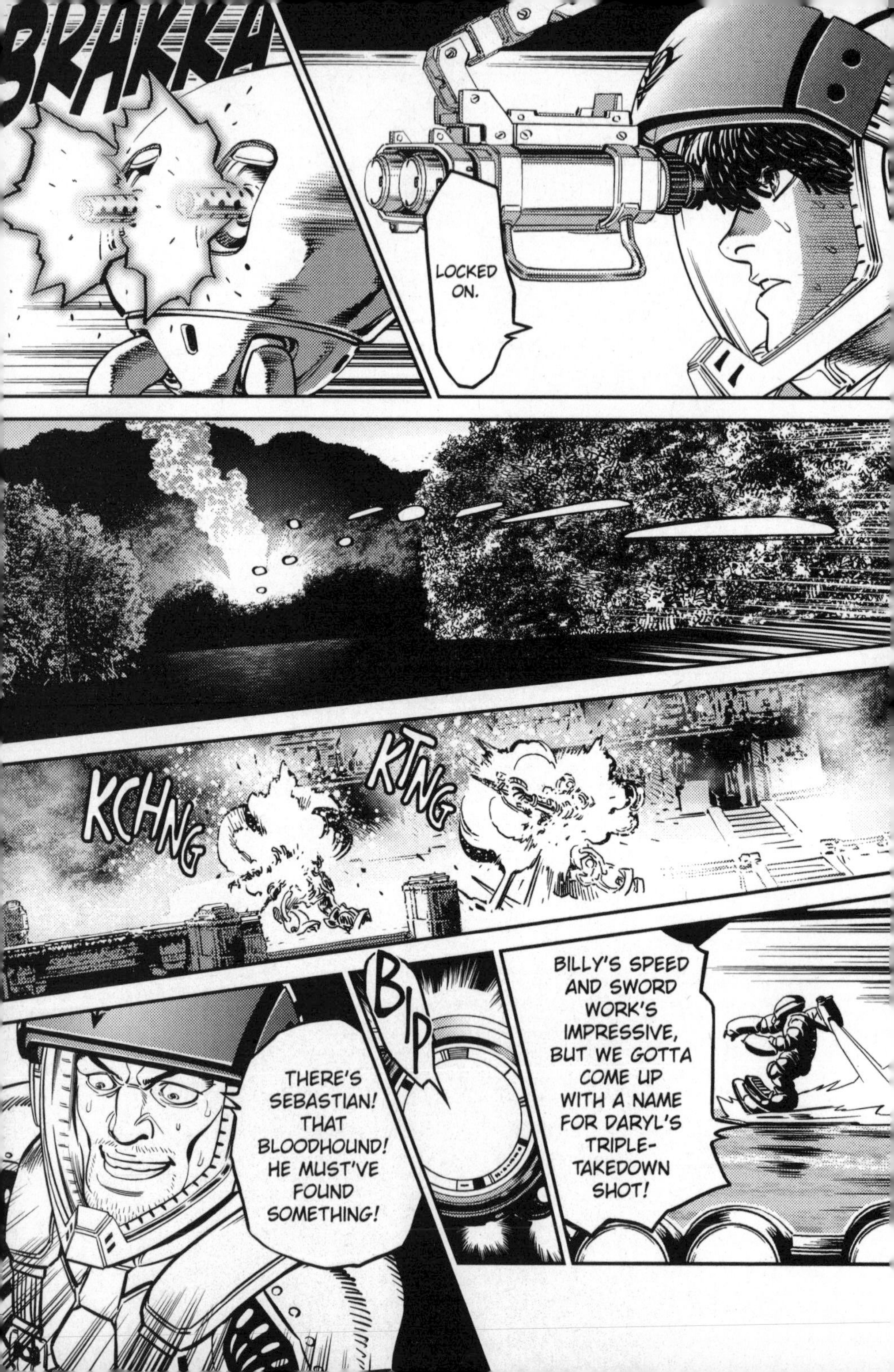
LOCKED ON.
BRAKKA
KTNG
KCHNG
BILLY'S SPEED AND SWORD WORK'S IMPRESSIVE, BUT WE GOTTA COME UP WITH A NAME FOR DARYL'S TRIPLE-TAKEDOWN SHOT!
BIP
THERE'S SEBASTIAN! THAT BLOODHOUND! HE MUST'VE FOUND SOMETHING!

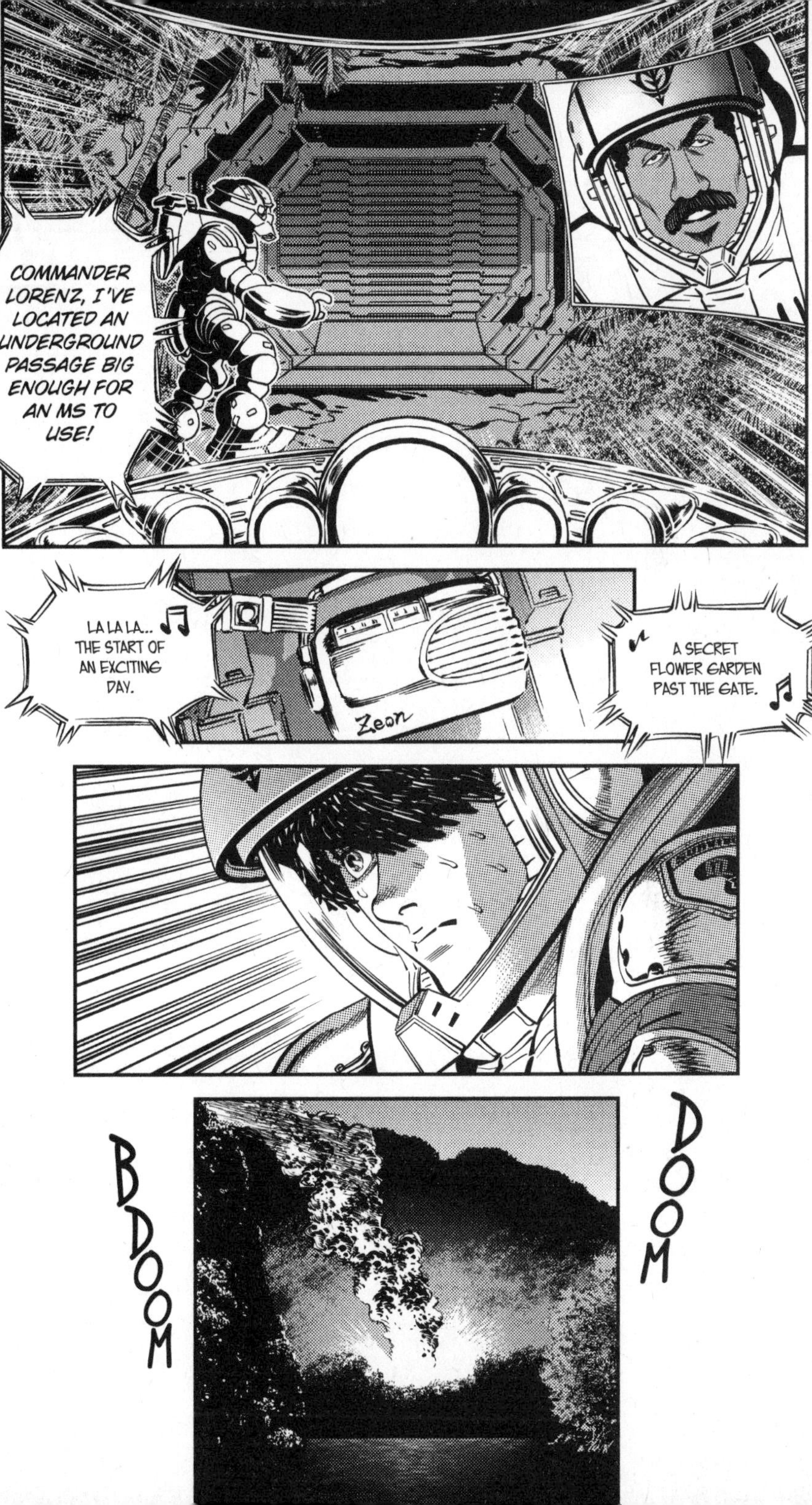
COMMANDER LORENZ, I'VE LOCATED AN UNDERGROUND PASSAGE BIG ENOUGH FOR AN MS TO USE!
A SECRET FLOWER GARDEN PAST THE GATE.
LA LA LA... THE START OF AN EXCITING DAY.
Zeon
DOOM
BDOOM

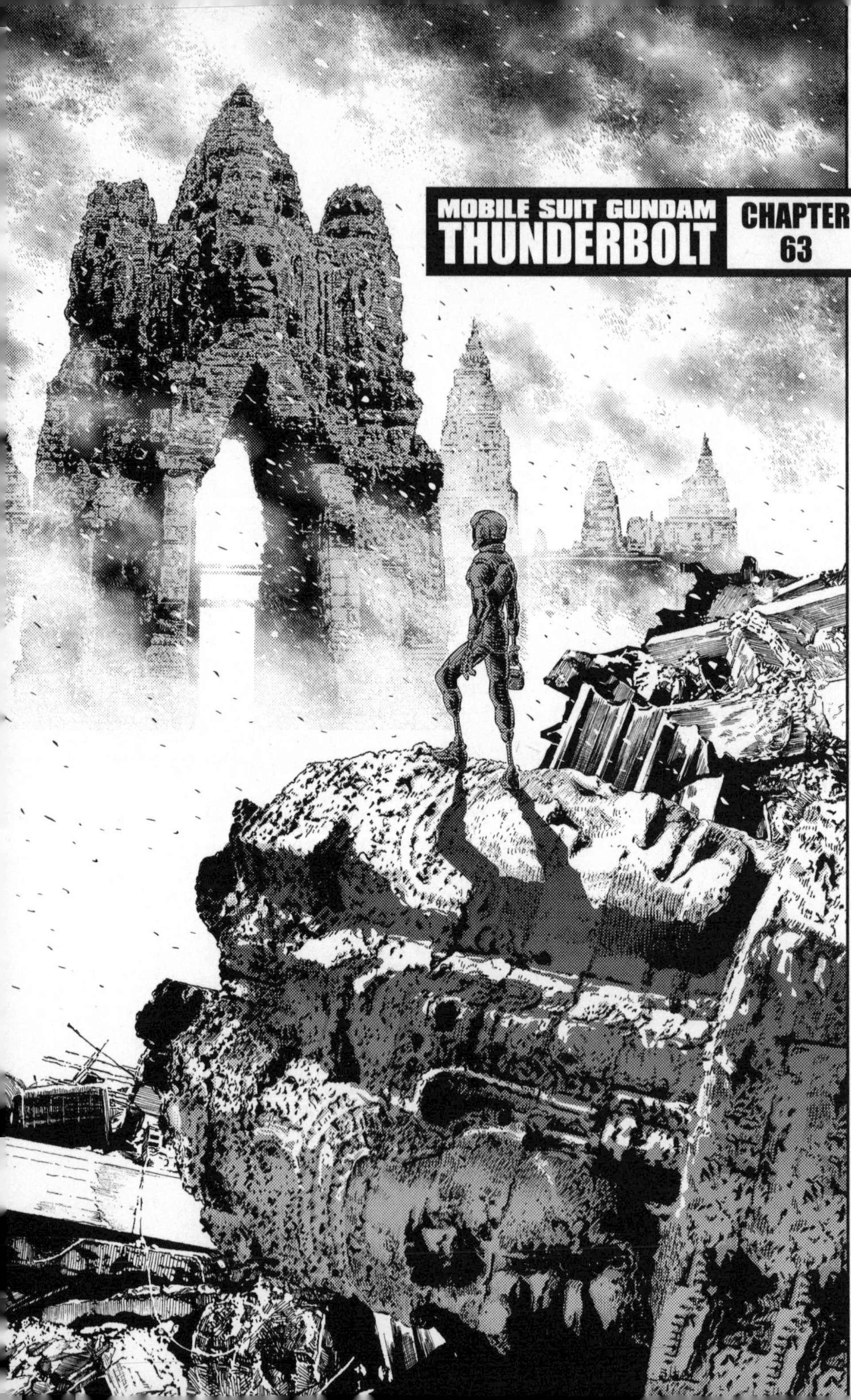
MOBILE SUIT GUNDAM
THUNDERBOLT
CHAPTER
63

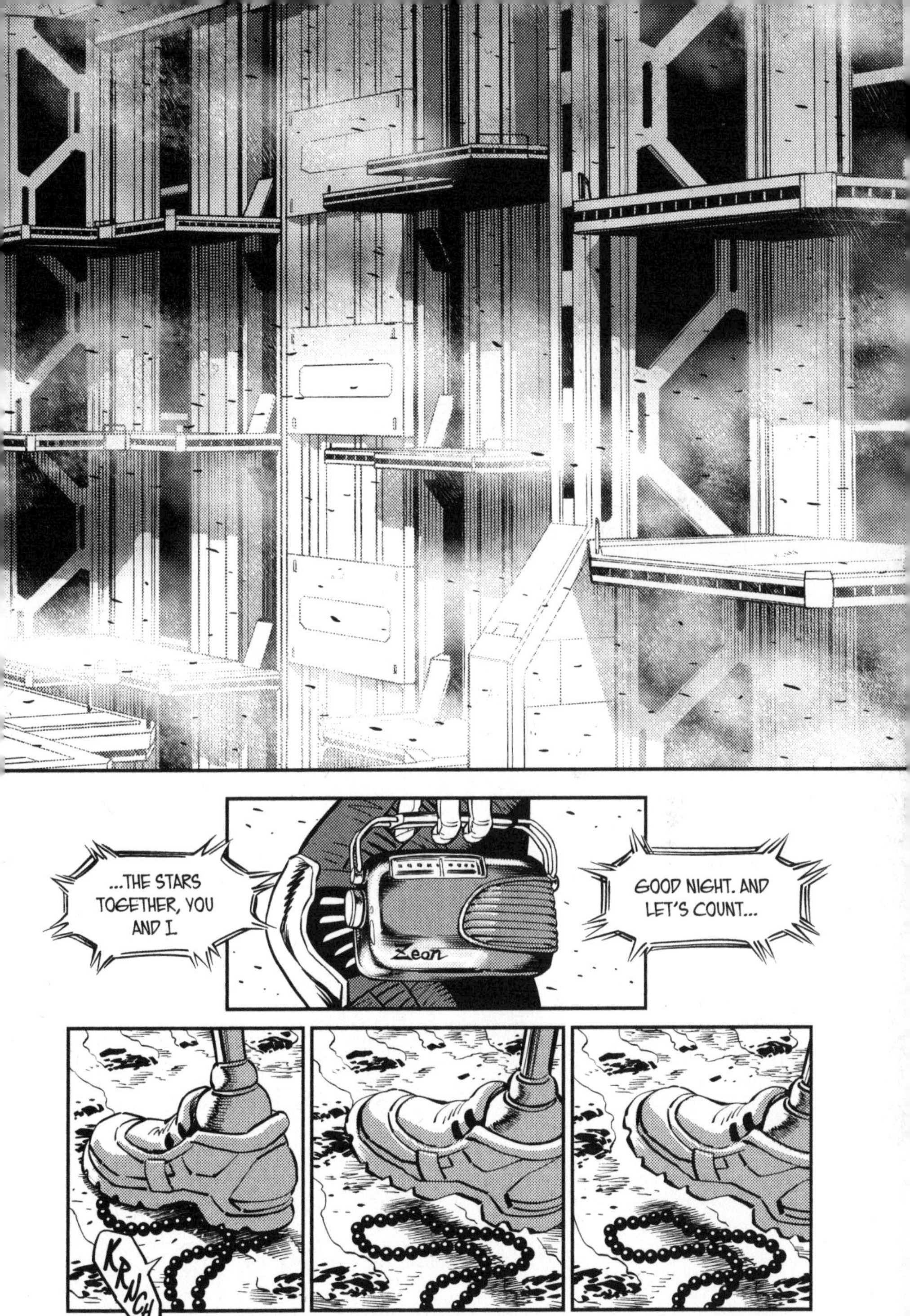
GOOD NIGHT. AND LET'S COUNT...
...THE STARS TOGETHER, YOU AND I.
KRNCH

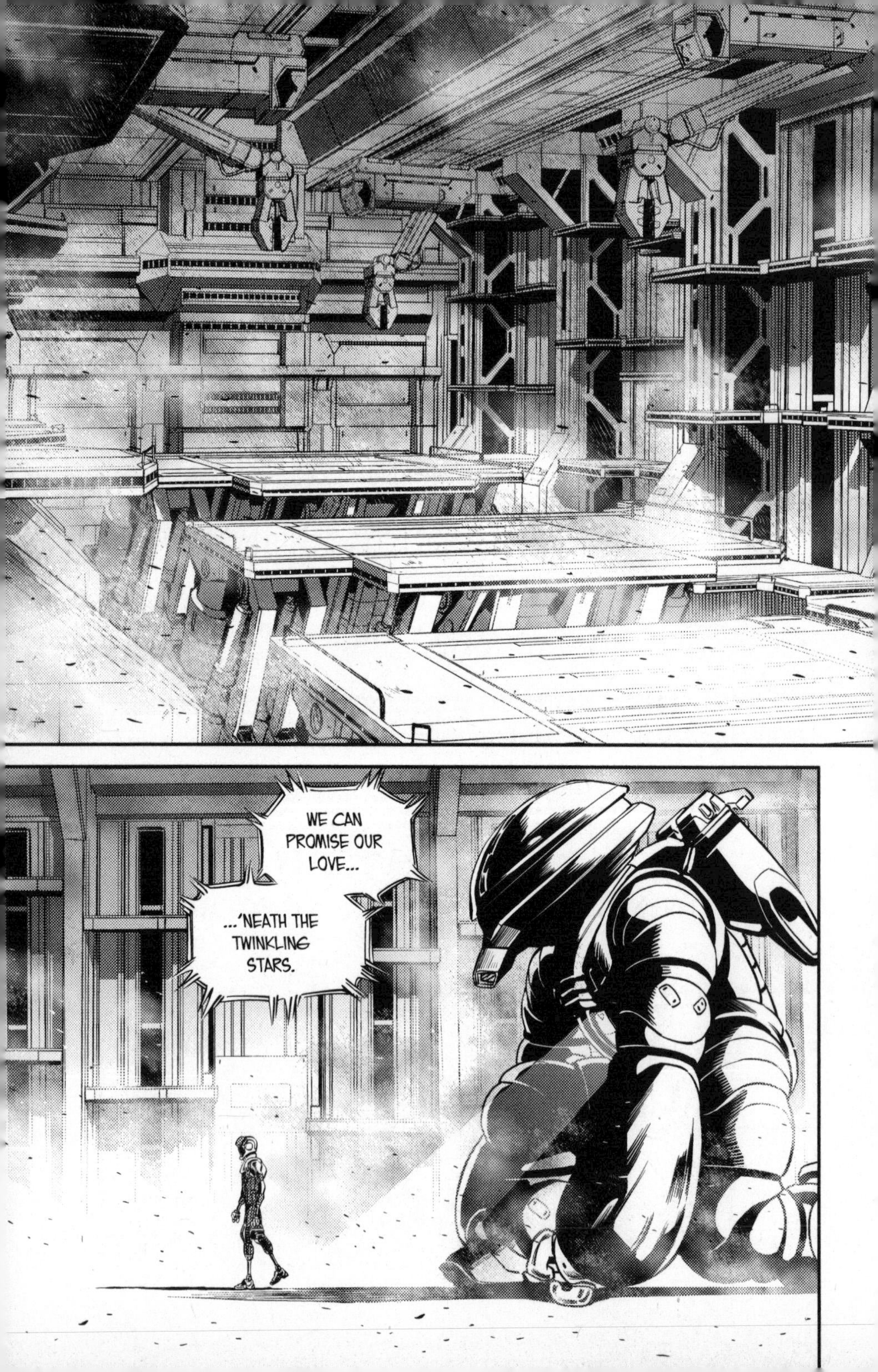
WE CAN PROMISE OUR LOVE...
...'NEATH THE TWINKLING STARS.

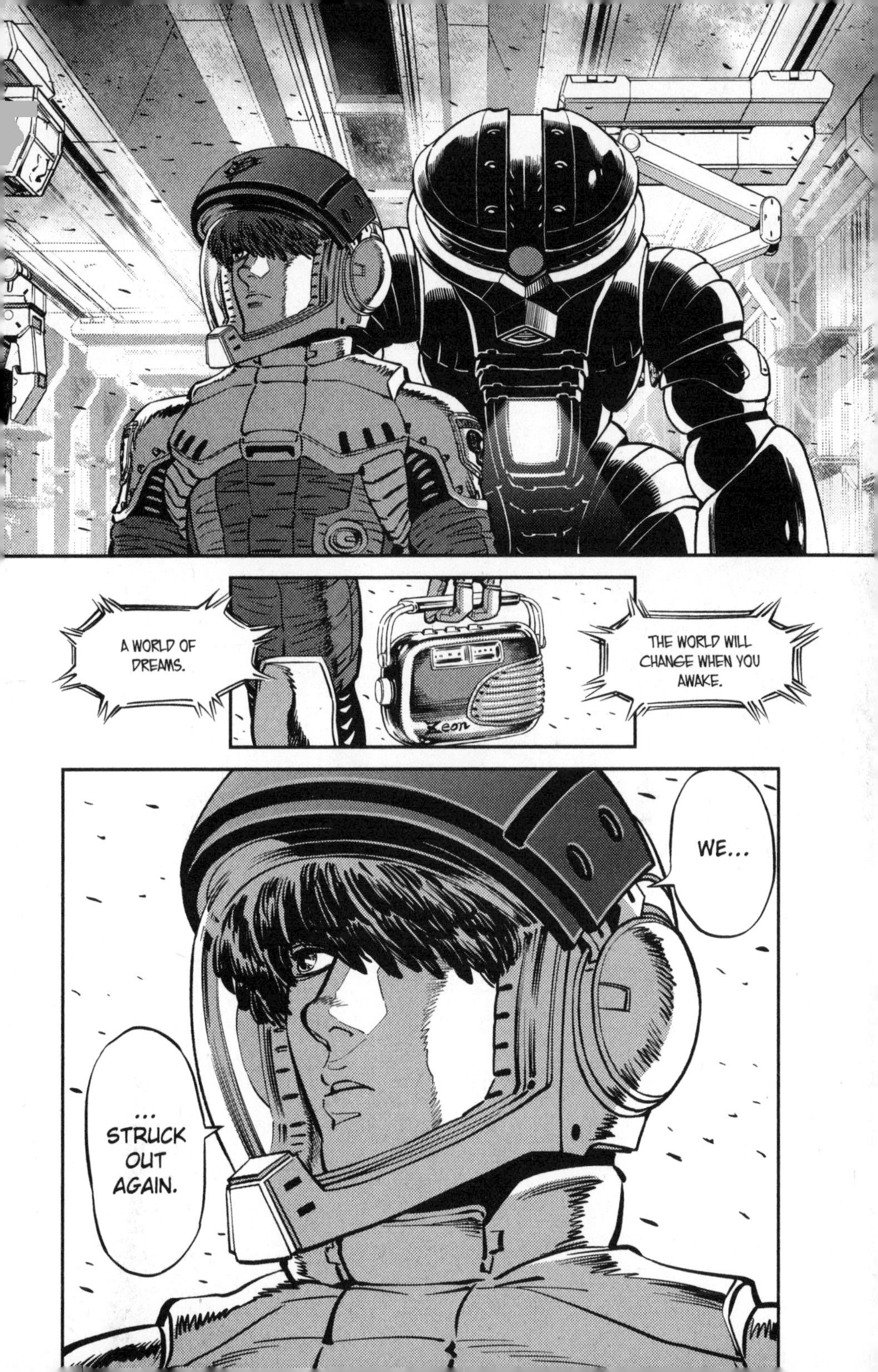
THE WORLD WILL CHANGE WHEN YOU AWAKE.
A WORLD OF DREAMS.
Zeon
WE...
...STRUCK OUT AGAIN.

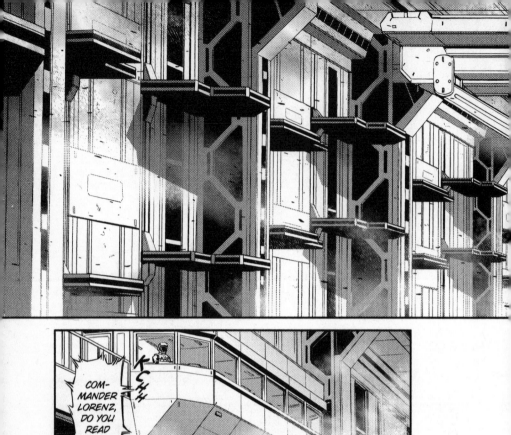

COMMANDER LORENZ, DO YOU READ ME?

I'M GOING THROUGH THE RECORDS IN THE CONTROL ROOM, BUT...

...I'M NOT FINDING ANYTHING RELATED TO THE PSYCHO ZAKU.

KCHH

SKCHH

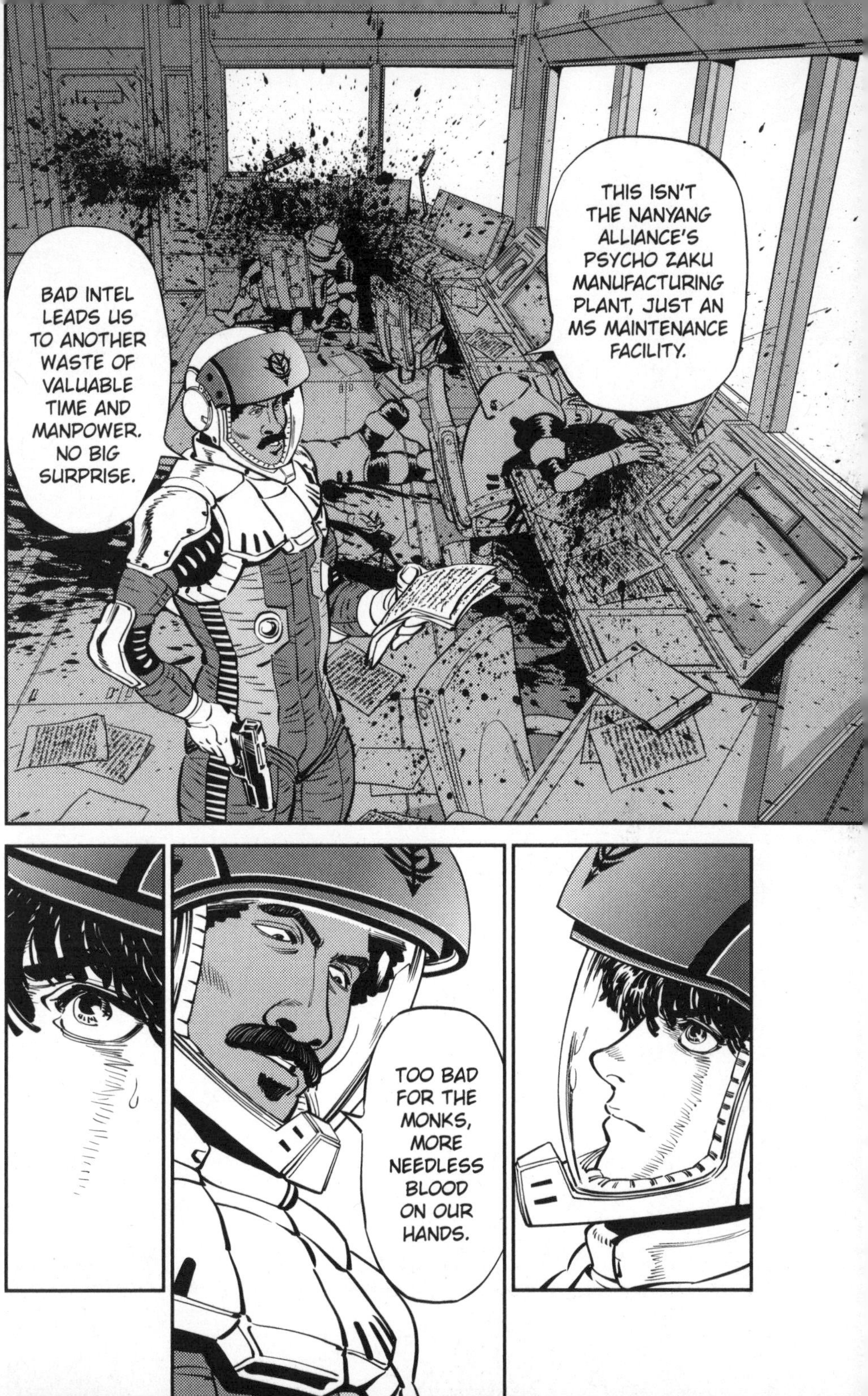
THIS ISN'T THE NANYANG ALLIANCE'S PSYCHO ZAKU MANUFACTURING PLANT, JUST AN MS MAINTENANCE FACILITY.
BAD INTEL LEADS US TO ANOTHER WASTE OF VALUABLE TIME AND MANPOWER. NO BIG SURPRISE.
TOO BAD FOR THE MONKS, MORE NEEDLESS BLOOD ON OUR HANDS.

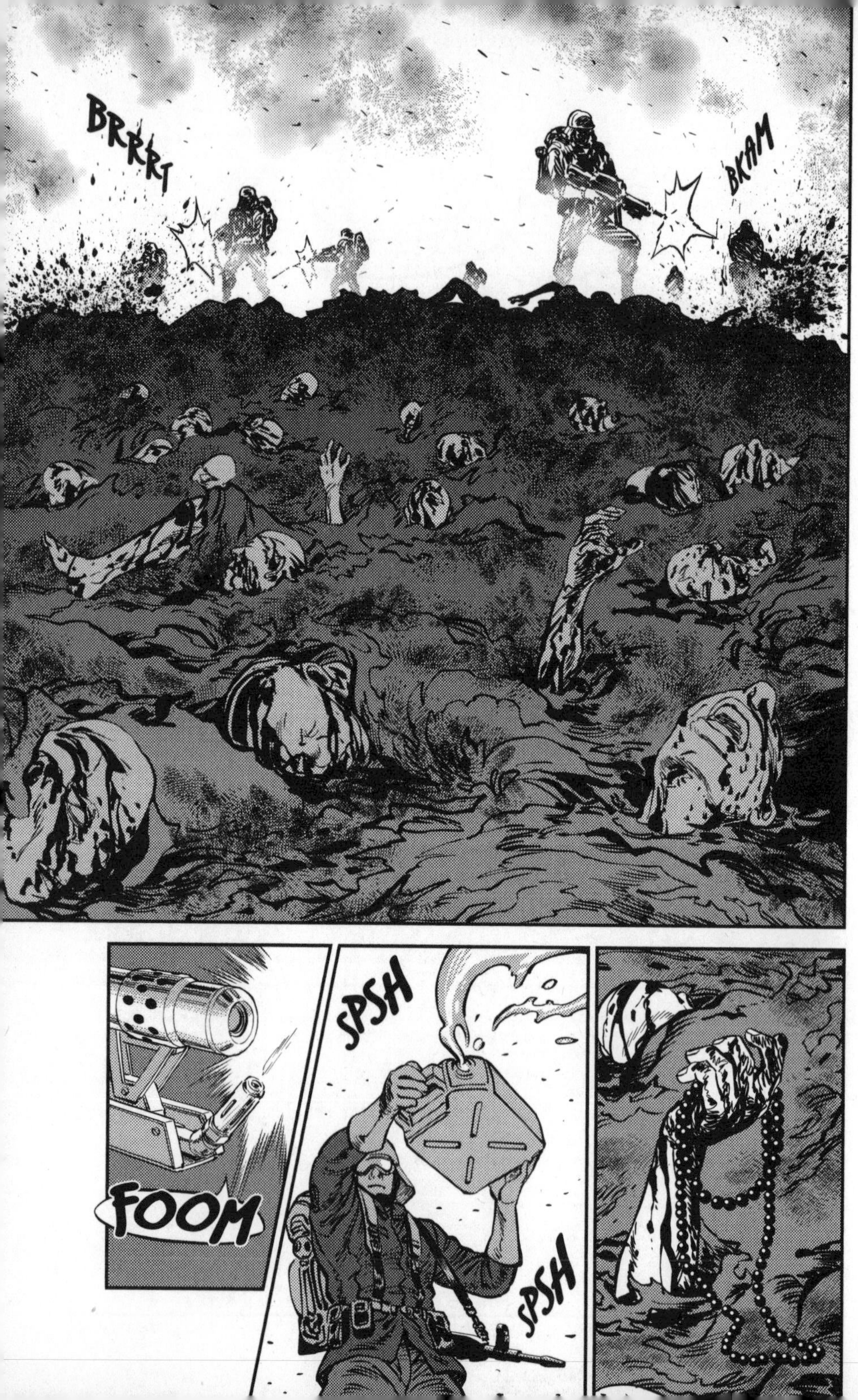
BKAM
BRRRT
SPSH
SPSH
FOOM

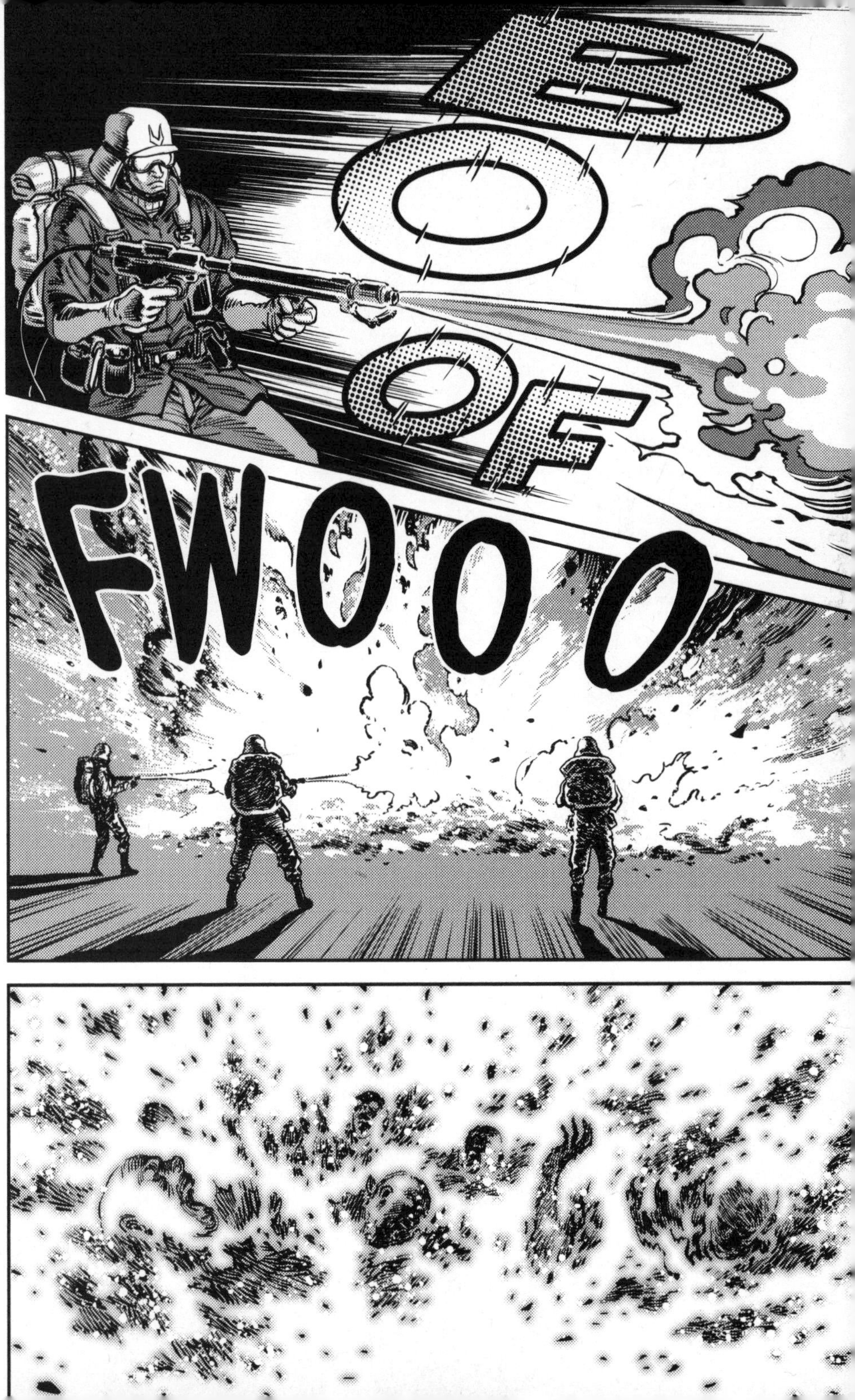
BOOF
FWOOO

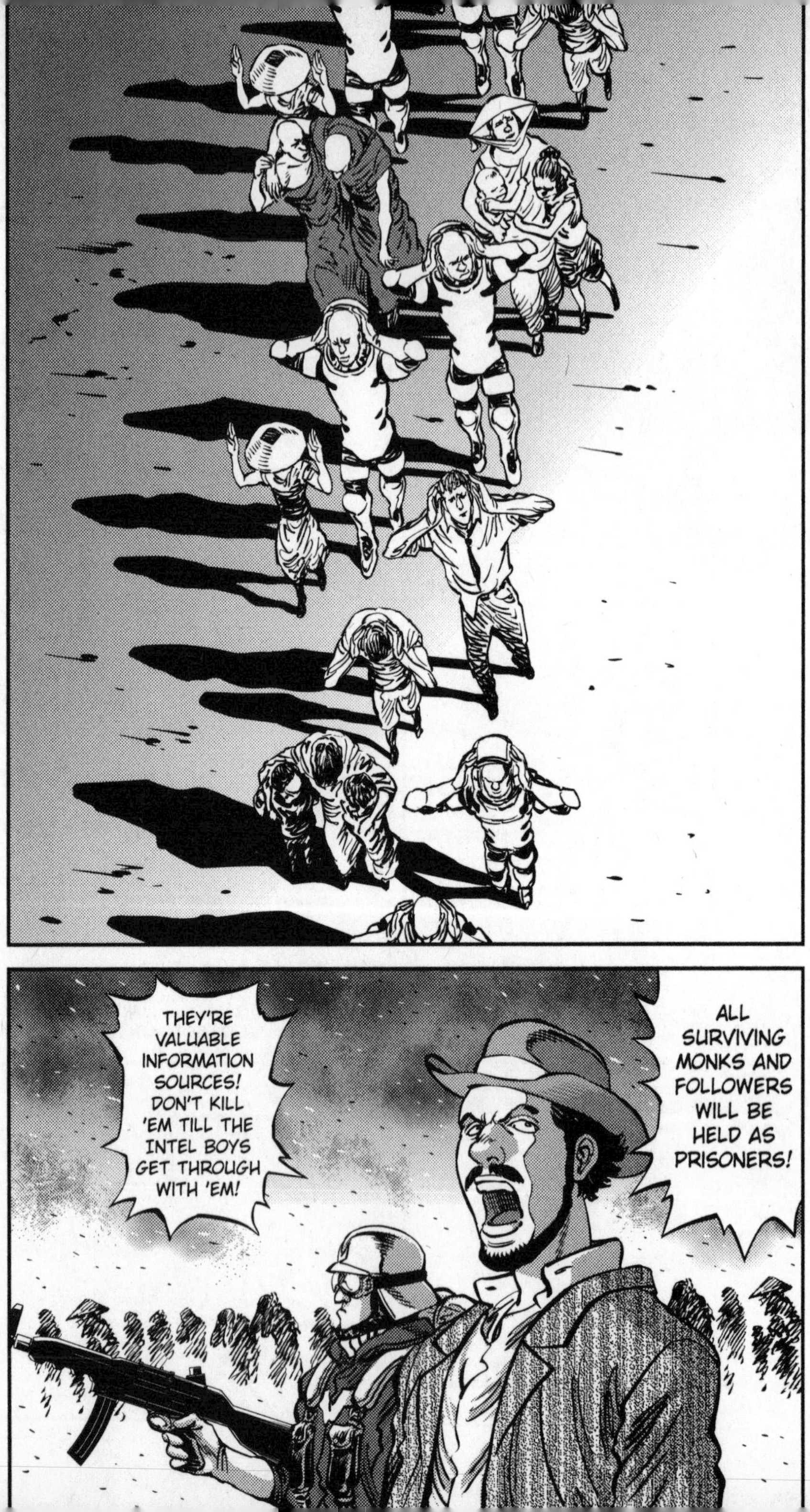
ALL SURVIVING MONKS AND FOLLOWERS WILL BE HELD AS PRISONERS!
THEY'RE VALUABLE INFORMATION SOURCES! DON'T KILL 'EM TILL THE INTEL BOYS GET THROUGH WITH 'EM!

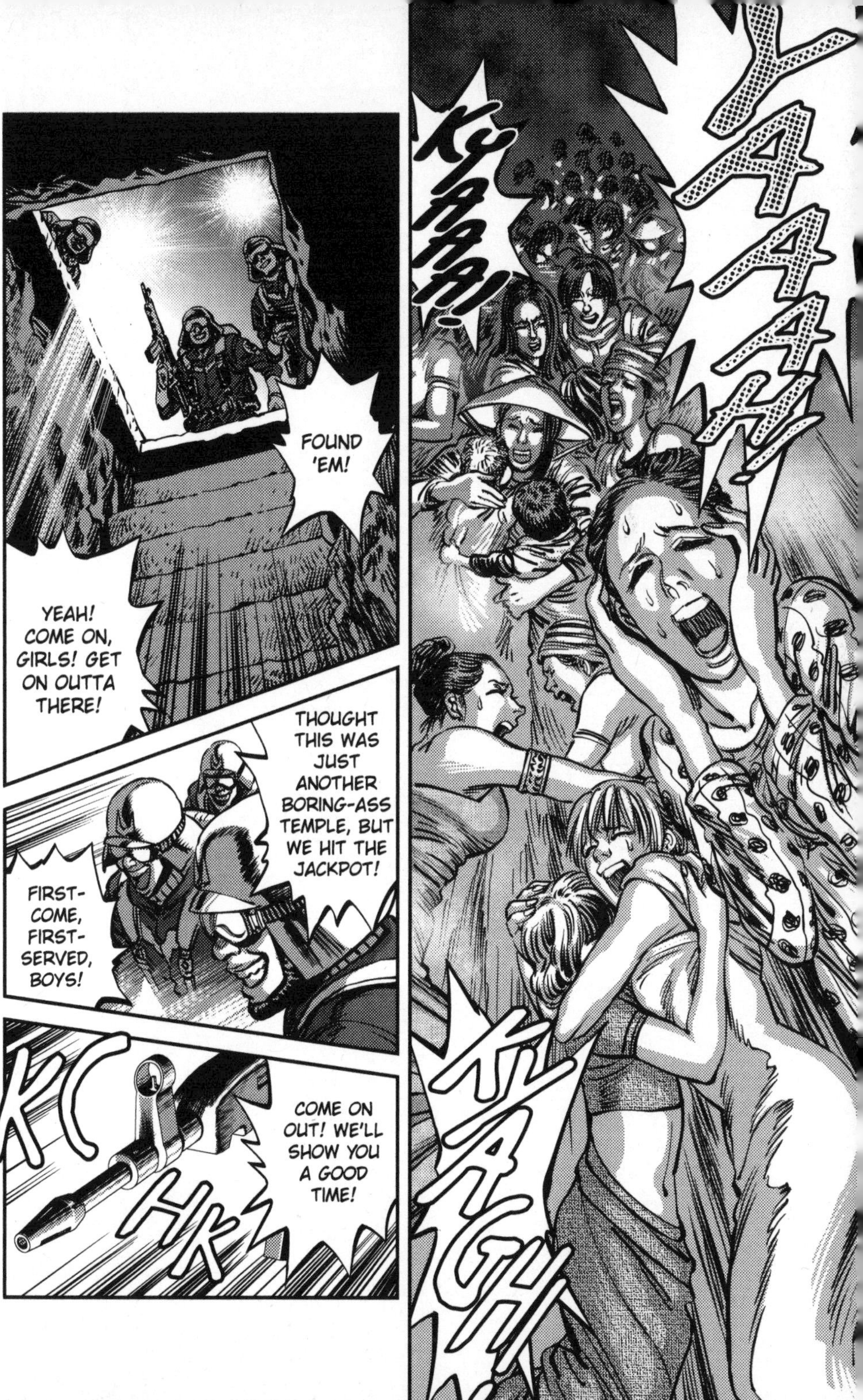
YAAAH!
KYAAAA!
KYAAGH!!
FOUND 'EM!
YEAH! COME ON, GIRLS! GET ON OUTTA THERE!
THOUGHT THIS WAS JUST ANOTHER BORING-ASS TEMPLE, BUT WE HIT THE JACKPOT!
FIRST-COME, FIRST-SERVED, BOYS!
COME ON OUT! WE'LL SHOW YOU A GOOD TIME!
KCHK

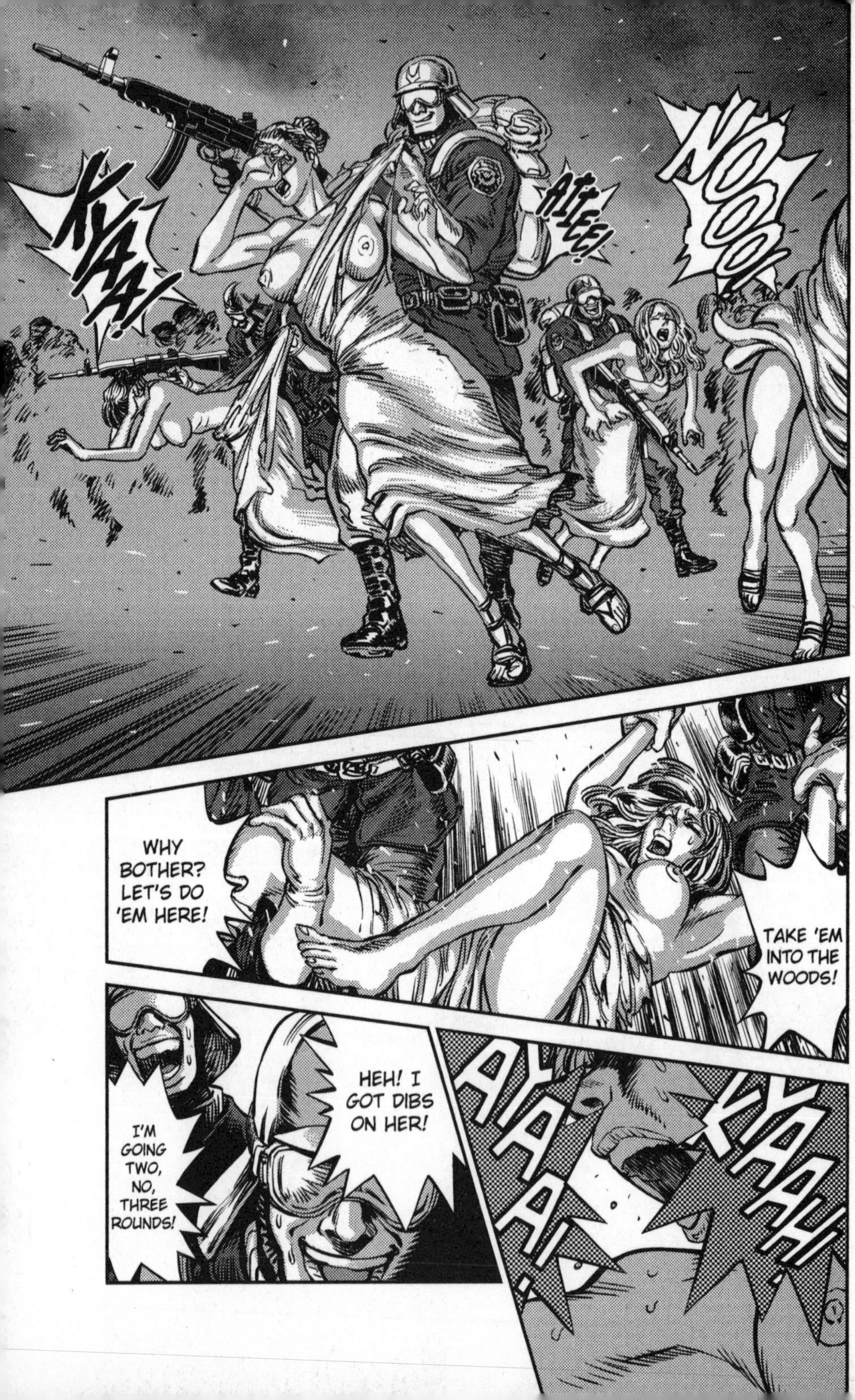
NOOOO!
AIIEE!
KYAAA!
TAKE 'EM INTO THE WOODS!
WHY BOTHER? LET'S DO 'EM HERE!
KYAAH!
AYAAA!
HEH! I GOT DIBS ON HER!
I'M GOING TWO, NO, THREE ROUNDS!

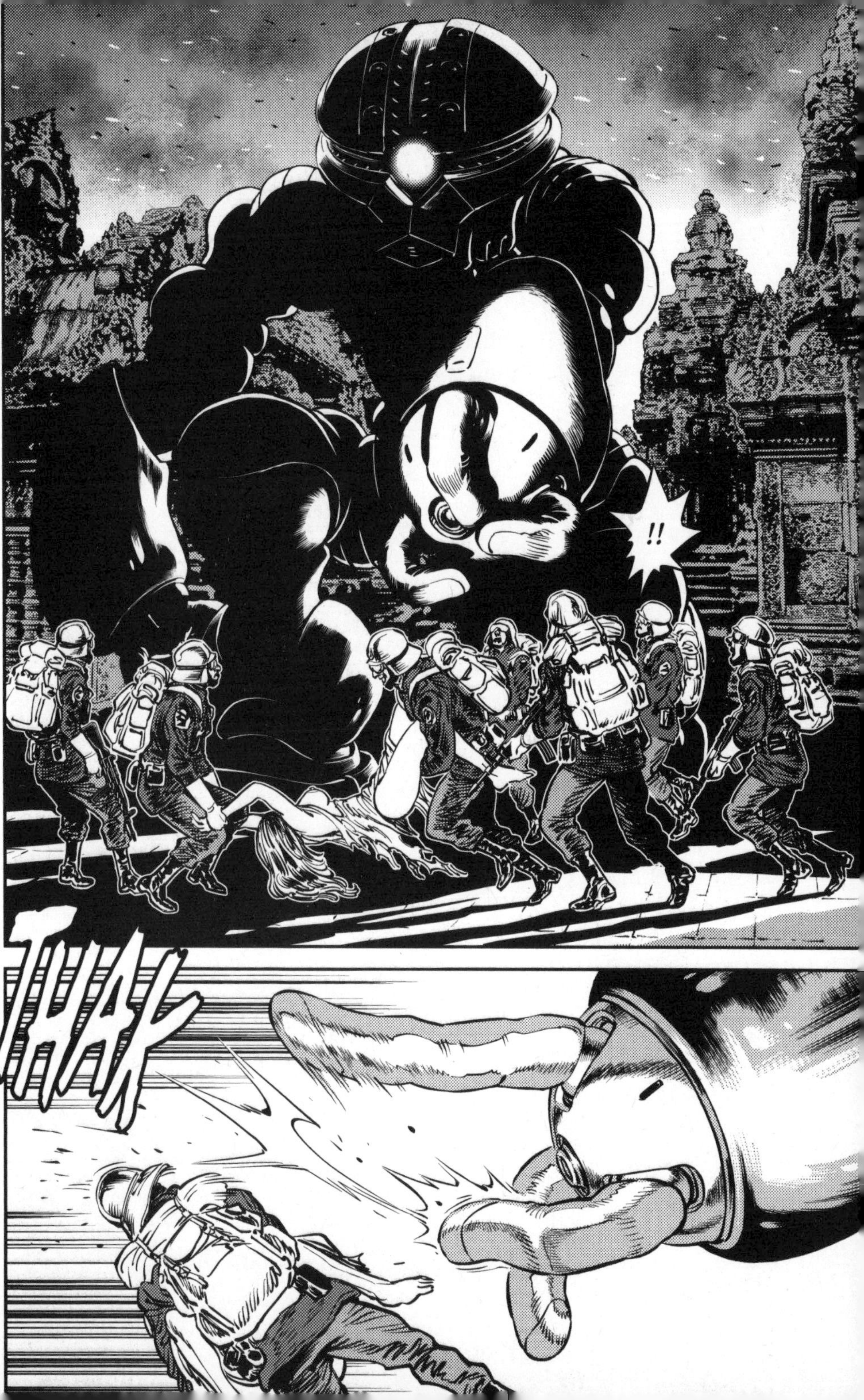
!!
THAK

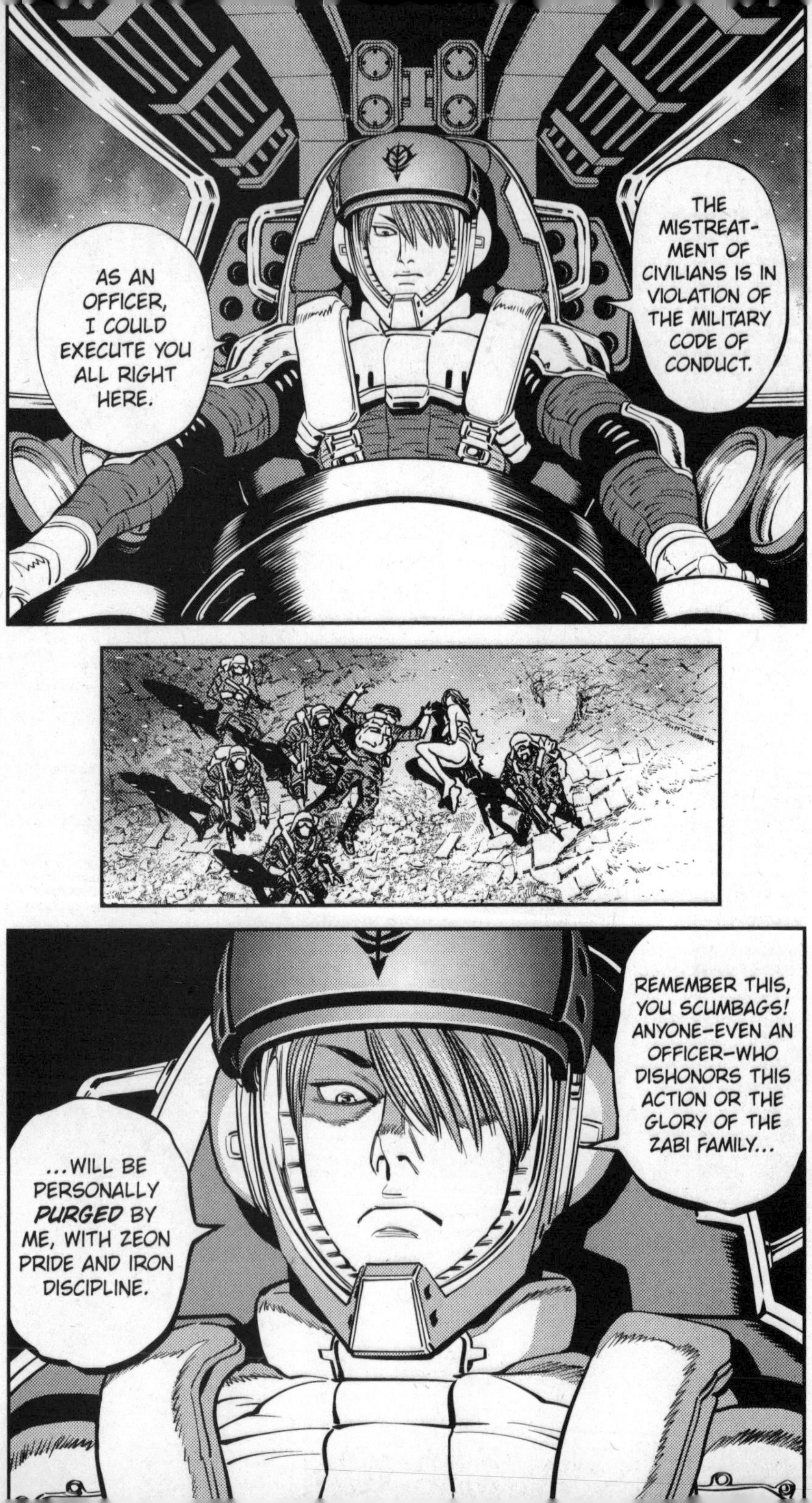
THE MISTREATMENT OF CIVILIANS IS IN VIOLATION OF THE MILITARY CODE OF CONDUCT.
AS AN OFFICER, I COULD EXECUTE YOU ALL RIGHT HERE.
REMEMBER THIS, YOU SCUMBAGS! ANYONE—EVEN AN OFFICER—WHO DISHONORS THIS ACTION OR THE GLORY OF THE ZABI FAMILY...
...WILL BE PERSONALLY *PURGED* BY ME, WITH ZEON PRIDE AND IRON DISCIPLINE.

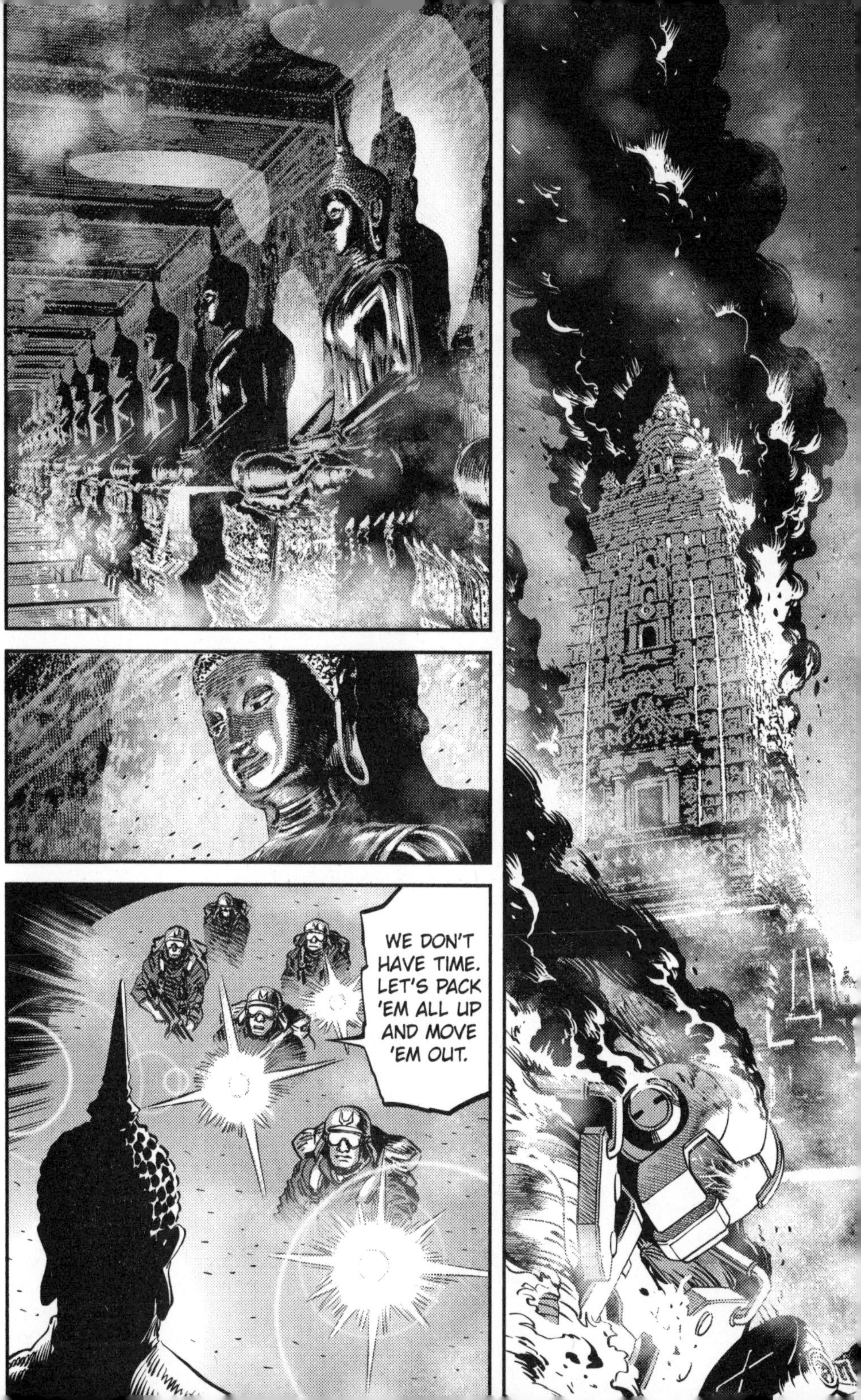
WE DON'T HAVE TIME. LET'S PACK 'EM ALL UP AND MOVE 'EM OUT.

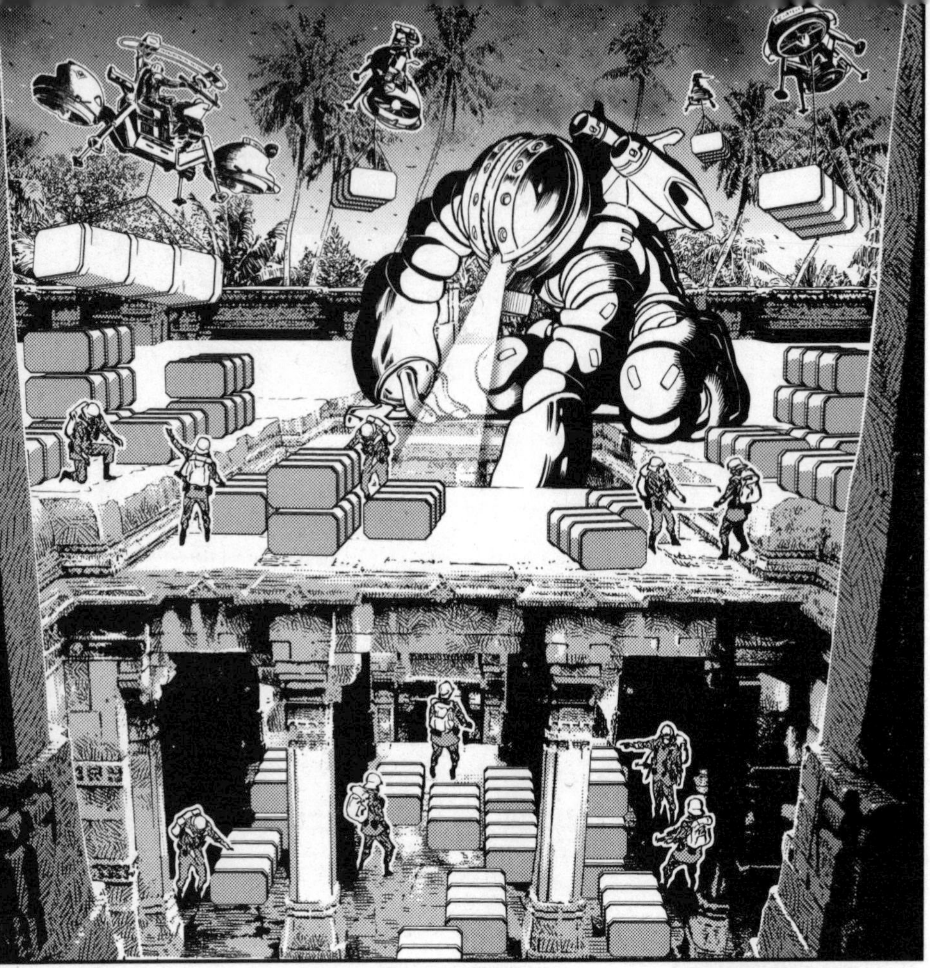
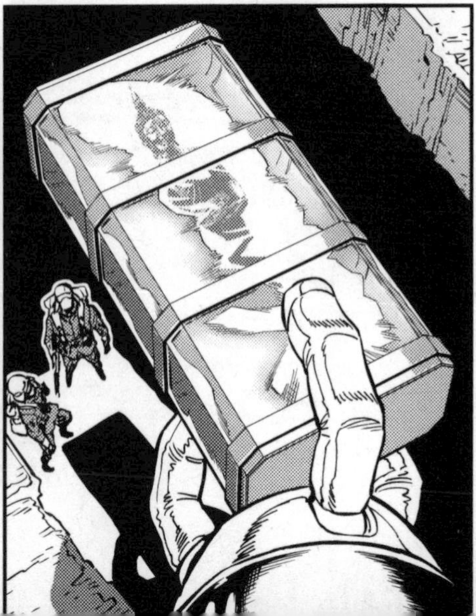
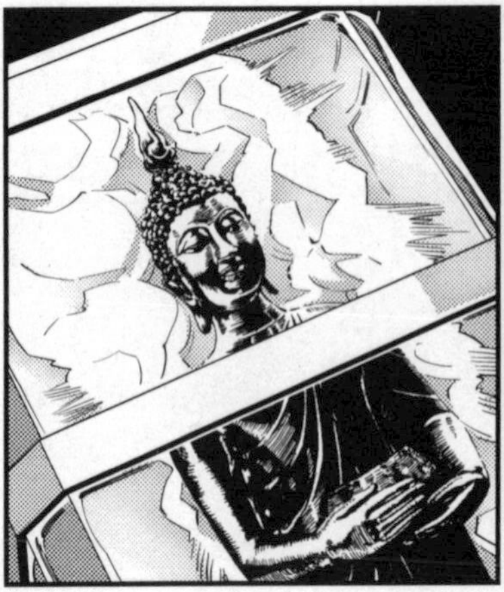

NAN-MAIDA...

I UNDERSTAND THE NEED TO PROTECT HISTORICAL HERITAGE FROM BEING DESTROYED BY WAR...

...BUT THIS FEELS LIKE GRAVE ROBBING. HOPE BUDDHA DON'T CURSE ME FOR THIS.

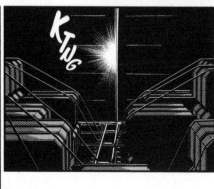

KTNG

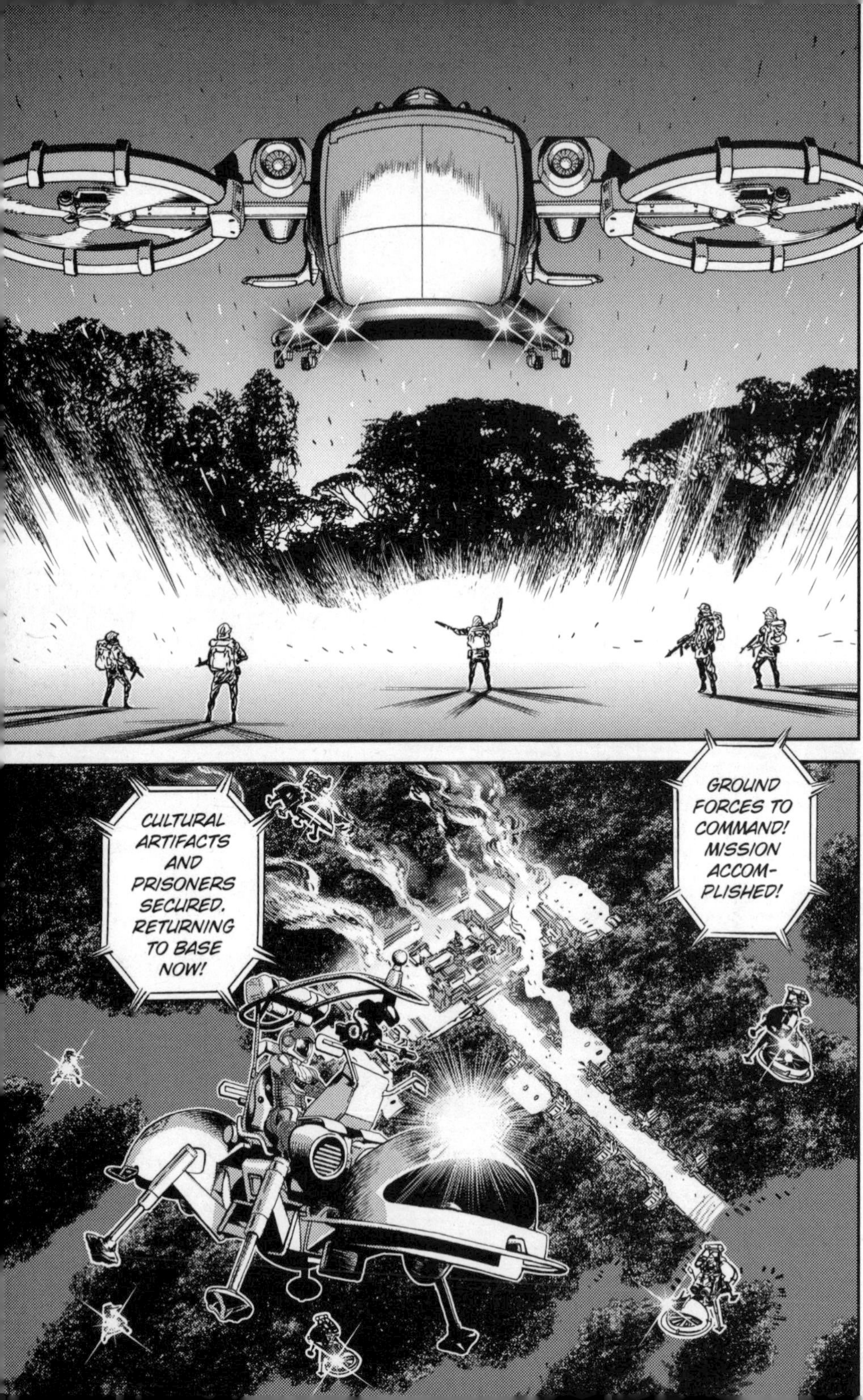
GROUND FORCES TO COMMAND! MISSION ACCOM-PLISHED!
CULTURAL ARTIFACTS AND PRISONERS SECURED. RETURNING TO BASE NOW!

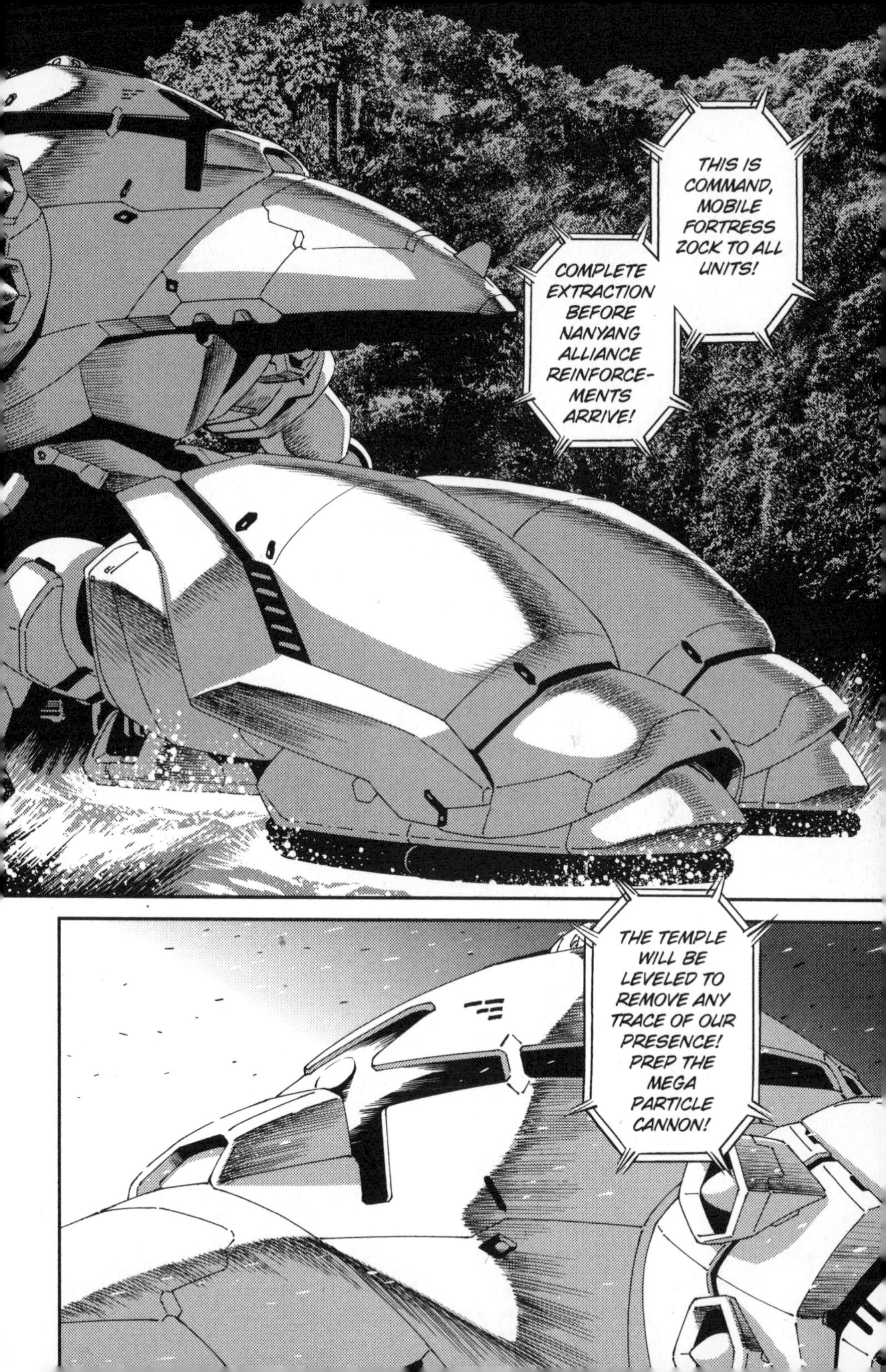
THIS IS COMMAND, MOBILE FORTRESS ZOCK TO ALL UNITS!
COMPLETE EXTRACTION BEFORE NANYANG ALLIANCE REINFORCE-MENTS ARRIVE!
THE TEMPLE WILL BE LEVELED TO REMOVE ANY TRACE OF OUR PRESENCE! PREP THE MEGA PARTICLE CANNON!

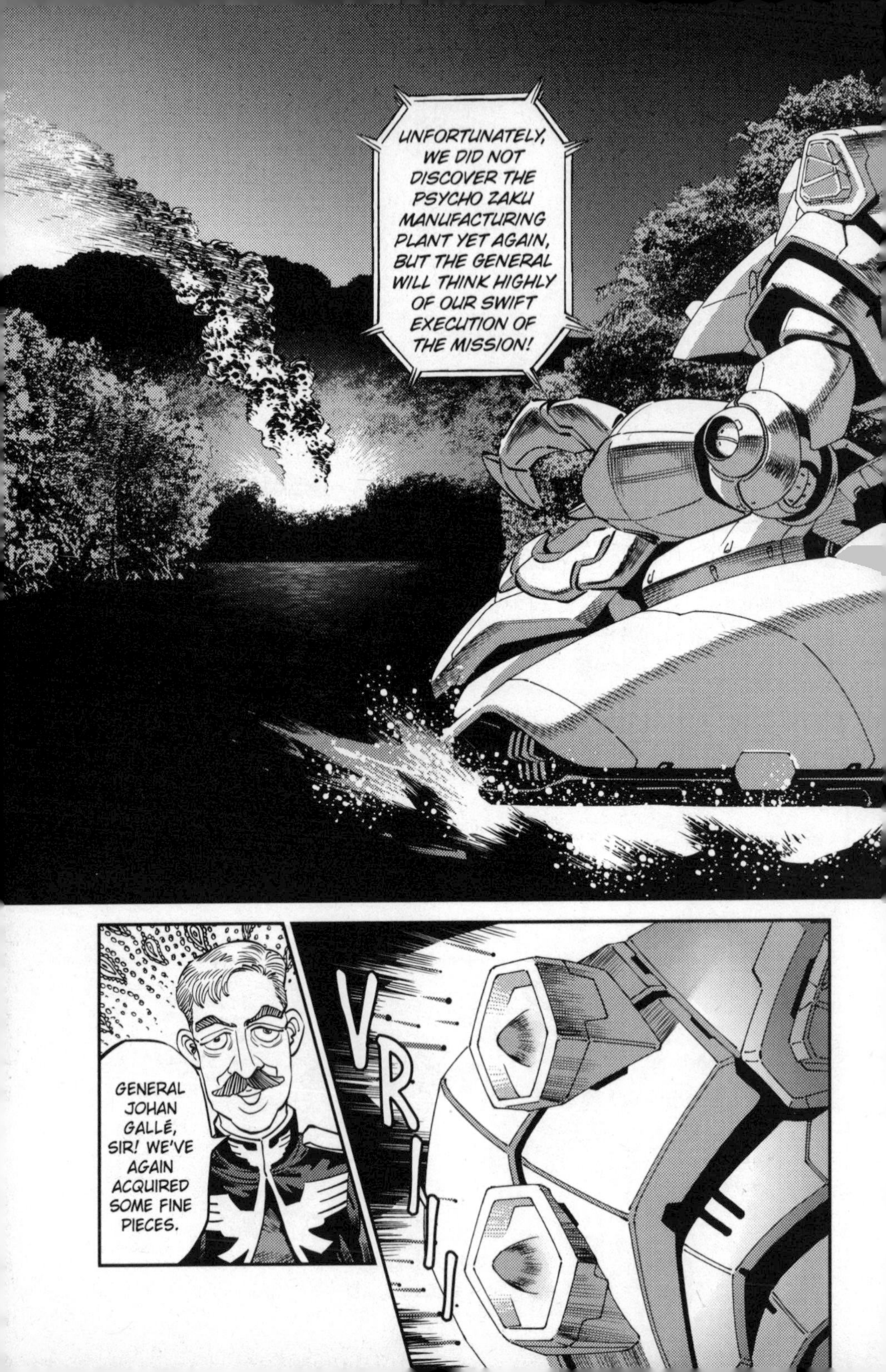
UNFORTUNATELY, WE DID NOT DISCOVER THE PSYCHO ZAKU MANUFACTURING PLANT YET AGAIN, BUT THE GENERAL WILL THINK HIGHLY OF OUR SWIFT EXECUTION OF THE MISSION!
VRI...
GENERAL JOHAN GALLÉ, SIR! WE'VE AGAIN ACQUIRED SOME FINE PIECES.

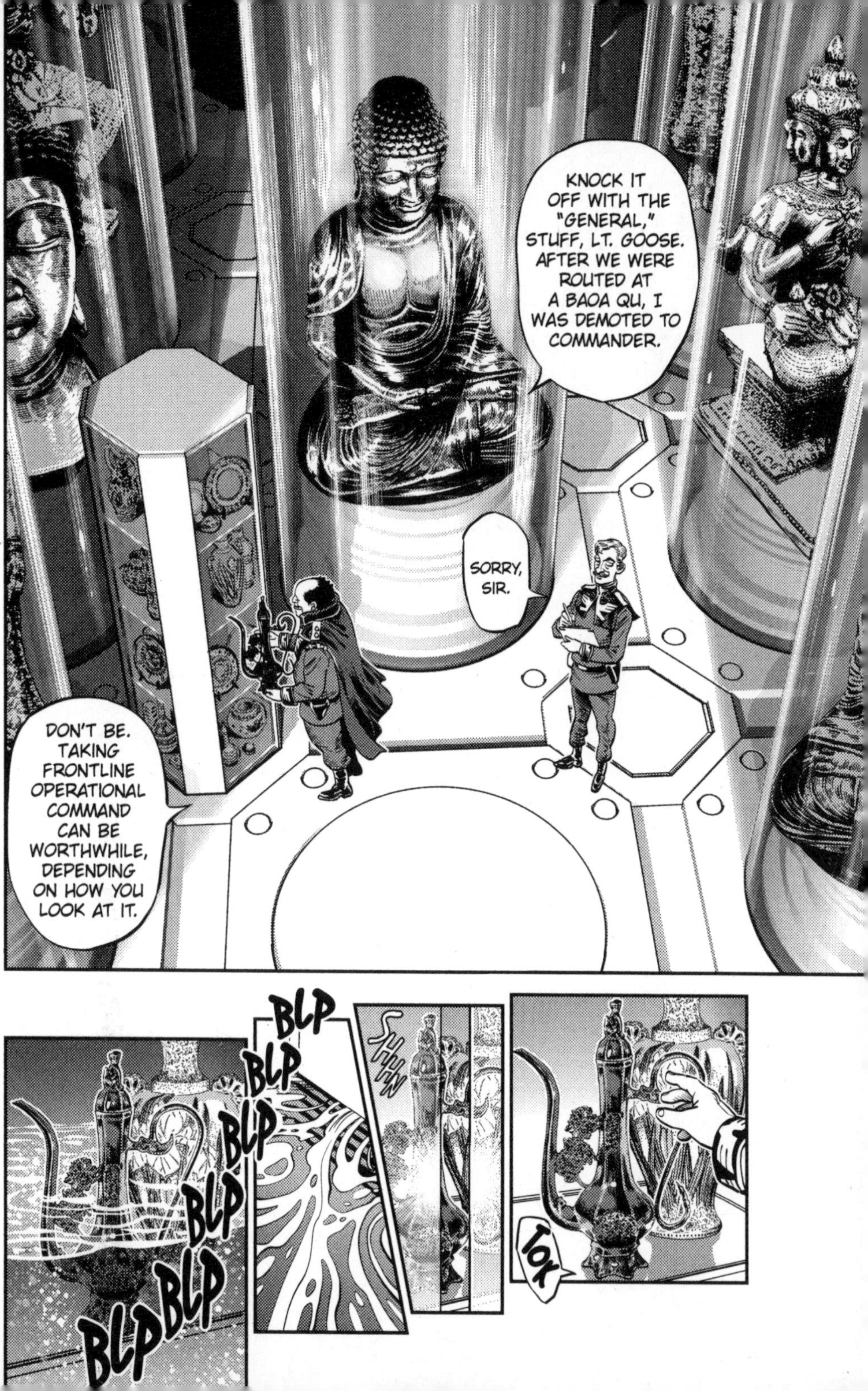
KNOCK IT OFF WITH THE "GENERAL," STUFF, LT. GOOSE. AFTER WE WERE ROUTED AT A BAOA QU, I WAS DEMOTED TO COMMANDER.
SORRY, SIR.
DON'T BE. TAKING FRONTLINE OPERATIONAL COMMAND CAN BE WORTHWHILE, DEPENDING ON HOW YOU LOOK AT IT.
TOK
SHHN
BLP
BLP
BLP
BLP
BLP
BLP
BLP

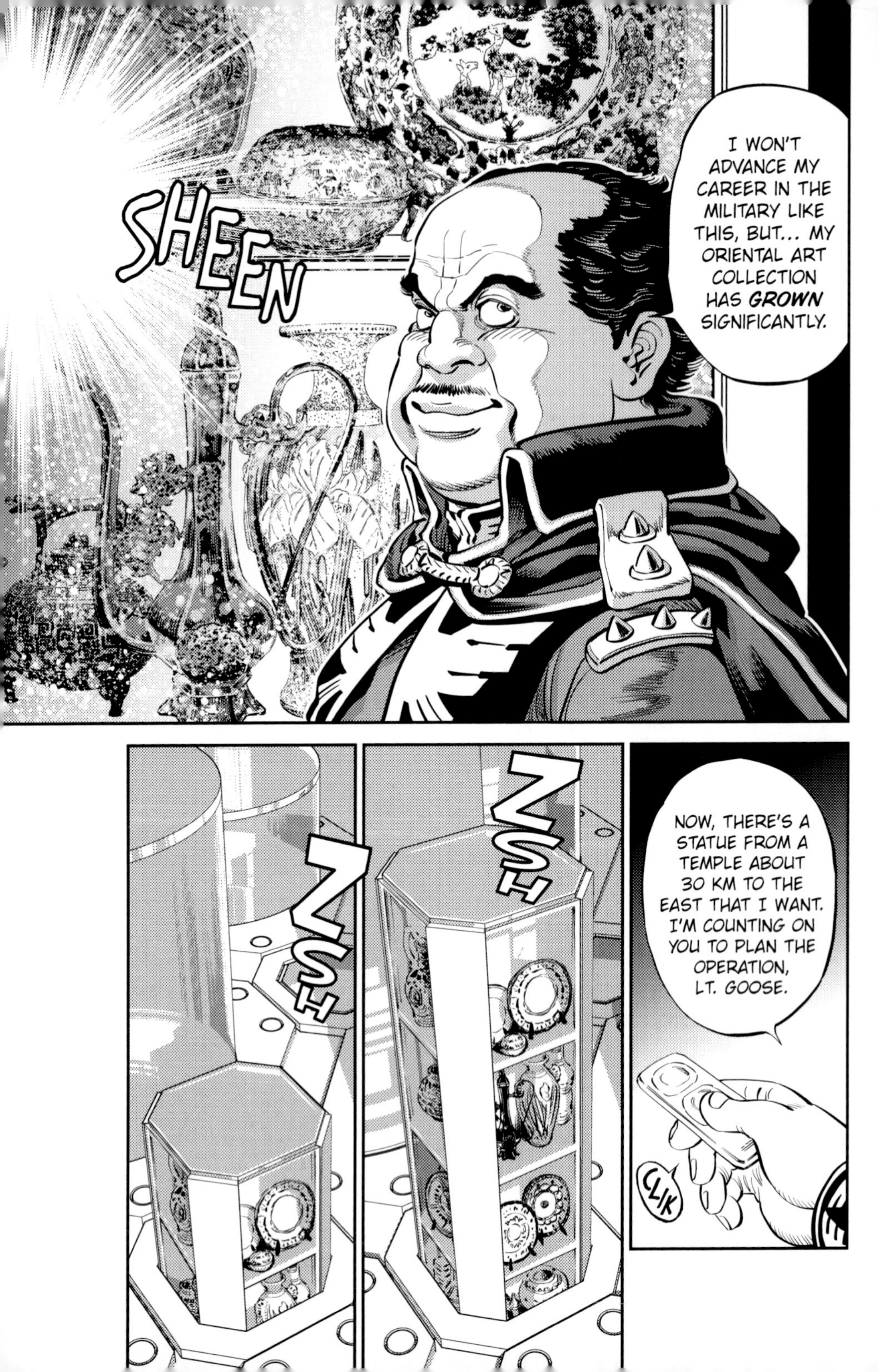
SHEEN
I WON'T ADVANCE MY CAREER IN THE MILITARY LIKE THIS, BUT... MY ORIENTAL ART COLLECTION HAS **GROWN** SIGNIFICANTLY.
NOW, THERE'S A STATUE FROM A TEMPLE ABOUT 30 KM TO THE EAST THAT I WANT. I'M COUNTING ON YOU TO PLAN THE OPERATION, LT. GOOSE.
CLIK
ZSH
ZSH

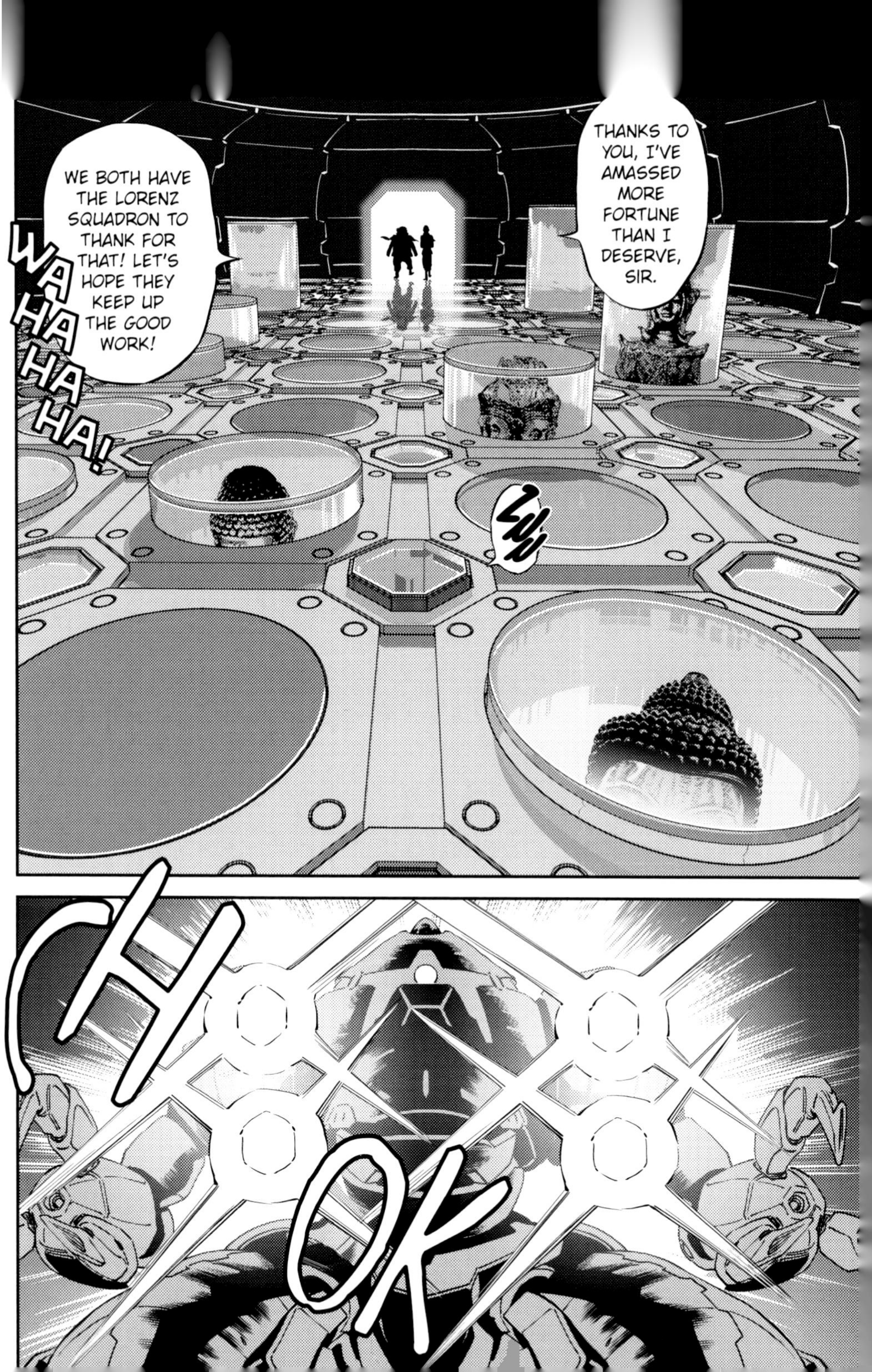
THANKS TO YOU, I'VE AMASSED MORE FORTUNE THAN I DESERVE, SIR.
WE BOTH HAVE THE LORENZ SQUADRON TO THANK FOR THAT! LET'S HOPE THEY KEEP UP THE GOOD WORK!
WAHAHAHAHA!
CH
OK

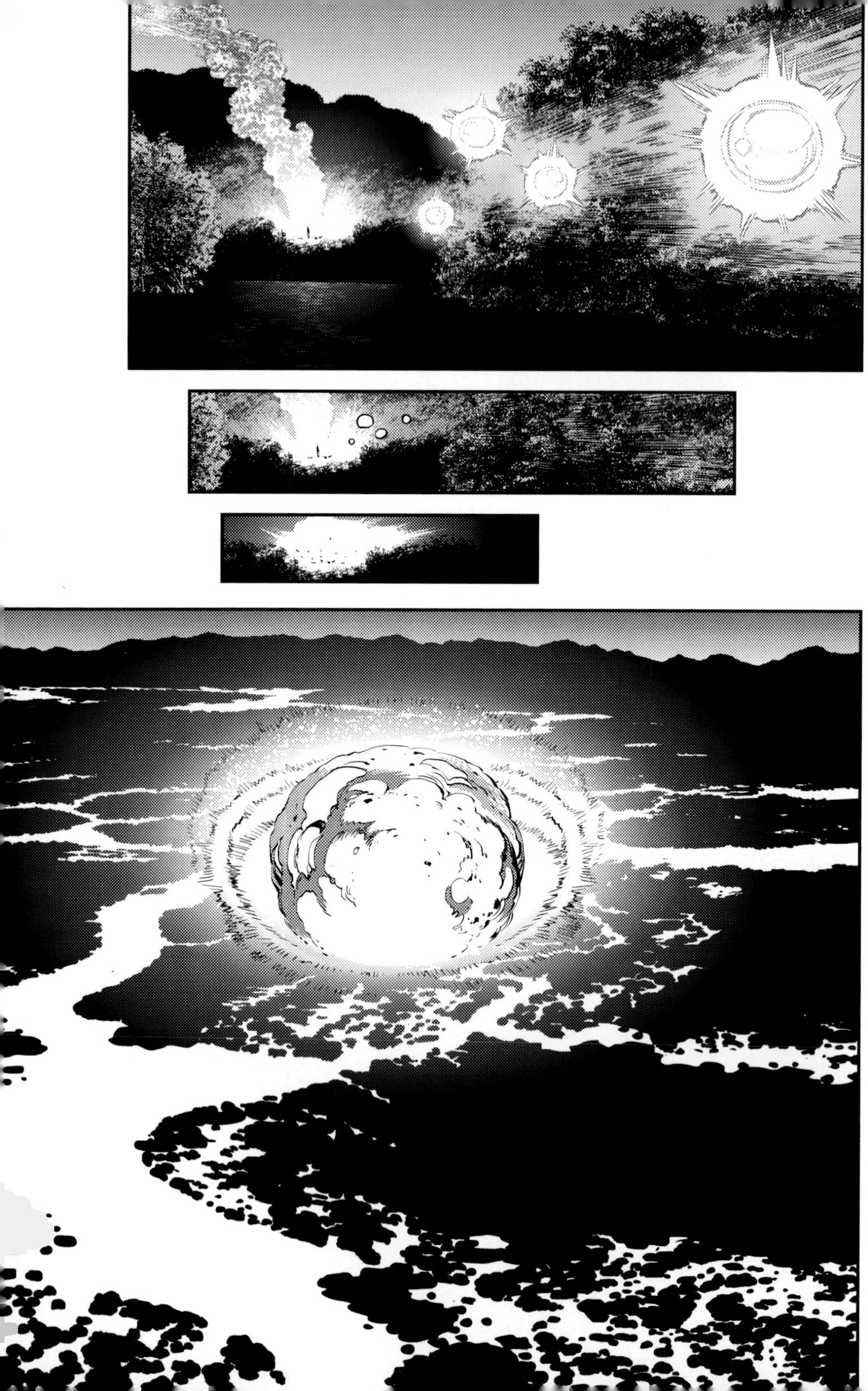

THAT TEMPLE WAS BUILT 800 YEARS AGO, BUT IT ONLY TAKES A SECOND TO TORCH IT. WAR REALLY IS A SIN.

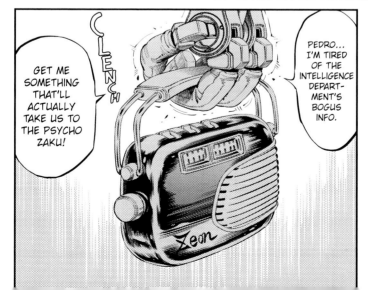

PEDRO... I'M TIRED OF THE INTELLIGENCE DEPARTMENT'S BOGUS INFO.

GET ME SOMETHING THAT'LL ACTUALLY TAKE US TO THE PSYCHO ZAKU!

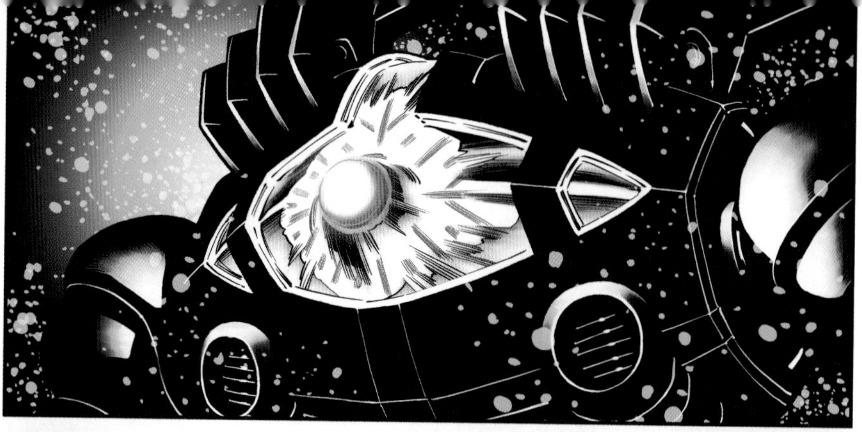

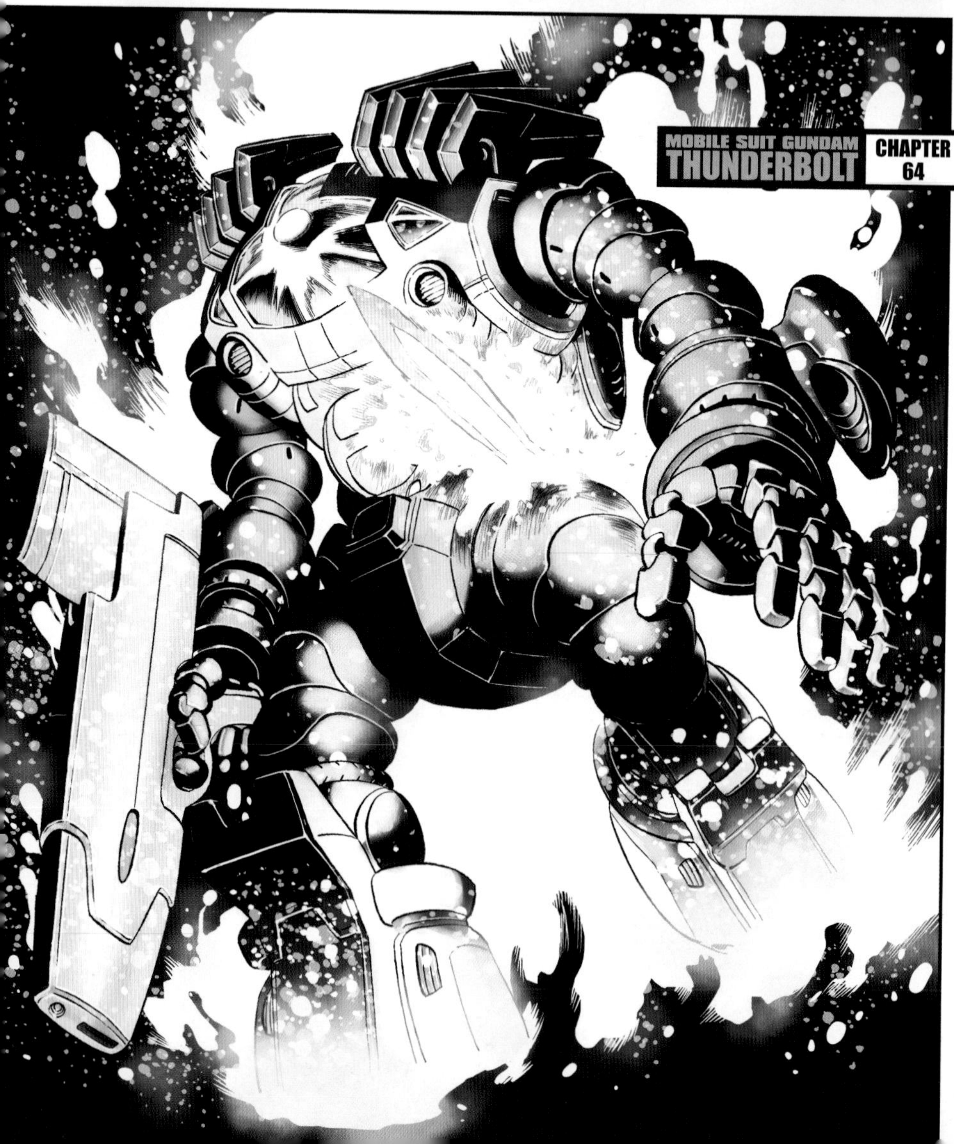
MOBILE SUIT GUNDAM THUNDERBOLT
CHAPTER 64

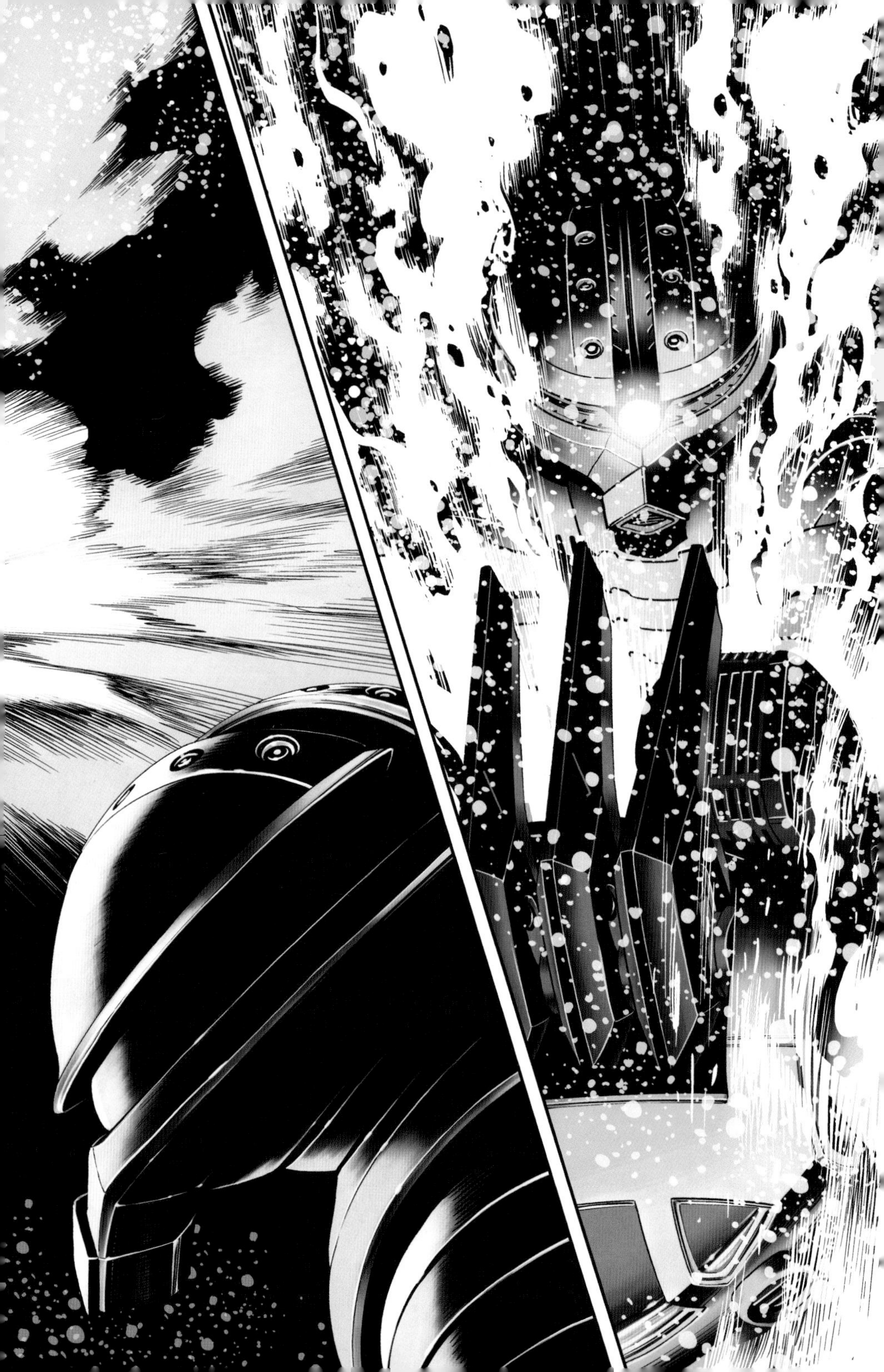

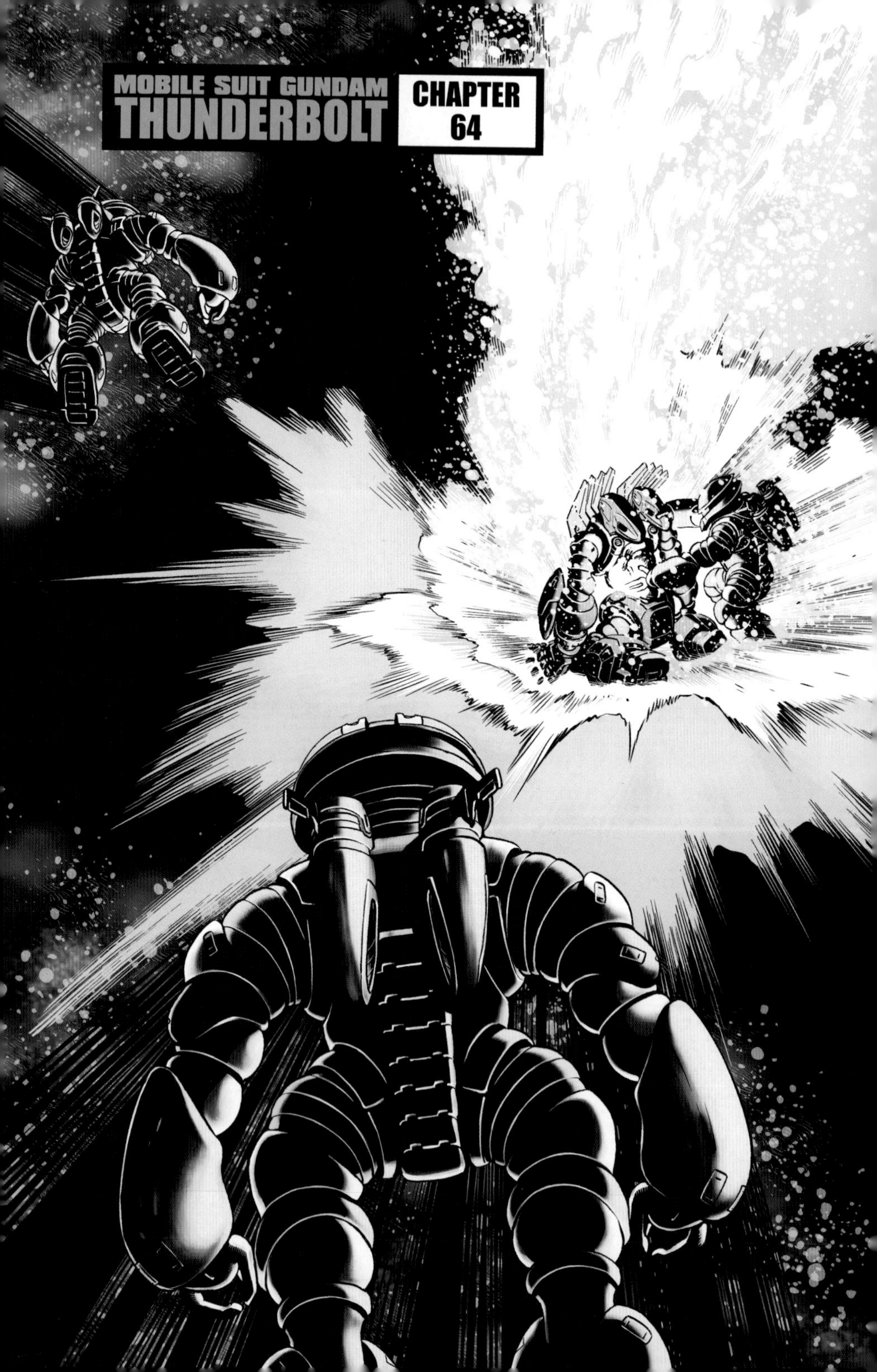
MOBILE SUIT GUNDAM
THUNDERBOLT
CHAPTER
64

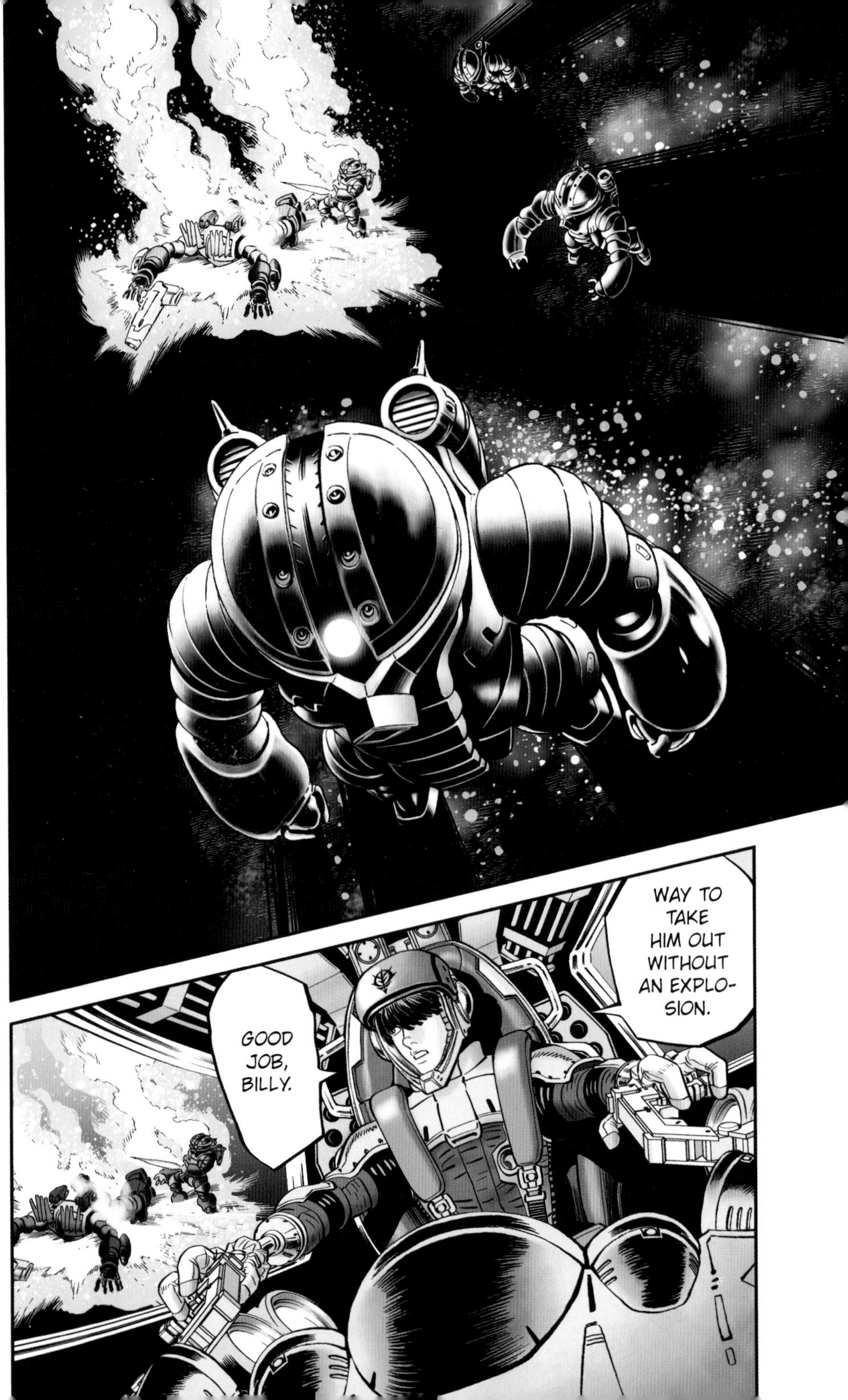
WAY TO TAKE HIM OUT WITHOUT AN EXPLOSION.
GOOD JOB, BILLY.

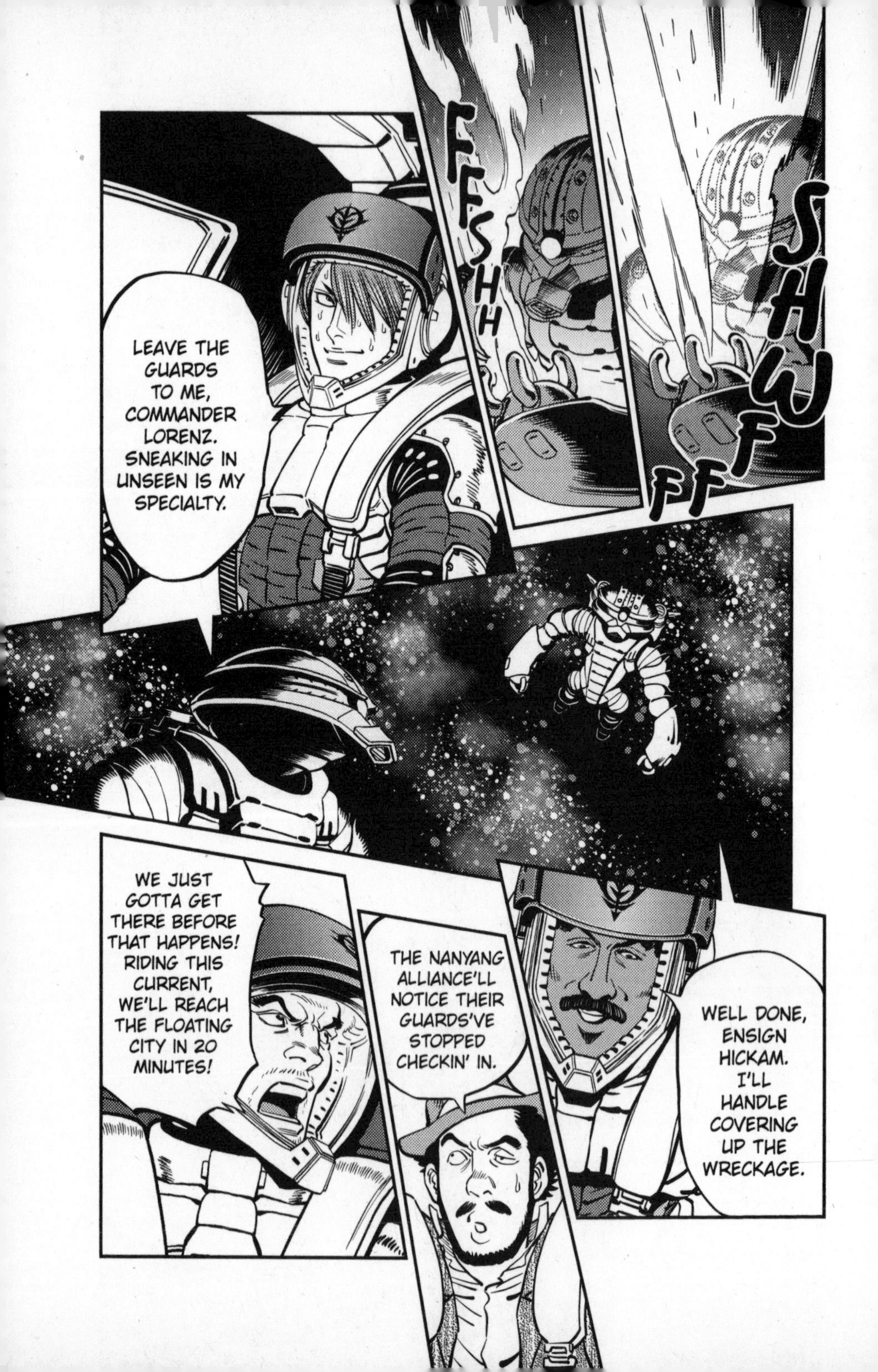
SHWFFF
FFSHH
LEAVE THE GUARDS TO ME, COMMANDER LORENZ. SNEAKING IN UNSEEN IS MY SPECIALTY.
WELL DONE, ENSIGN HICKAM. I'LL HANDLE COVERING UP THE WRECKAGE.
THE NANYANG ALLIANCE'LL NOTICE THEIR GUARDS'VE STOPPED CHECKIN' IN.
WE JUST GOTTA GET THERE BEFORE THAT HAPPENS! RIDING THIS CURRENT, WE'LL REACH THE FLOATING CITY IN 20 MINUTES!

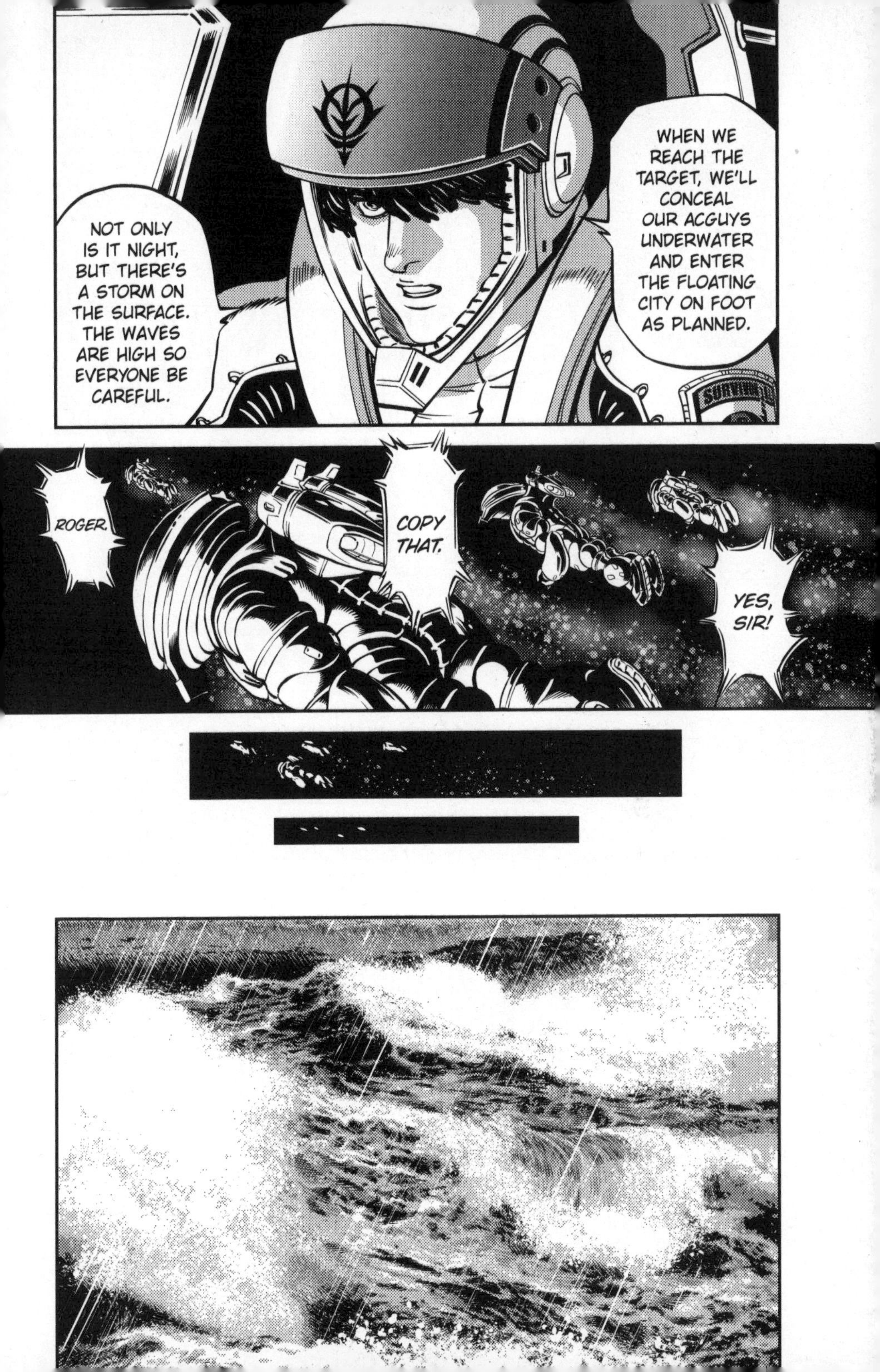
WHEN WE REACH THE TARGET, WE'LL CONCEAL OUR ACGUYS UNDERWATER AND ENTER THE FLOATING CITY ON FOOT AS PLANNED.
NOT ONLY IS IT NIGHT, BUT THERE'S A STORM ON THE SURFACE. THE WAVES ARE HIGH SO EVERYONE BE CAREFUL.
YES, SIR!
COPY THAT.
ROGER.

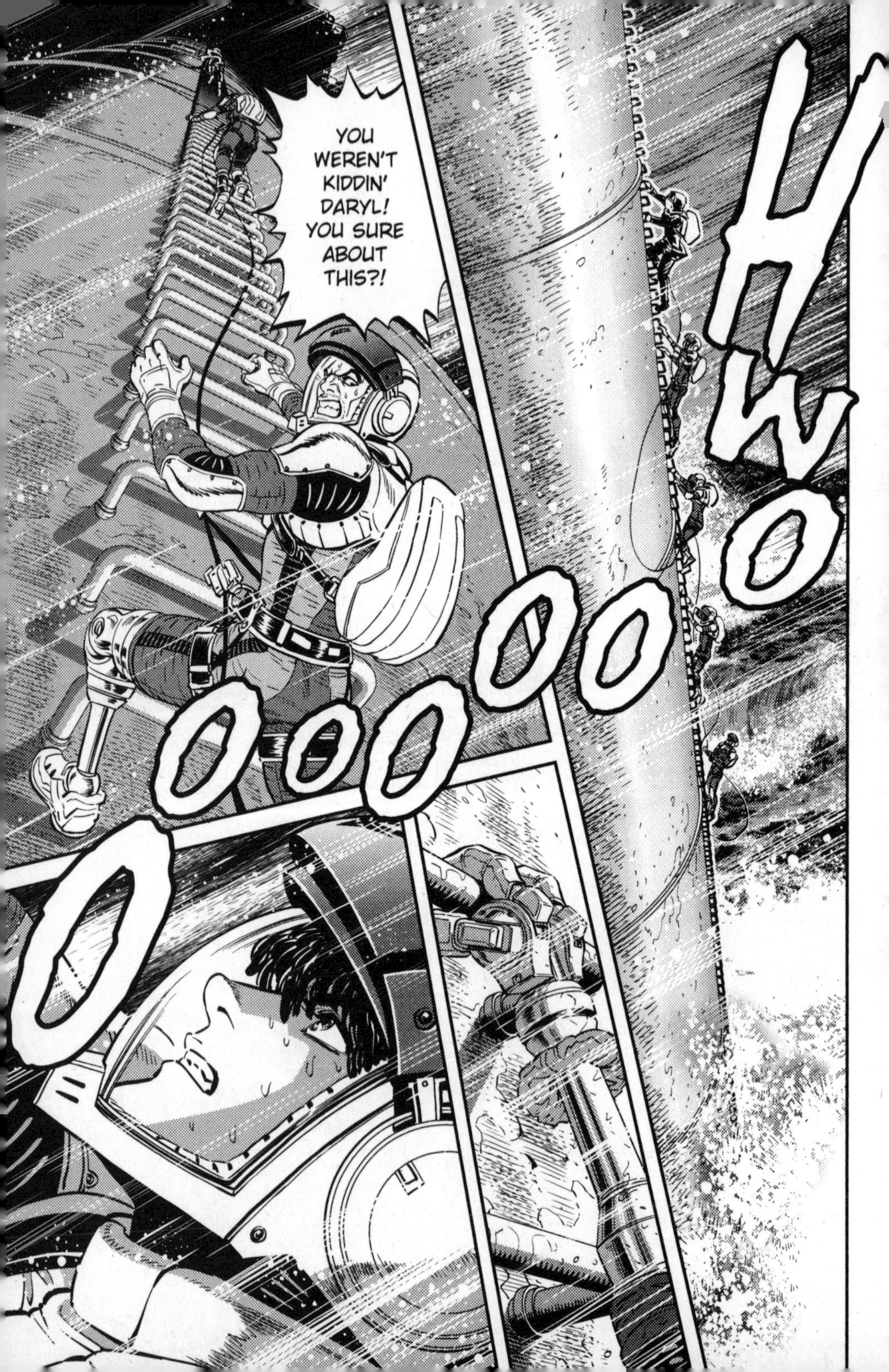
YOU WEREN'T KIDDIN' DARYL! YOU SURE ABOUT THIS?!
HWOOOOOOOO

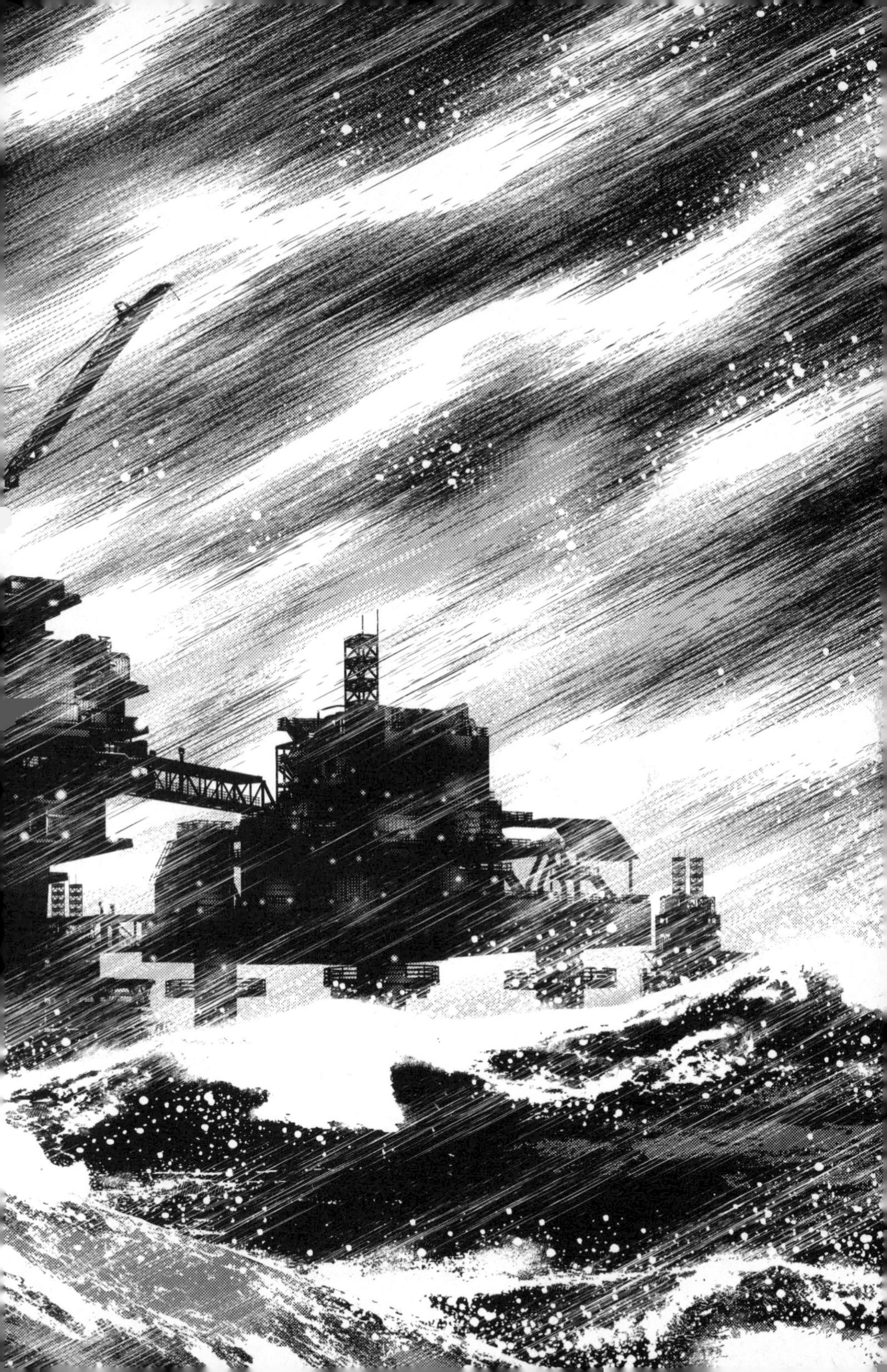

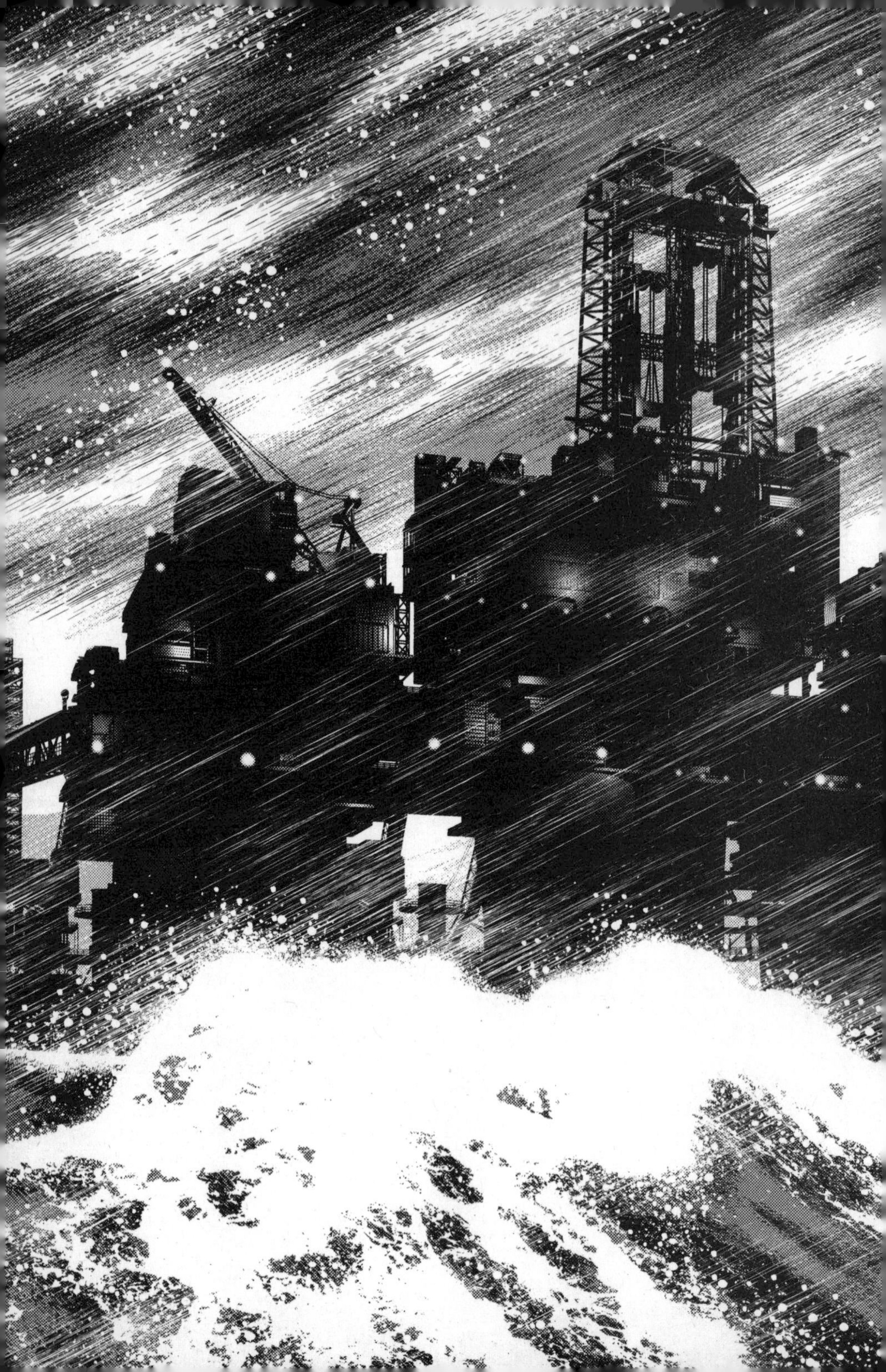

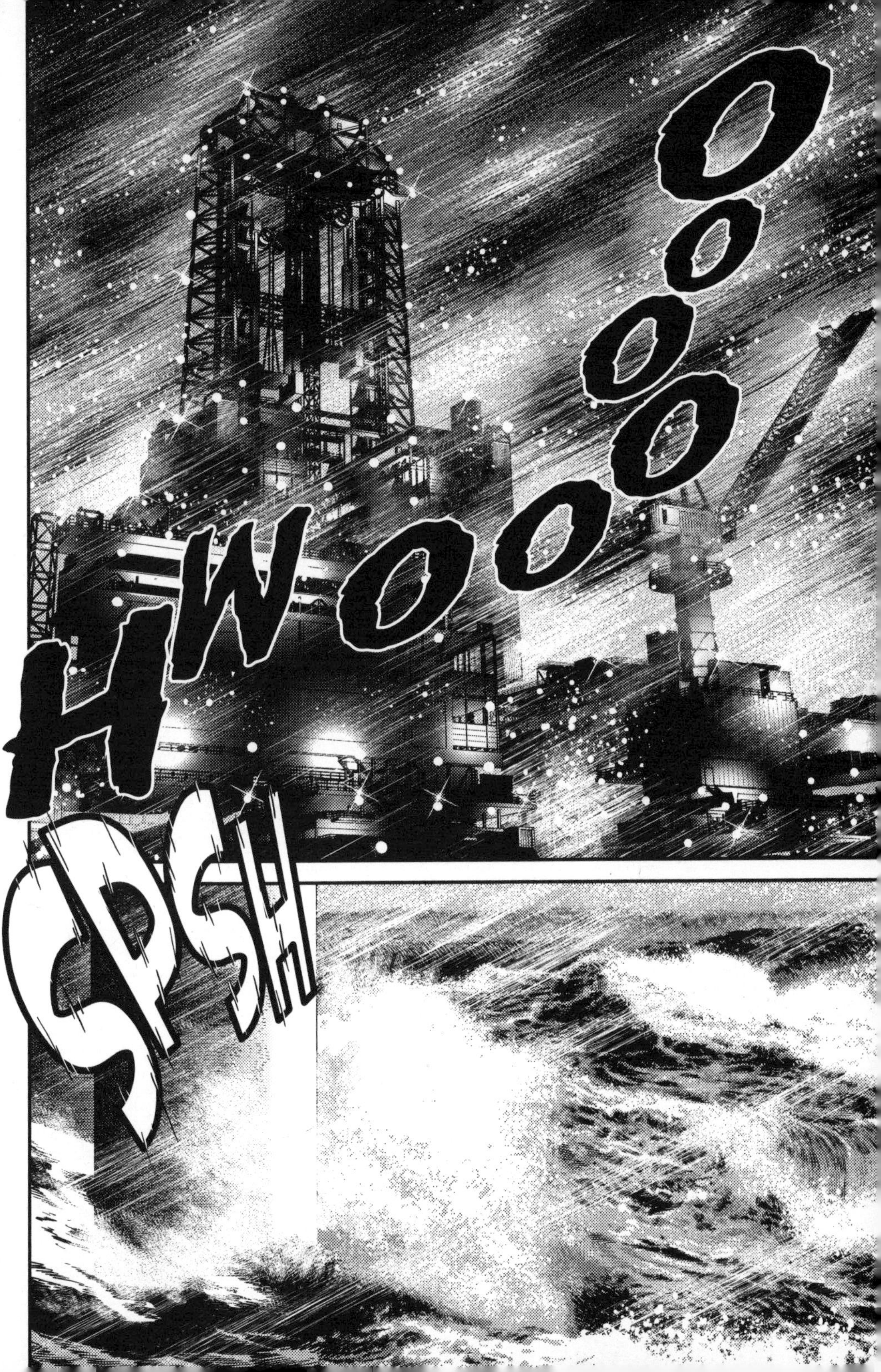
HWOOOOOO
SPSH

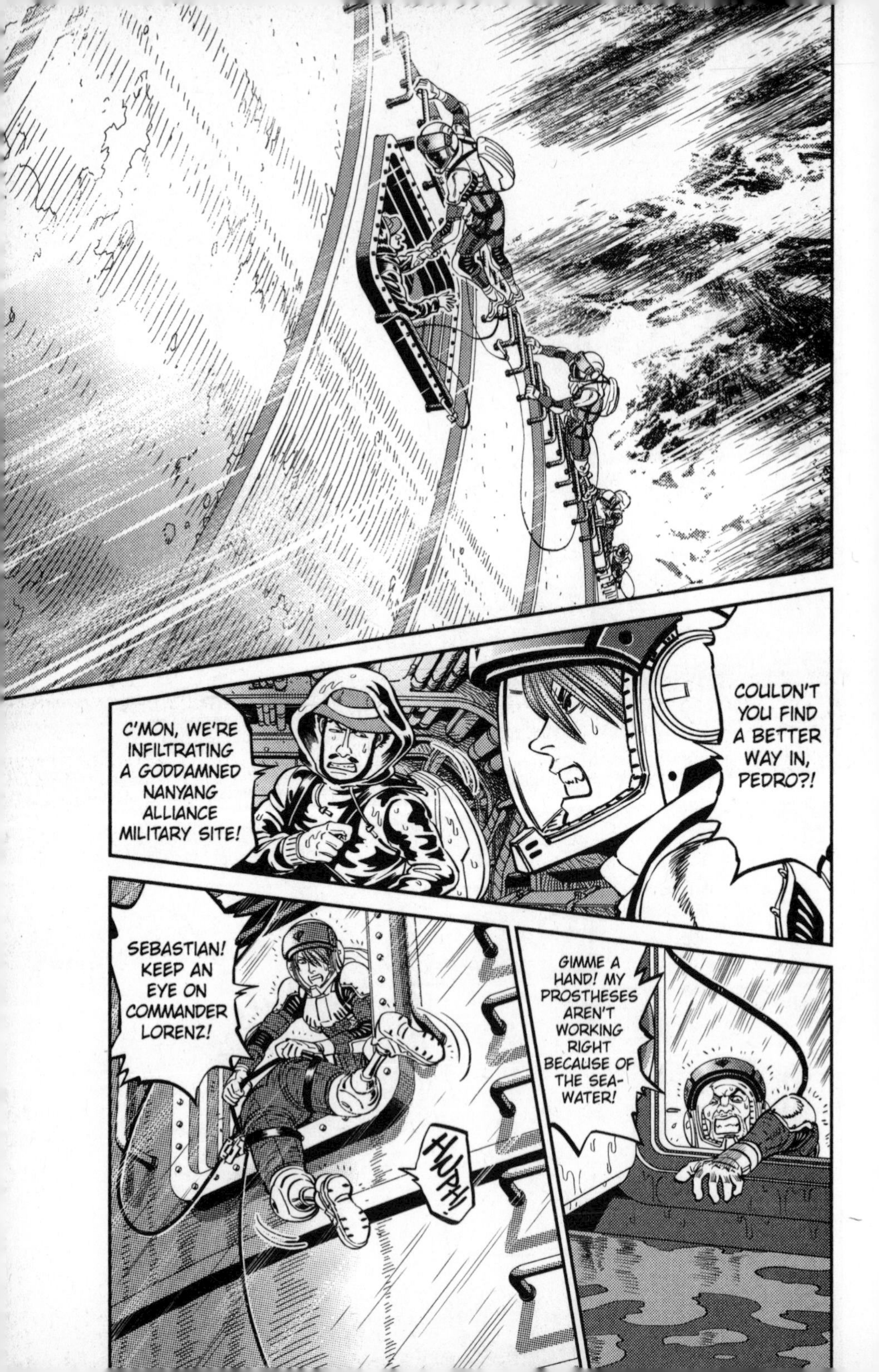
COULDN'T YOU FIND A BETTER WAY IN, PEDRO?!
C'MON, WE'RE INFILTRATING A GODDAMNED NANYANG ALLIANCE MILITARY SITE!
GIMME A HAND! MY PROSTHESES AREN'T WORKING RIGHT BECAUSE OF THE SEA-WATER!
SEBASTIAN! KEEP AN EYE ON COMMANDER LORENZ!
HUPH!

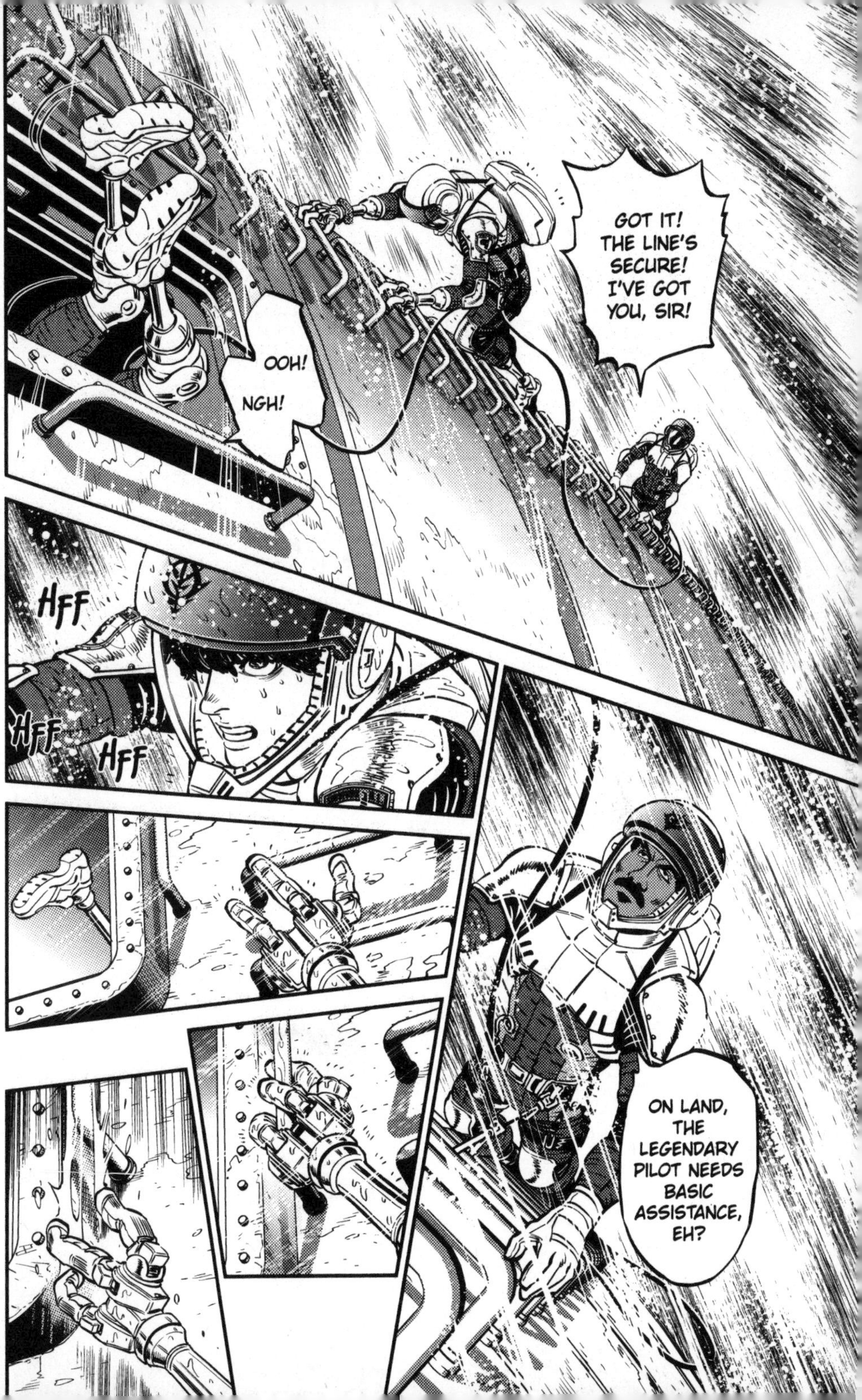
GOT IT! THE LINE'S SECURE! I'VE GOT YOU, SIR!
OOH!
NGH!
ON LAND, THE LEGENDARY PILOT NEEDS BASIC ASSISTANCE, EH?
HFF
HFF
HFF

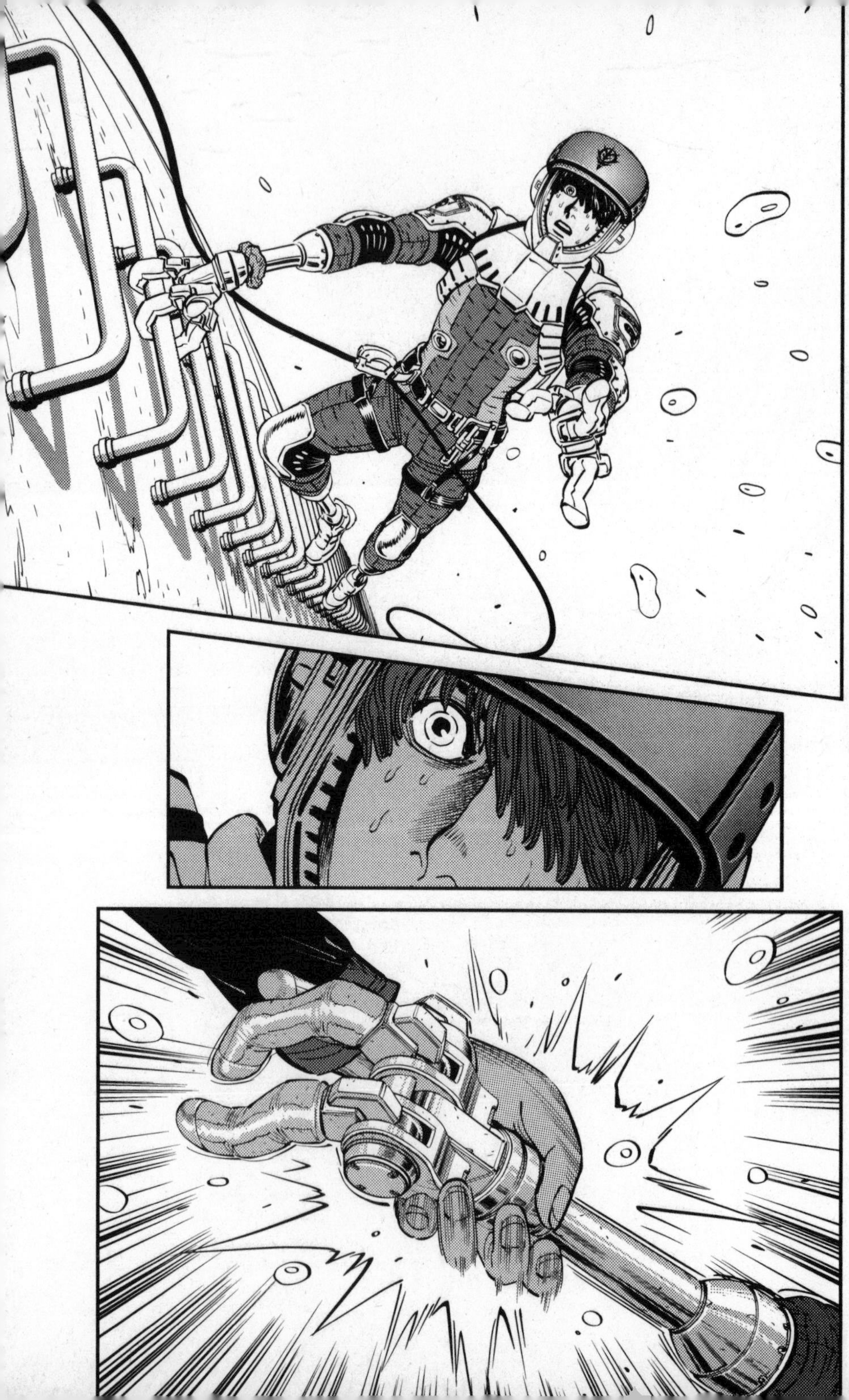

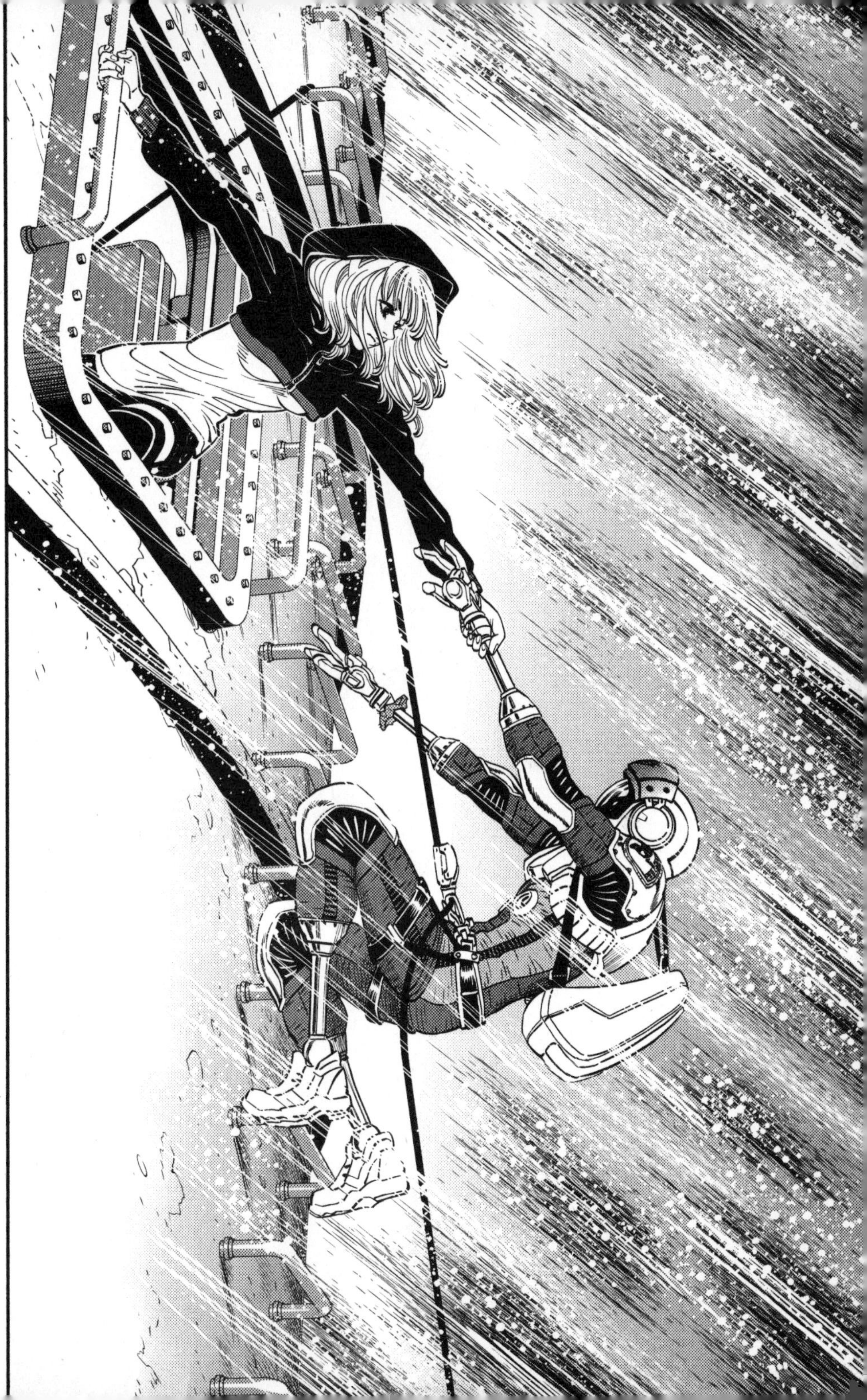

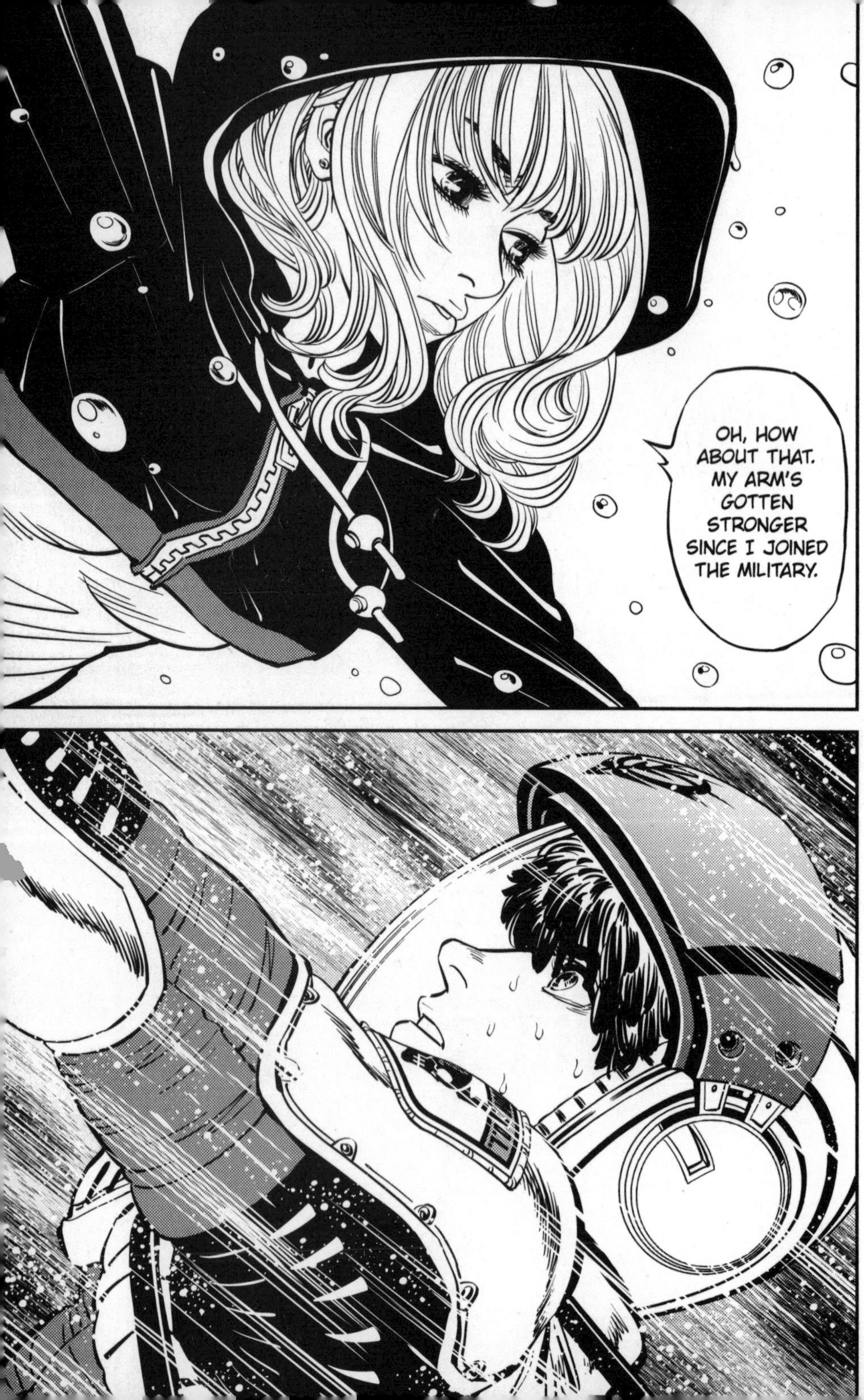
OH, HOW ABOUT THAT. MY ARM'S GOTTEN STRONGER SINCE I JOINED THE MILITARY.

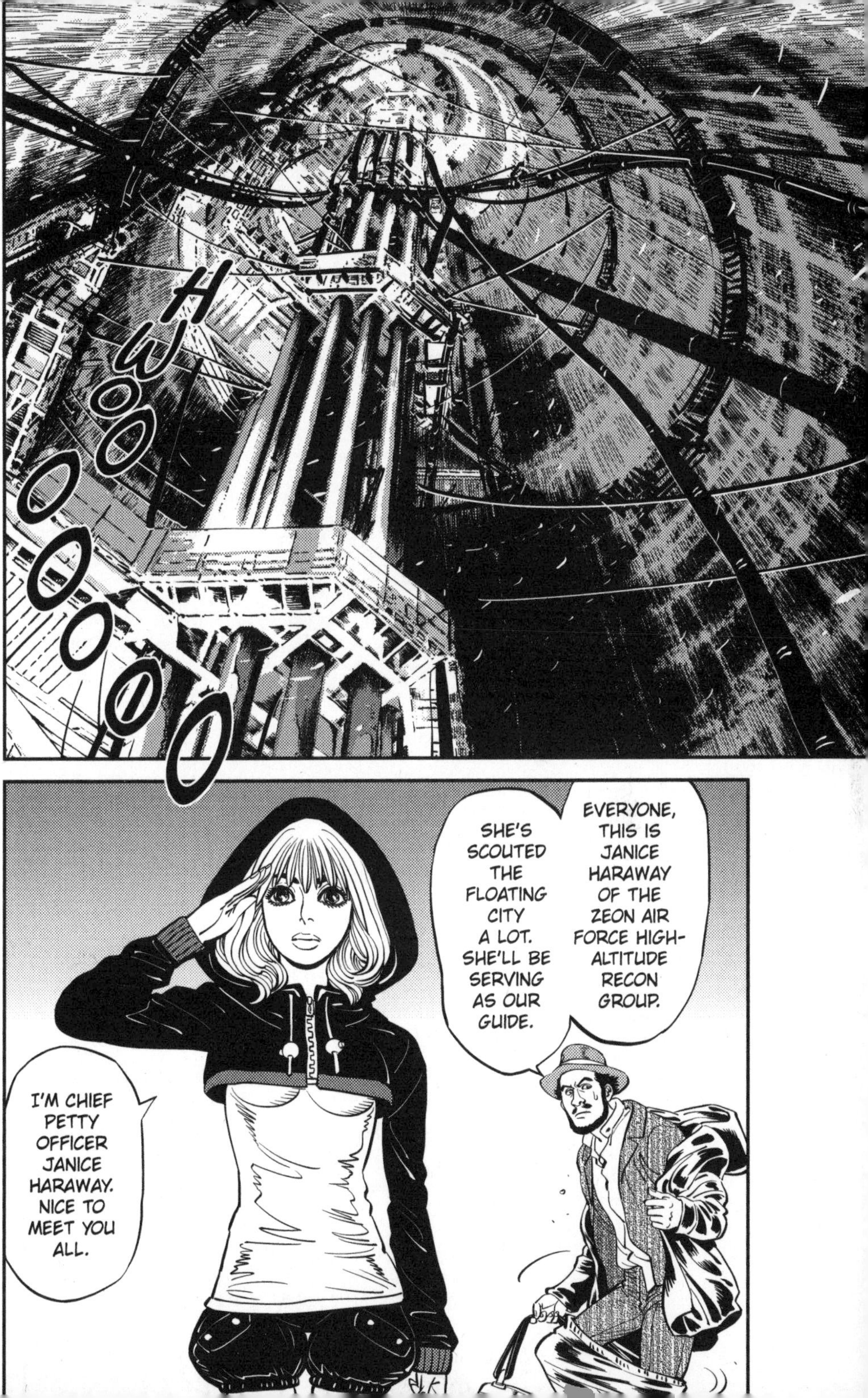
HWOOOOOOOOO
EVERYONE, THIS IS JANICE HARAWAY OF THE ZEON AIR FORCE HIGH-ALTITUDE RECON GROUP.
SHE'S SCOUTED THE FLOATING CITY A LOT. SHE'LL BE SERVING AS OUR GUIDE.
I'M CHIEF PETTY OFFICER JANICE HARAWAY. NICE TO MEET YOU ALL.

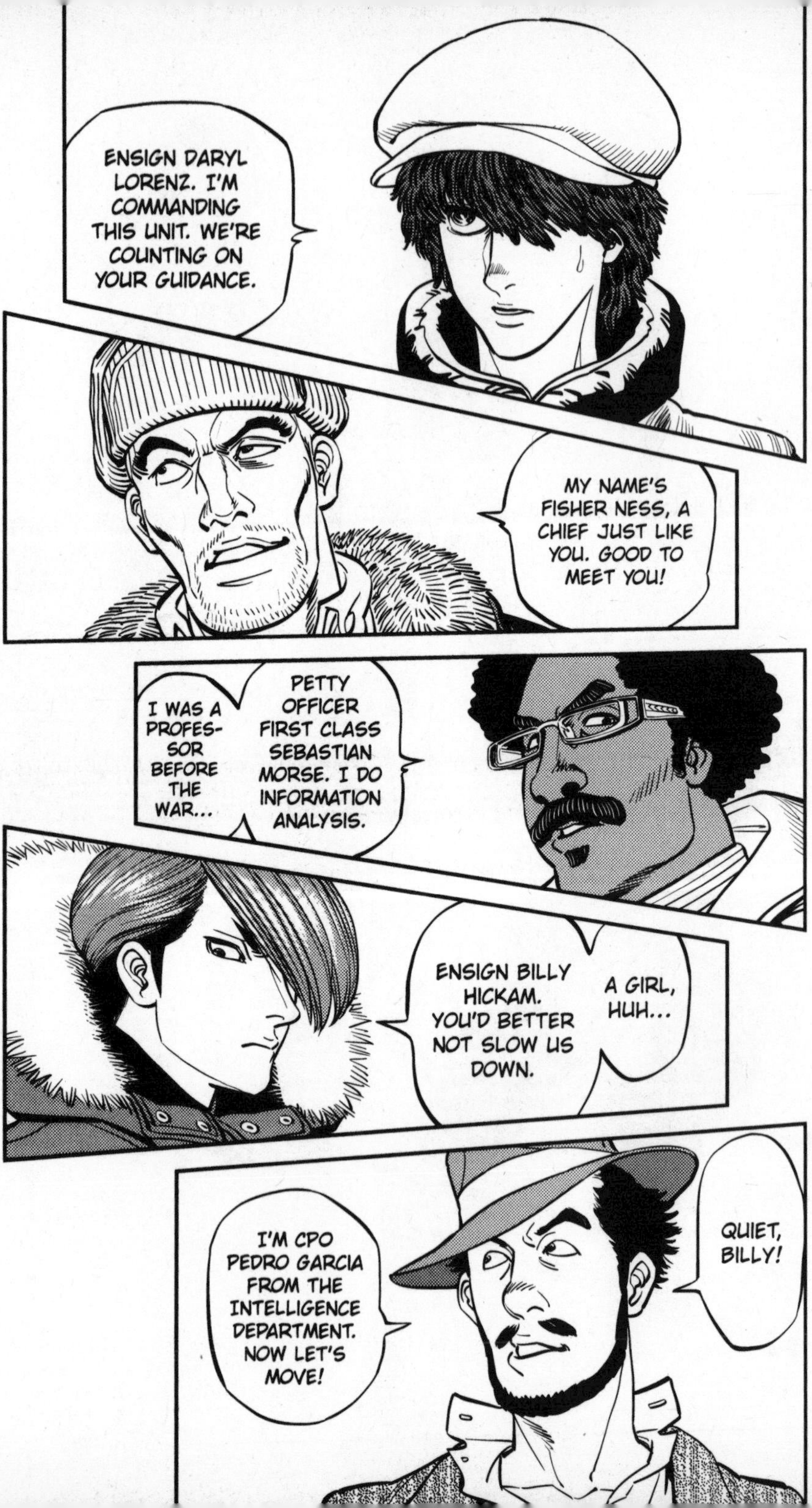
ENSIGN DARYL LORENZ. I'M COMMANDING THIS UNIT. WE'RE COUNTING ON YOUR GUIDANCE.
MY NAME'S FISHER NESS, A CHIEF JUST LIKE YOU. GOOD TO MEET YOU!
PETTY OFFICER FIRST CLASS SEBASTIAN MORSE. I DO INFORMATION ANALYSIS.
I WAS A PROFES-SOR BEFORE THE WAR...
A GIRL, HUH...
ENSIGN BILLY HICKAM. YOU'D BETTER NOT SLOW US DOWN.
QUIET, BILLY!
I'M CPO PEDRO GARCIA FROM THE INTELLIGENCE DEPARTMENT. NOW LET'S MOVE!

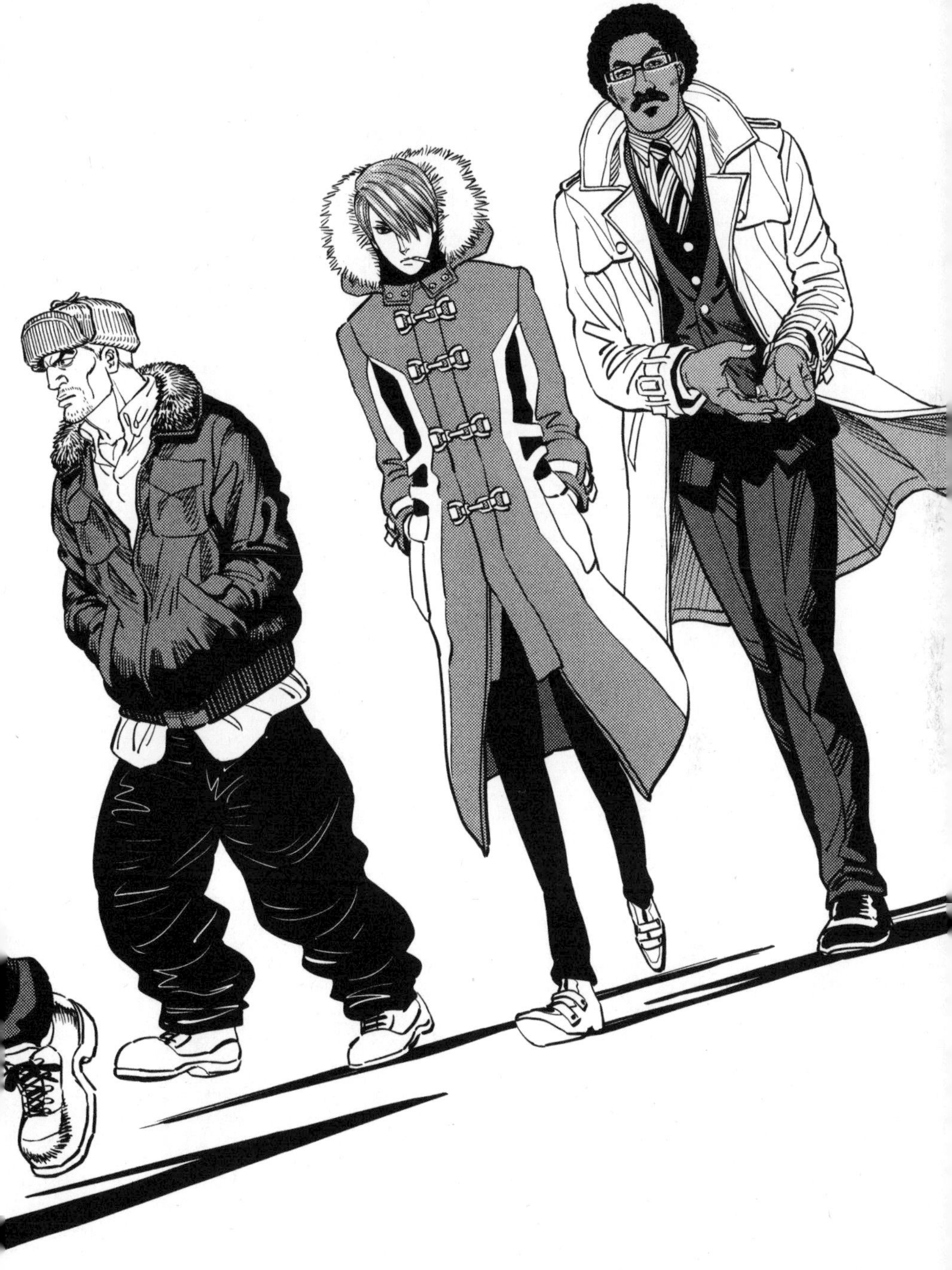

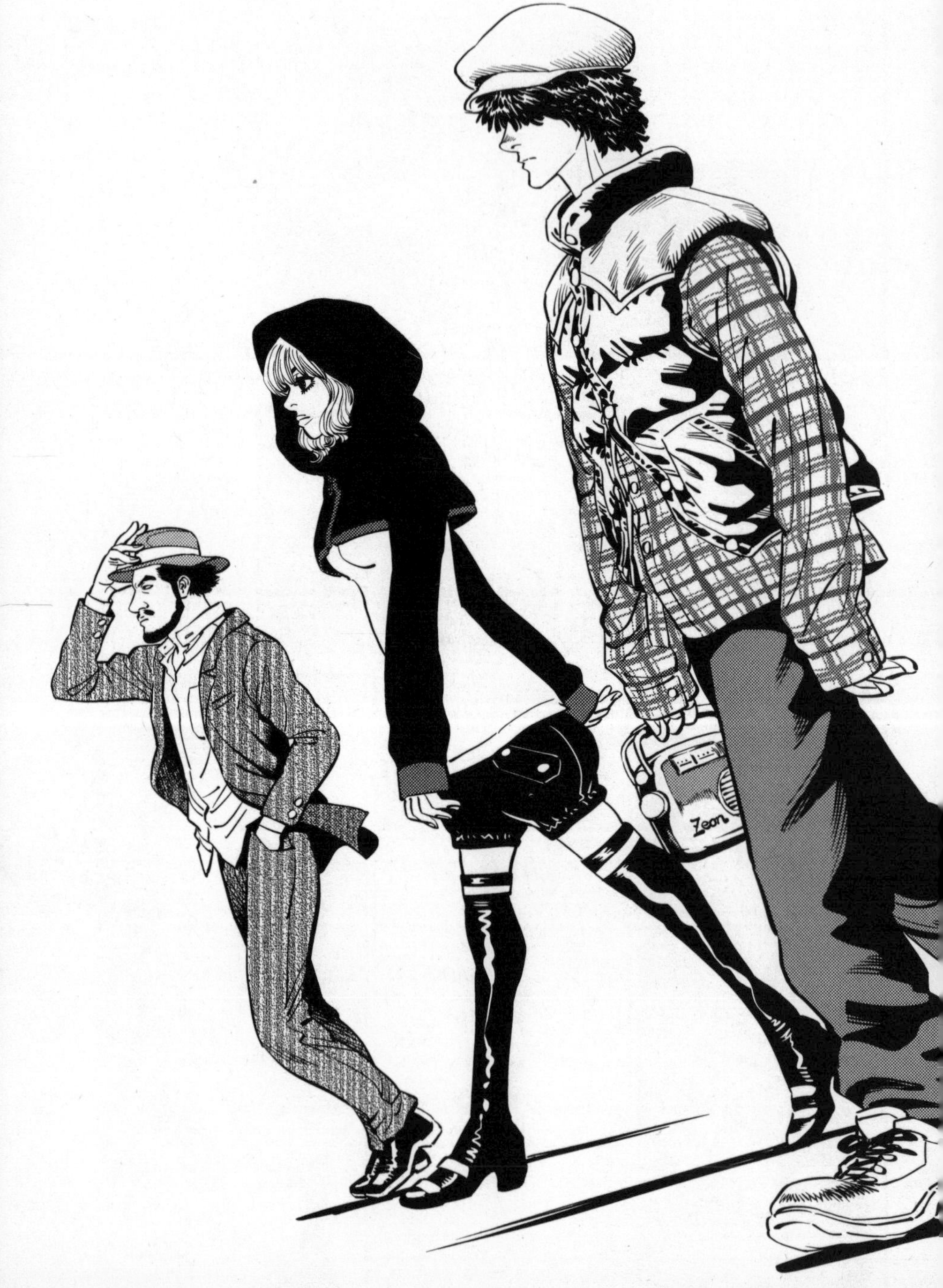
Zeon

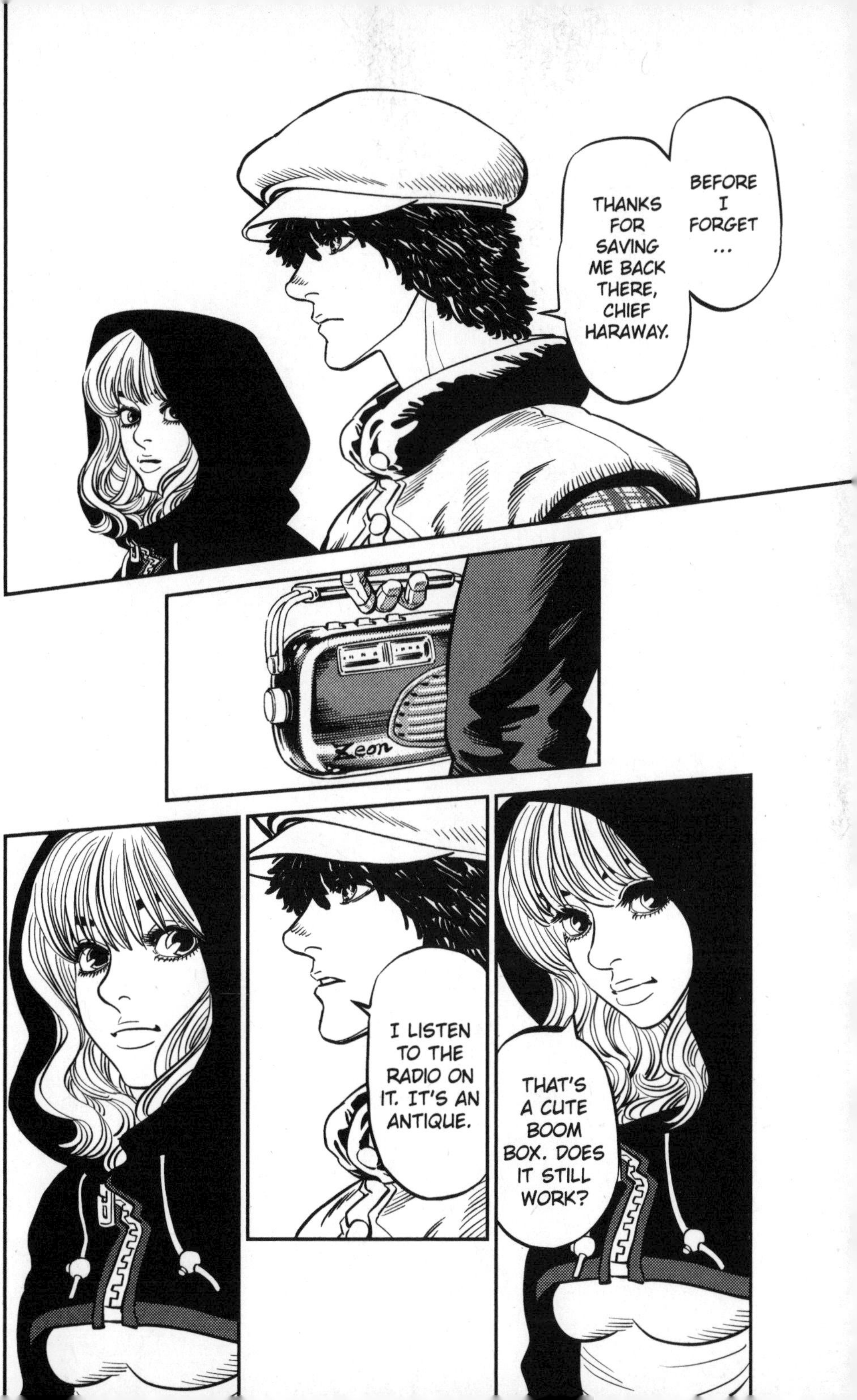
BEFORE I FORGET...
THANKS FOR SAVING ME BACK THERE, CHIEF HARAWAY.
Zeon
THAT'S A CUTE BOOM BOX. DOES IT STILL WORK?
I LISTEN TO THE RADIO ON IT. IT'S AN ANTIQUE.

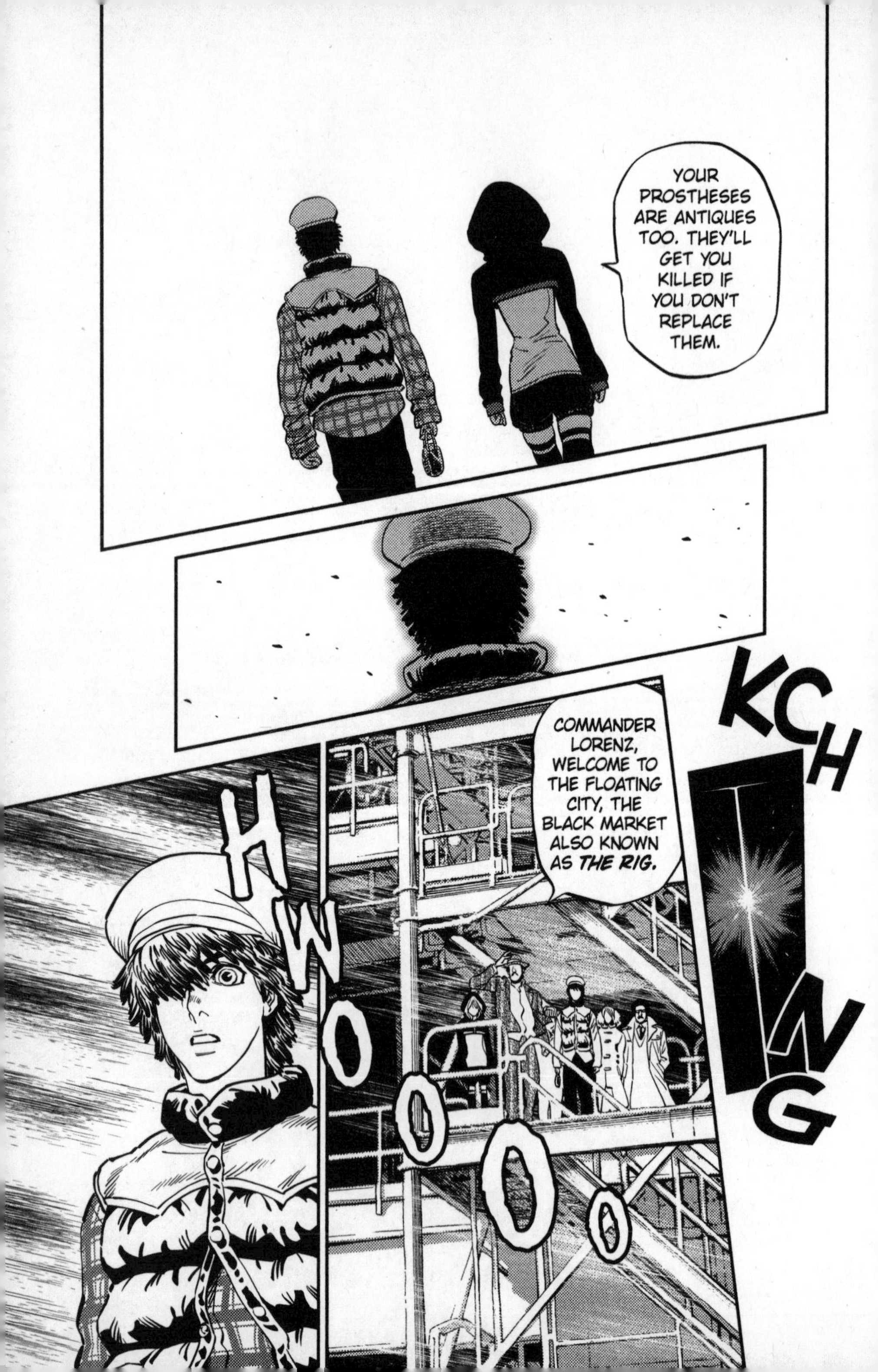
YOUR PROSTHESES ARE ANTIQUES TOO. THEY'LL GET YOU KILLED IF YOU DON'T REPLACE THEM.
KCHING
COMMANDER LORENZ, WELCOME TO THE FLOATING CITY, THE BLACK MARKET ALSO KNOWN AS *THE RIG.*
HWOOOOO

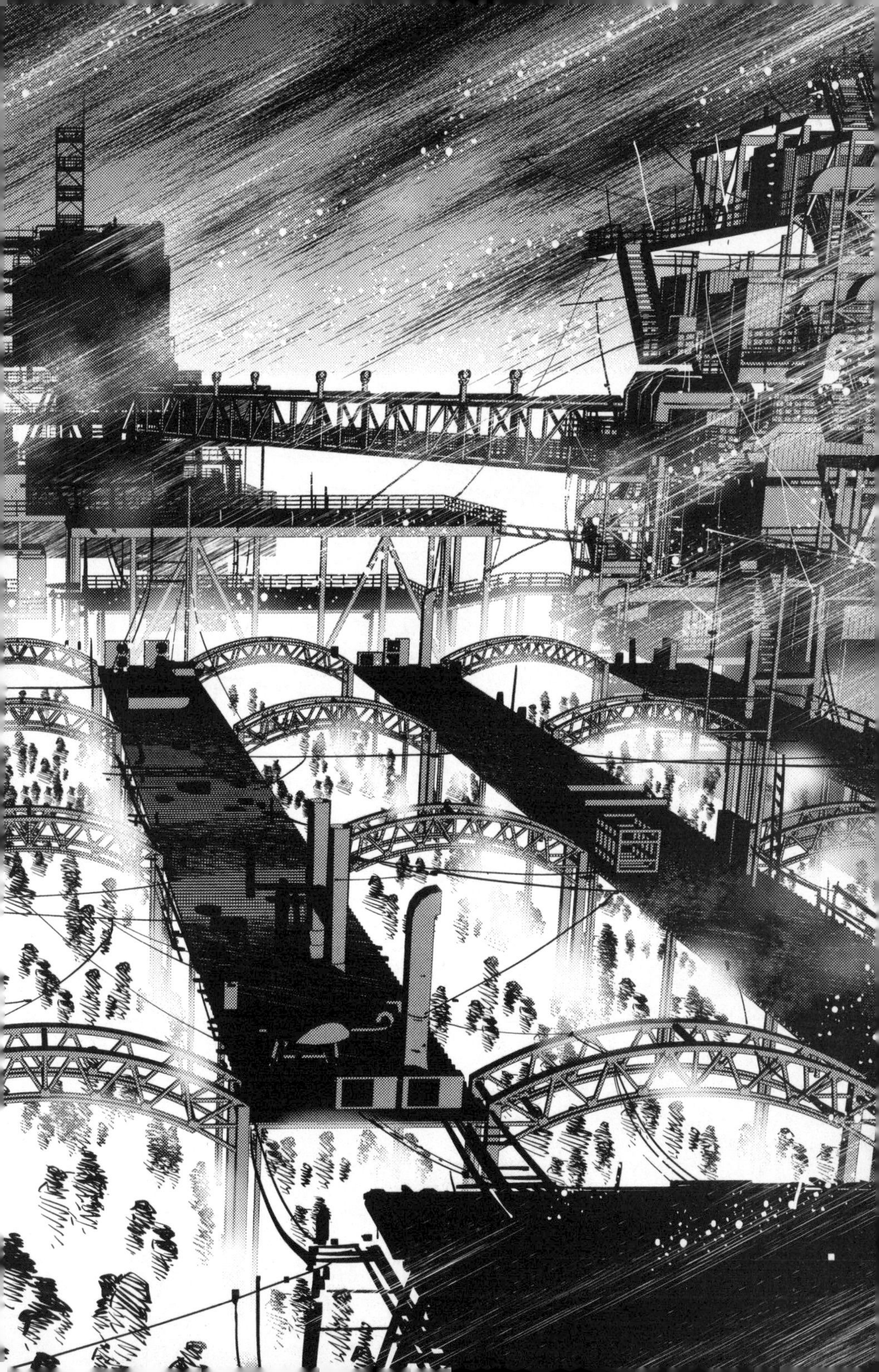

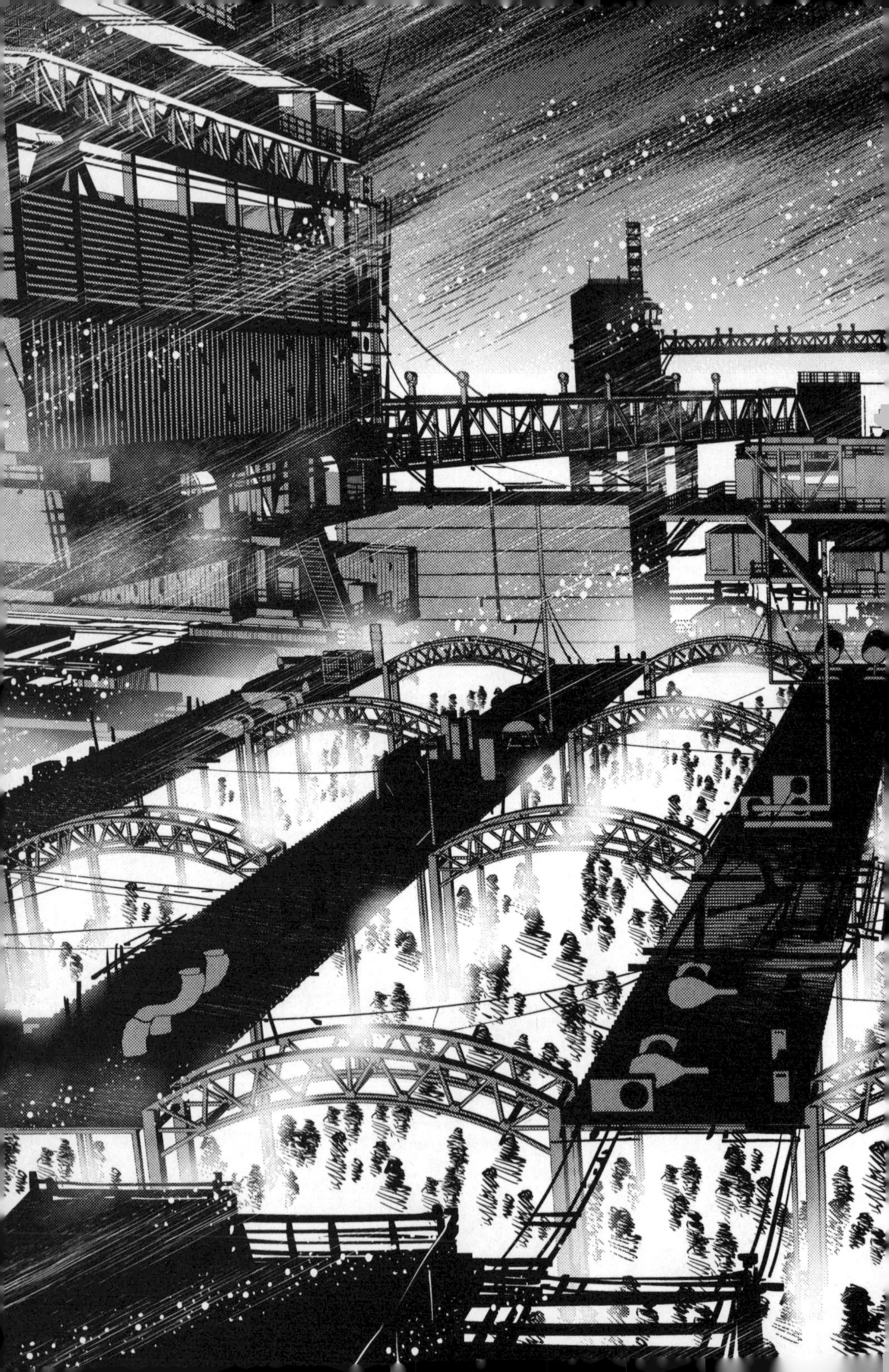

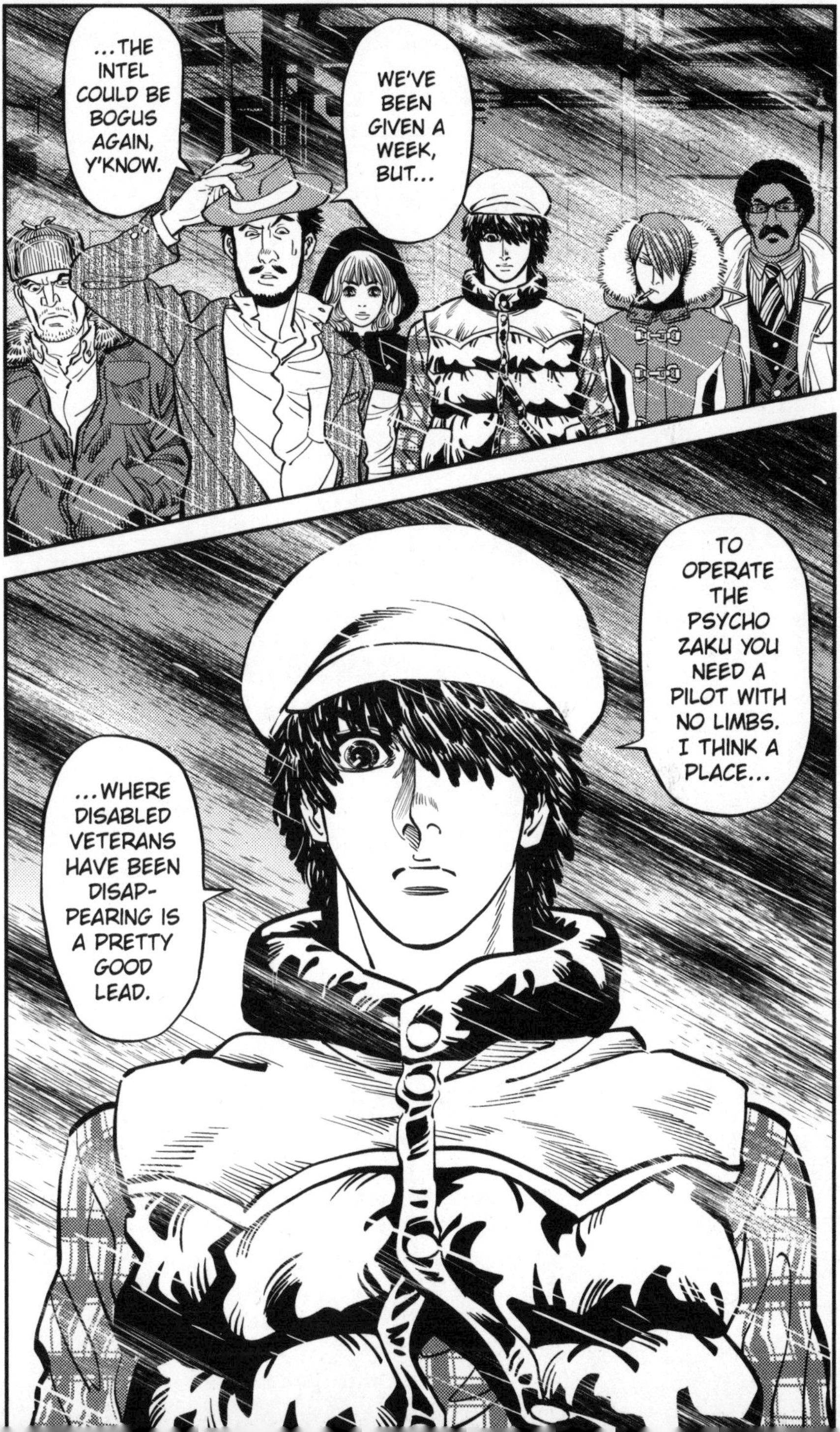
WE'VE BEEN GIVEN A WEEK, BUT...
...THE INTEL COULD BE BOGUS AGAIN, Y'KNOW.
TO OPERATE THE PSYCHO ZAKU YOU NEED A PILOT WITH NO LIMBS. I THINK A PLACE...
...WHERE DISABLED VETERANS HAVE BEEN DISAP-PEARING IS A PRETTY GOOD LEAD.

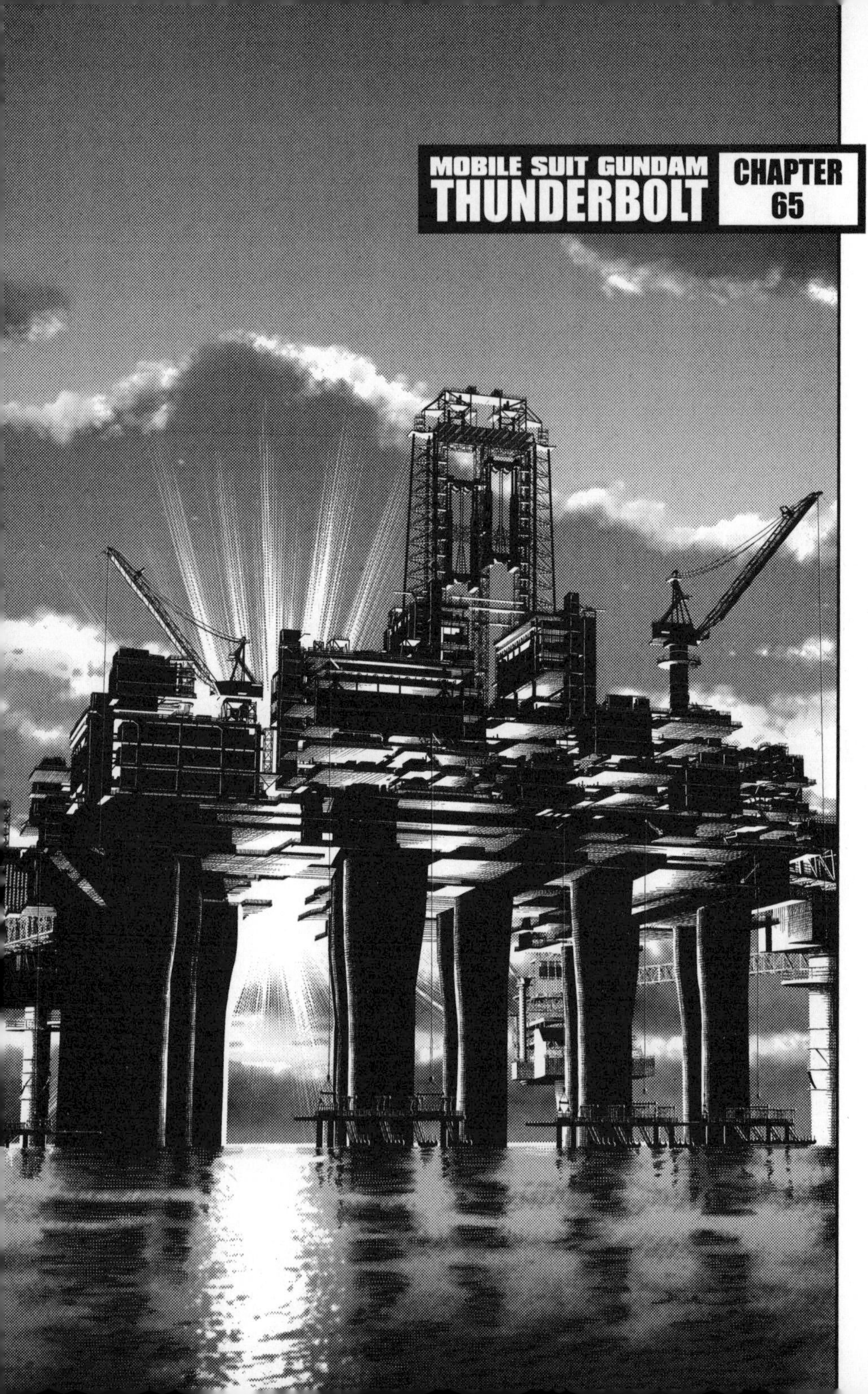
MOBILE SUIT GUNDAM
THUNDERBOLT
CHAPTER
65

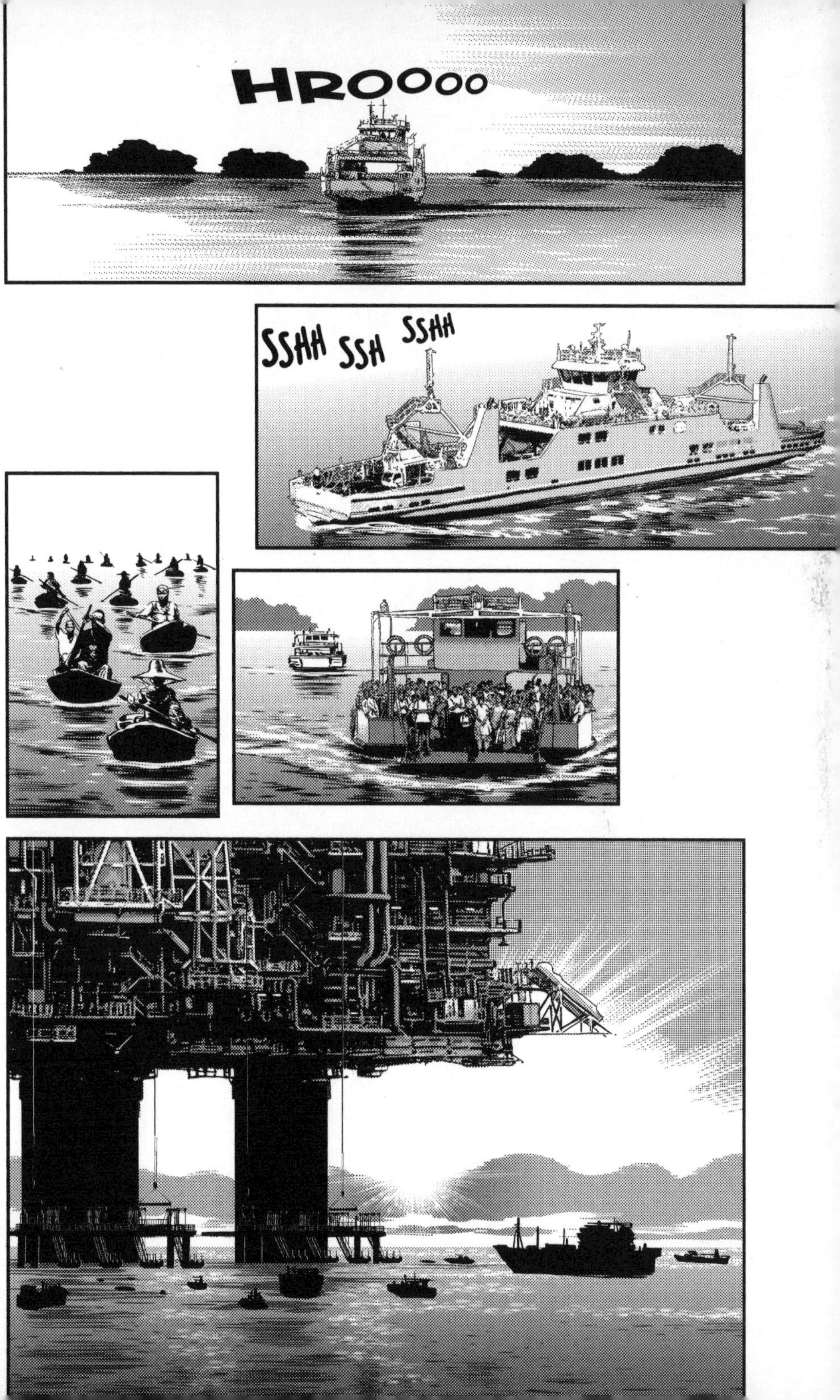
HROOoo
SSHH SSH SSHH

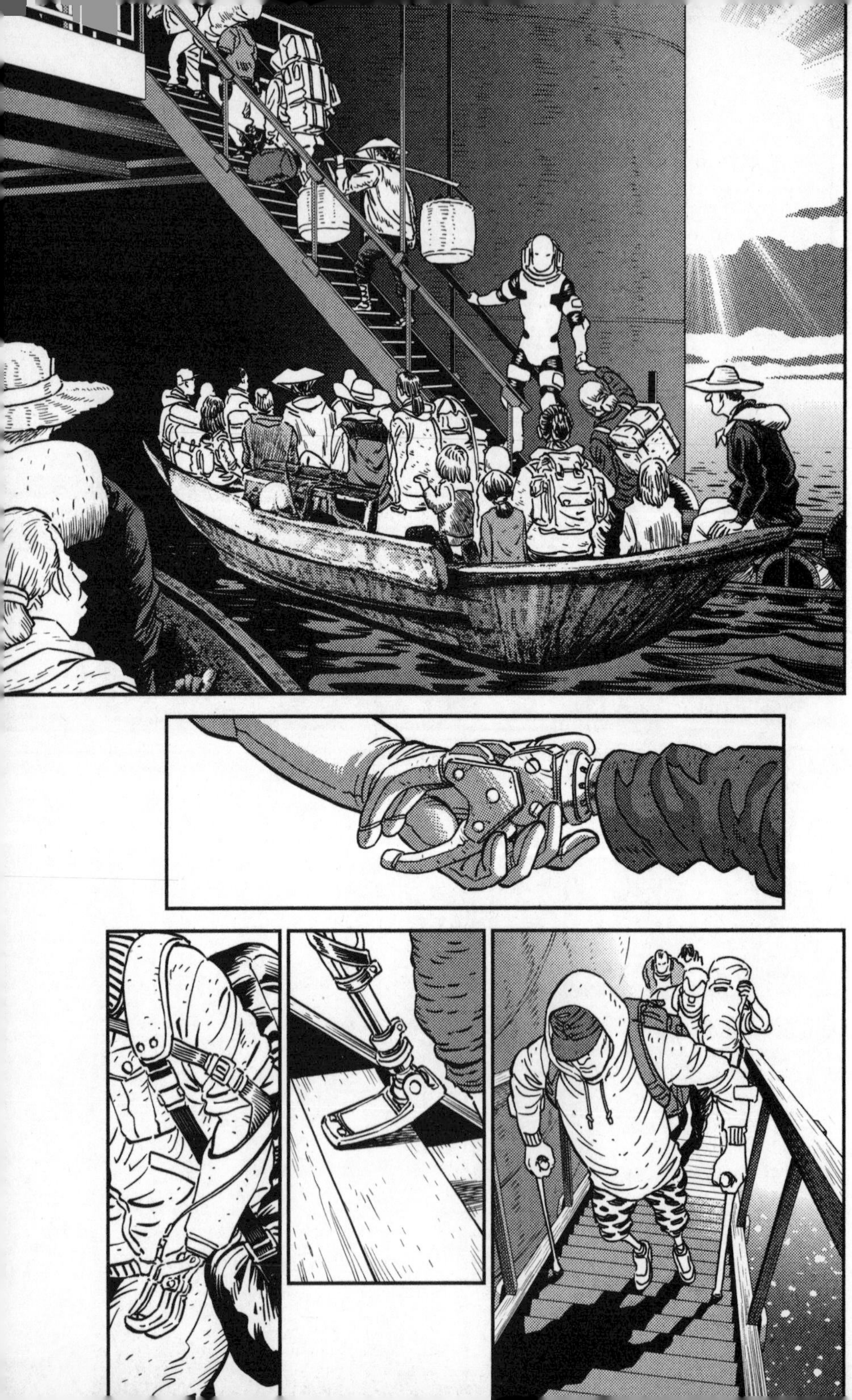

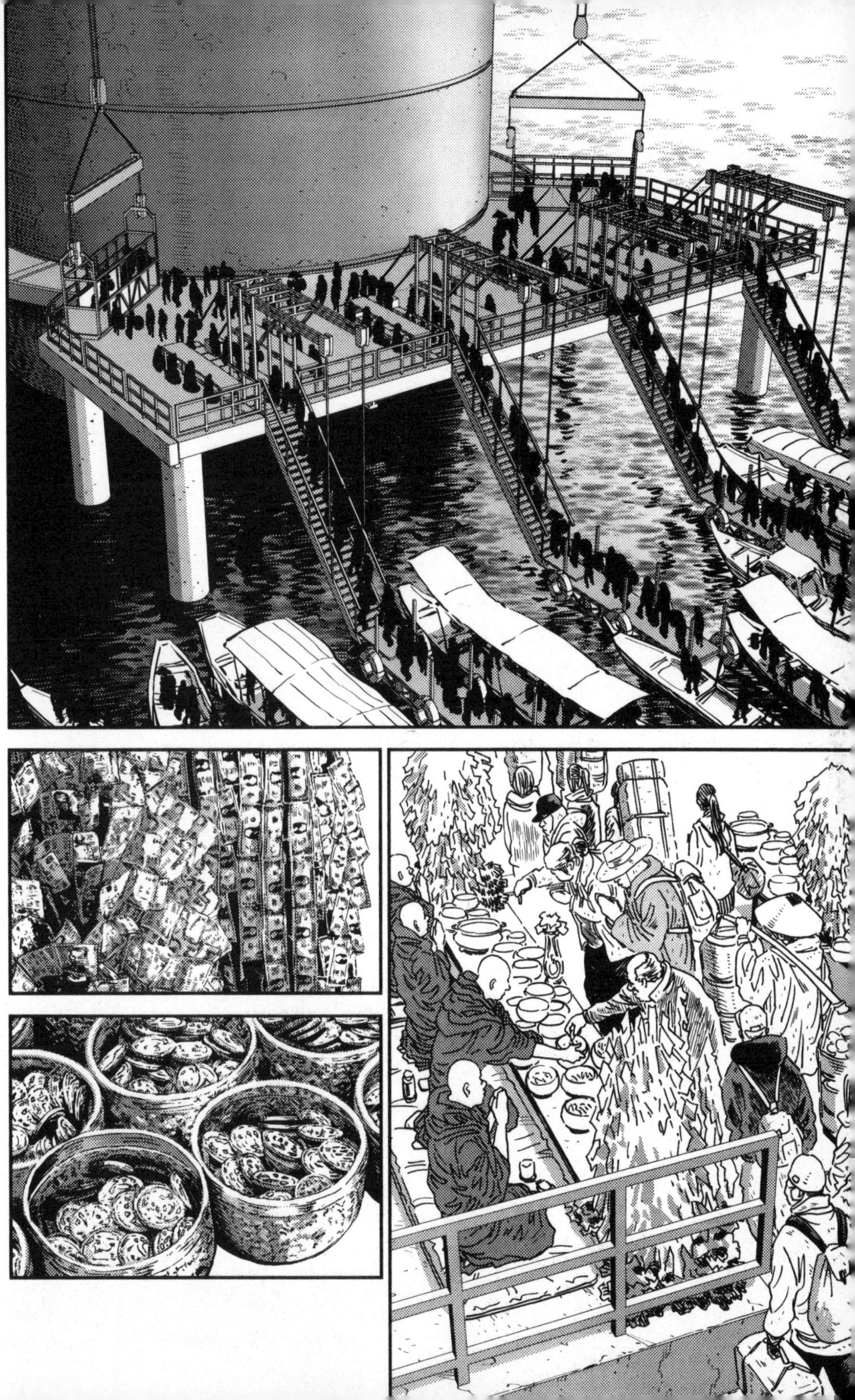

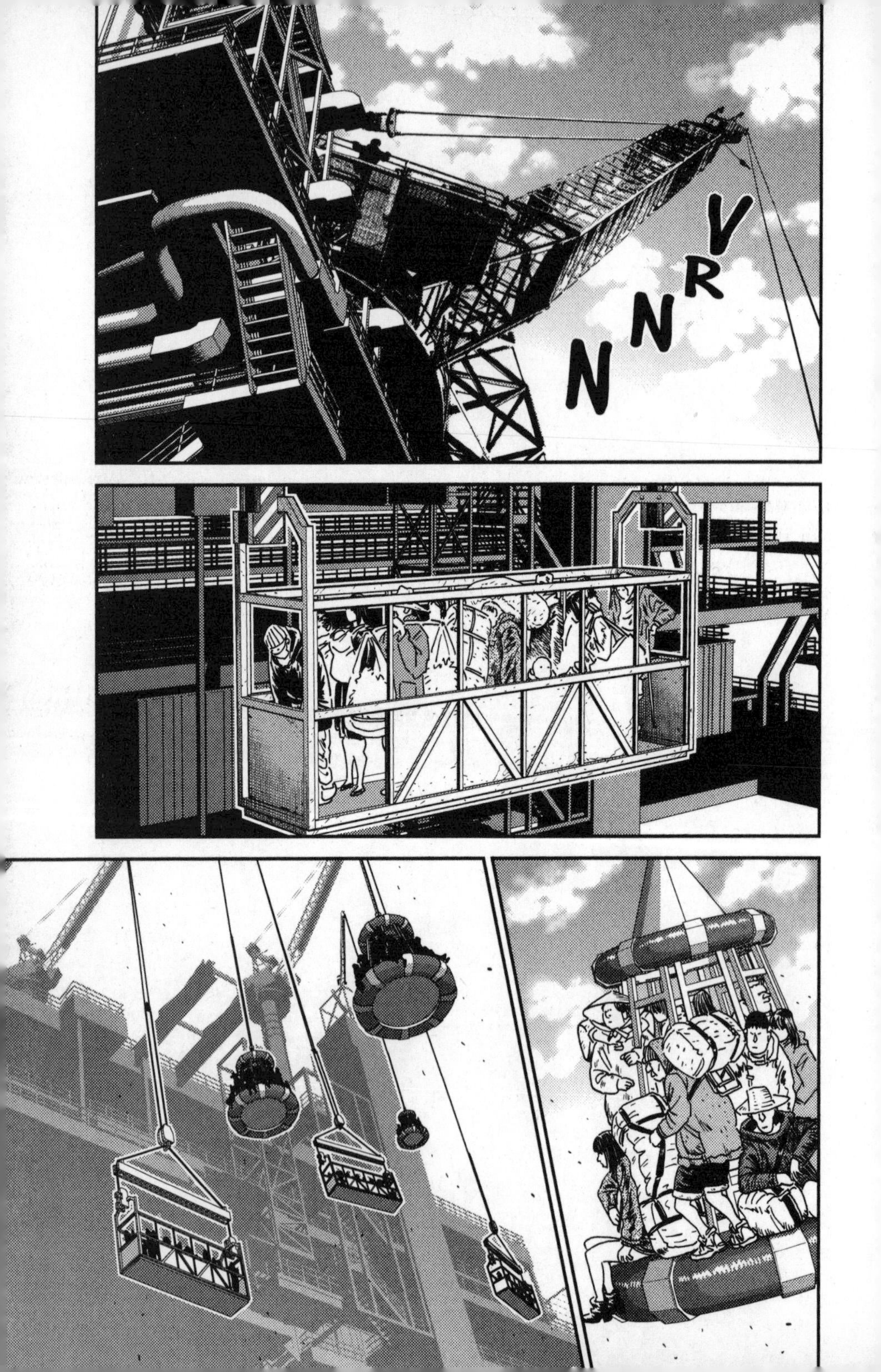
NNRV

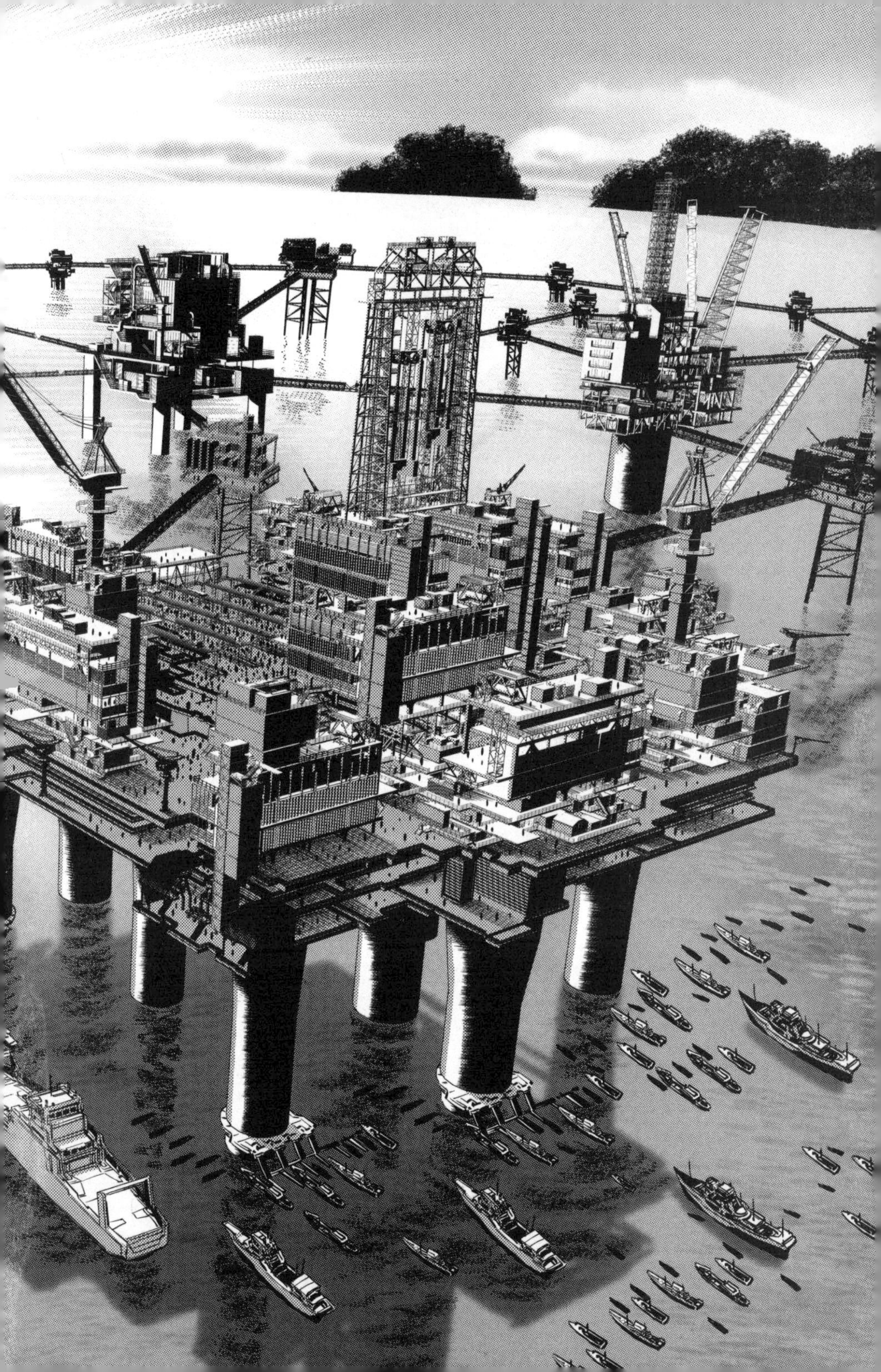

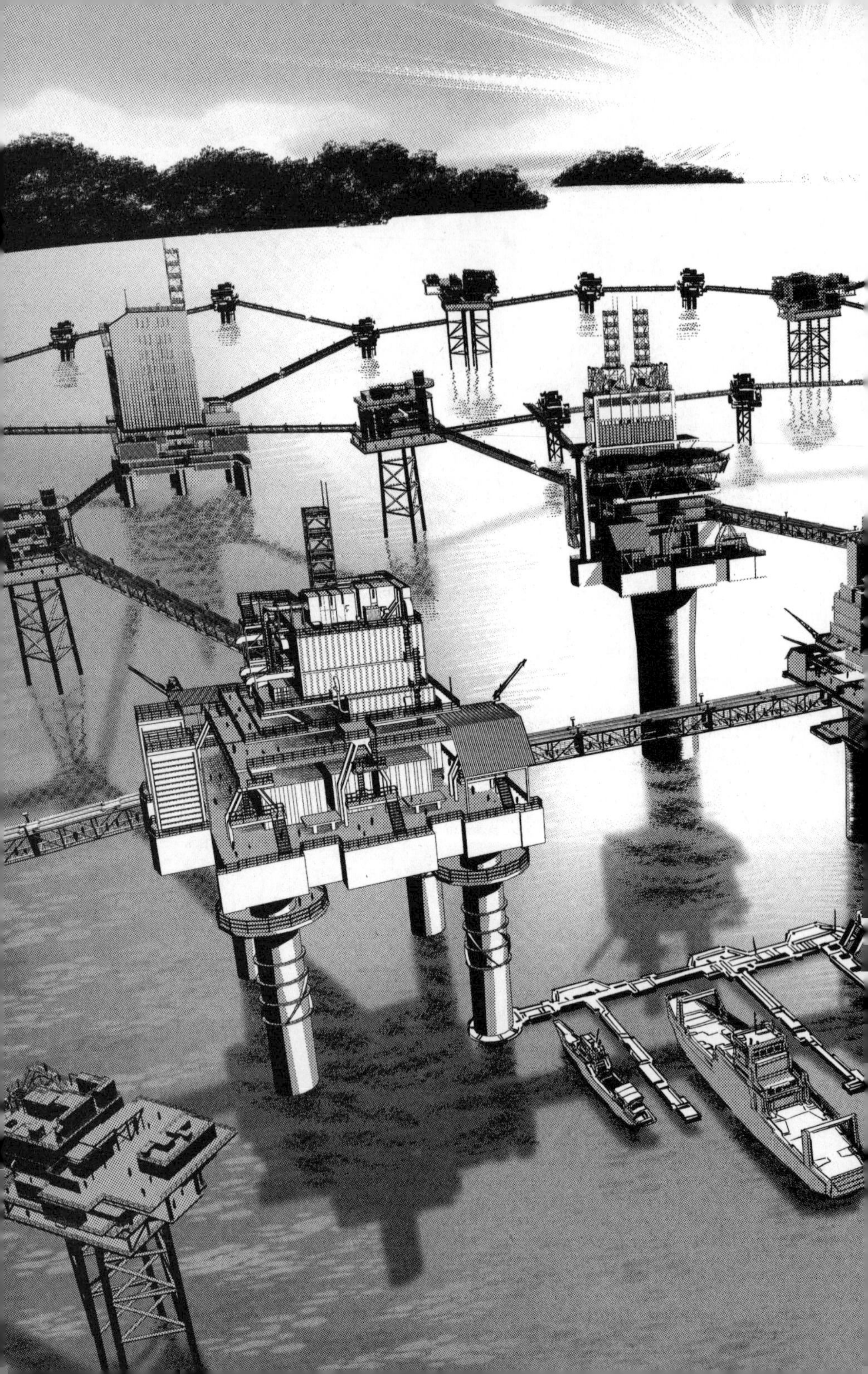

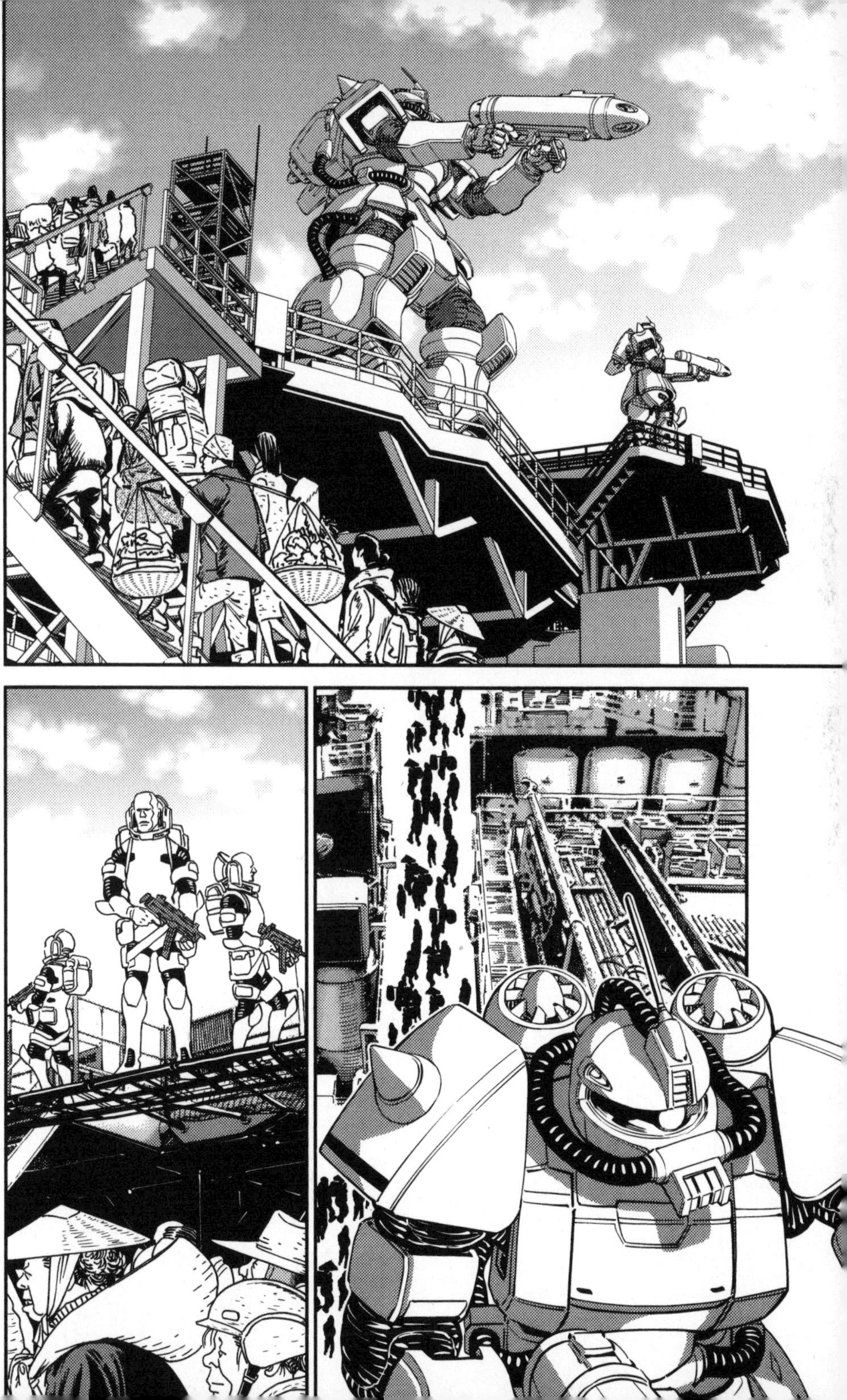

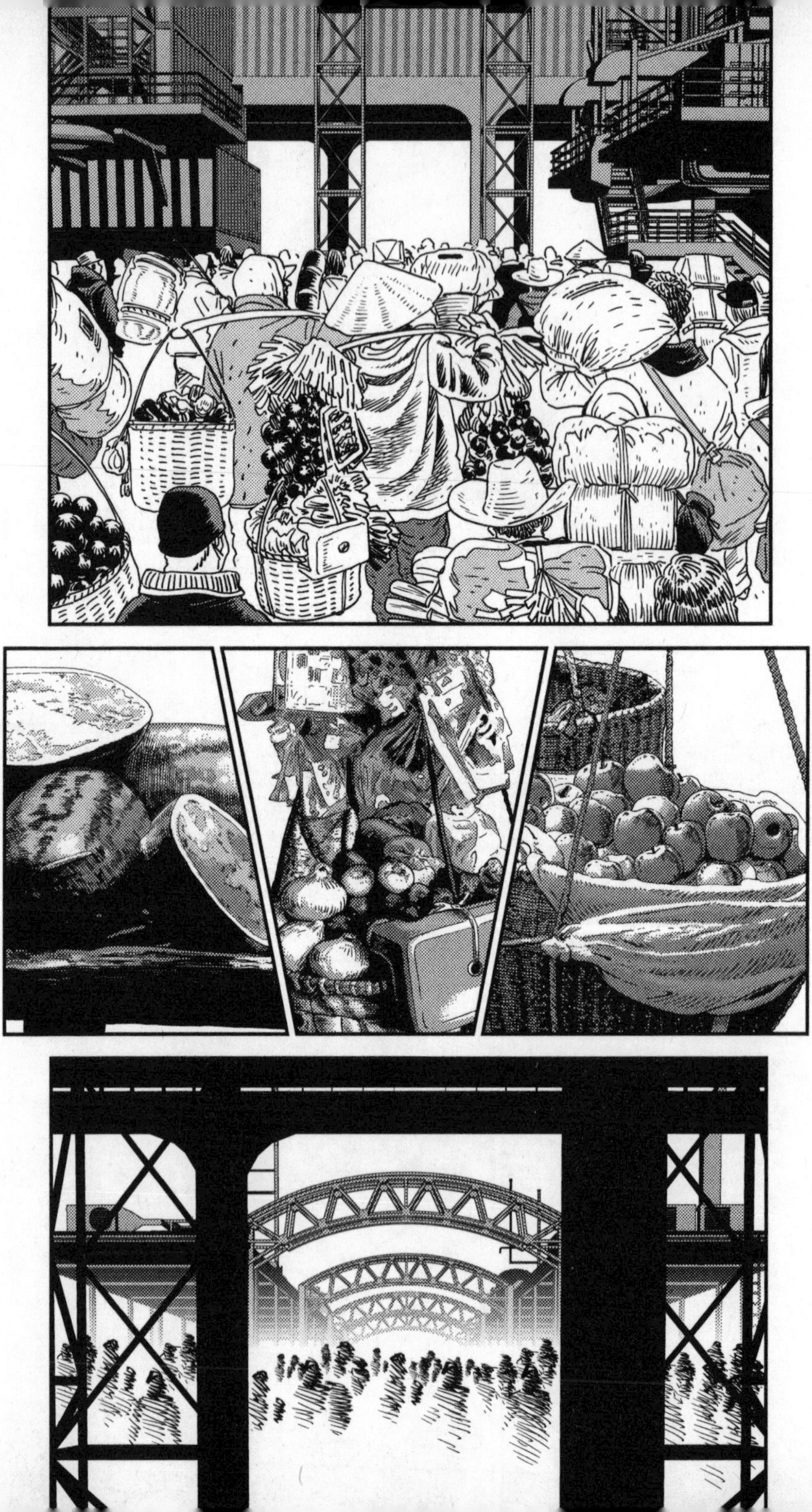

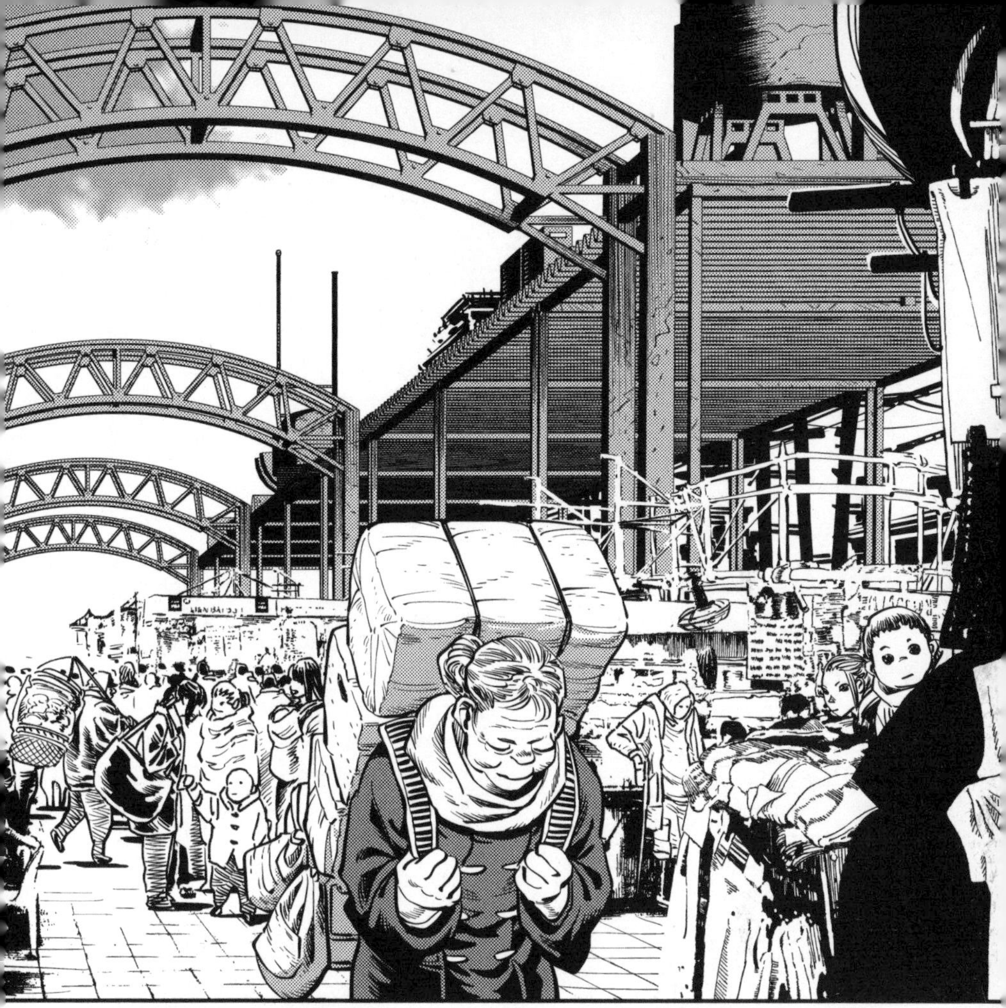
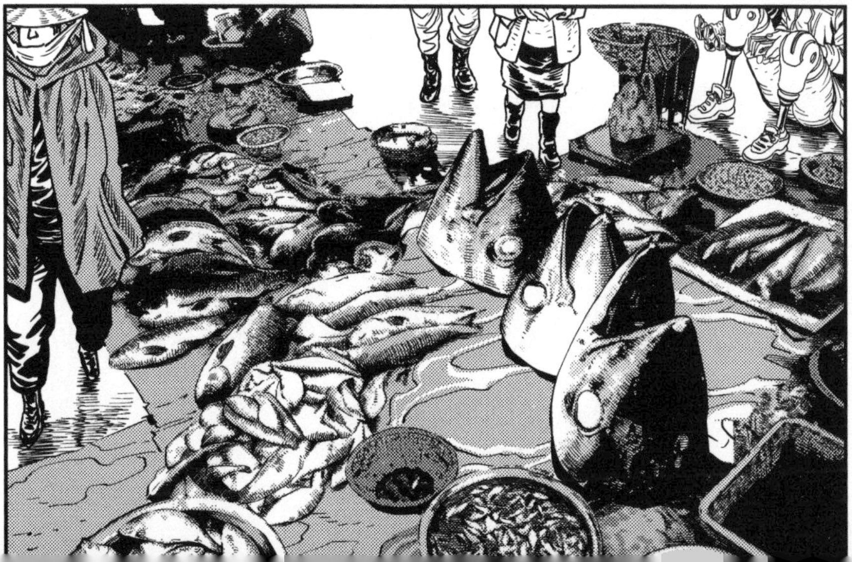

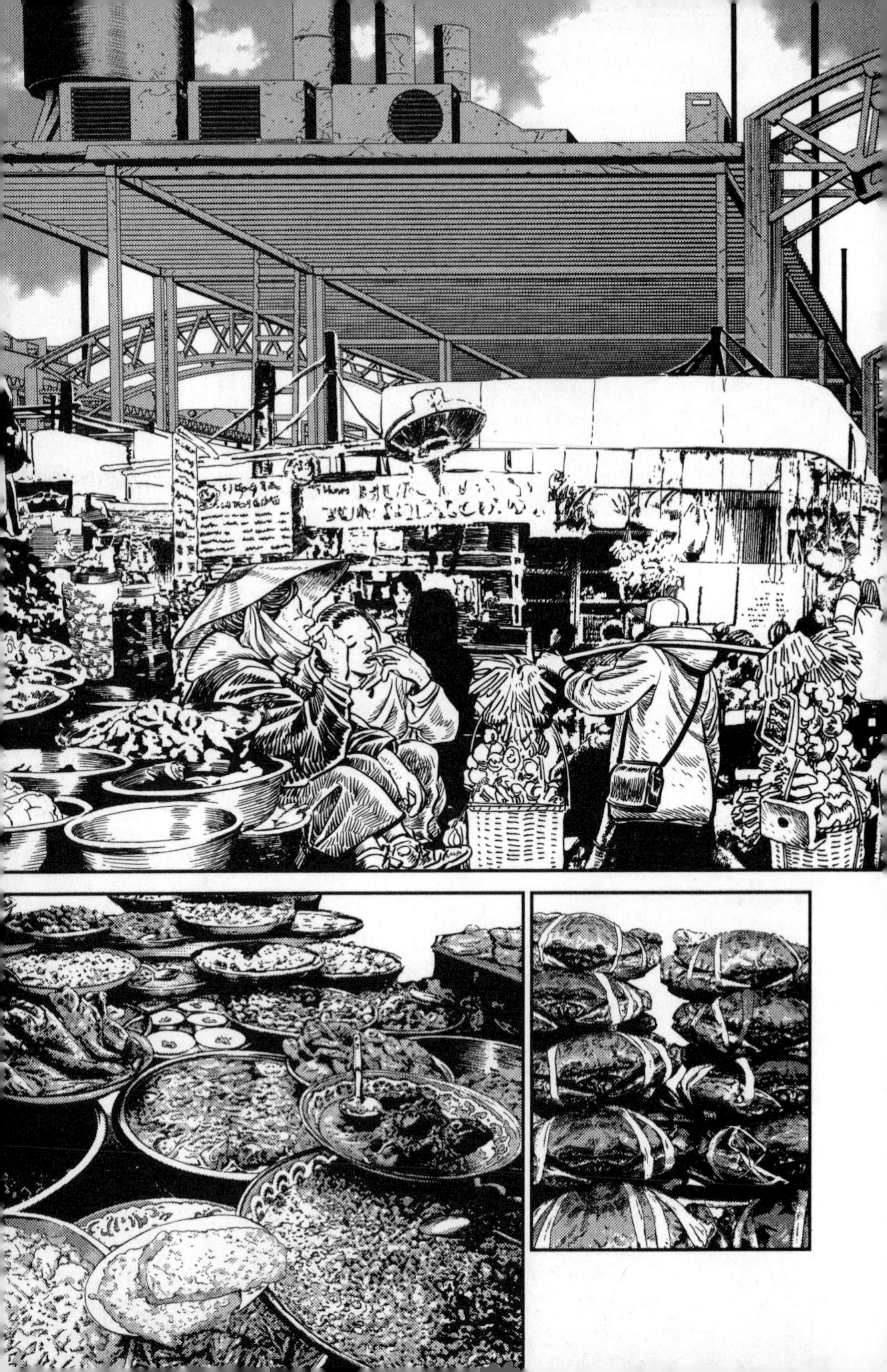

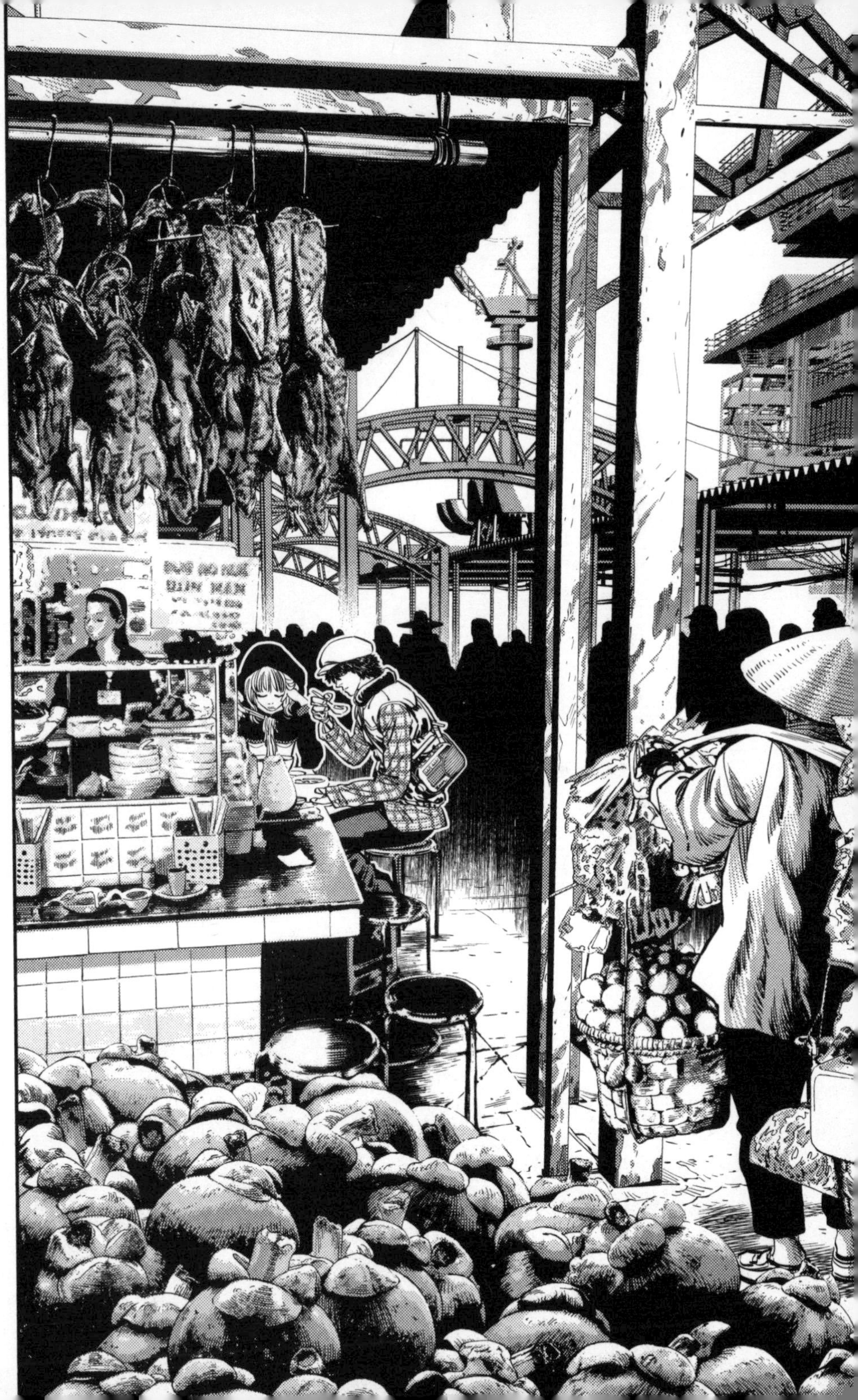

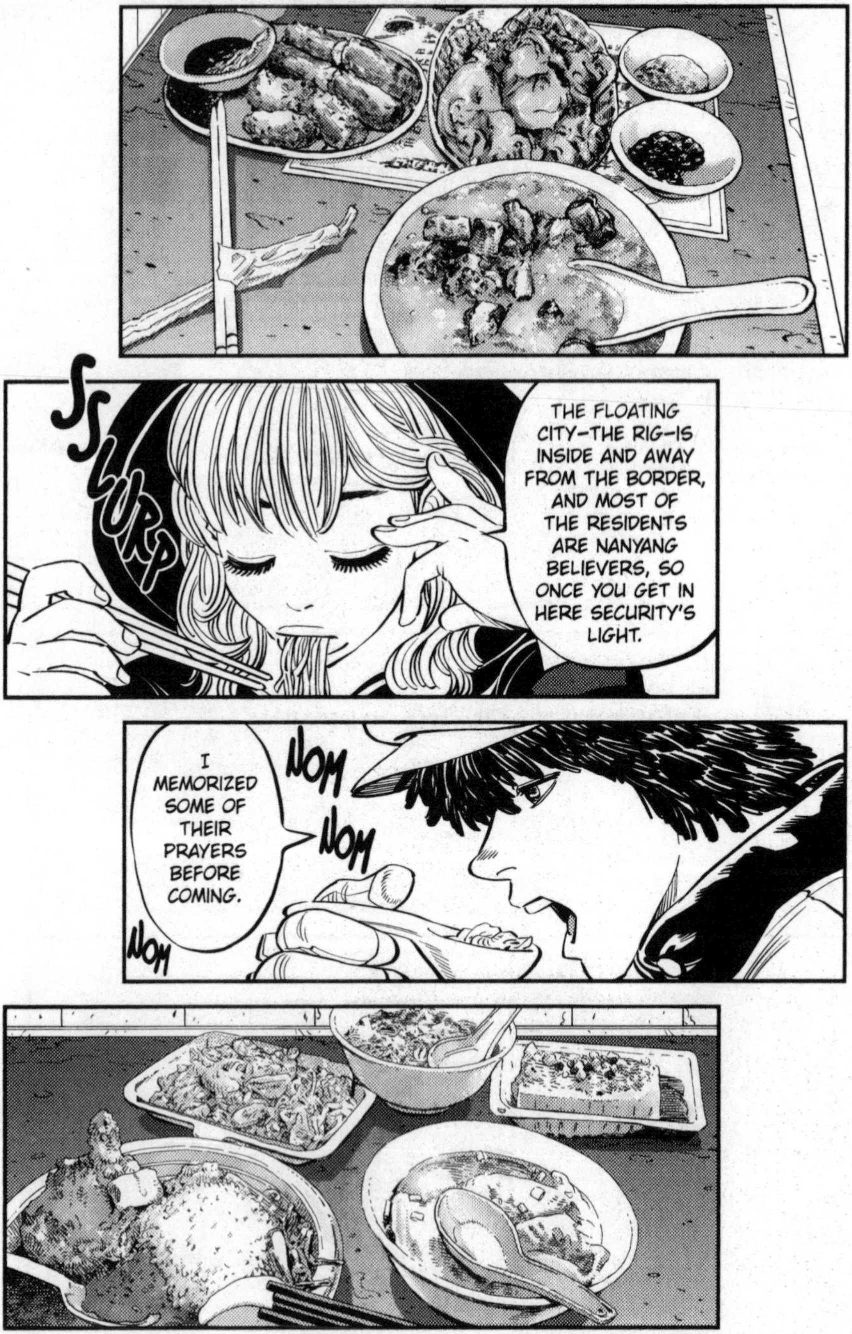
THE FLOATING CITY—THE RIG—IS INSIDE AND AWAY FROM THE BORDER, AND MOST OF THE RESIDENTS ARE NANYANG BELIEVERS, SO ONCE YOU GET IN HERE SECURITY'S LIGHT.
SSLURP
NOM
NOM
I MEMORIZED SOME OF THEIR PRAYERS BEFORE COMING.
NOM

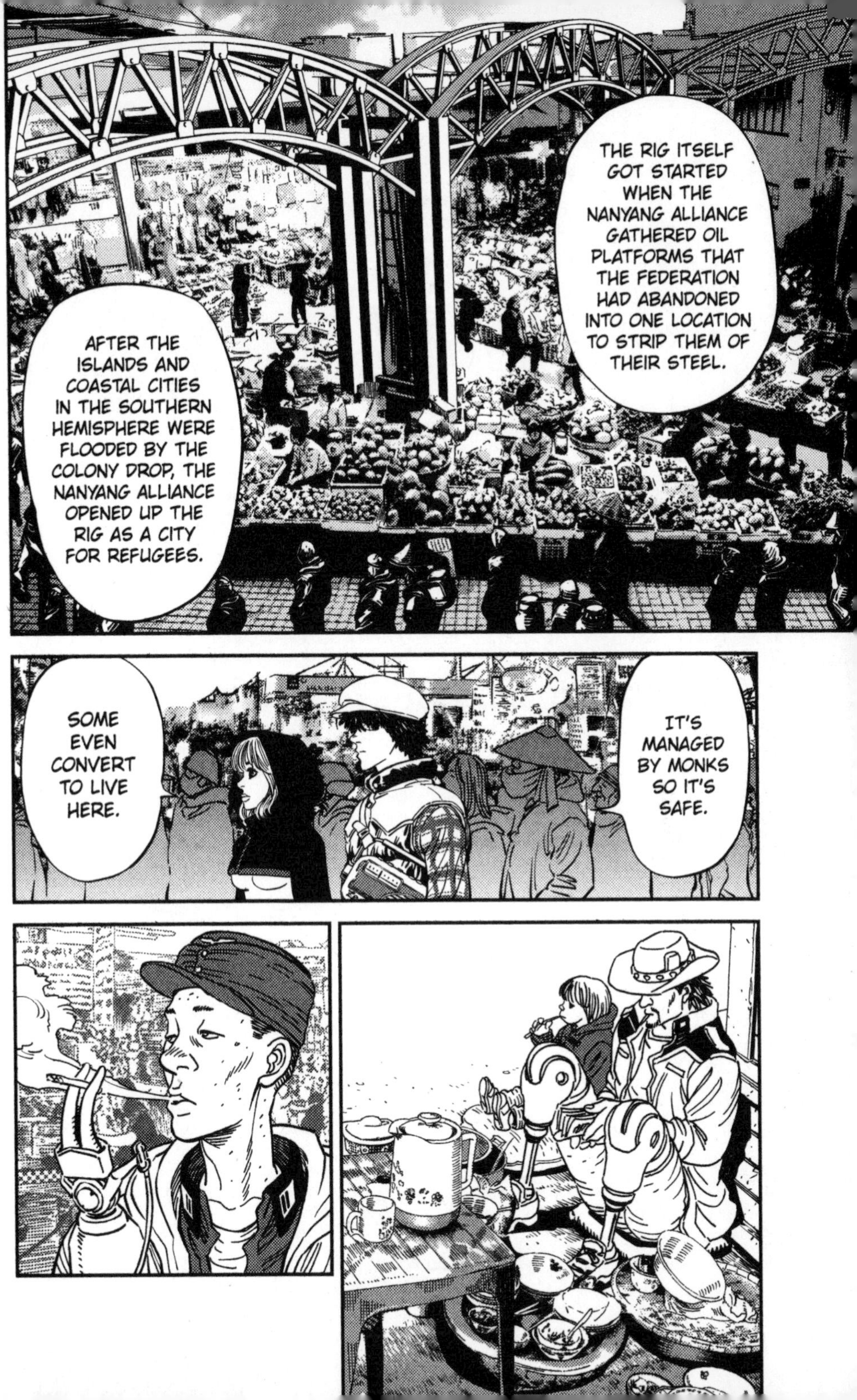
THE RIG ITSELF GOT STARTED WHEN THE NANYANG ALLIANCE GATHERED OIL PLATFORMS THAT THE FEDERATION HAD ABANDONED INTO ONE LOCATION TO STRIP THEM OF THEIR STEEL.
AFTER THE ISLANDS AND COASTAL CITIES IN THE SOUTHERN HEMISPHERE WERE FLOODED BY THE COLONY DROP, THE NANYANG ALLIANCE OPENED UP THE RIG AS A CITY FOR REFUGEES.
IT'S MANAGED BY MONKS SO IT'S SAFE.
SOME EVEN CONVERT TO LIVE HERE.

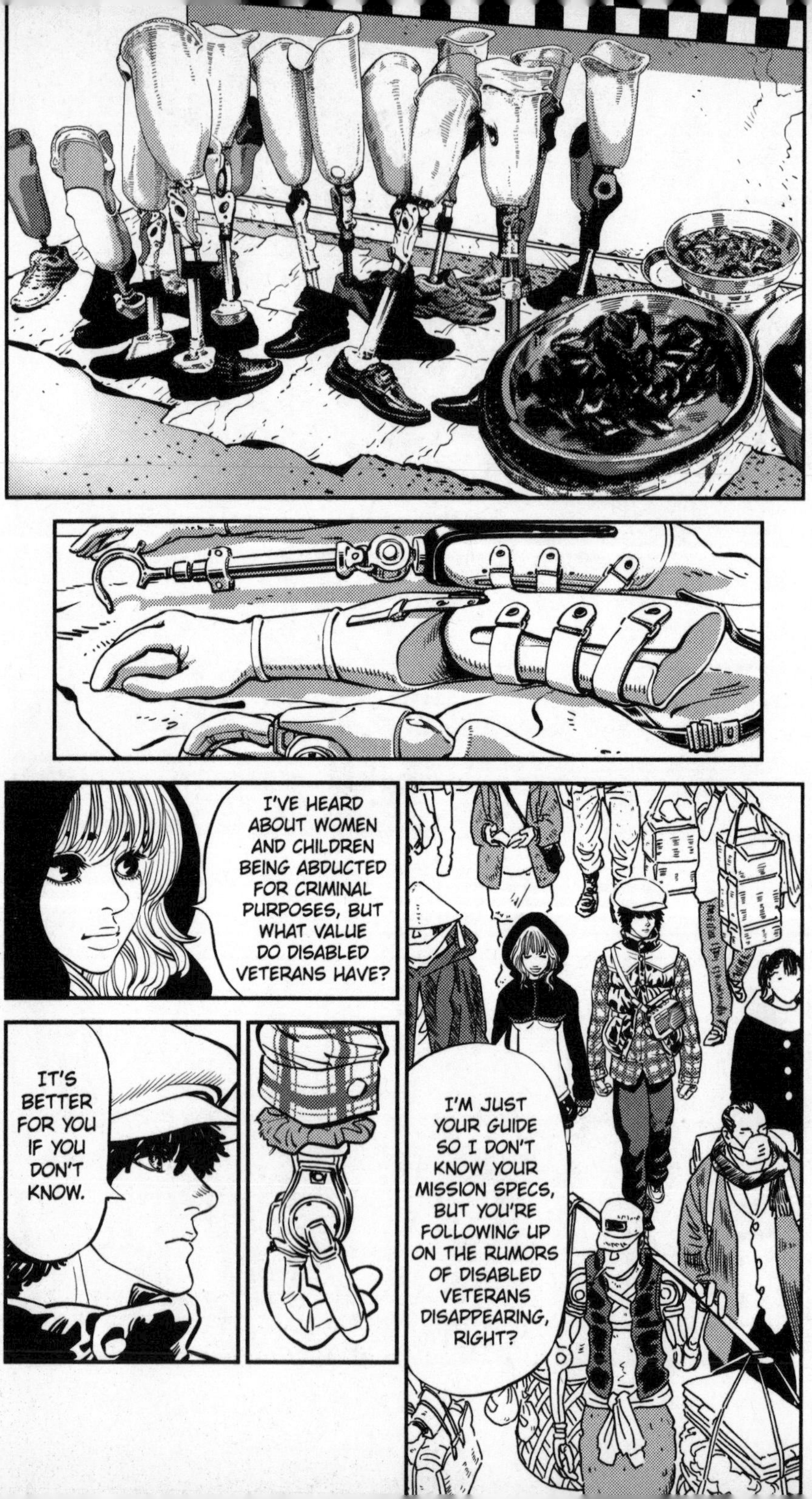
I'M JUST YOUR GUIDE SO I DON'T KNOW YOUR MISSION SPECS, BUT YOU'RE FOLLOWING UP ON THE RUMORS OF DISABLED VETERANS DISAPPEARING, RIGHT?
I'VE HEARD ABOUT WOMEN AND CHILDREN BEING ABDUCTED FOR CRIMINAL PURPOSES, BUT WHAT VALUE DO DISABLED VETERANS HAVE?
IT'S BETTER FOR YOU IF YOU DON'T KNOW.

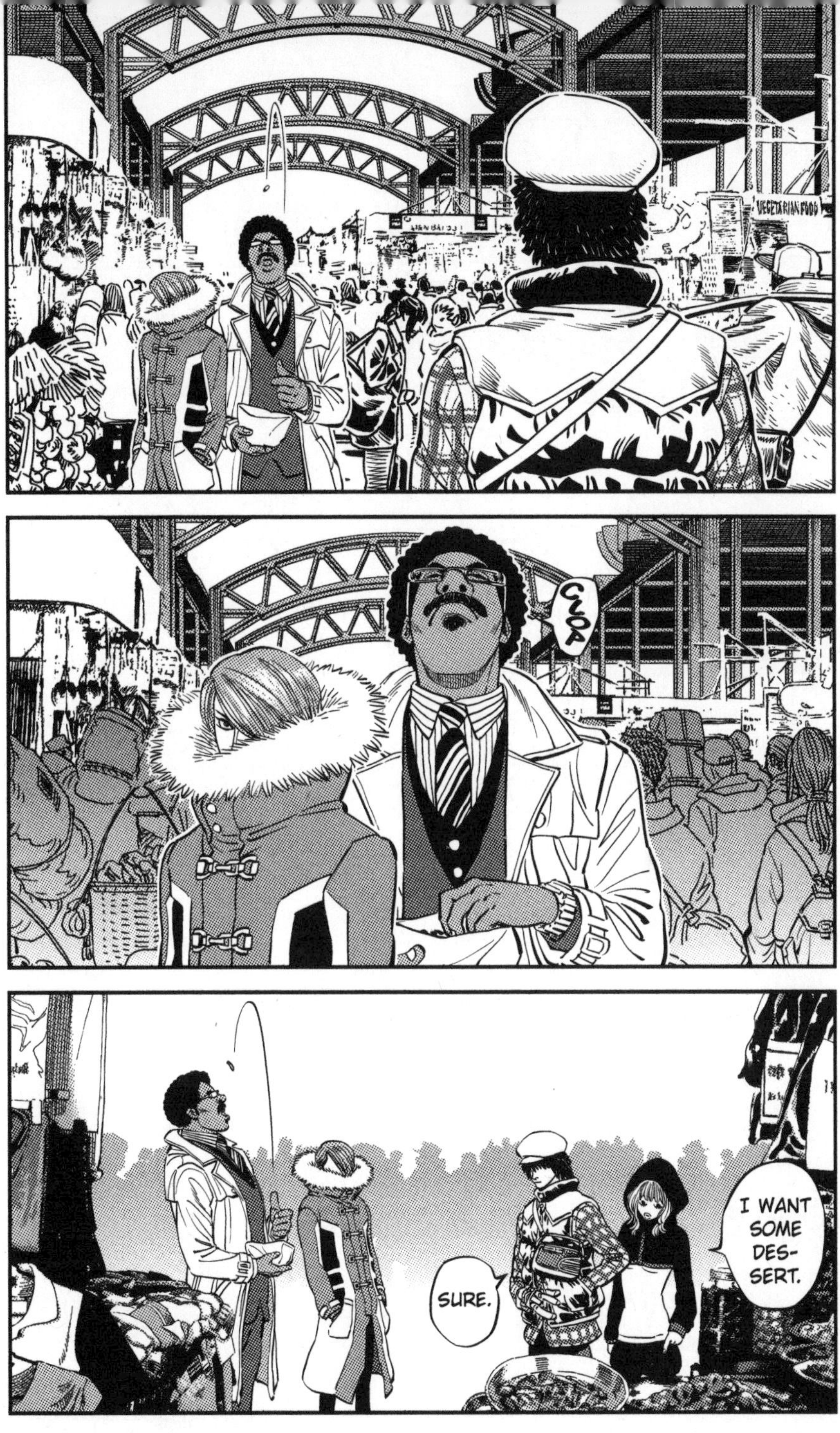
VEGETARIAN FOOD
CLOP
I WANT SOME DES-SERT.
SURE.

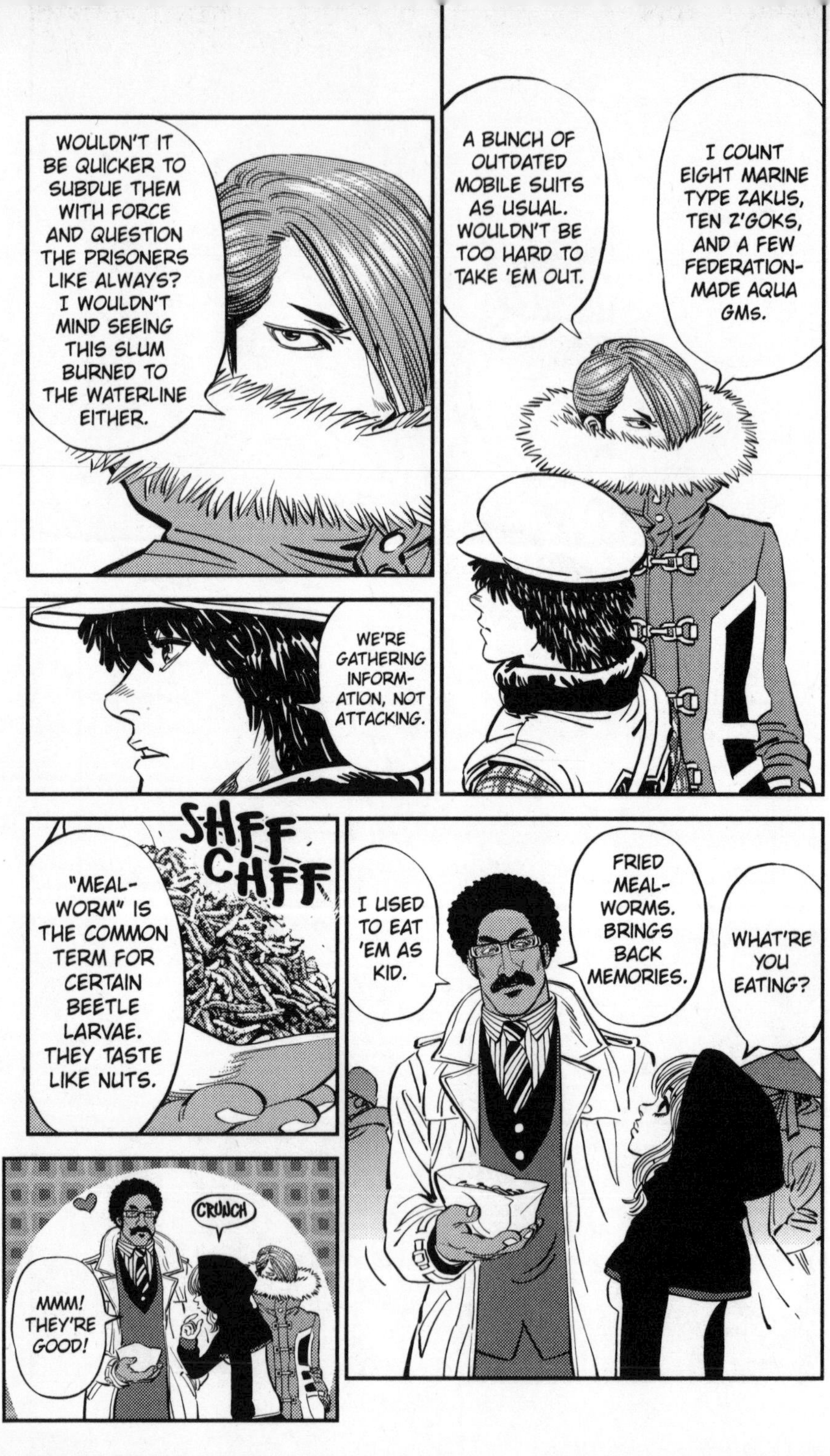
I COUNT EIGHT MARINE TYPE ZAKUS, TEN Z'GOKS, AND A FEW FEDERATION-MADE AQUA GMS.
A BUNCH OF OUTDATED MOBILE SUITS AS USUAL. WOULDN'T BE TOO HARD TO TAKE 'EM OUT.
WOULDN'T IT BE QUICKER TO SUBDUE THEM WITH FORCE AND QUESTION THE PRISONERS LIKE ALWAYS? I WOULDN'T MIND SEEING THIS SLUM BURNED TO THE WATERLINE EITHER.
WE'RE GATHERING INFORMATION, NOT ATTACKING.
WHAT'RE YOU EATING?
FRIED MEALWORMS. BRINGS BACK MEMORIES.
I USED TO EAT 'EM AS KID.
SHFF CHFF
"MEALWORM" IS THE COMMON TERM FOR CERTAIN BEETLE LARVAE. THEY TASTE LIKE NUTS.
CRUNCH
MMM! THEY'RE GOOD!

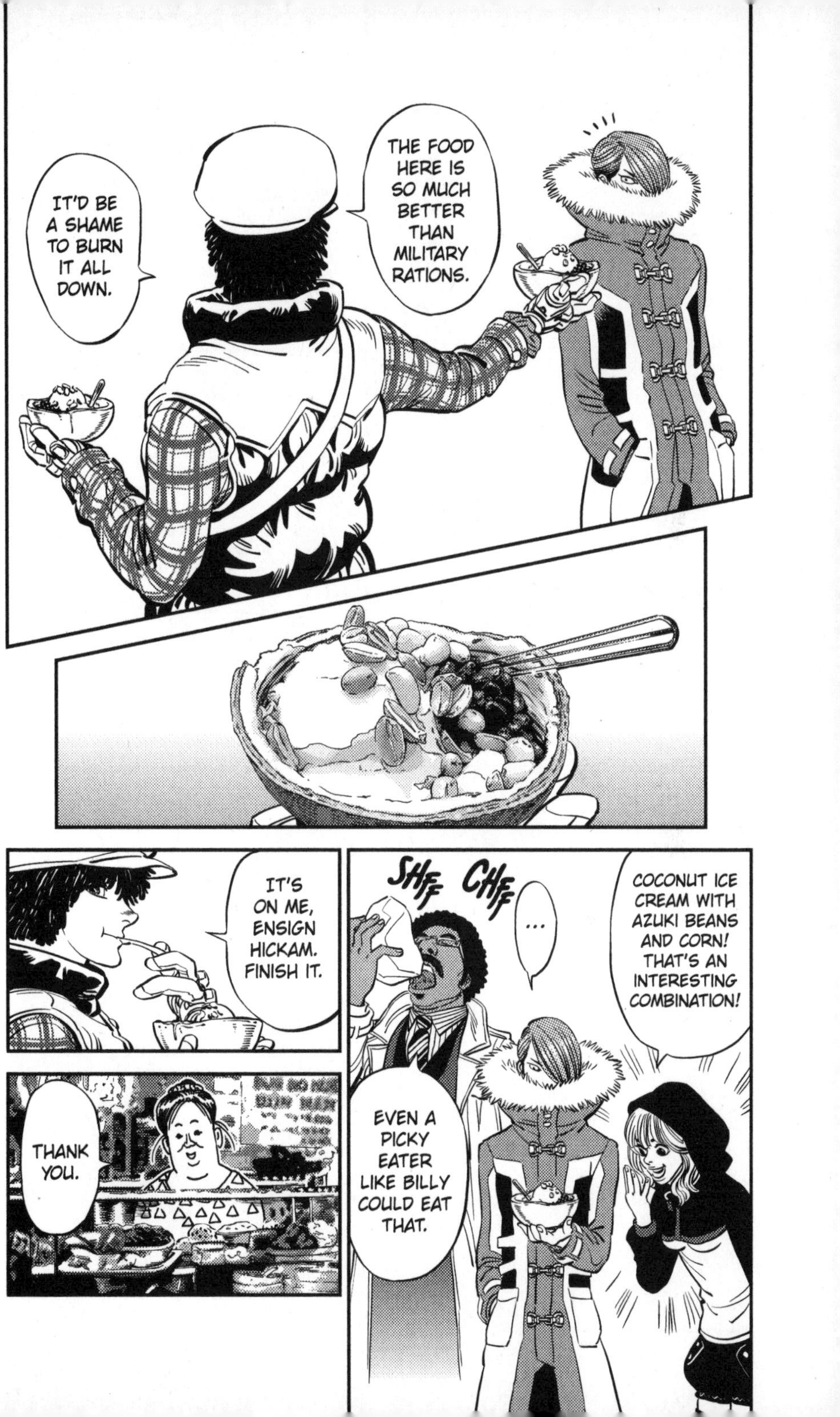
THE FOOD HERE IS SO MUCH BETTER THAN MILITARY RATIONS.
IT'D BE A SHAME TO BURN IT ALL DOWN.
COCONUT ICE CREAM WITH AZUKI BEANS AND CORN! THAT'S AN INTERESTING COMBINATION!
SHFF CHFF
...
EVEN A PICKY EATER LIKE BILLY COULD EAT THAT.
IT'S ON ME, ENSIGN HICKAM. FINISH IT.
THANK YOU.

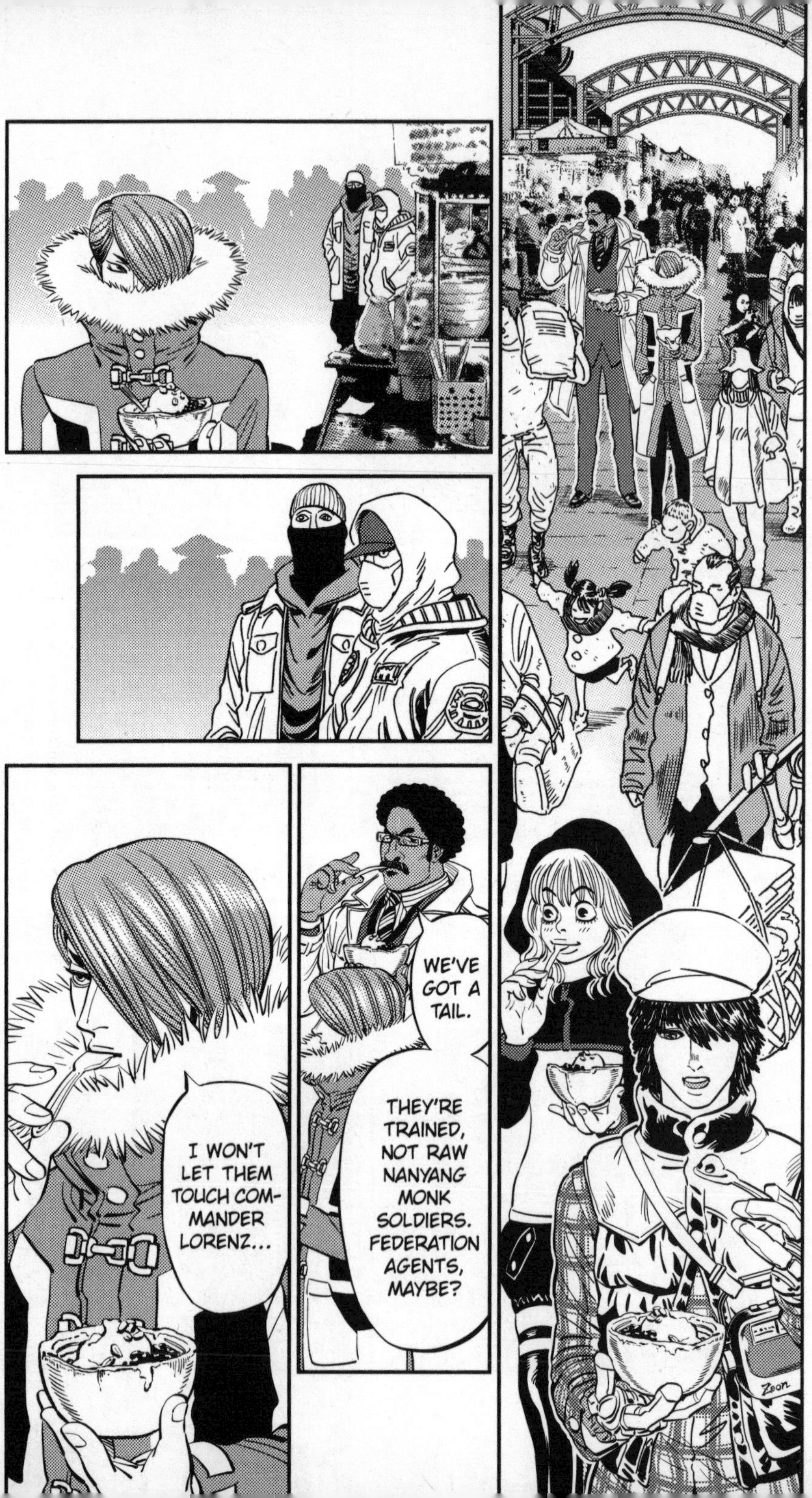
WE'VE GOT A TAIL.
THEY'RE TRAINED, NOT RAW NANYANG MONK SOLDIERS. FEDERATION AGENTS, MAYBE?
I WON'T LET THEM TOUCH COM-MANDER LORENZ...

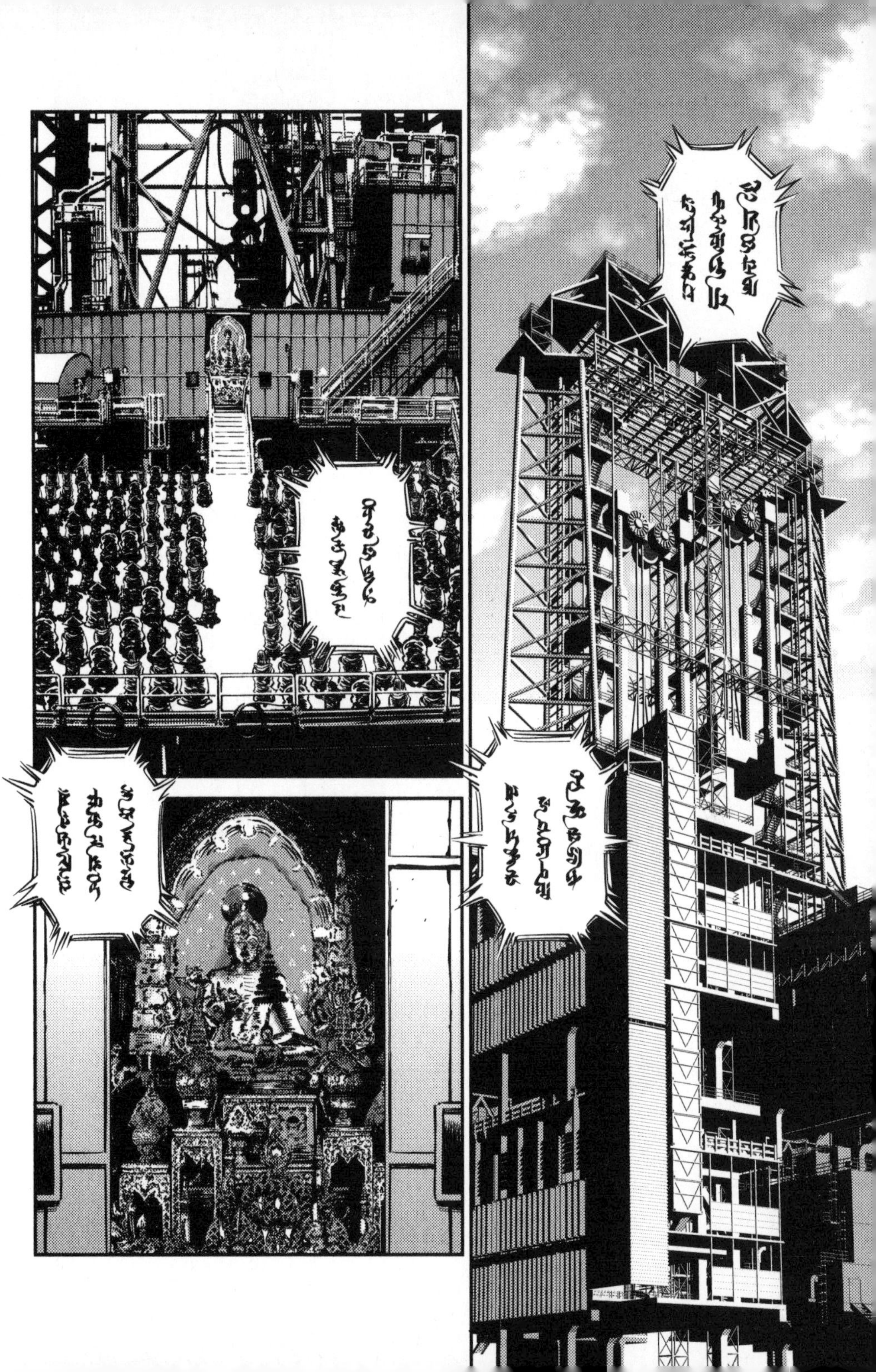

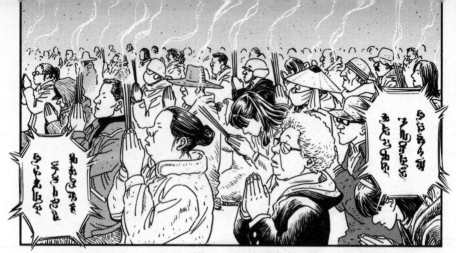

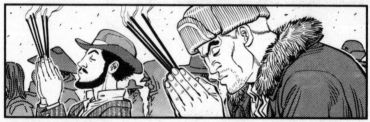

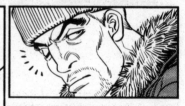

IT'S A TEMPLE, THAT'S FOR SURE.
THE CRANE IS THE PAGODA AND THE STORAGE SPACE IS THE MAIN SHRINE. THE MONKS LIVE IN THE SHRINE OFFICE IN THE BACK.
LOOKS LIKE THE SPECIAL GUEST HAS ARRIVED.

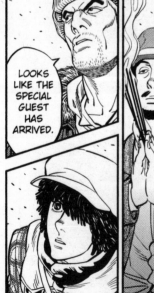

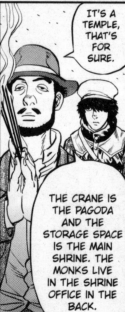

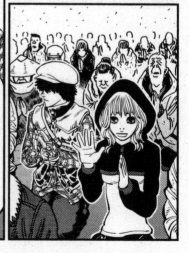

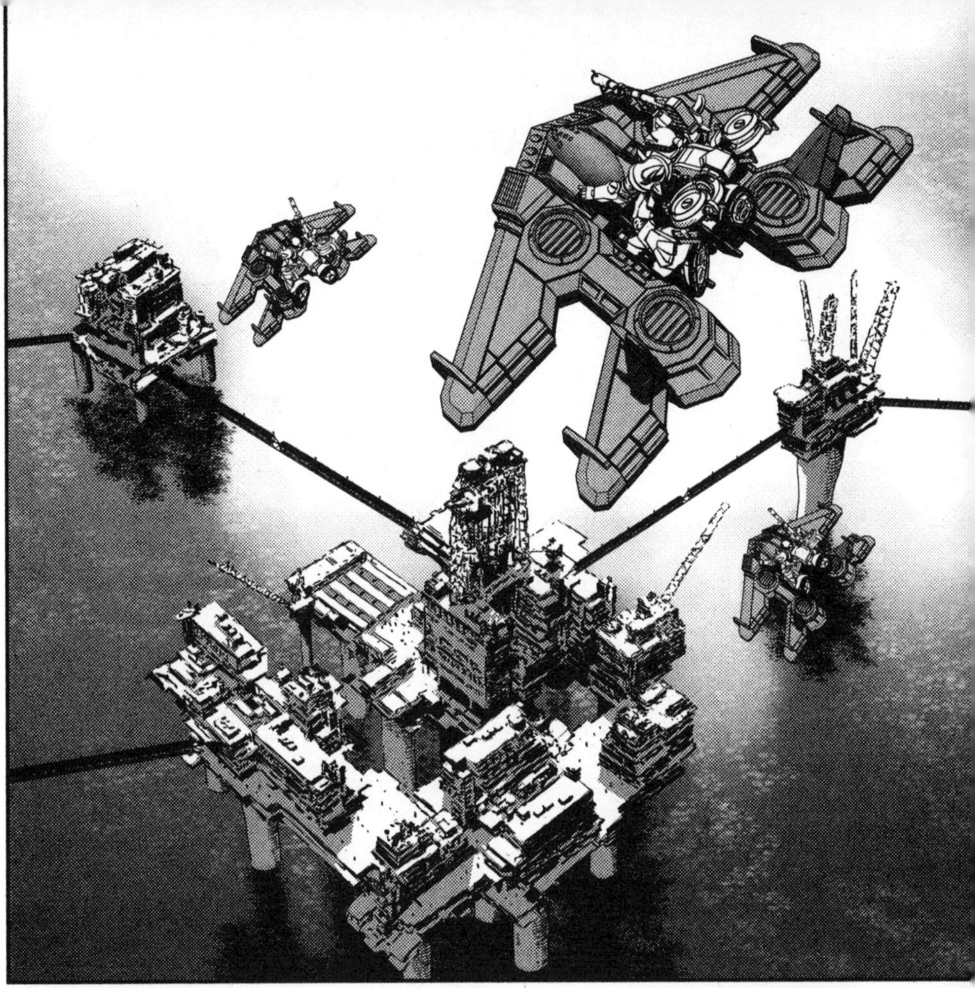
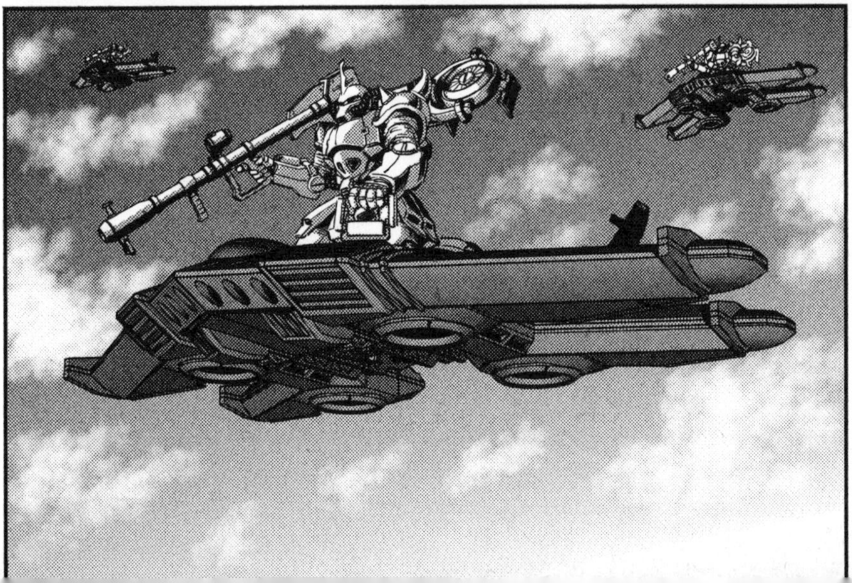

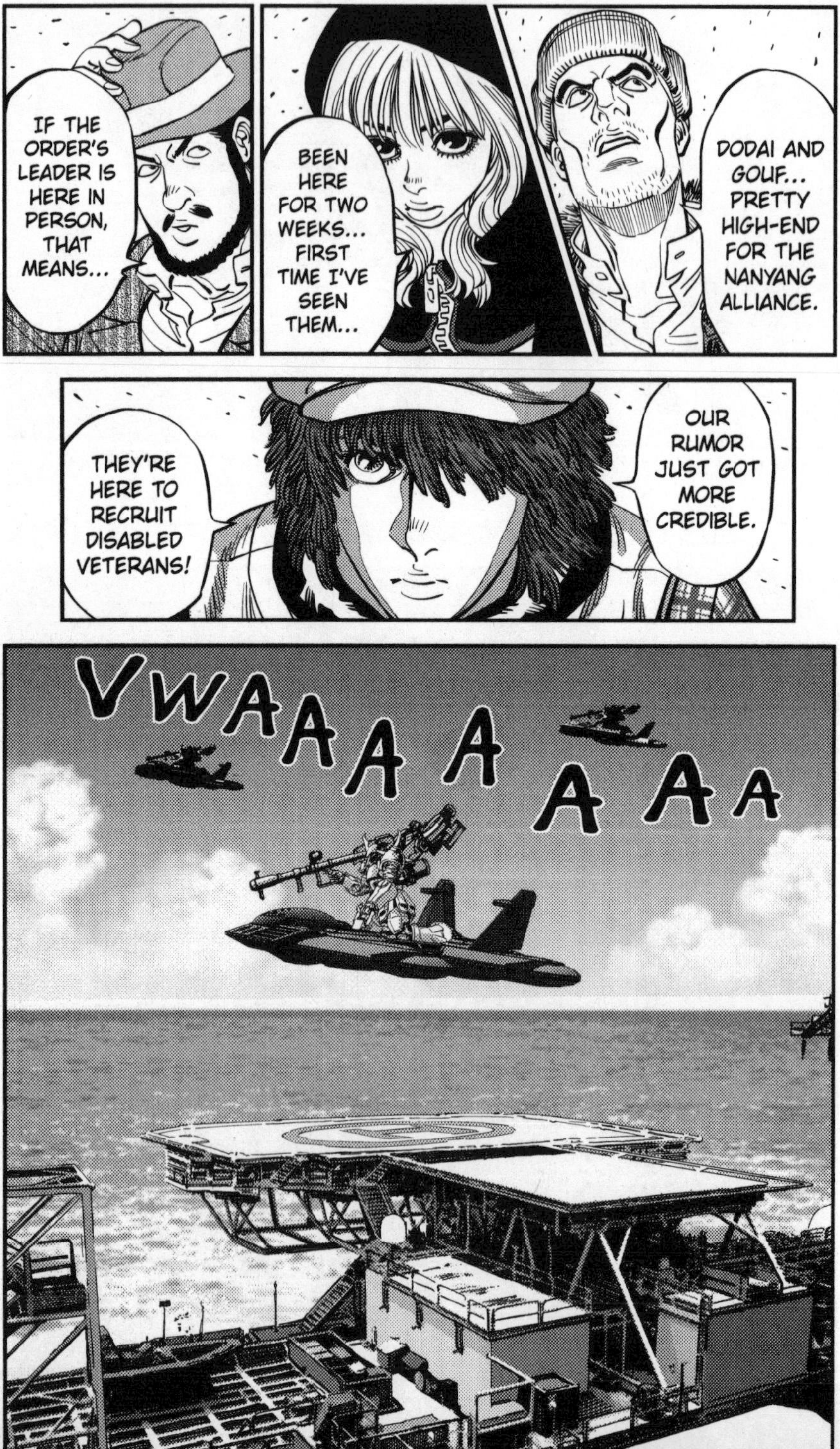
DODAI AND GOUF... PRETTY HIGH-END FOR THE NANYANG ALLIANCE.
BEEN HERE FOR TWO WEEKS... FIRST TIME I'VE SEEN THEM...
IF THE ORDER'S LEADER IS HERE IN PERSON, THAT MEANS...
OUR RUMOR JUST GOT MORE CREDIBLE.
THEY'RE HERE TO RECRUIT DISABLED VETERANS!
VWAAAAAAAA

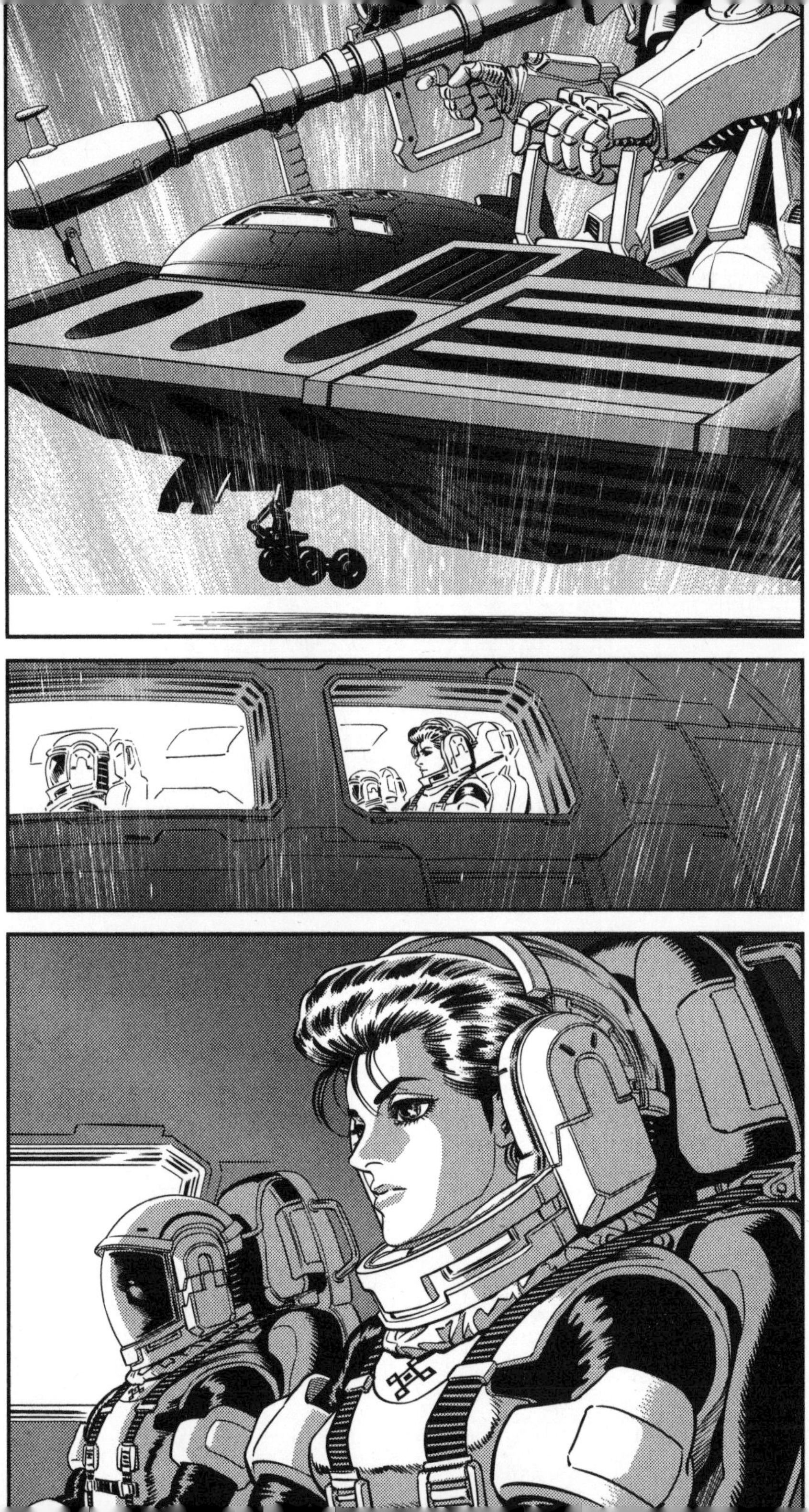

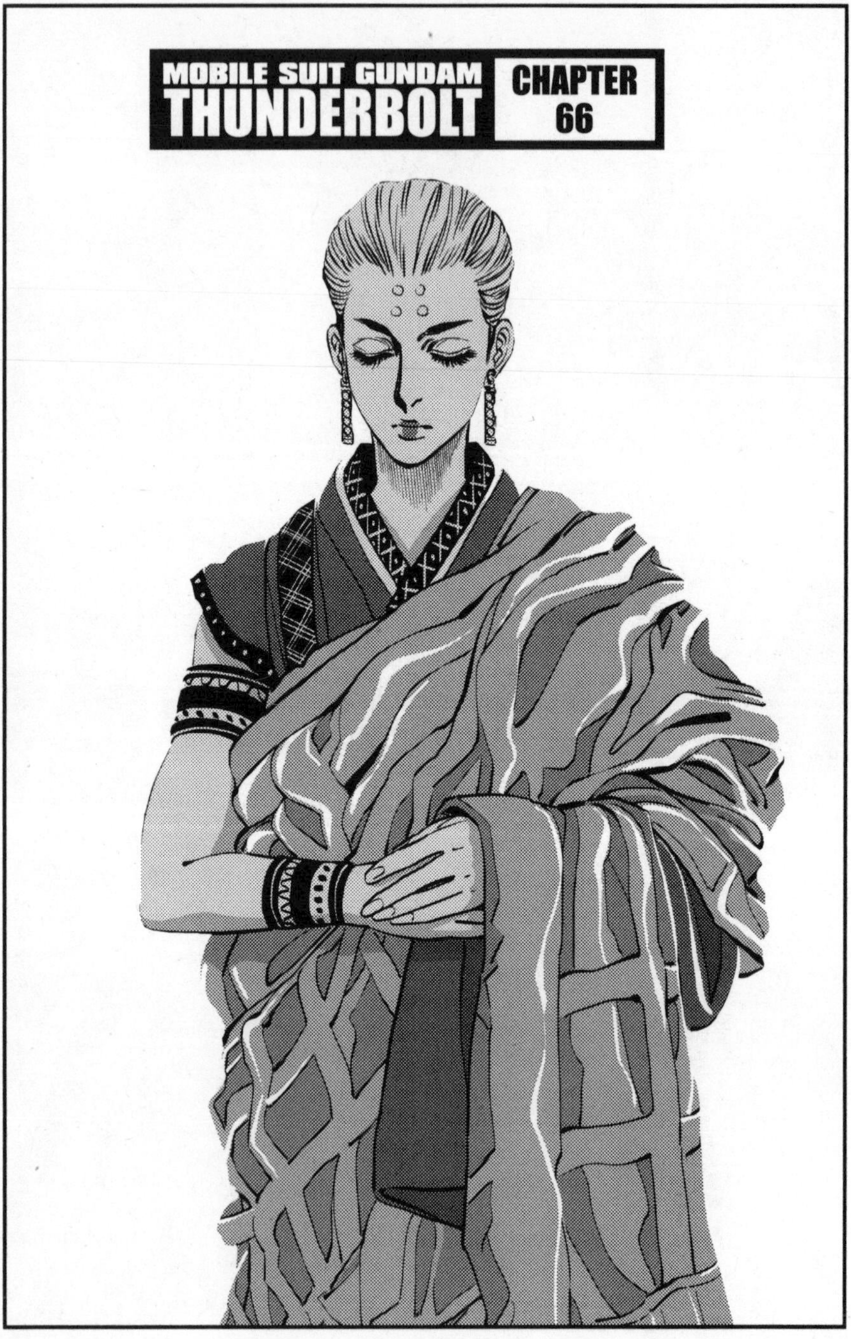
MOBILE SUIT GUNDAM
THUNDERBOLT
CHAPTER
66

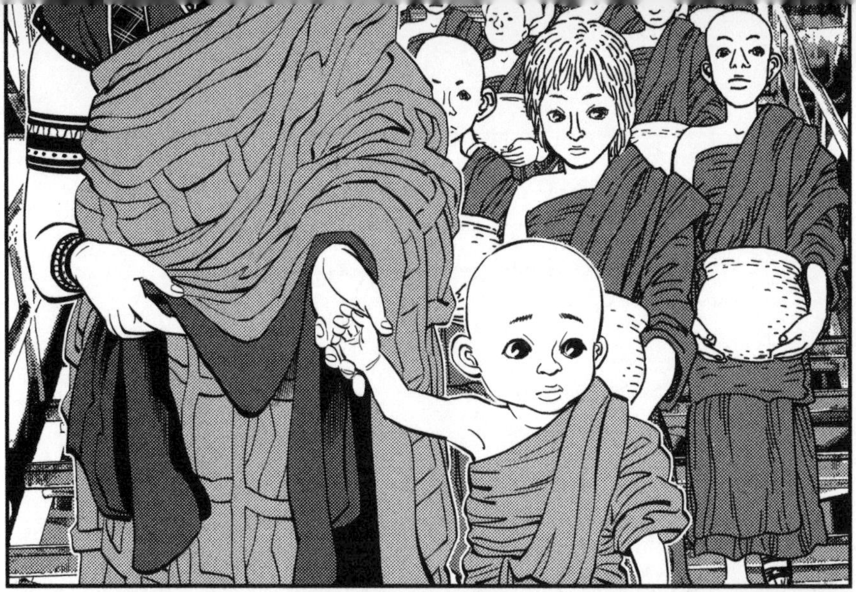
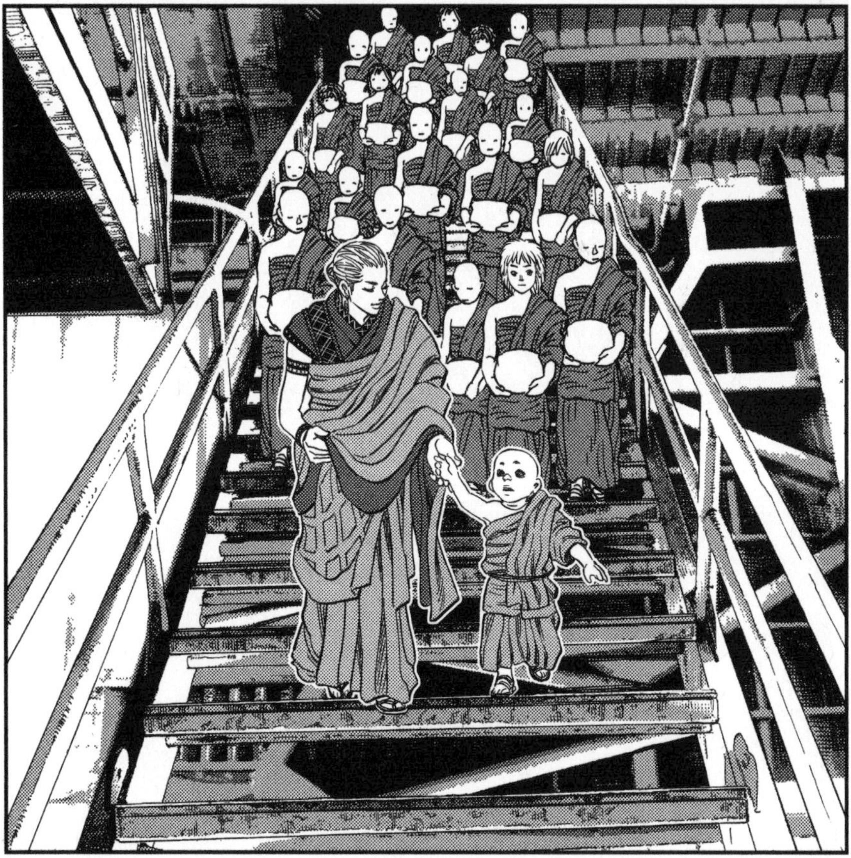

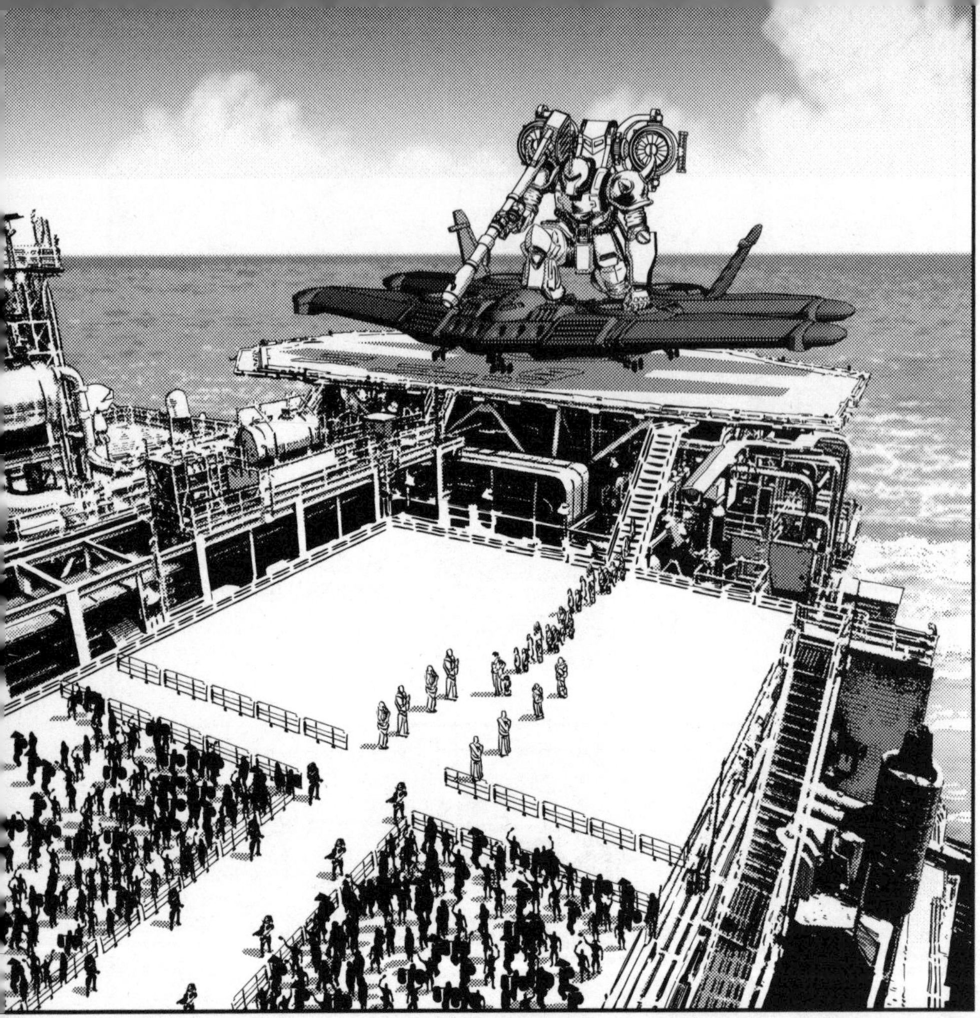
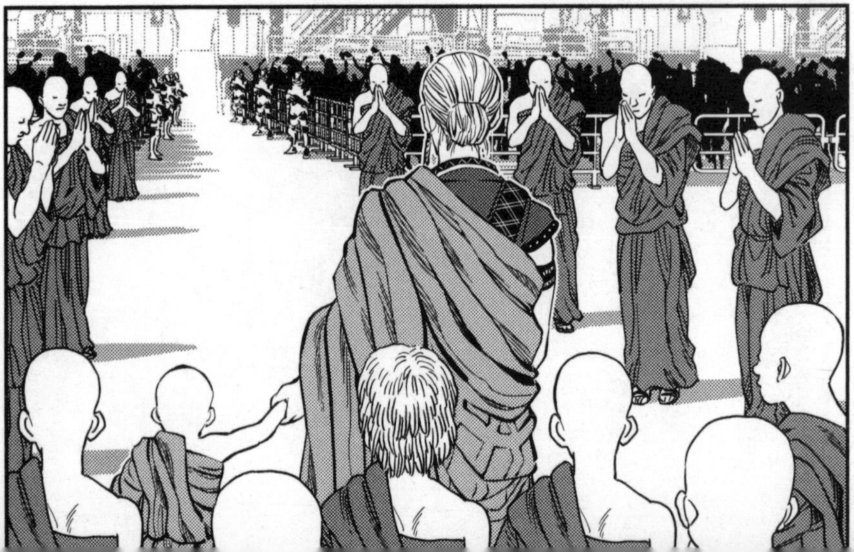

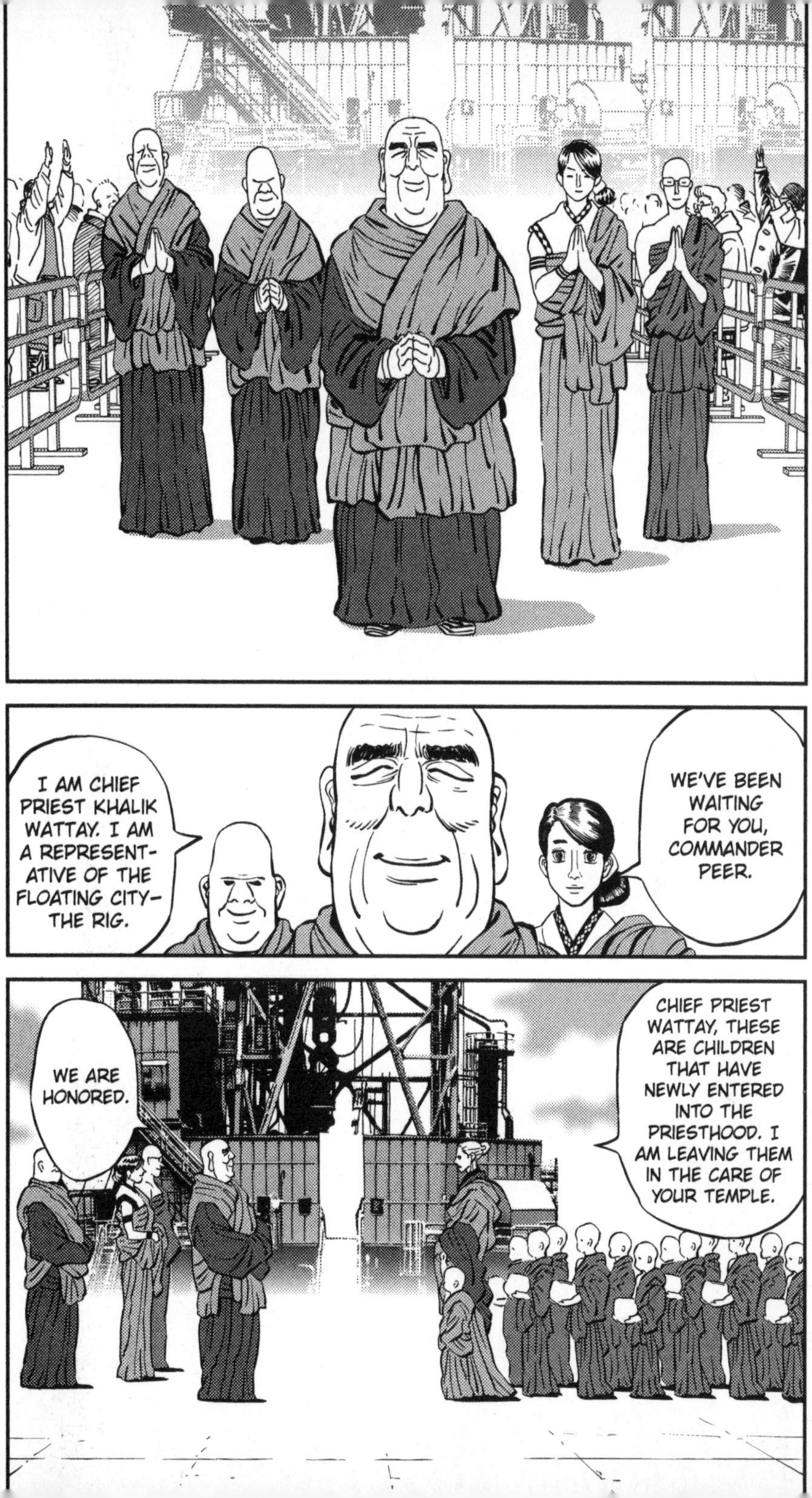
WE'VE BEEN WAITING FOR YOU, COMMANDER PEER.
I AM CHIEF PRIEST KHALIK WATTAY. I AM A REPRESENT-ATIVE OF THE FLOATING CITY-THE RIG.
CHIEF PRIEST WATTAY, THESE ARE CHILDREN THAT HAVE NEWLY ENTERED INTO THE PRIESTHOOD. I AM LEAVING THEM IN THE CARE OF YOUR TEMPLE.
WE ARE HONORED.

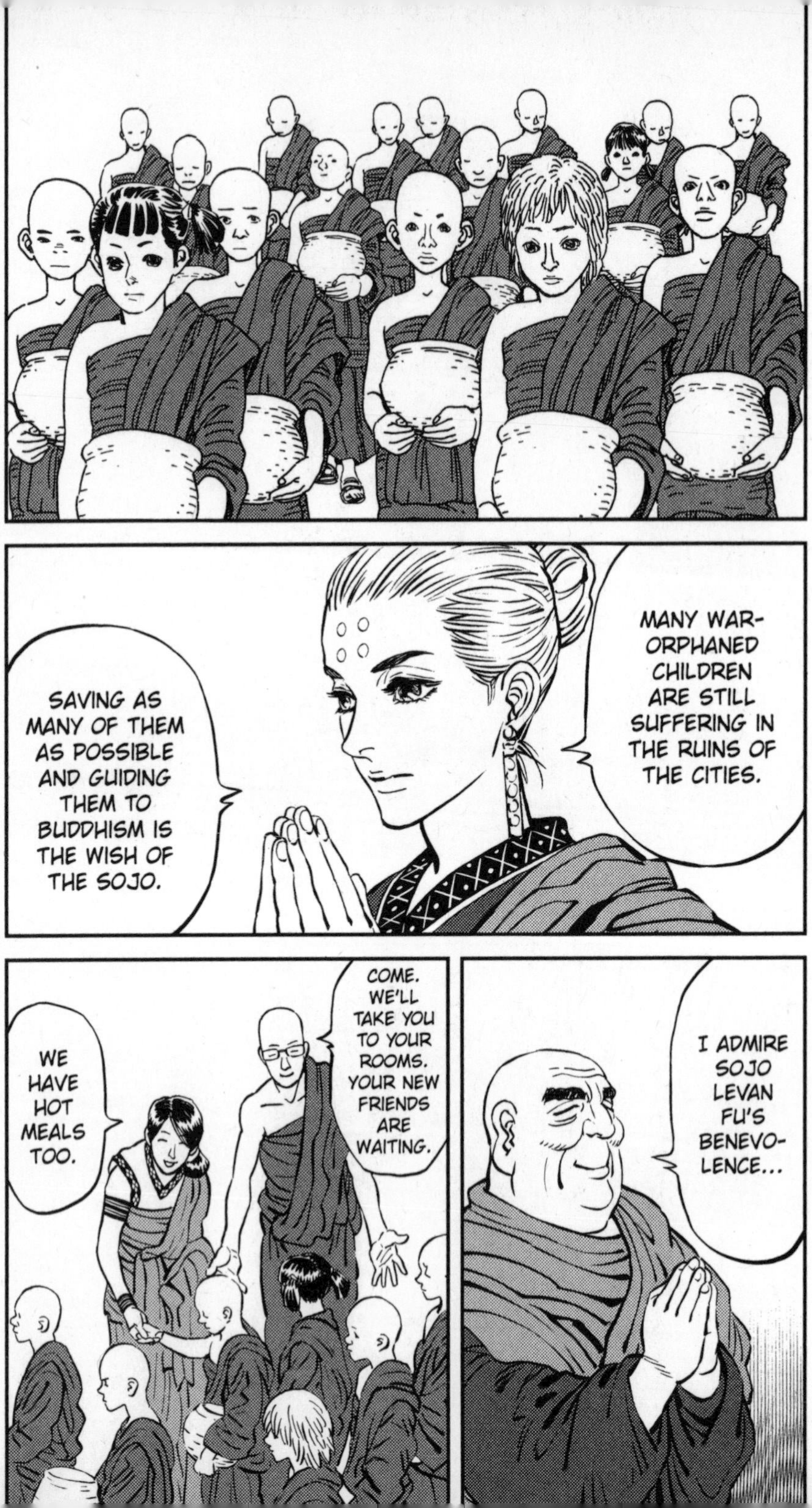
MANY WAR-ORPHANED CHILDREN ARE STILL SUFFERING IN THE RUINS OF THE CITIES.
SAVING AS MANY OF THEM AS POSSIBLE AND GUIDING THEM TO BUDDHISM IS THE WISH OF THE SOJO.
I ADMIRE SOJO LEVAN FU'S BENEVOLENCE...
COME. WE'LL TAKE YOU TO YOUR ROOMS. YOUR NEW FRIENDS ARE WAITING.
WE HAVE HOT MEALS TOO.

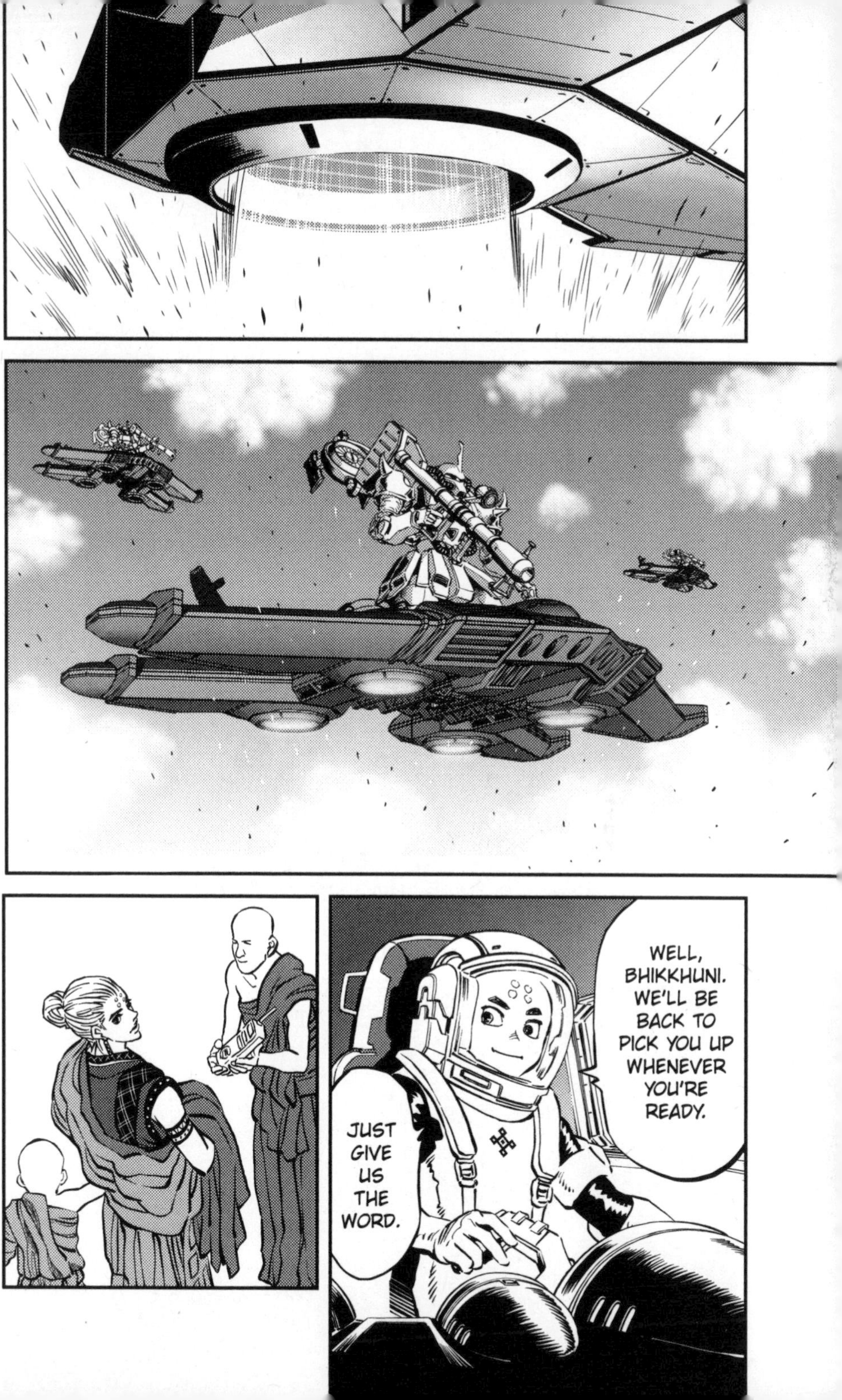
WELL, BHIKKHUNI. WE'LL BE BACK TO PICK YOU UP WHENEVER YOU'RE READY.
JUST GIVE US THE WORD.

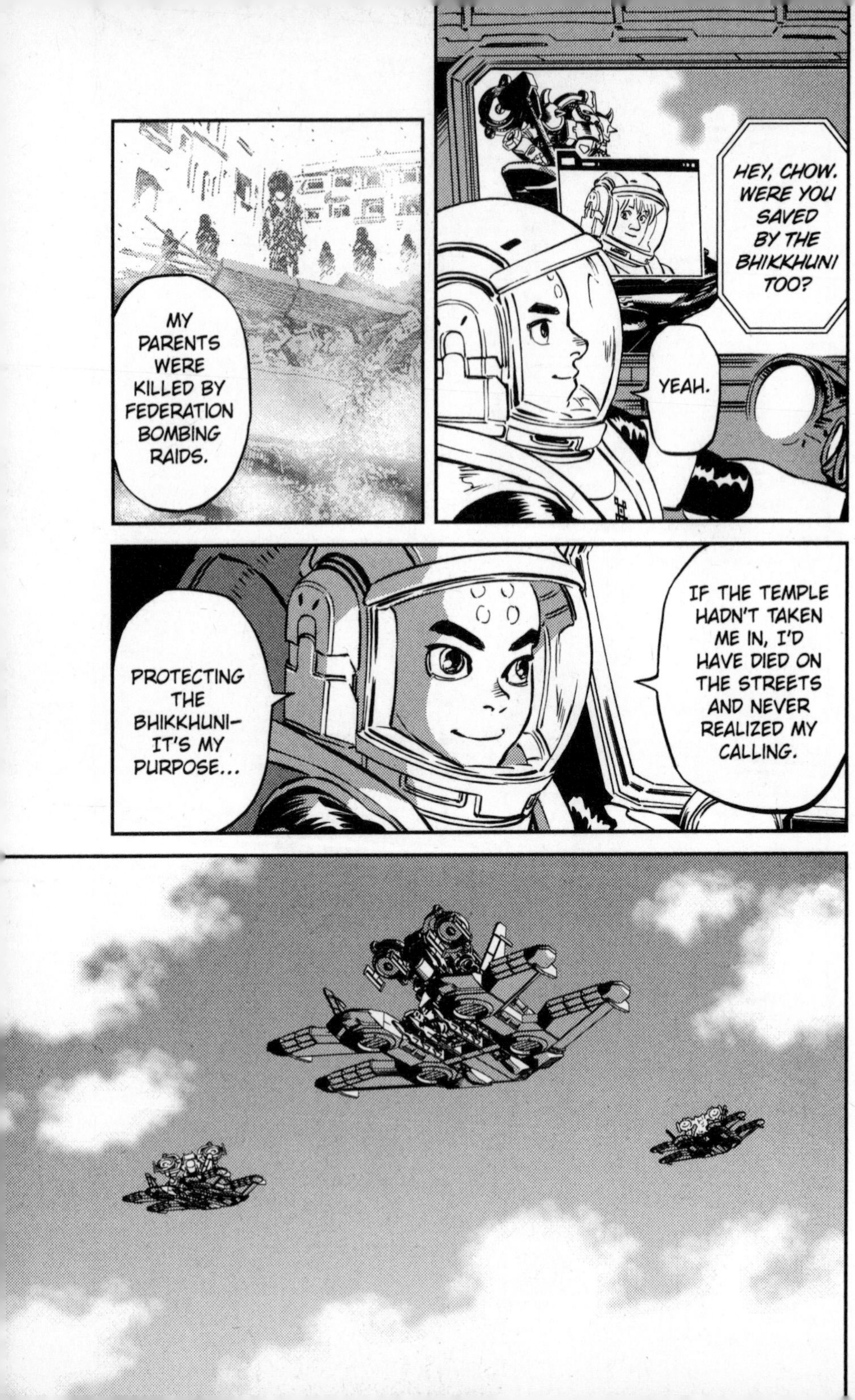
HEY, CHOW. WERE YOU SAVED BY THE BHIKKHUNI TOO?
YEAH.
MY PARENTS WERE KILLED BY FEDERATION BOMBING RAIDS.
IF THE TEMPLE HADN'T TAKEN ME IN, I'D HAVE DIED ON THE STREETS AND NEVER REALIZED MY CALLING.
PROTECTING THE BHIKKHUNI— IT'S MY PURPOSE...

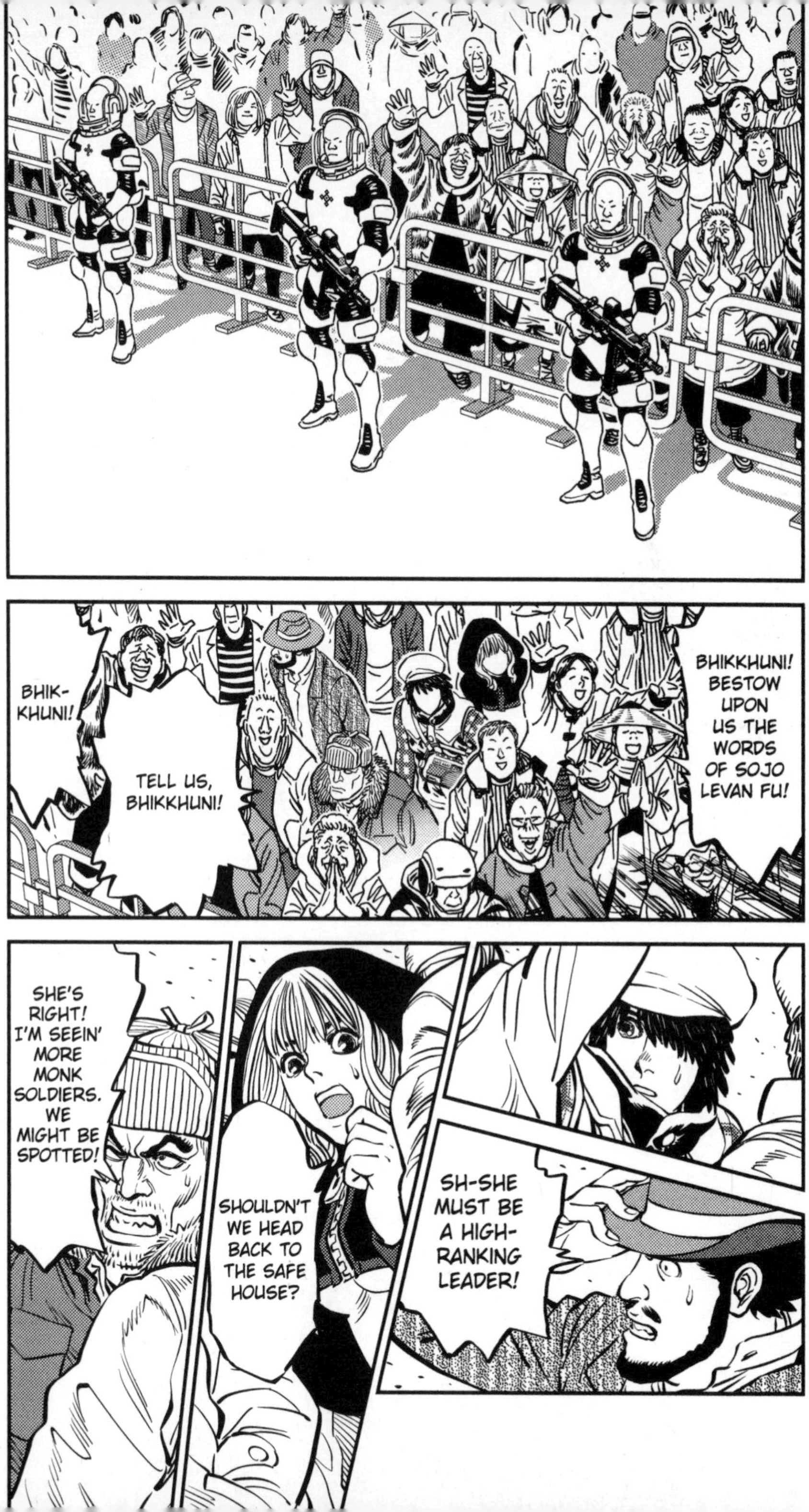
BHIKKHUNI! BESTOW UPON US THE WORDS OF SOJO LEVAN FU!
TELL US, BHIKKHUNI!
BHIK-KHUNI!
SH-SHE MUST BE A HIGH-RANKING LEADER!
SHOULDN'T WE HEAD BACK TO THE SAFE HOUSE?
SHE'S RIGHT! I'M SEEIN' MORE MONK SOLDIERS. WE MIGHT BE SPOTTED!

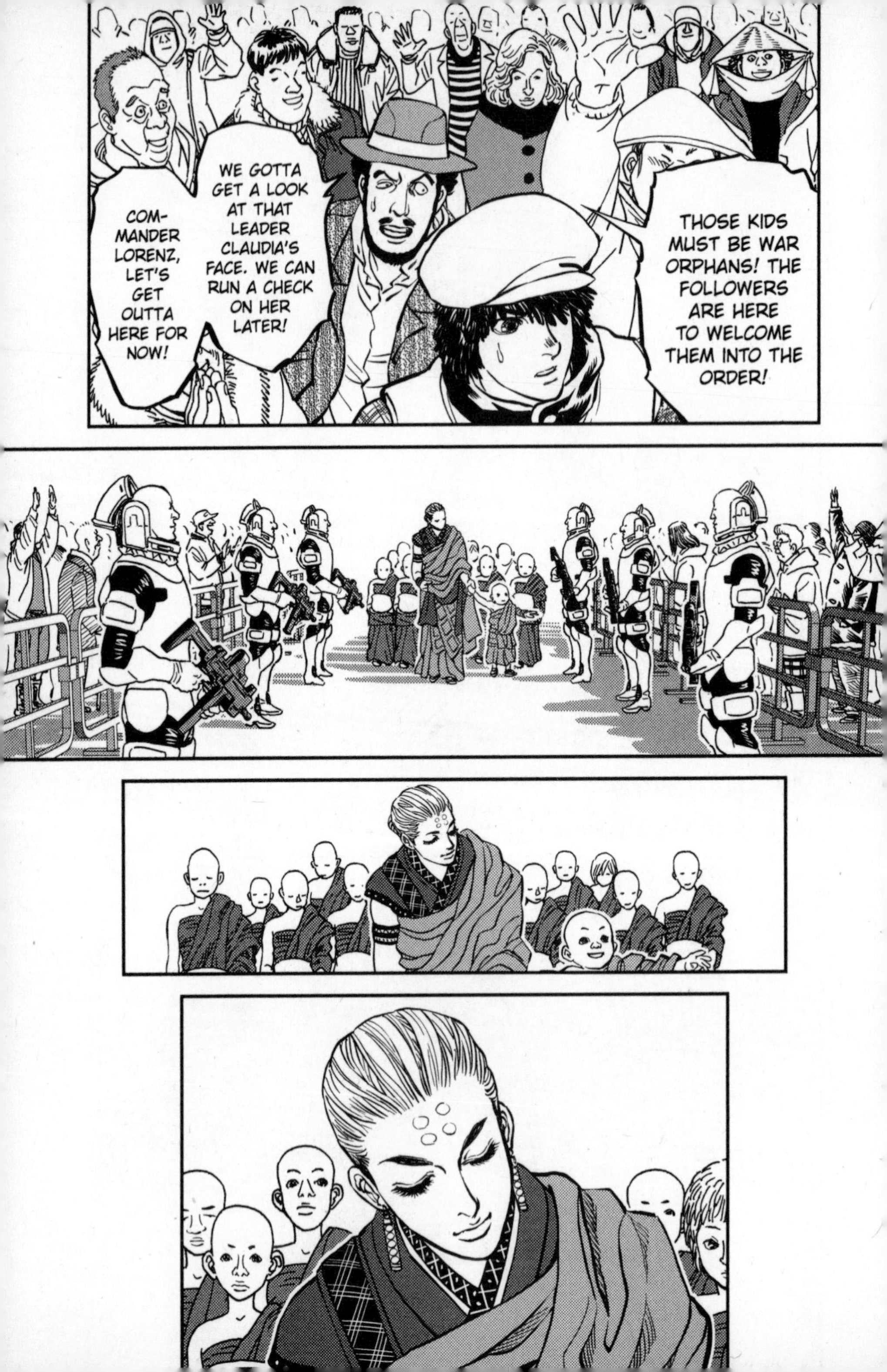
THOSE KIDS MUST BE WAR ORPHANS! THE FOLLOWERS ARE HERE TO WELCOME THEM INTO THE ORDER!
WE GOTTA GET A LOOK AT THAT LEADER CLAUDIA'S FACE. WE CAN RUN A CHECK ON HER LATER!
COM-MANDER LORENZ, LET'S GET OUTTA HERE FOR NOW!

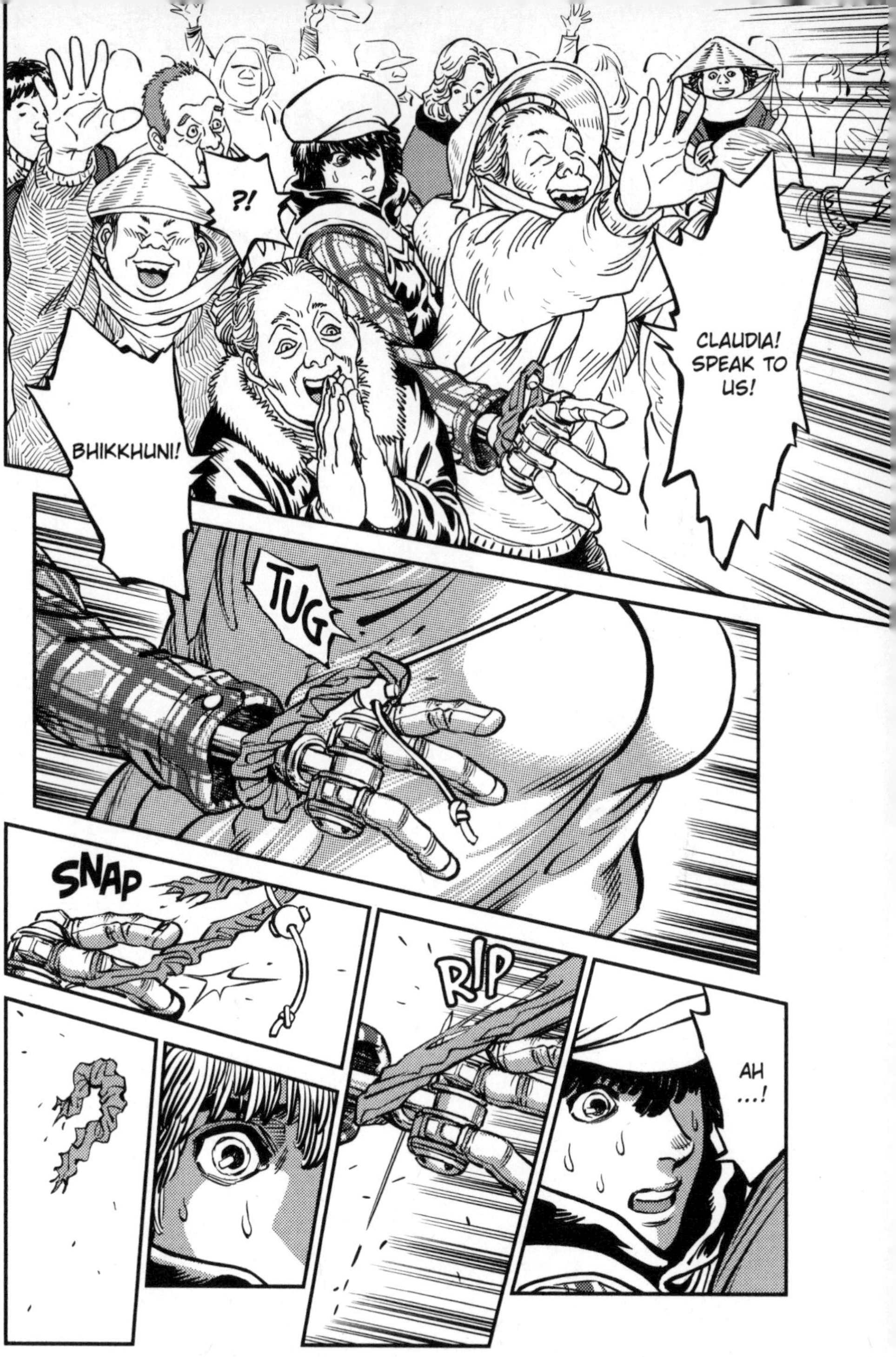
CLAUDIA! SPEAK TO US!
?!
BHIKKHUNI!
TUG
AH ...!
RIP
SNAP

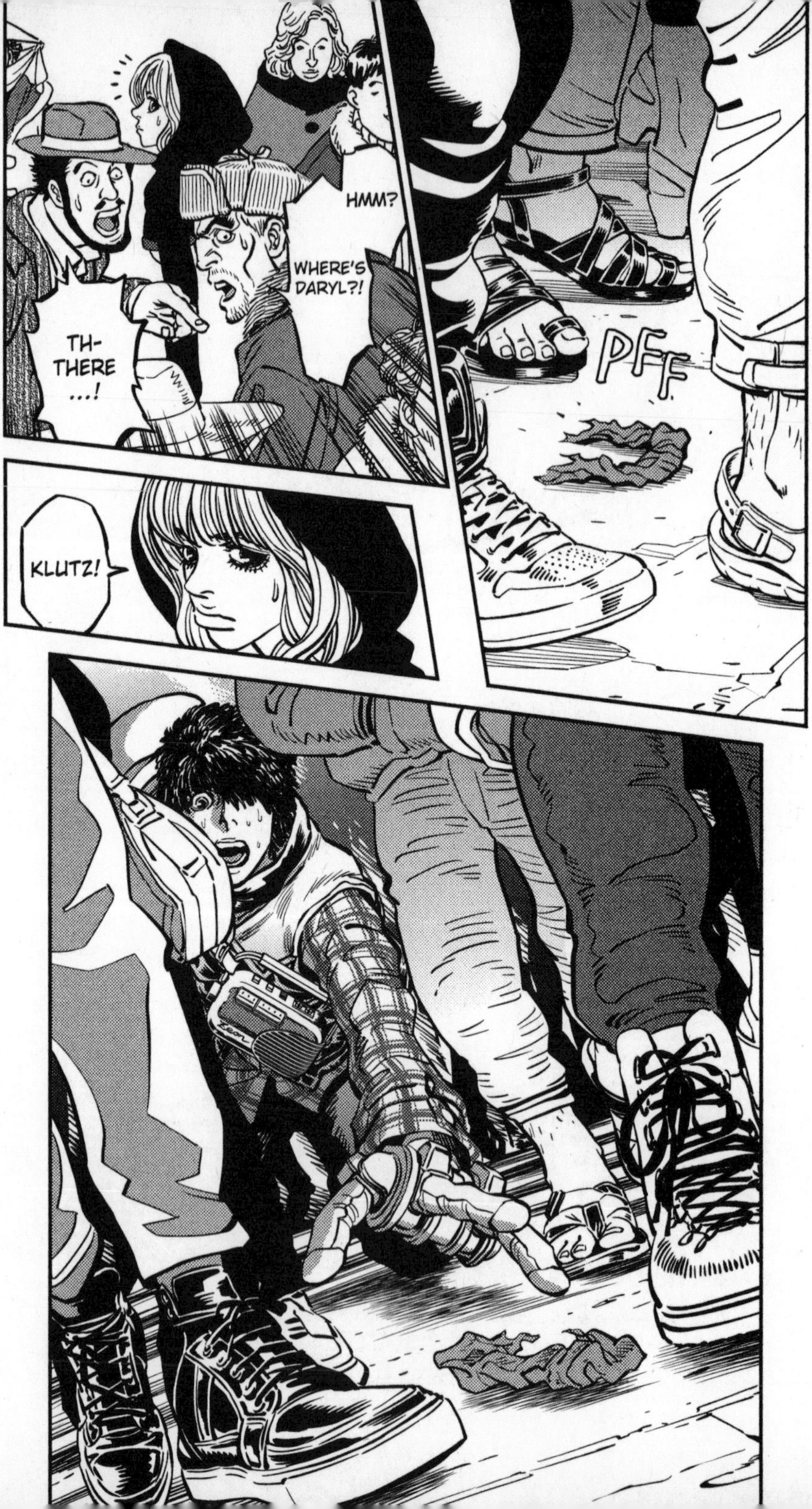
PFF
HMM?
WHERE'S DARYL?!
TH-THERE ...!
KLUTZ!

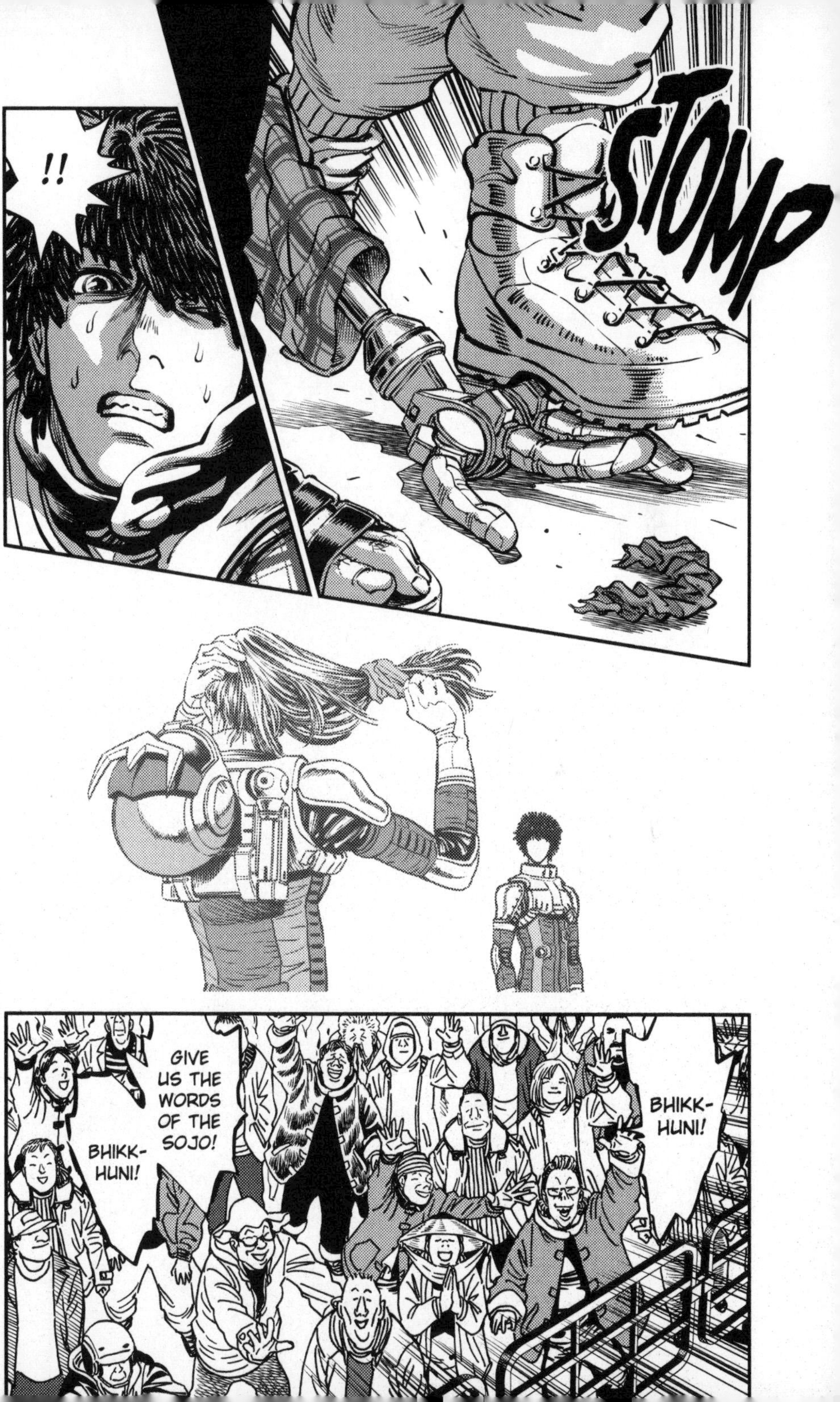
STOMP
!!
BHIKK-
HUNI!
GIVE
US THE
WORDS
OF THE
SOJO!
BHIKK-
HUNI!

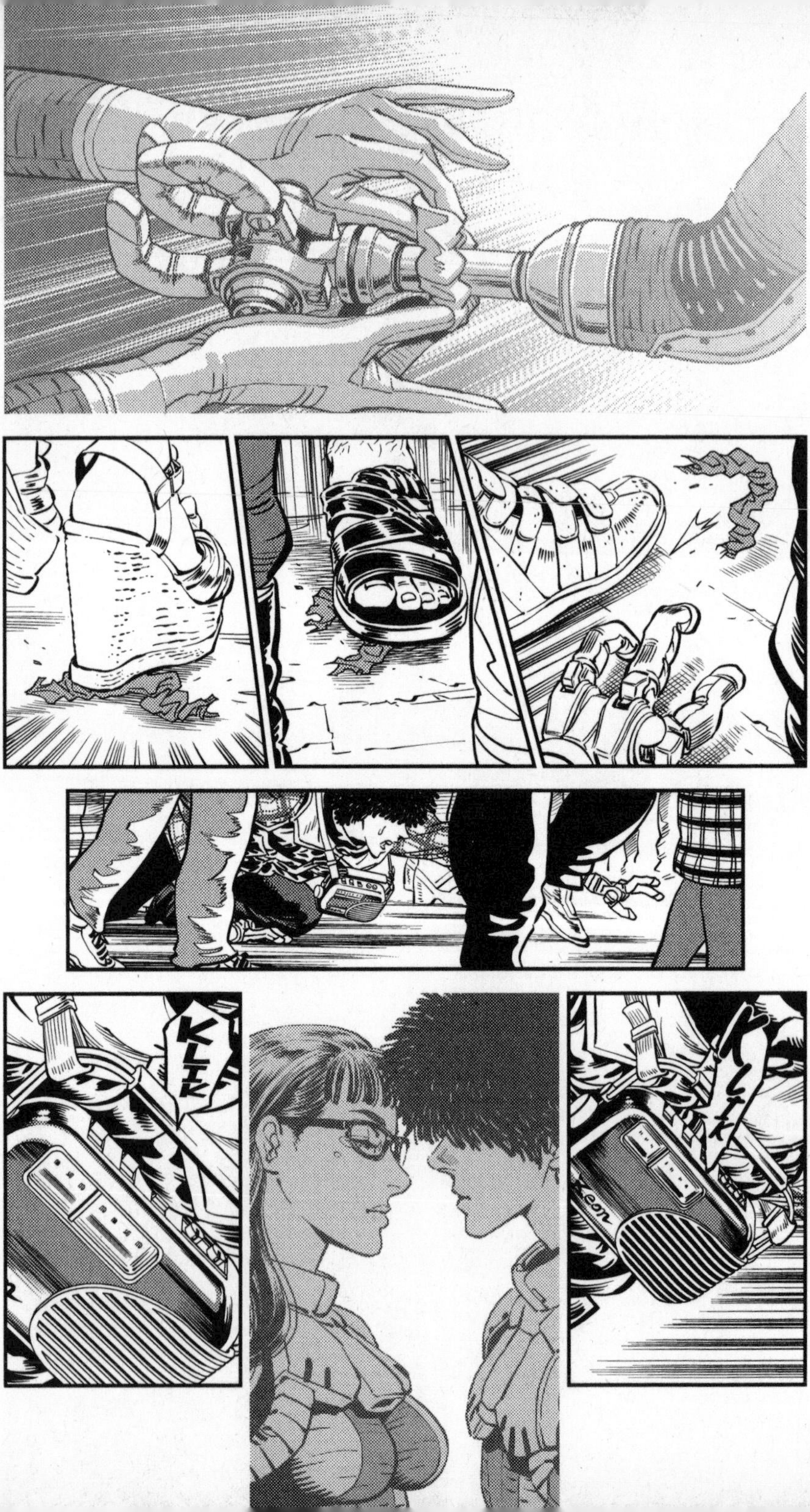
KLIK
KLIK

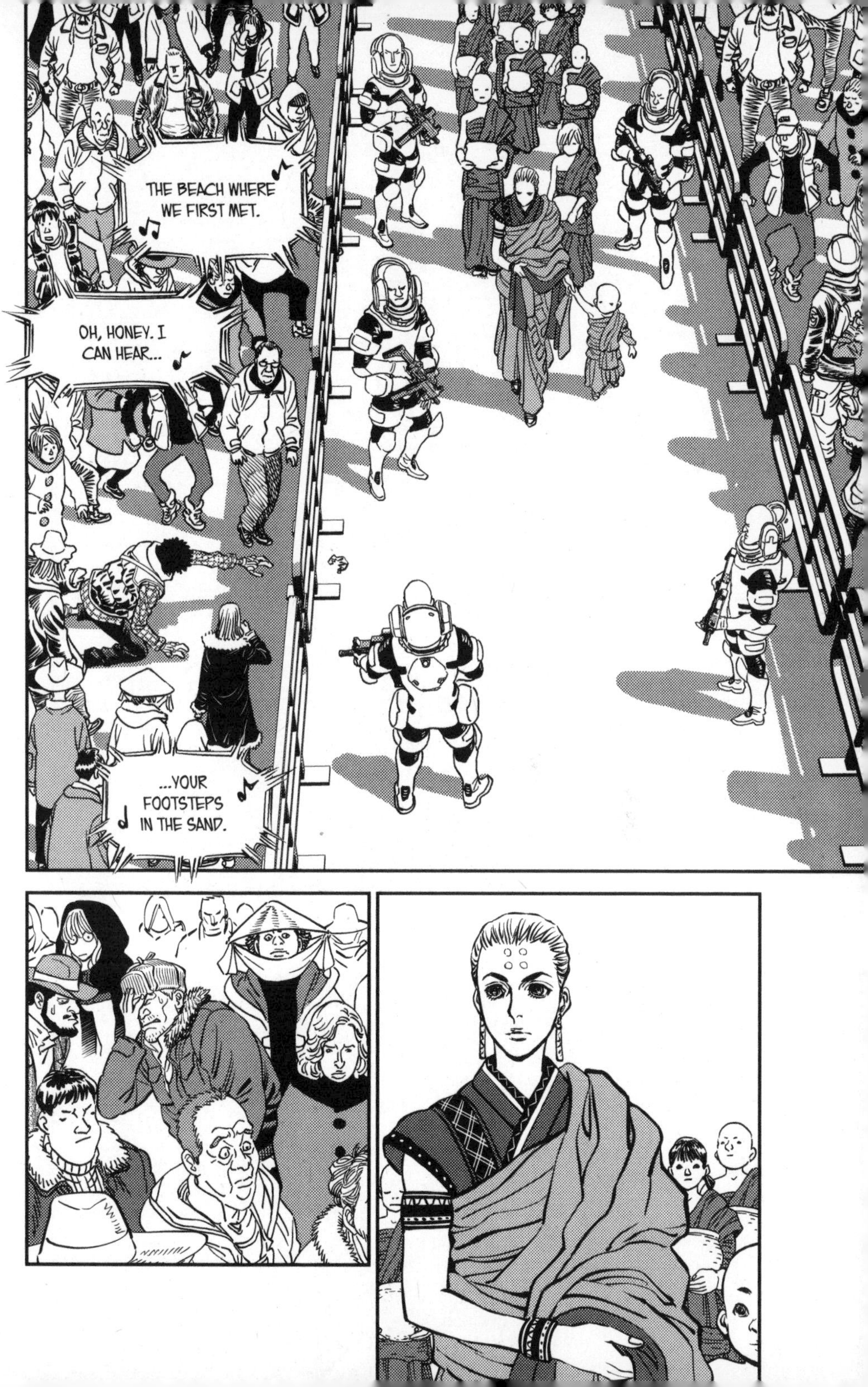
THE BEACH WHERE WE FIRST MET.
OH, HONEY. I CAN HEAR...
...YOUR FOOTSTEPS IN THE SAND.

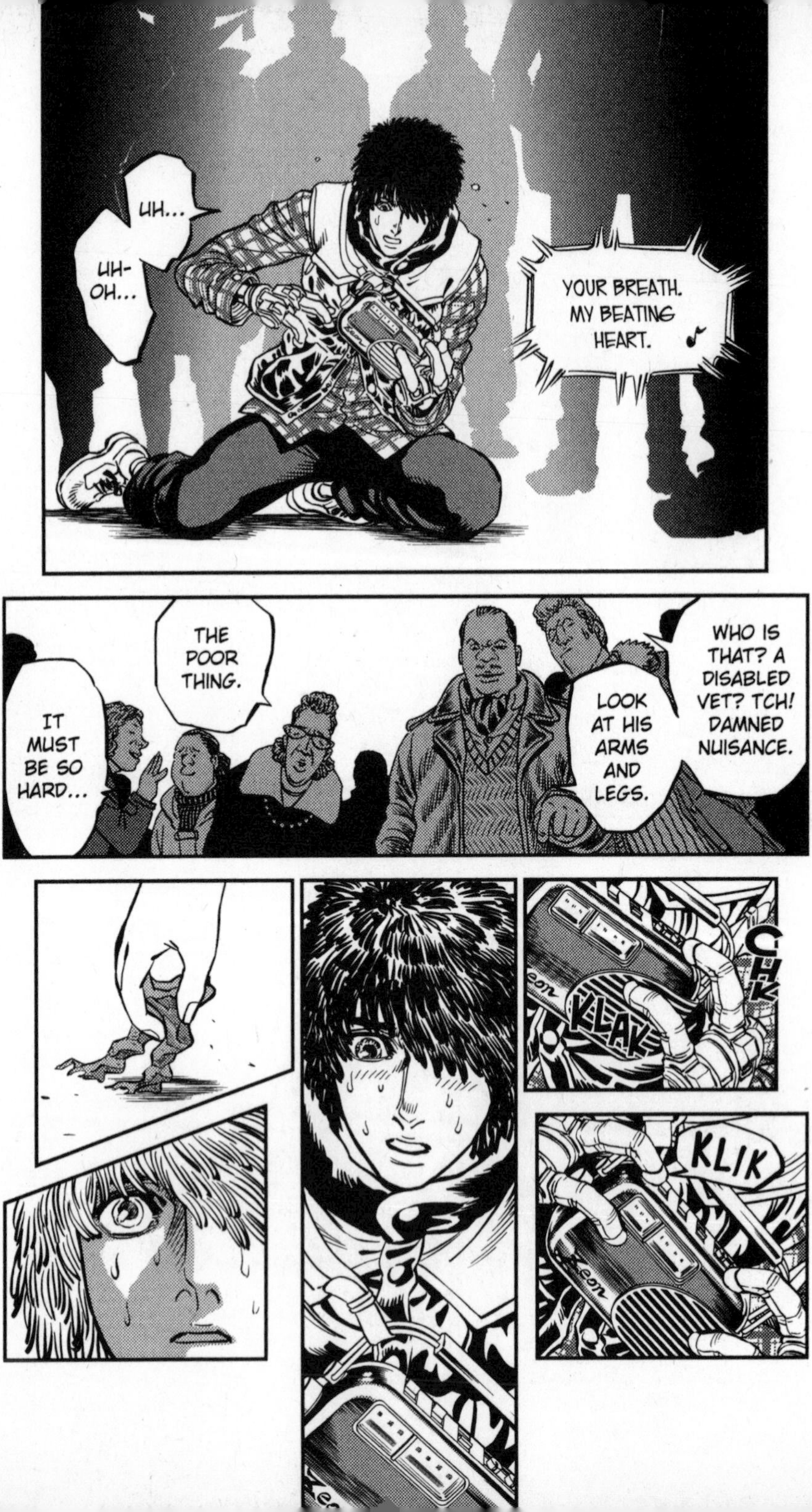
YOUR BREATH. MY BEATING HEART. ♪
UH...
UH-OH...
WHO IS THAT? A DISABLED VET? TCH! DAMNED NUISANCE.
LOOK AT HIS ARMS AND LEGS.
THE POOR THING.
IT MUST BE SO HARD...
CHK
KLAK
KLIK

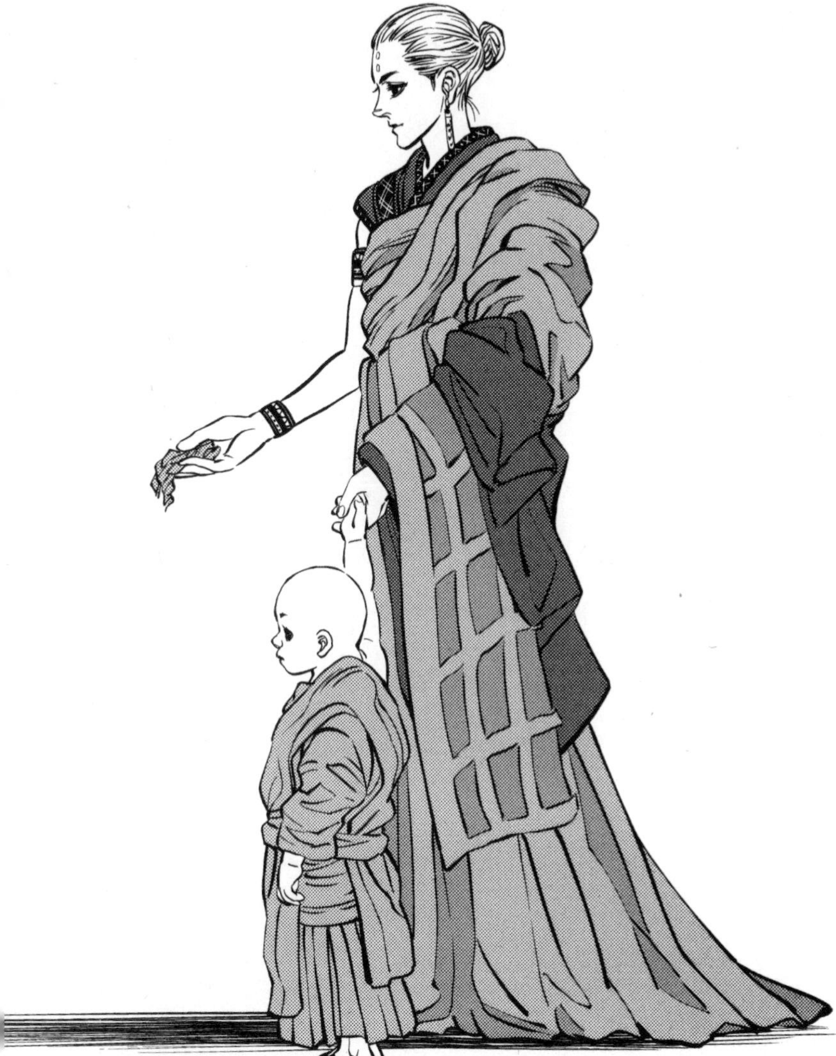

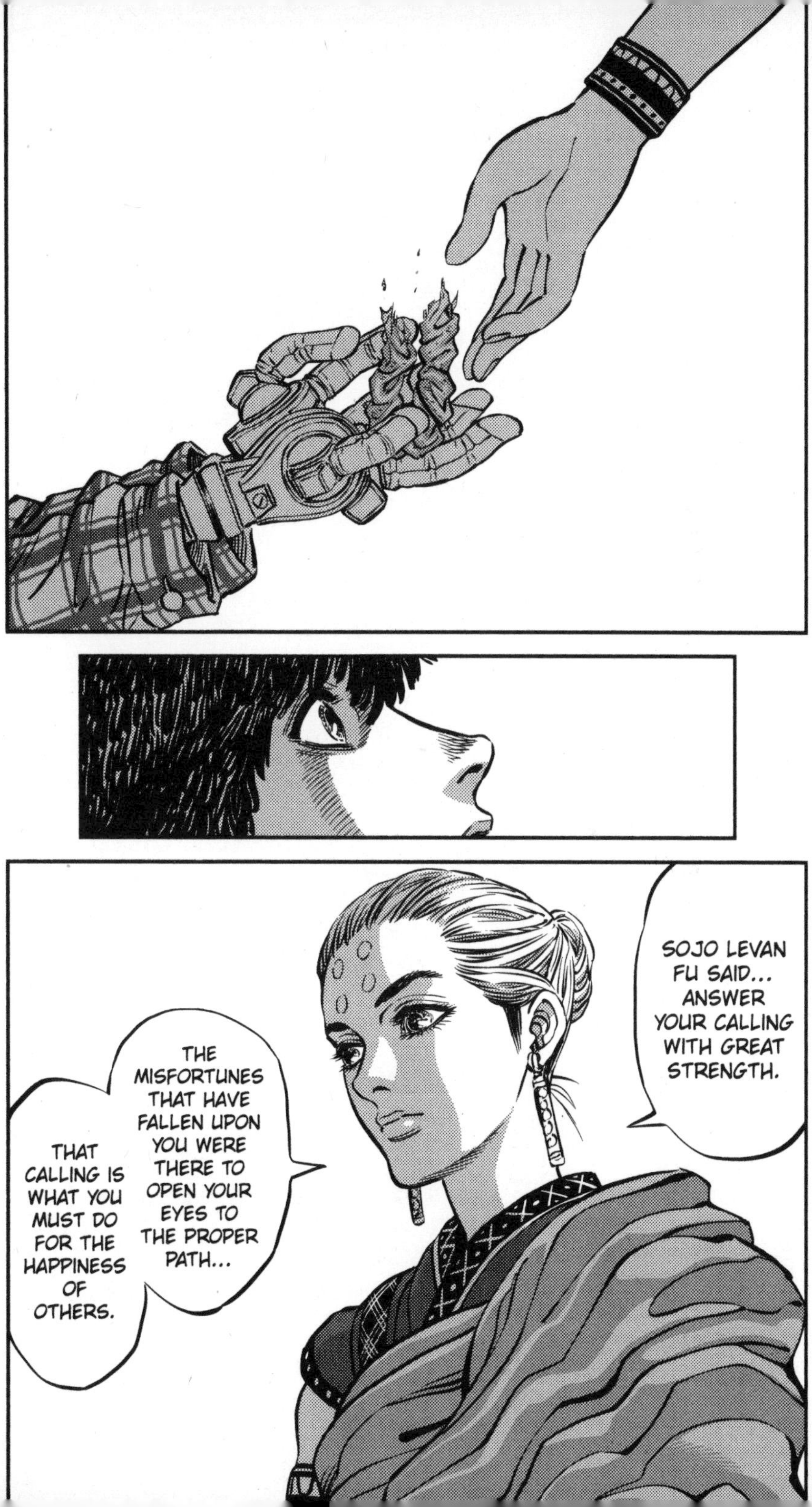
SOJO LEVAN FU SAID... ANSWER YOUR CALLING WITH GREAT STRENGTH.
THE MISFORTUNES THAT HAVE FALLEN UPON YOU WERE THERE TO OPEN YOUR EYES TO THE PROPER PATH...
THAT CALLING IS WHAT YOU MUST DO FOR THE HAPPINESS OF OTHERS.

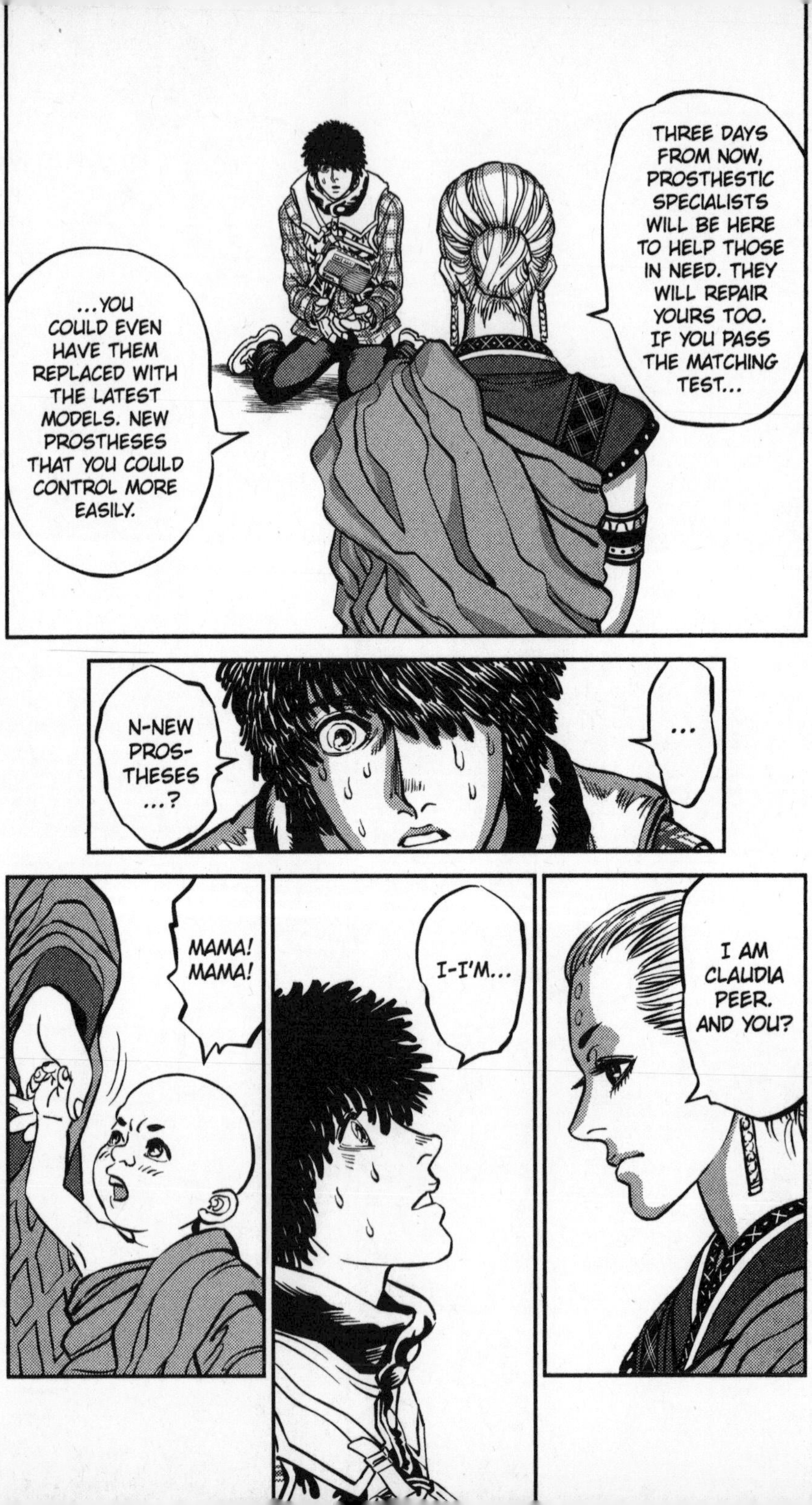
THREE DAYS FROM NOW, PROSTHESTIC SPECIALISTS WILL BE HERE TO HELP THOSE IN NEED. THEY WILL REPAIR YOURS TOO. IF YOU PASS THE MATCHING TEST...
...YOU COULD EVEN HAVE THEM REPLACED WITH THE LATEST MODELS. NEW PROSTHESES THAT YOU COULD CONTROL MORE EASILY.
...
N-NEW PROS-THESES ...?
I AM CLAUDIA PEER. AND YOU?
I-I'M...
MAMA! MAMA!

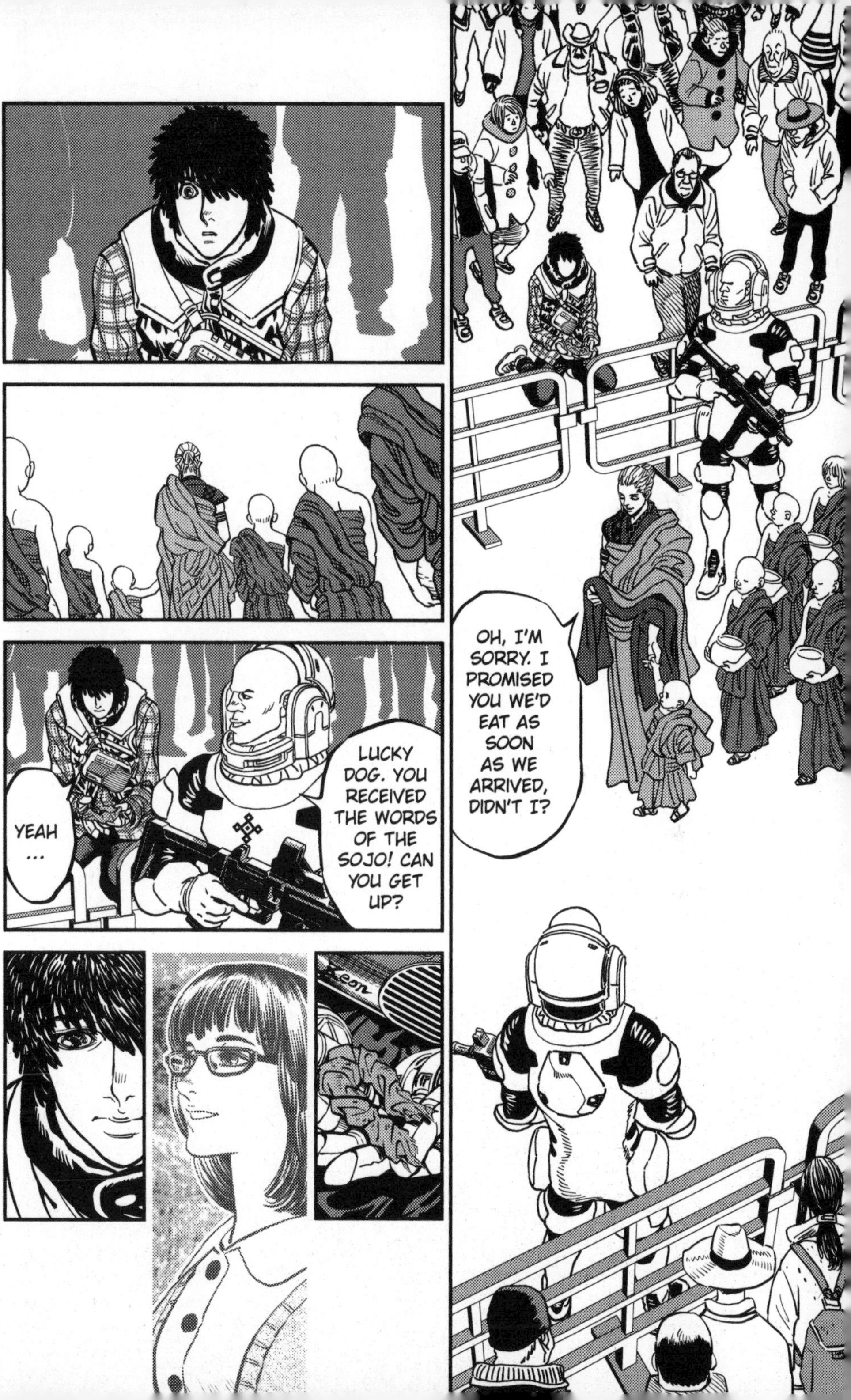
OH, I'M SORRY. I PROMISED YOU WE'D EAT AS SOON AS WE ARRIVED, DIDN'T I?
LUCKY DOG. YOU RECEIVED THE WORDS OF THE SOJO! CAN YOU GET UP?
YEAH ...

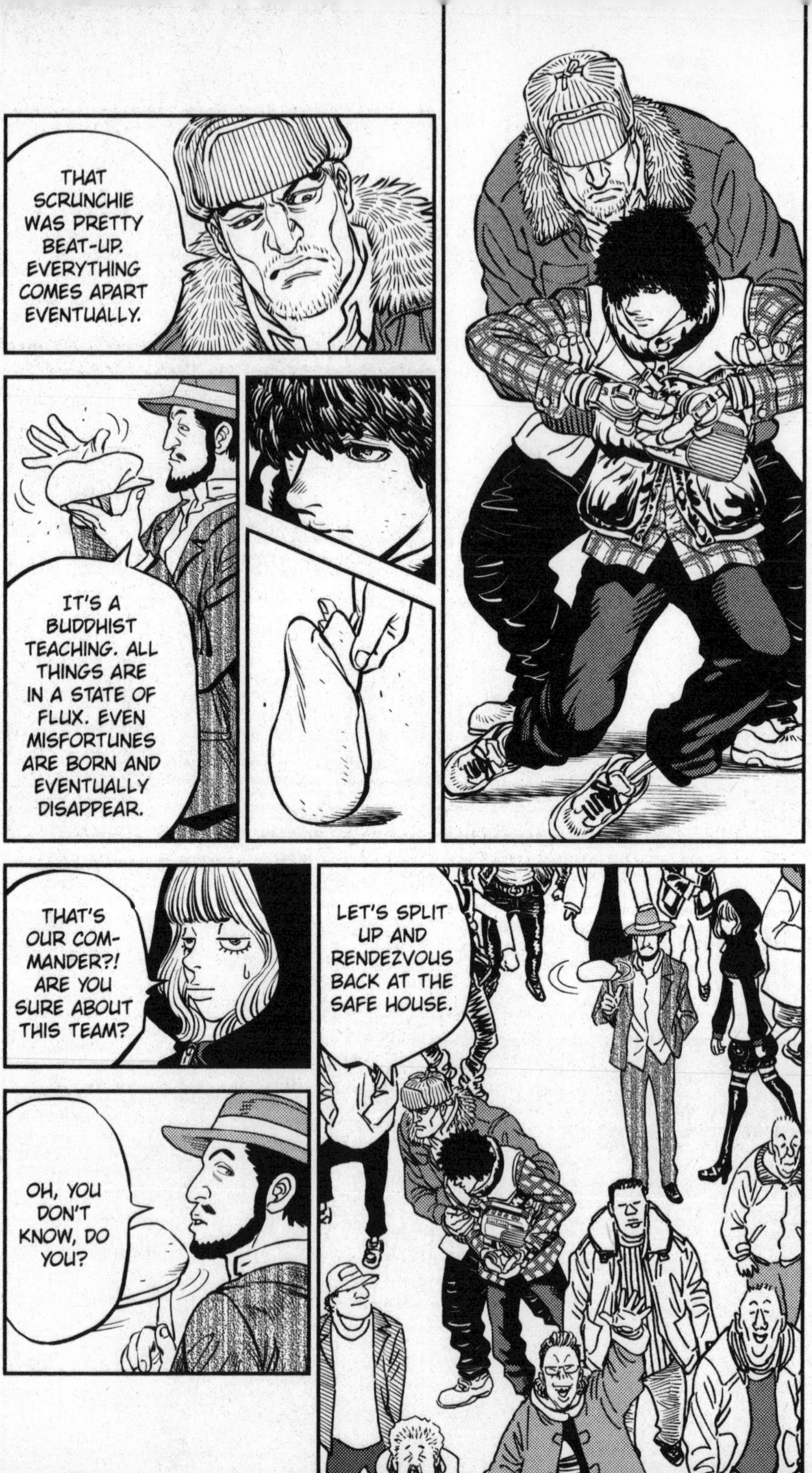
THAT SCRUNCHIE WAS PRETTY BEAT-UP. EVERYTHING COMES APART EVENTUALLY.
IT'S A BUDDHIST TEACHING. ALL THINGS ARE IN A STATE OF FLUX. EVEN MISFORTUNES ARE BORN AND EVENTUALLY DISAPPEAR.
LET'S SPLIT UP AND RENDEZVOUS BACK AT THE SAFE HOUSE.
THAT'S OUR COM-MANDER?! ARE YOU SURE ABOUT THIS TEAM?
OH, YOU DON'T KNOW, DO YOU?

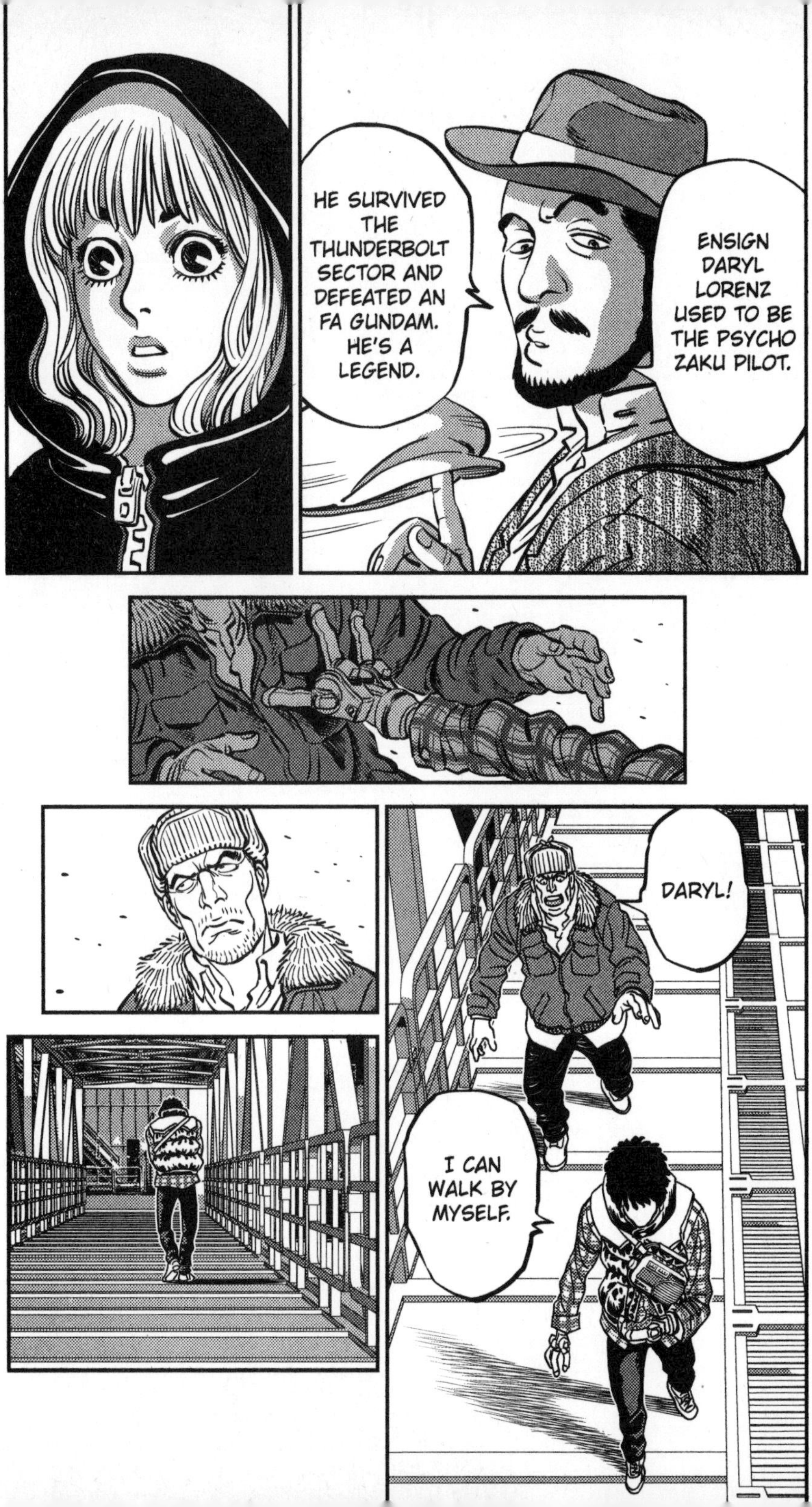
ENSIGN DARYL LORENZ USED TO BE THE PSYCHO ZAKU PILOT.
HE SURVIVED THE THUNDERBOLT SECTOR AND DEFEATED AN FA GUNDAM. HE'S A LEGEND.
DARYL!
I CAN WALK BY MYSELF.

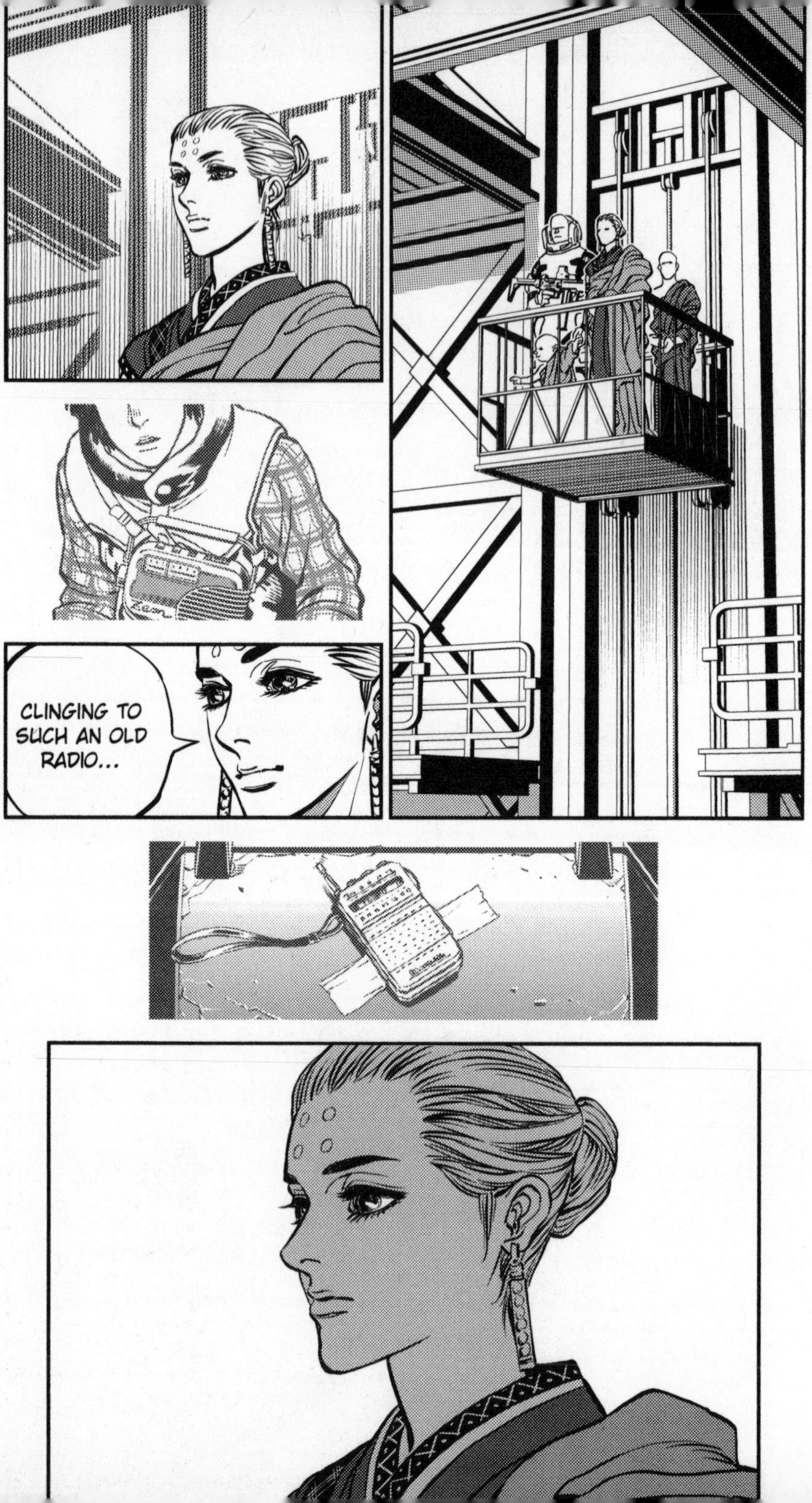
CLINGING TO SUCH AN OLD RADIO...

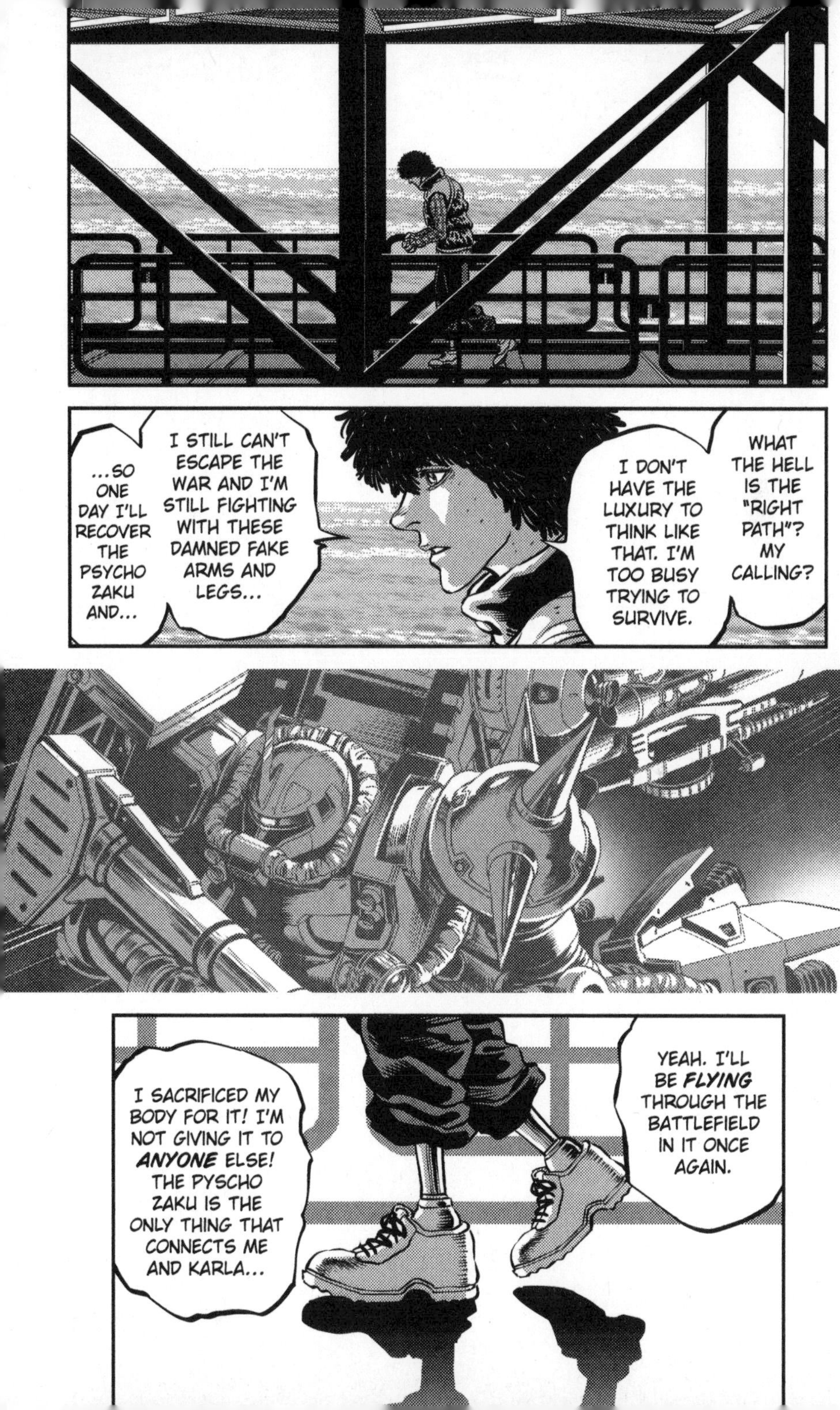
WHAT THE HELL IS THE "RIGHT PATH"? MY CALLING?
I DON'T HAVE THE LUXURY TO THINK LIKE THAT. I'M TOO BUSY TRYING TO SURVIVE.
I STILL CAN'T ESCAPE THE WAR AND I'M STILL FIGHTING WITH THESE DAMNED FAKE ARMS AND LEGS...
...SO ONE DAY I'LL RECOVER THE PSYCHO ZAKU AND...
YEAH. I'LL BE ***FLYING*** THROUGH THE BATTLEFIELD IN IT ONCE AGAIN.
I SACRIFICED MY BODY FOR IT! I'M NOT GIVING IT TO ***ANYONE*** ELSE! THE PYSCHO ZAKU IS THE ONLY THING THAT CONNECTS ME AND KARLA...

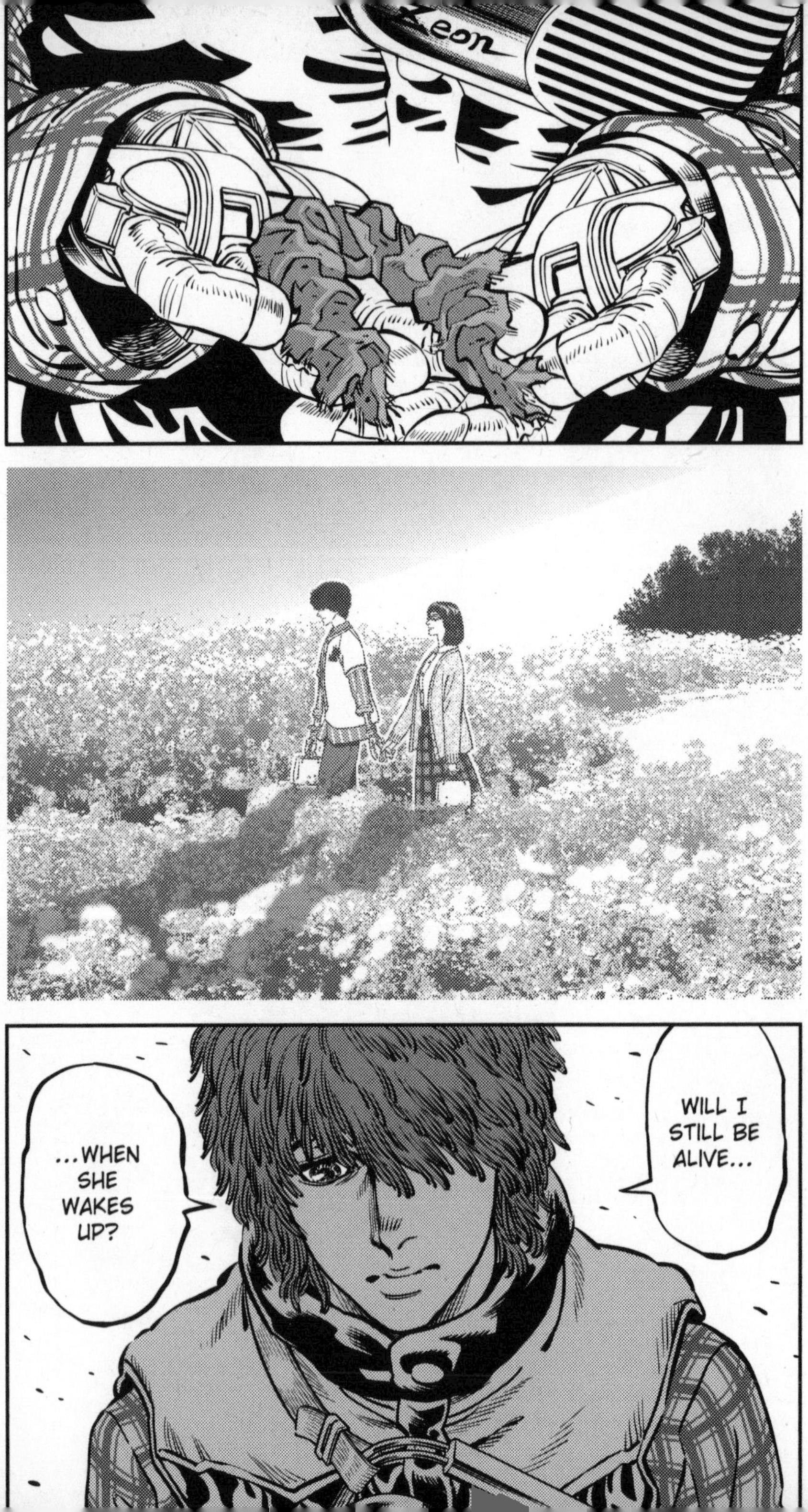
WILL I STILL BE ALIVE...
...WHEN SHE WAKES UP?

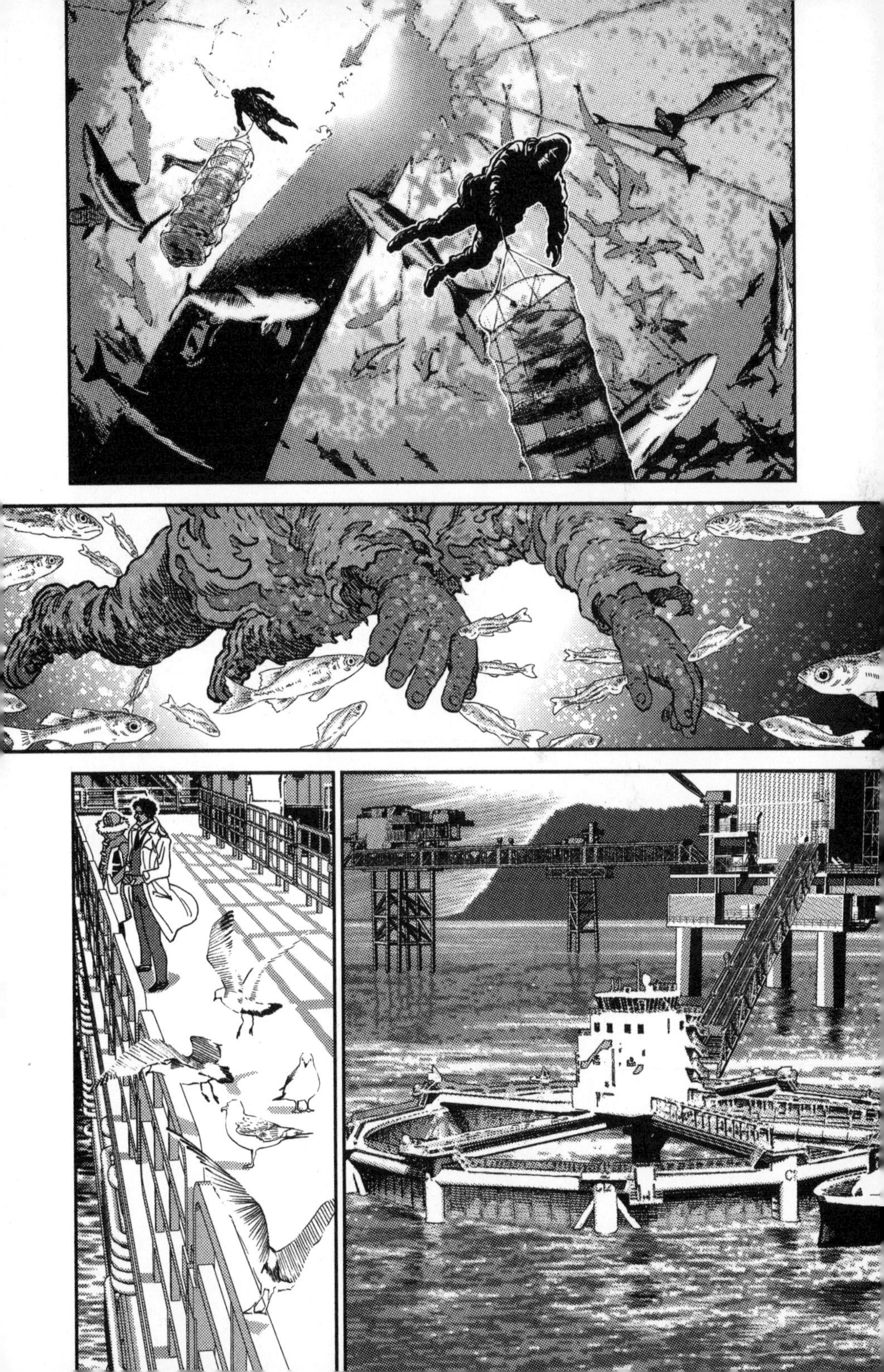

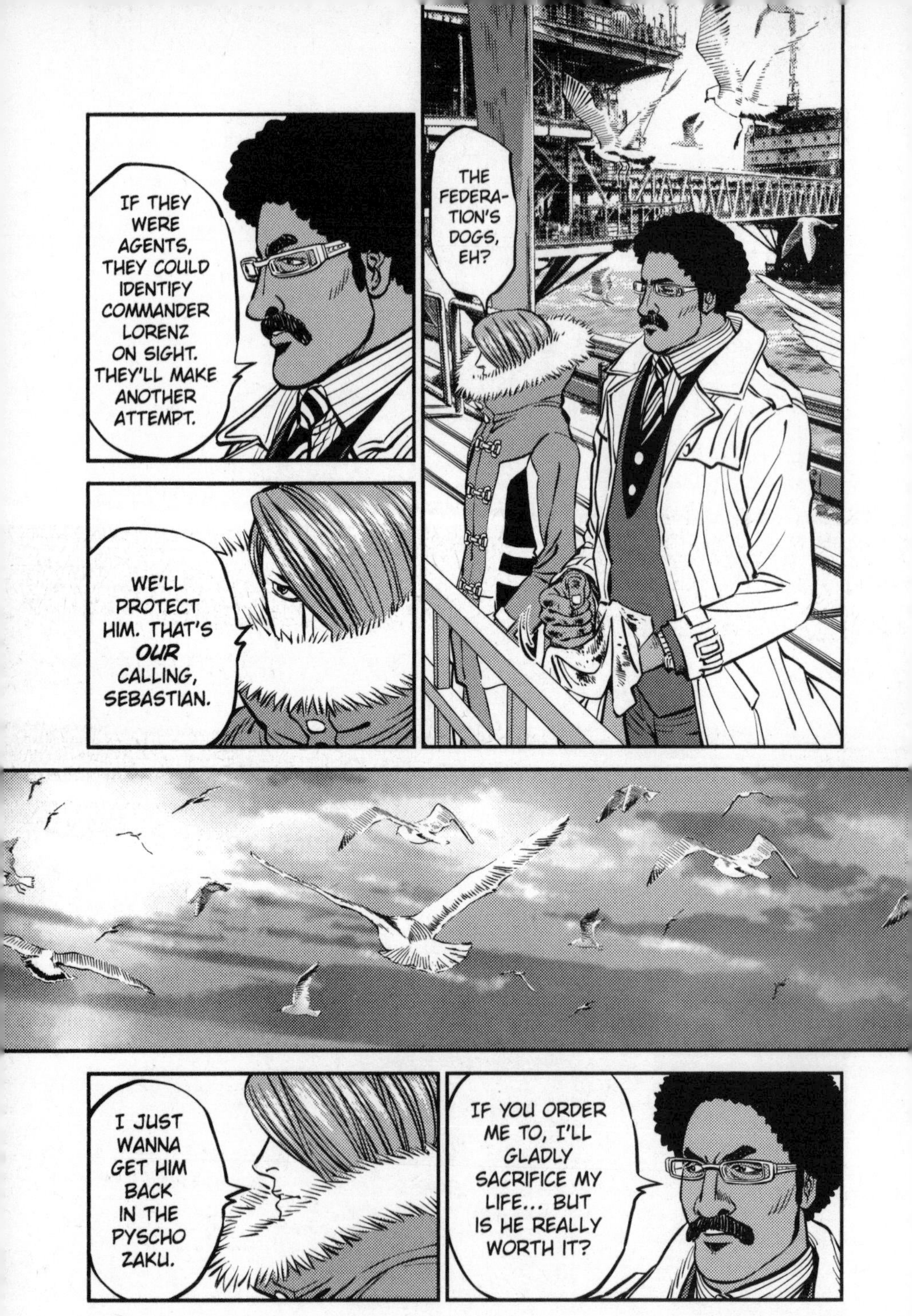
THE FEDERATION'S DOGS, EH?
IF THEY WERE AGENTS, THEY COULD IDENTIFY COMMANDER LORENZ ON SIGHT. THEY'LL MAKE ANOTHER ATTEMPT.
WE'LL PROTECT HIM. THAT'S *OUR* CALLING, SEBASTIAN.
IF YOU ORDER ME TO, I'LL GLADLY SACRIFICE MY LIFE... BUT IS HE REALLY WORTH IT?
I JUST WANNA GET HIM BACK IN THE PYSCHO ZAKU.

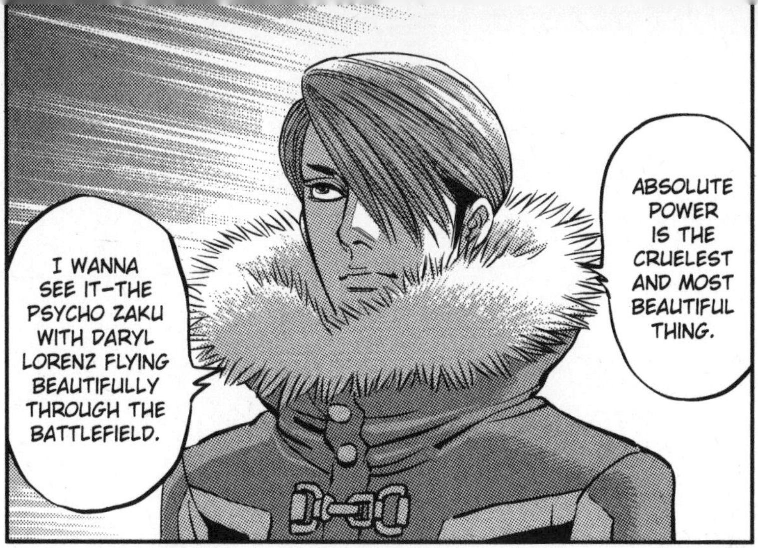
ABSOLUTE POWER IS THE CRUELEST AND MOST BEAUTIFUL THING.
I WANNA SEE IT—THE PSYCHO ZAKU WITH DARYL LORENZ FLYING BEAUTIFULLY THROUGH THE BATTLEFIELD.

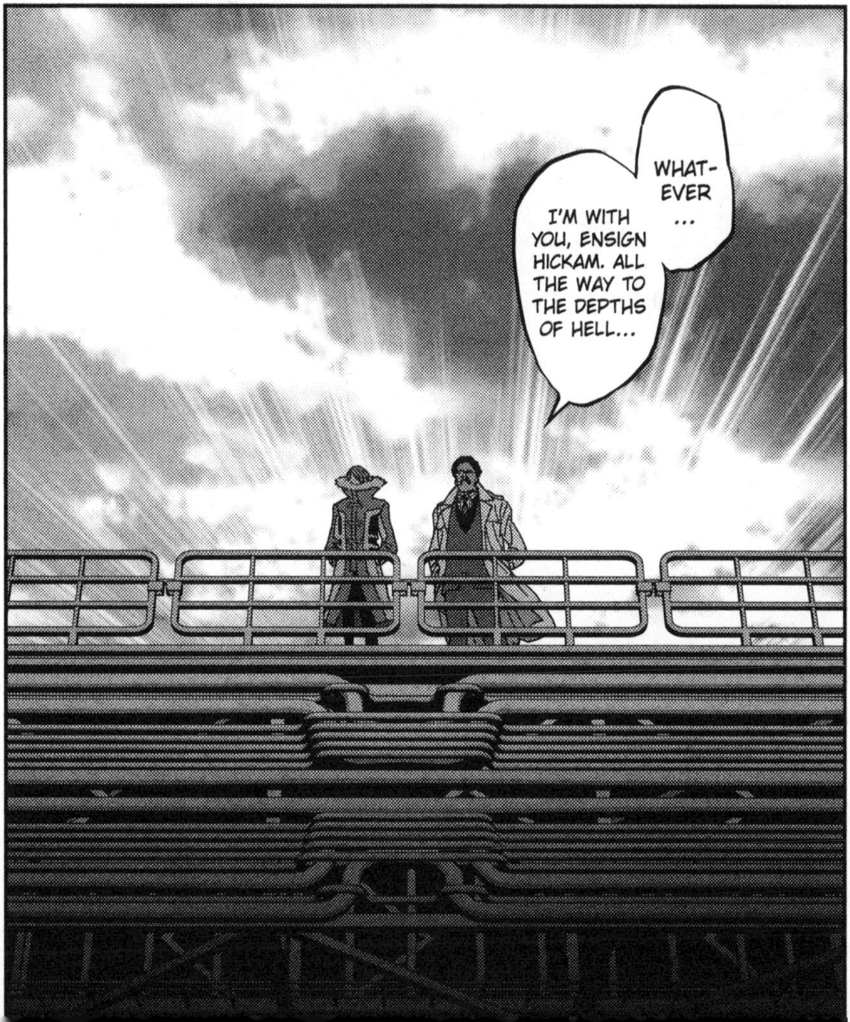
WHAT-EVER...
I'M WITH YOU, ENSIGN HICKAM. ALL THE WAY TO THE DEPTHS OF HELL...

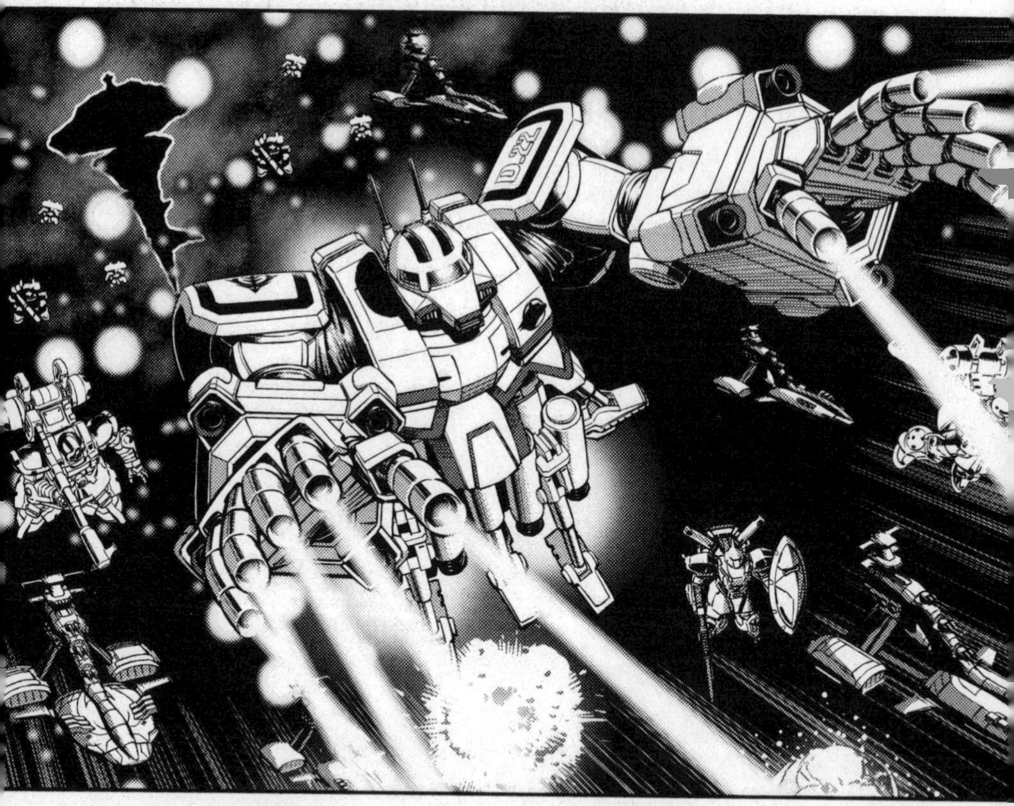
D-22

MOBILE SUIT GUNDAM
THUNDERBOLT

CHAPTER 67

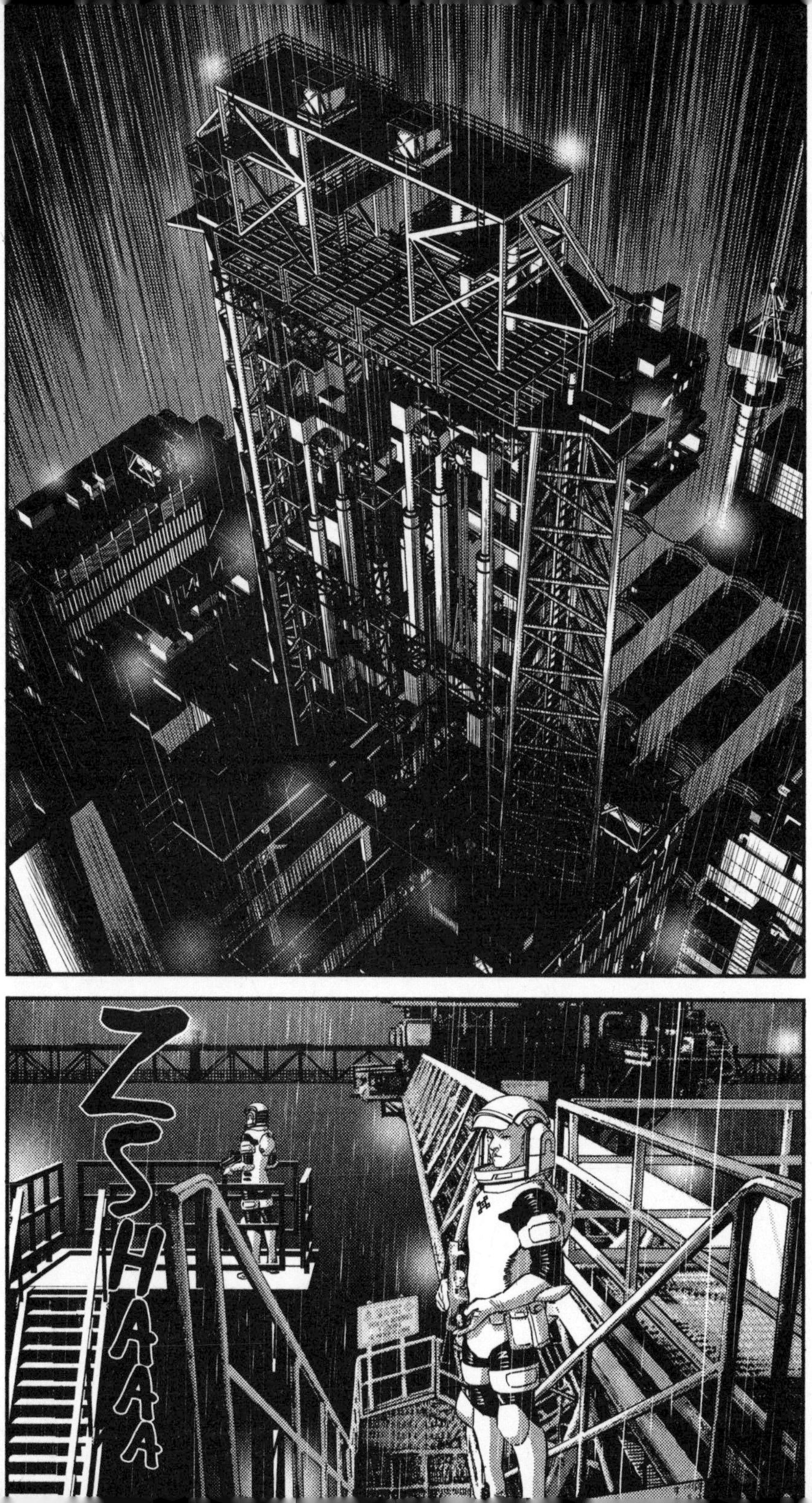
ZSHAAAA

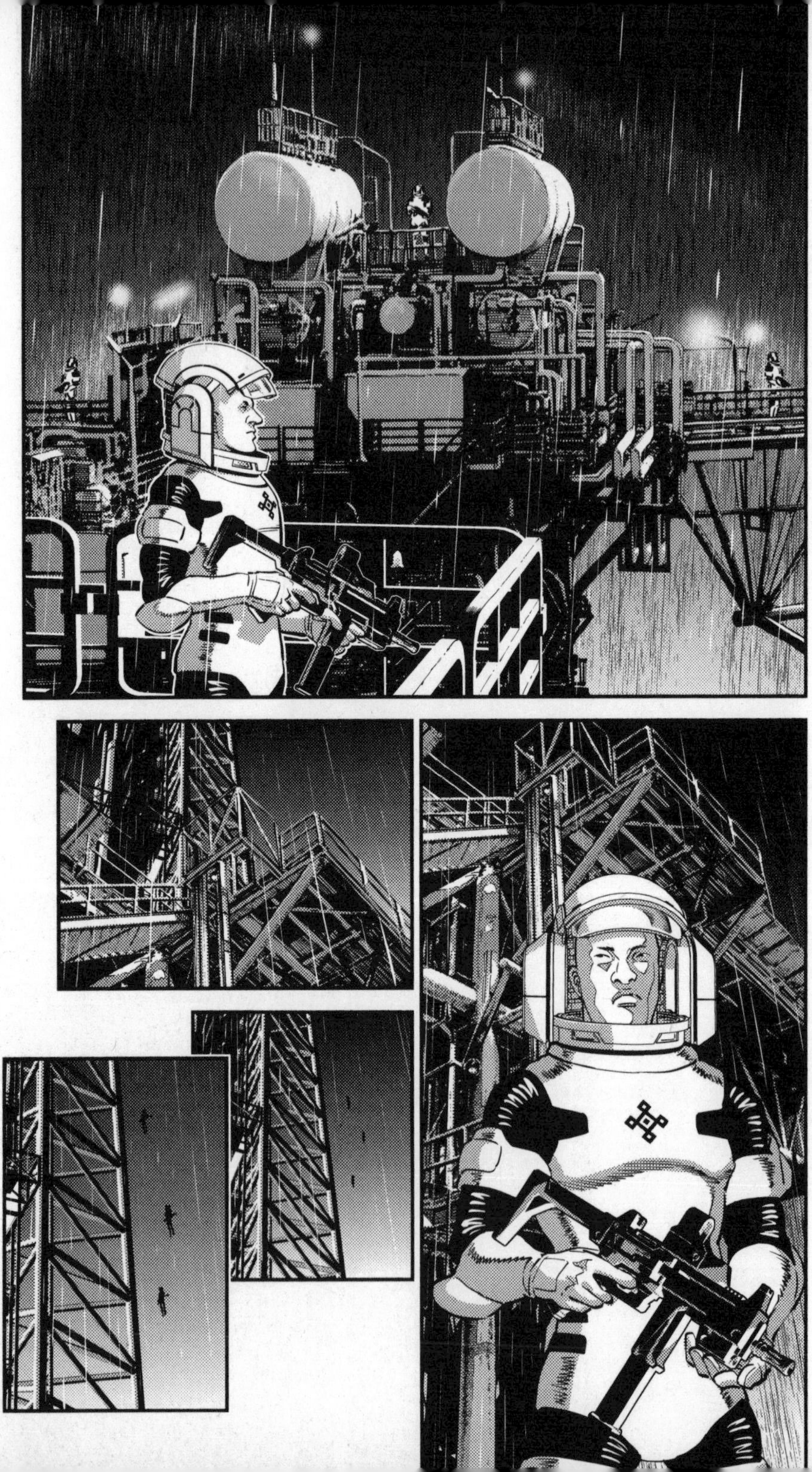

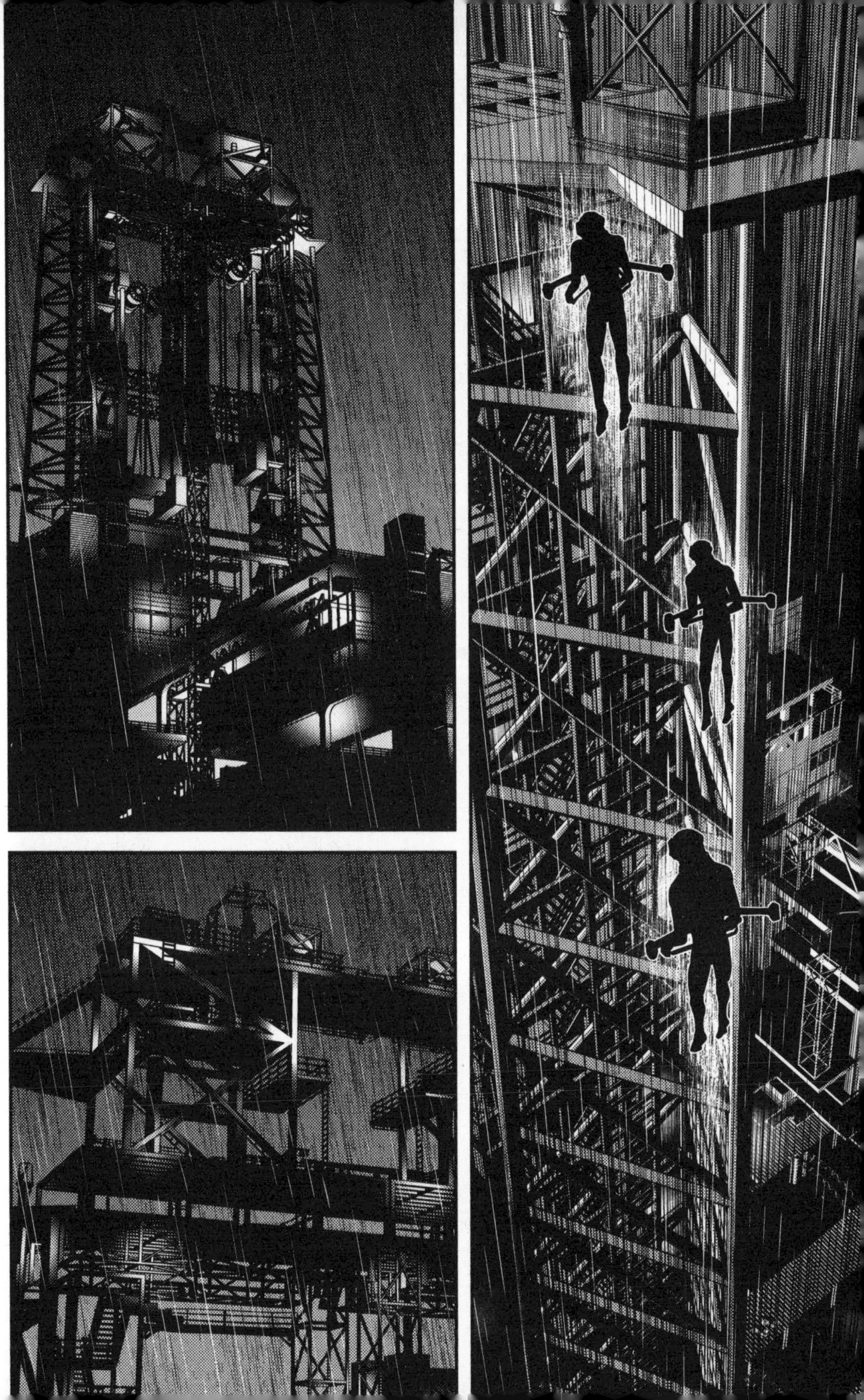

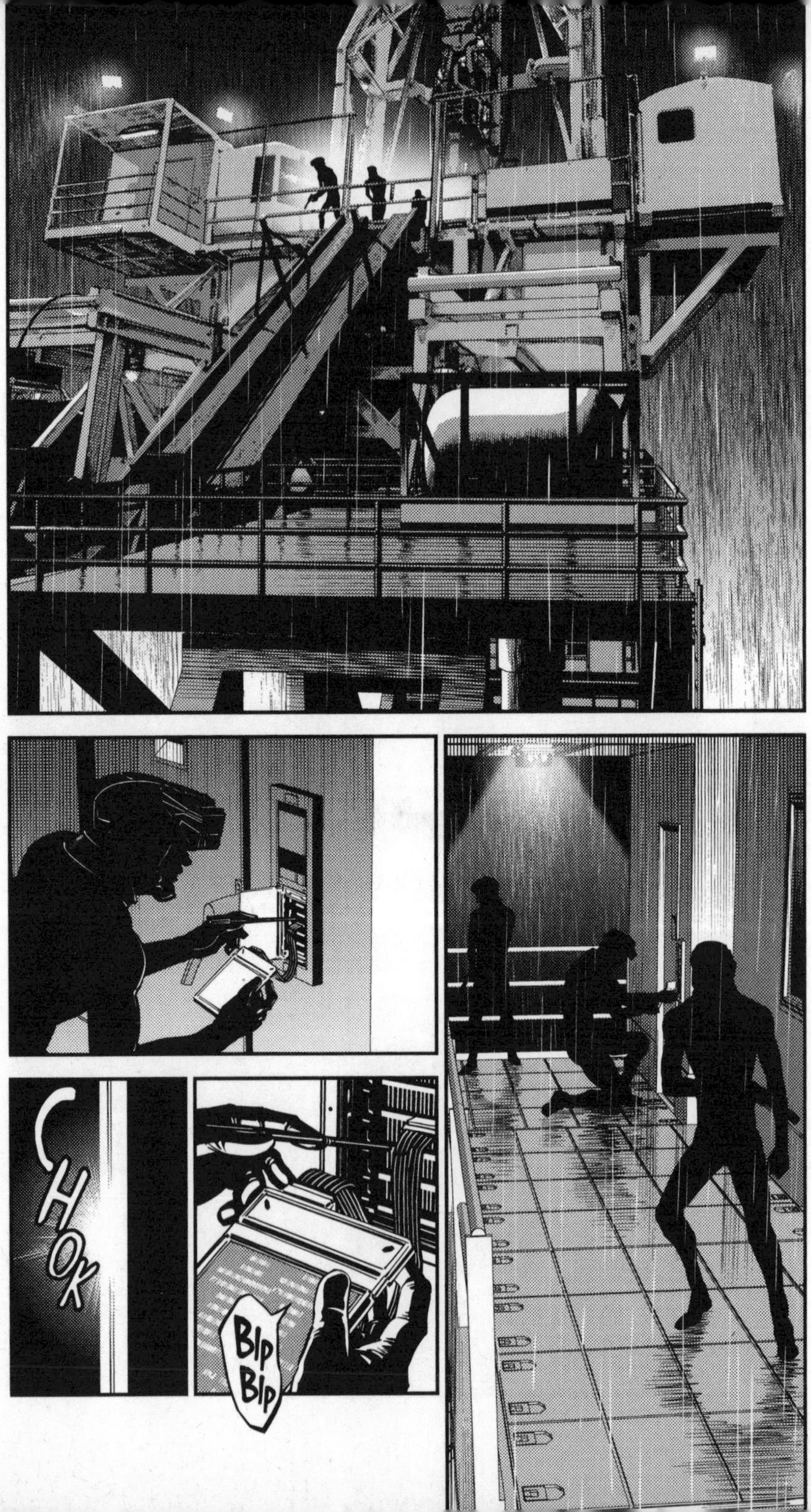
BLIP BLIP
CHOK

CHK

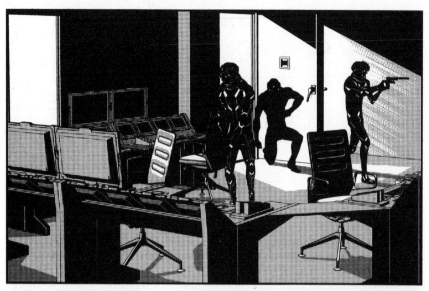

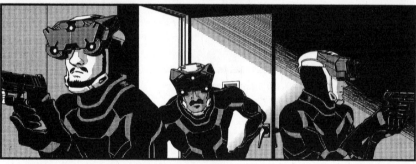

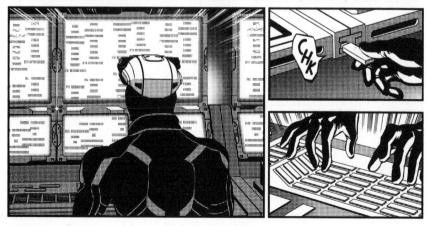

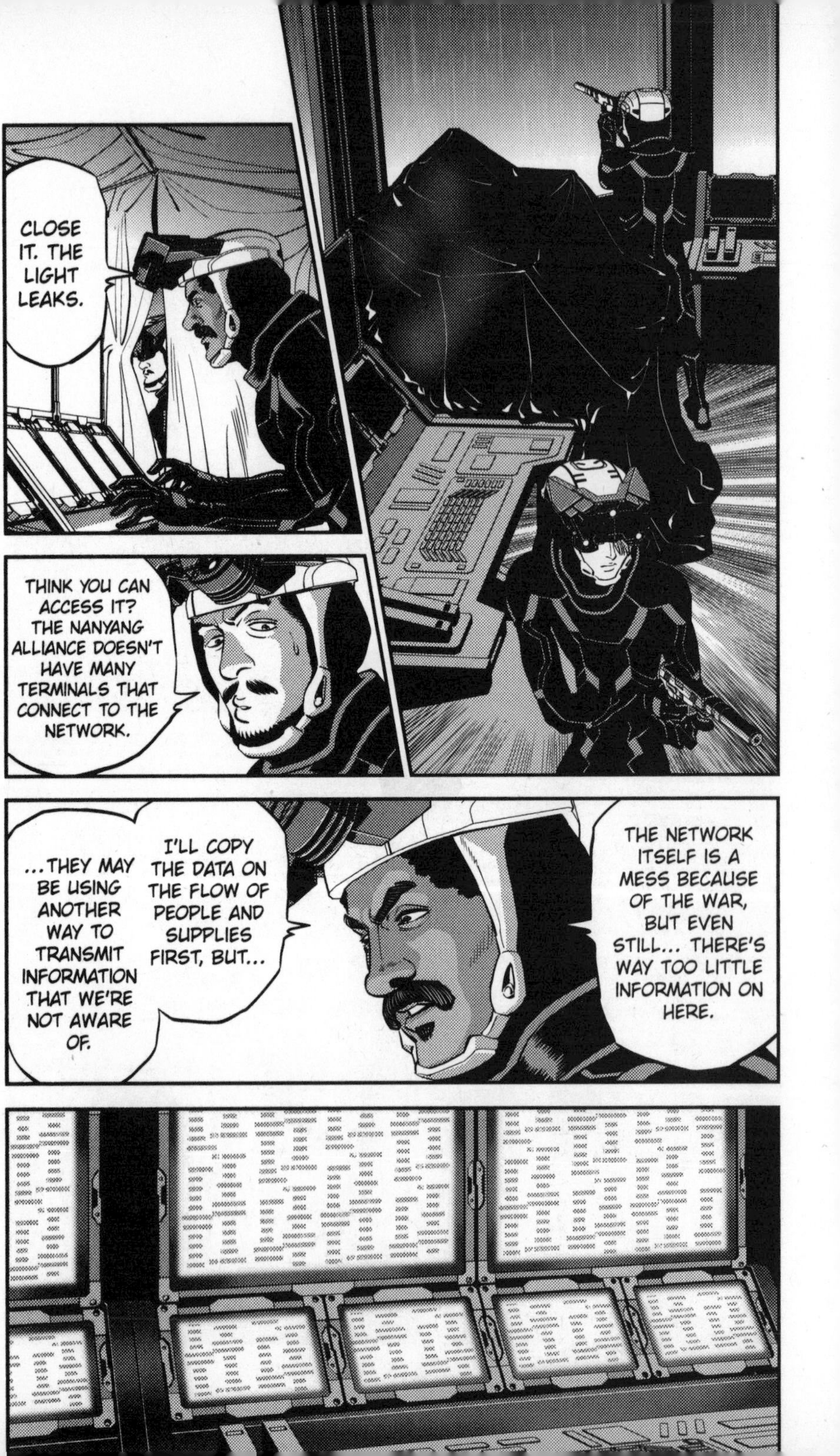
CLOSE IT. THE LIGHT LEAKS.
THINK YOU CAN ACCESS IT? THE NANYANG ALLIANCE DOESN'T HAVE MANY TERMINALS THAT CONNECT TO THE NETWORK.
THE NETWORK ITSELF IS A MESS BECAUSE OF THE WAR, BUT EVEN STILL... THERE'S WAY TOO LITTLE INFORMATION ON HERE.
I'LL COPY THE DATA ON THE FLOW OF PEOPLE AND SUPPLIES FIRST, BUT...
...THEY MAY BE USING ANOTHER WAY TO TRANSMIT INFORMATION THAT WE'RE NOT AWARE OF.

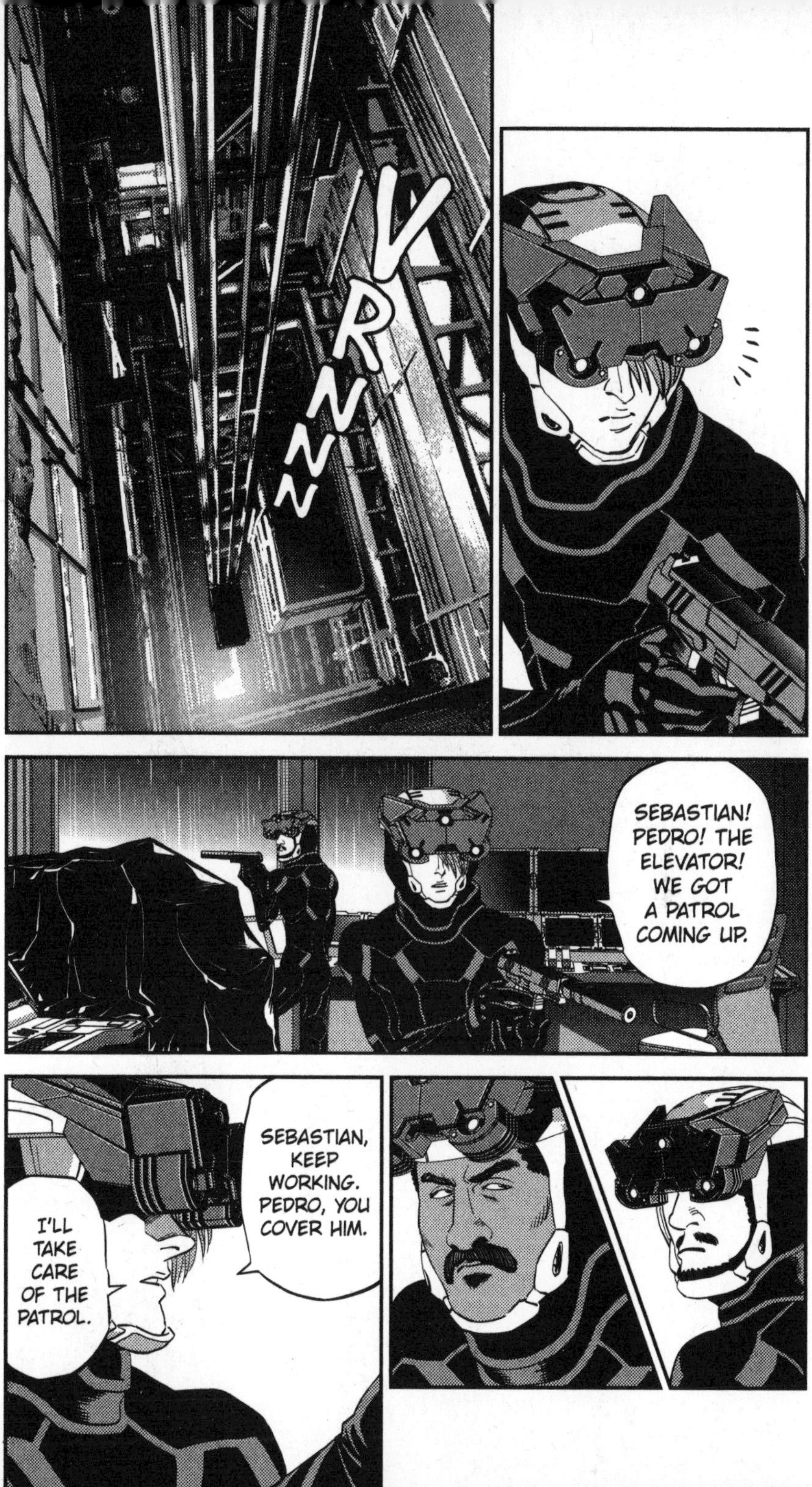
VRNNNN
SEBASTIAN! PEDRO! THE ELEVATOR! WE GOT A PATROL COMING UP.
SEBASTIAN, KEEP WORKING. PEDRO, YOU COVER HIM.
I'LL TAKE CARE OF THE PATROL.

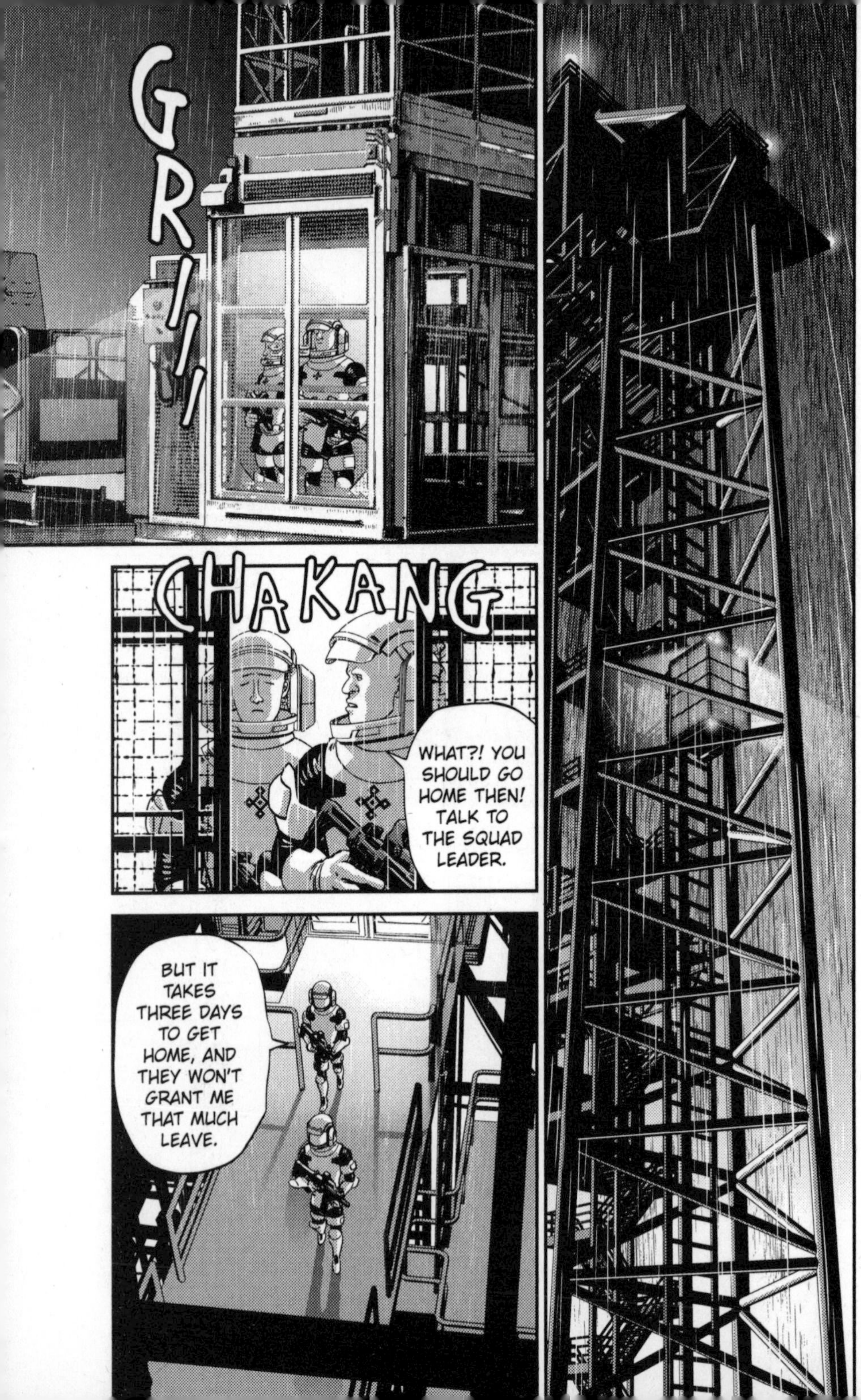
GRIIII
CHAKANG
WHAT?! YOU SHOULD GO HOME THEN! TALK TO THE SQUAD LEADER.
BUT IT TAKES THREE DAYS TO GET HOME, AND THEY WON'T GRANT ME THAT MUCH LEAVE.

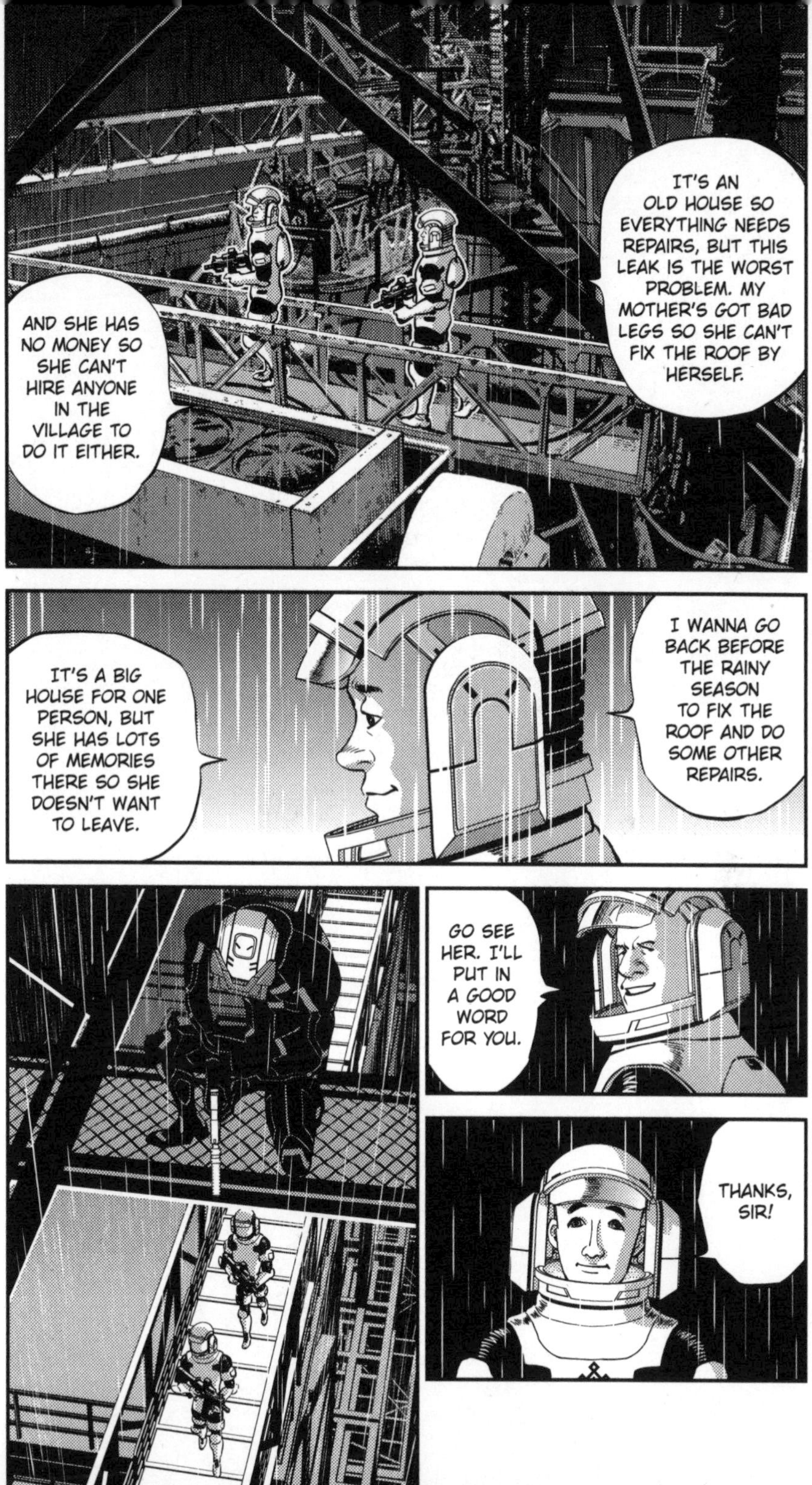
IT'S AN OLD HOUSE SO EVERYTHING NEEDS REPAIRS, BUT THIS LEAK IS THE WORST PROBLEM. MY MOTHER'S GOT BAD LEGS SO SHE CAN'T FIX THE ROOF BY HERSELF.
AND SHE HAS NO MONEY SO SHE CAN'T HIRE ANYONE IN THE VILLAGE TO DO IT EITHER.
I WANNA GO BACK BEFORE THE RAINY SEASON TO FIX THE ROOF AND DO SOME OTHER REPAIRS.
IT'S A BIG HOUSE FOR ONE PERSON, BUT SHE HAS LOTS OF MEMORIES THERE SO SHE DOESN'T WANT TO LEAVE.
GO SEE HER. I'LL PUT IN A GOOD WORD FOR YOU.
THANKS, SIR!

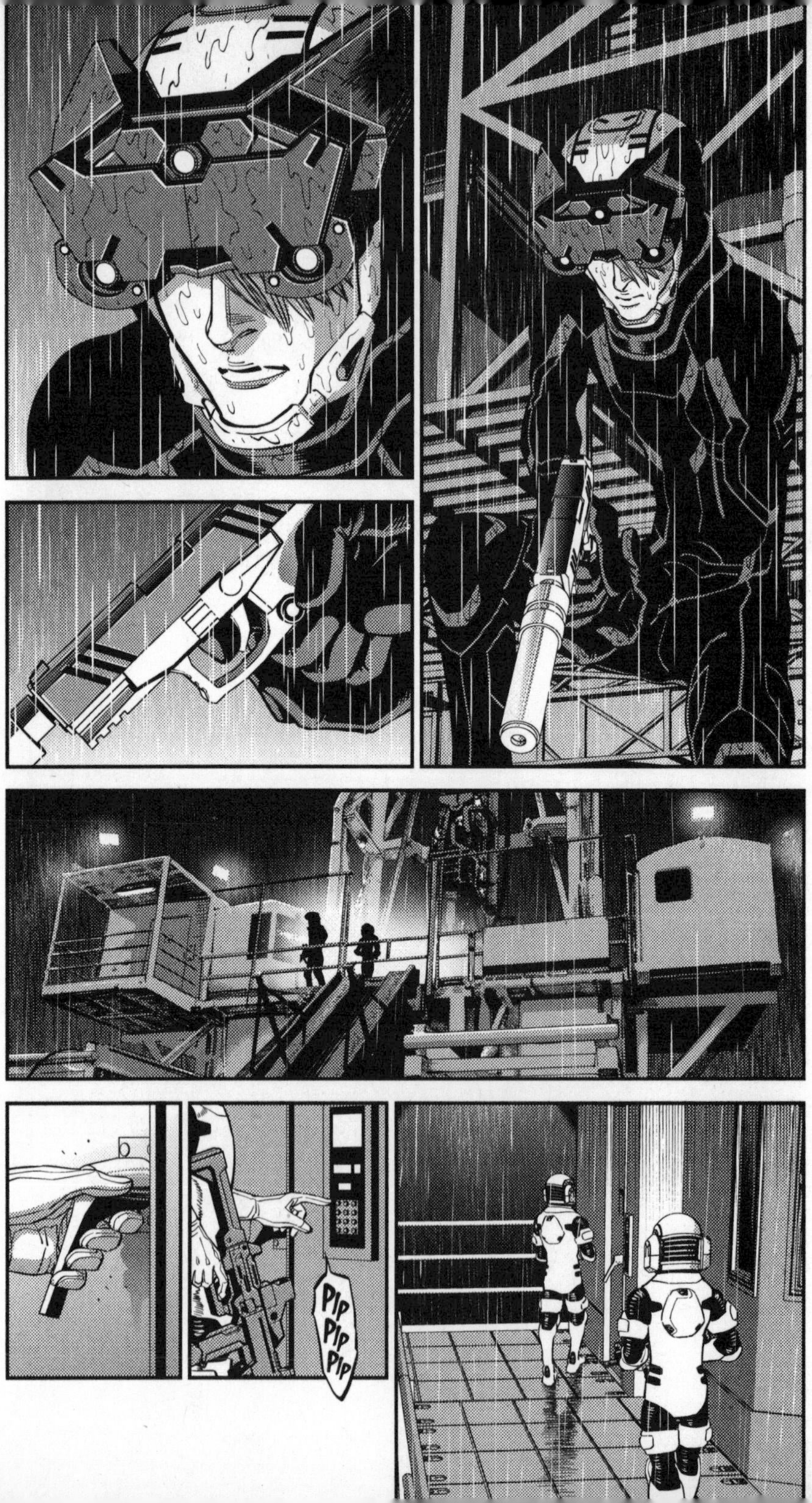
PIP PIP PIP

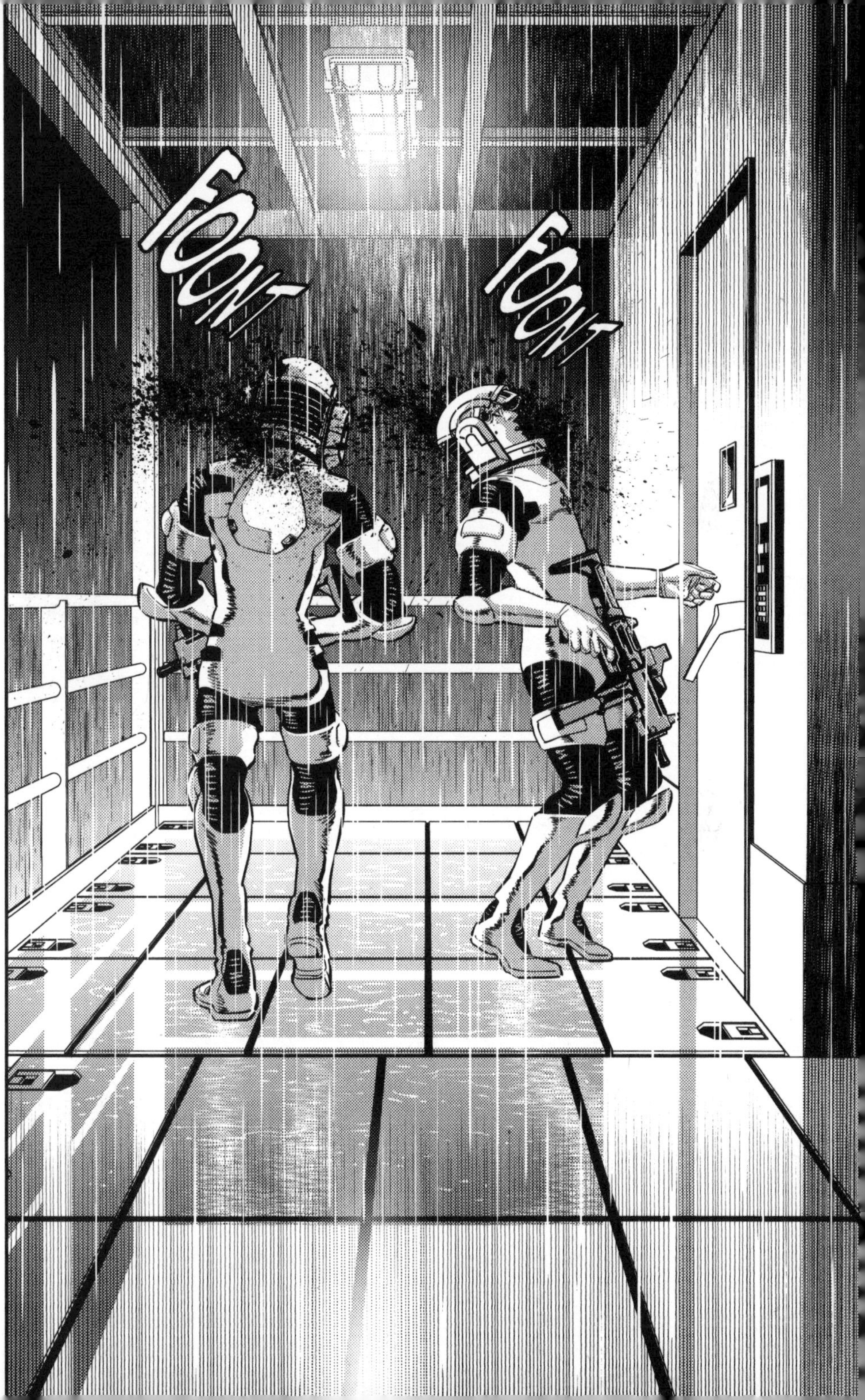
FOOM
FOOM

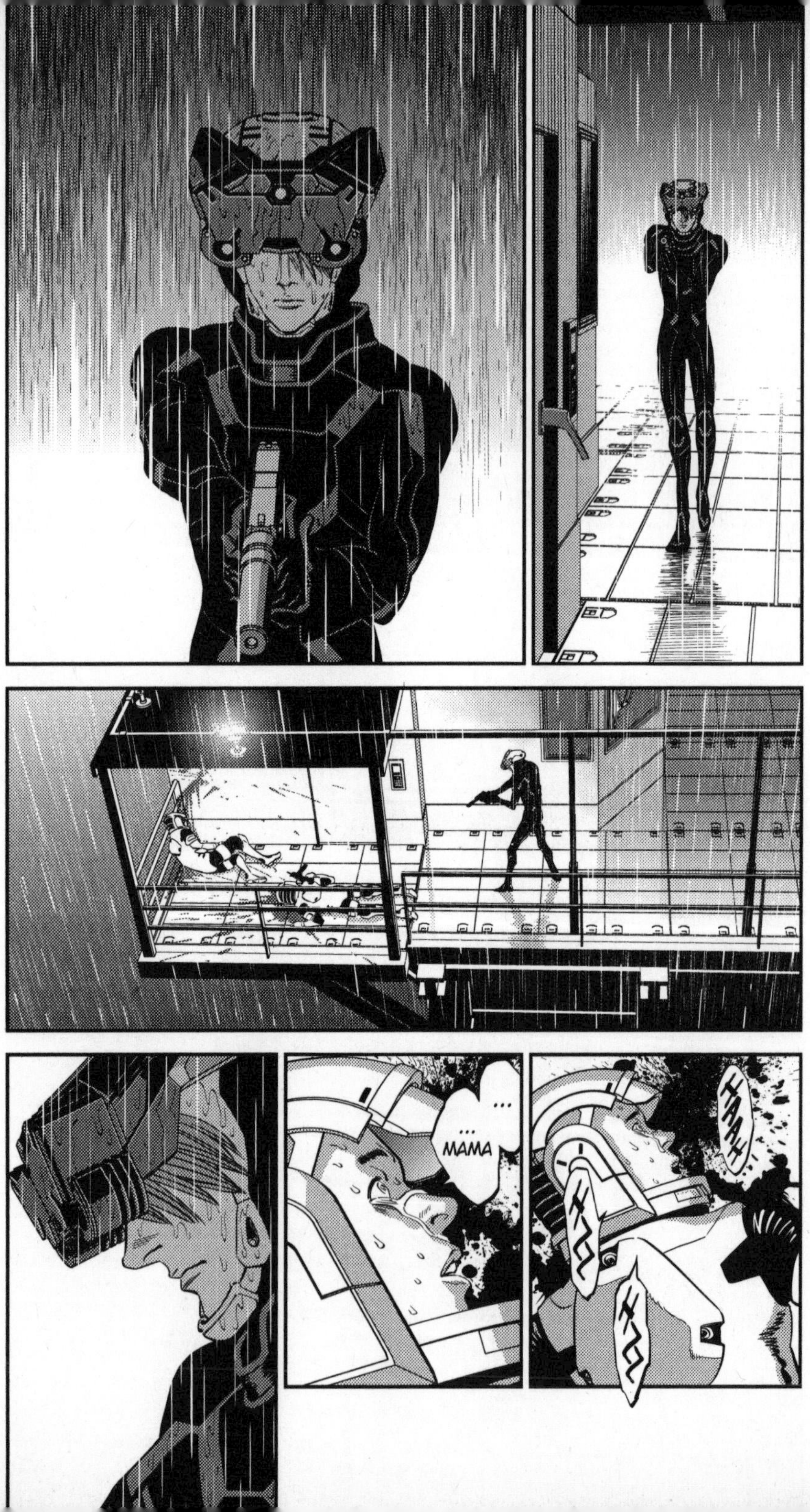
HAAH
...
...MAMA

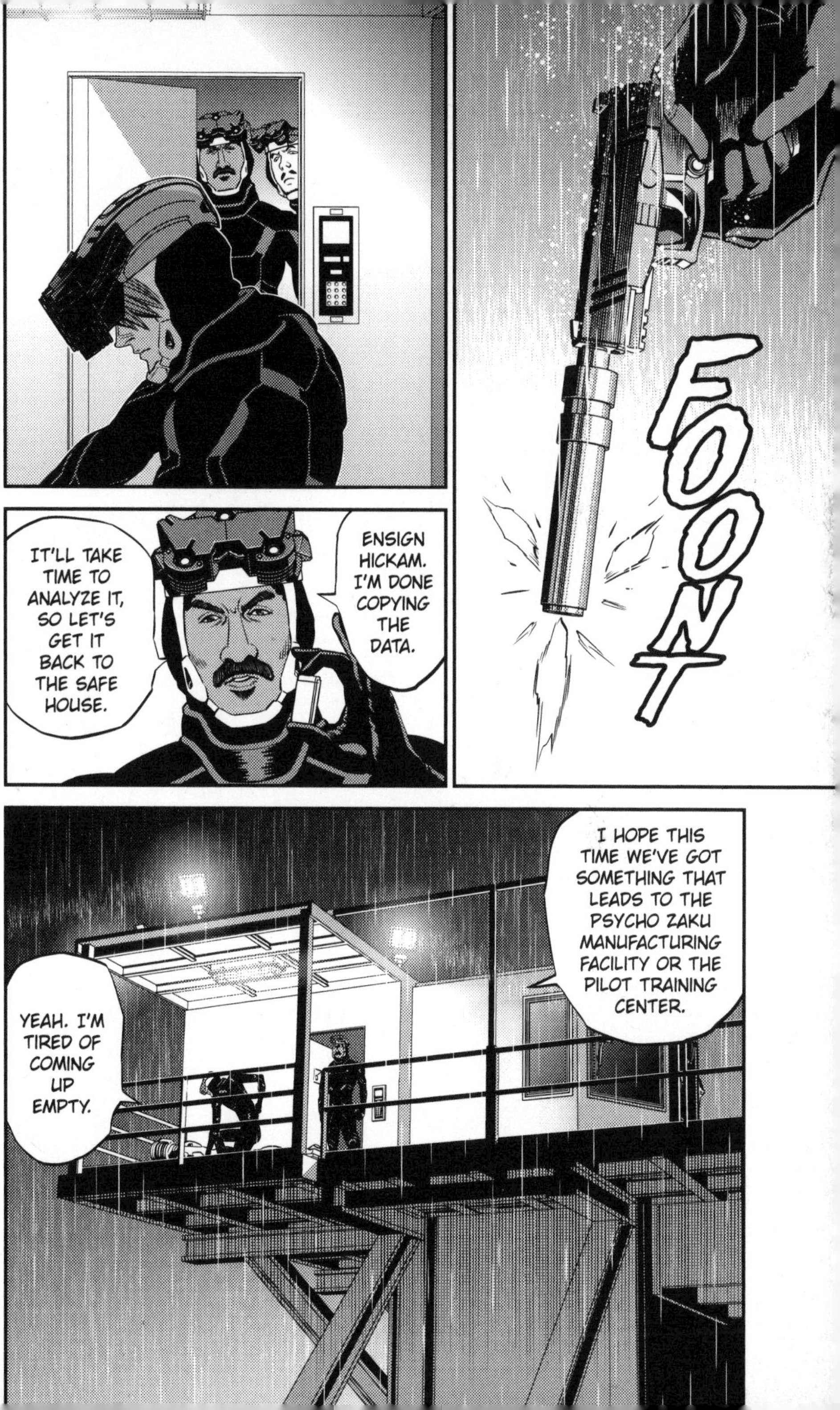
FOONT
ENSIGN HICKAM. I'M DONE COPYING THE DATA.
IT'LL TAKE TIME TO ANALYZE IT, SO LET'S GET IT BACK TO THE SAFE HOUSE.
I HOPE THIS TIME WE'VE GOT SOMETHING THAT LEADS TO THE PSYCHO ZAKU MANUFACTURING FACILITY OR THE PILOT TRAINING CENTER.
YEAH. I'M TIRED OF COMING UP EMPTY.

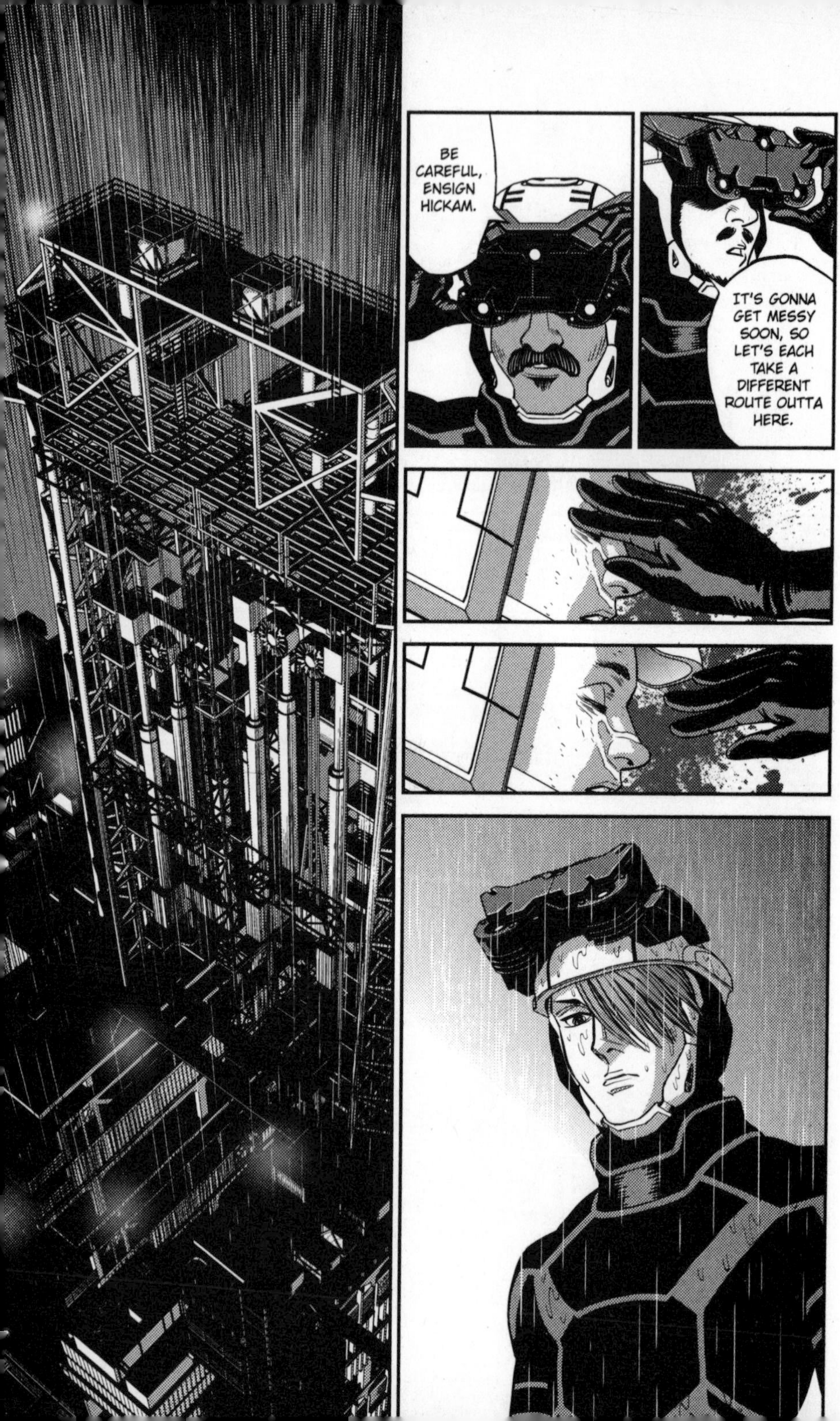
IT'S GONNA GET MESSY SOON, SO LET'S EACH TAKE A DIFFERENT ROUTE OUTTA HERE.
BE CAREFUL, ENSIGN HICKAM.

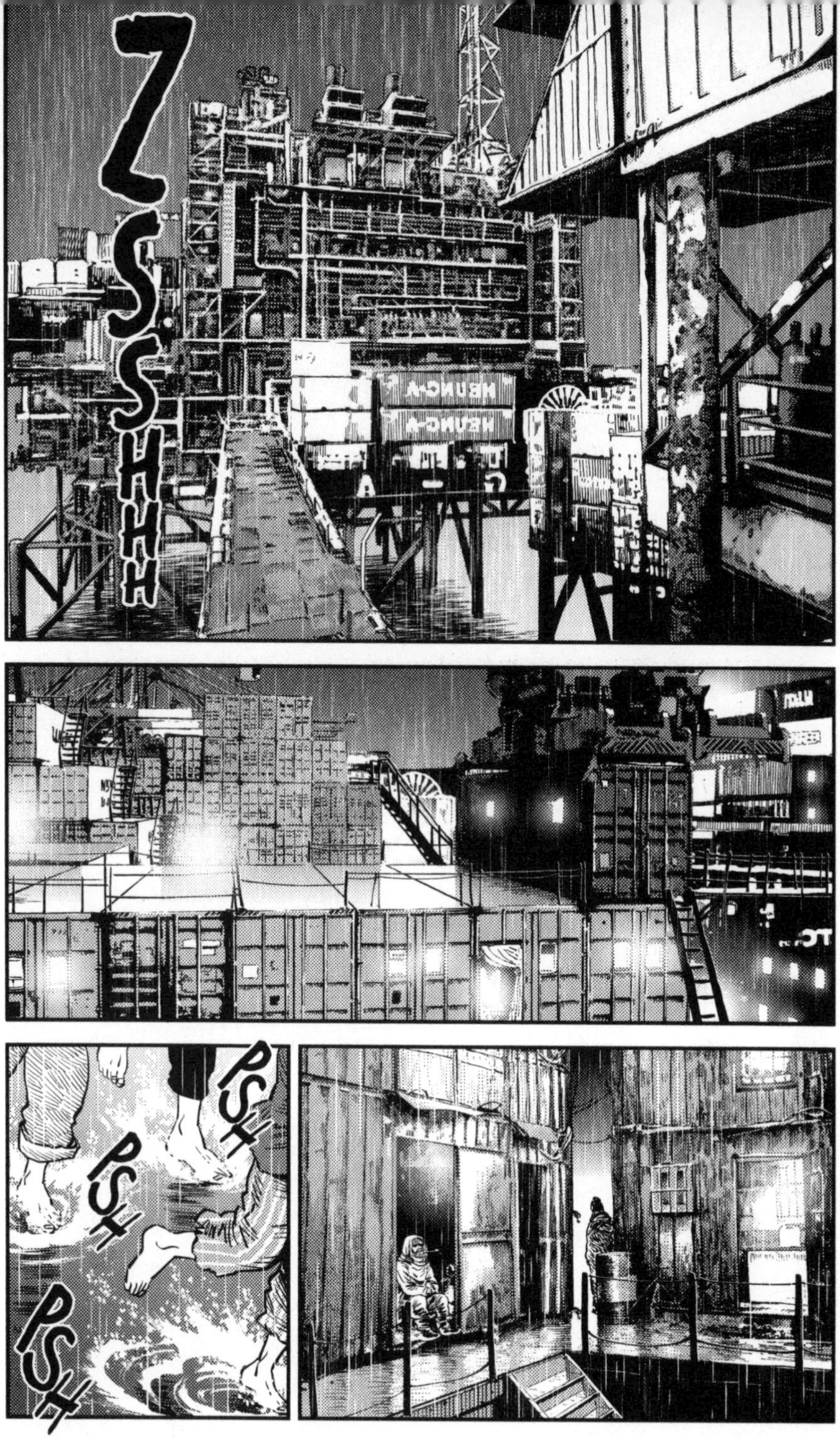
ZSSSHHH
PSH
PSH
PSH

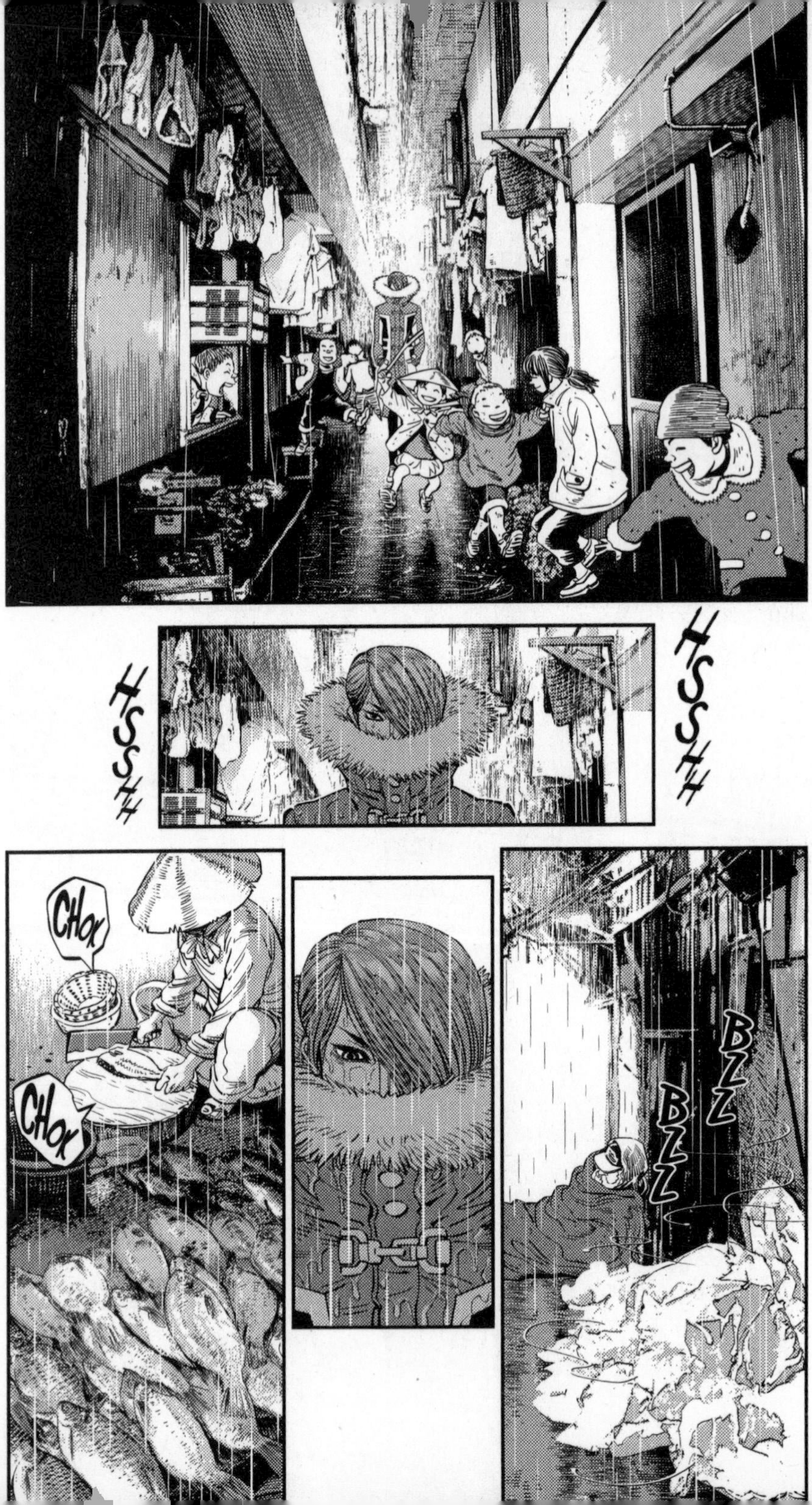
HSSHH
HSSHH
BZZ
BZZ
CHOK
CHOK

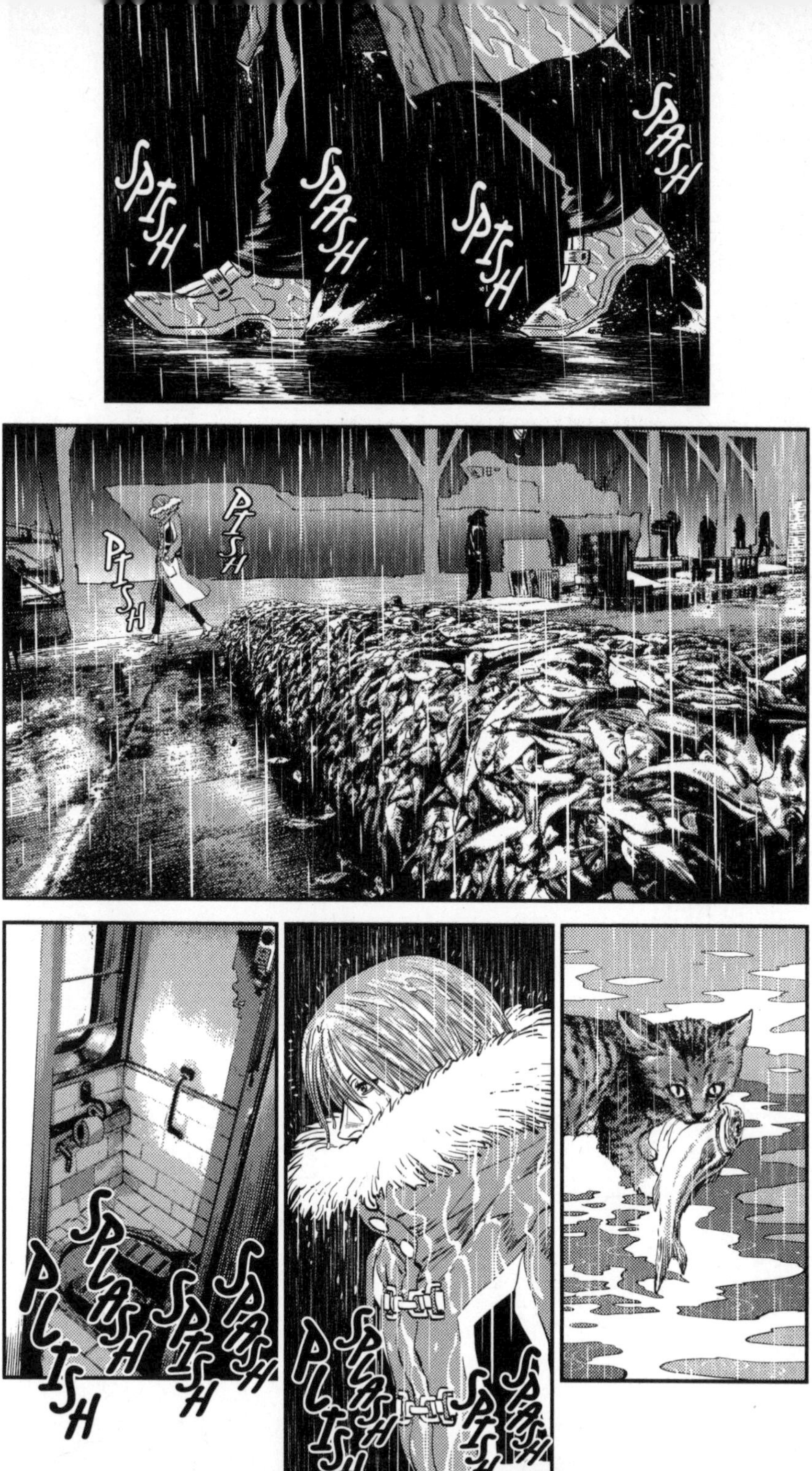
SPASH
SPISH
SPASH
SPISH
PISH
PISH
SPASH
SPISH
SPLASH
PLISH
SPASH
SPISH
SPLASH
PLISH

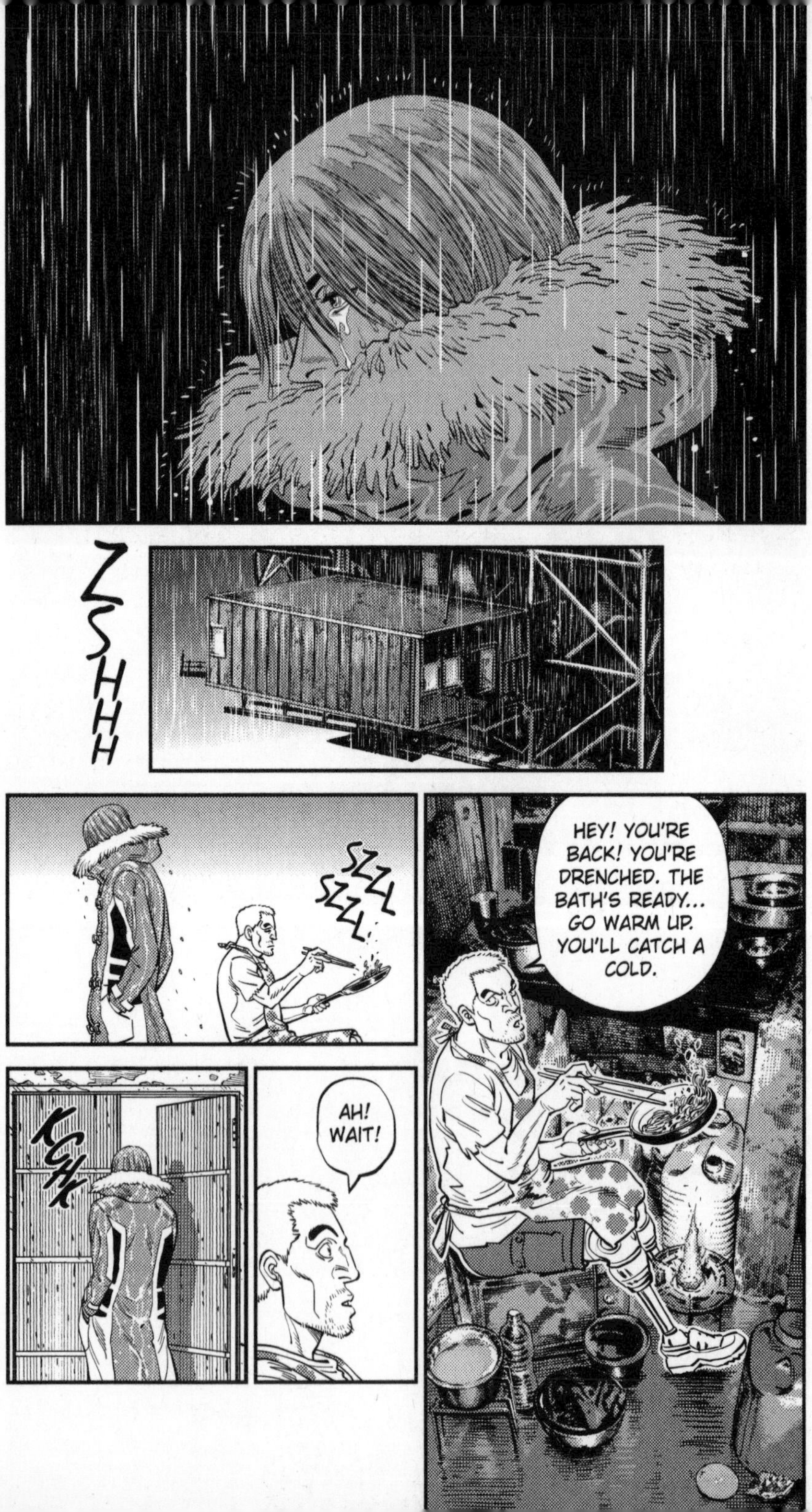
ZSHHH
HEY! YOU'RE BACK! YOU'RE DRENCHED. THE BATH'S READY... GO WARM UP. YOU'LL CATCH A COLD.
SZZL SZZL
AH! WAIT!
KCHK

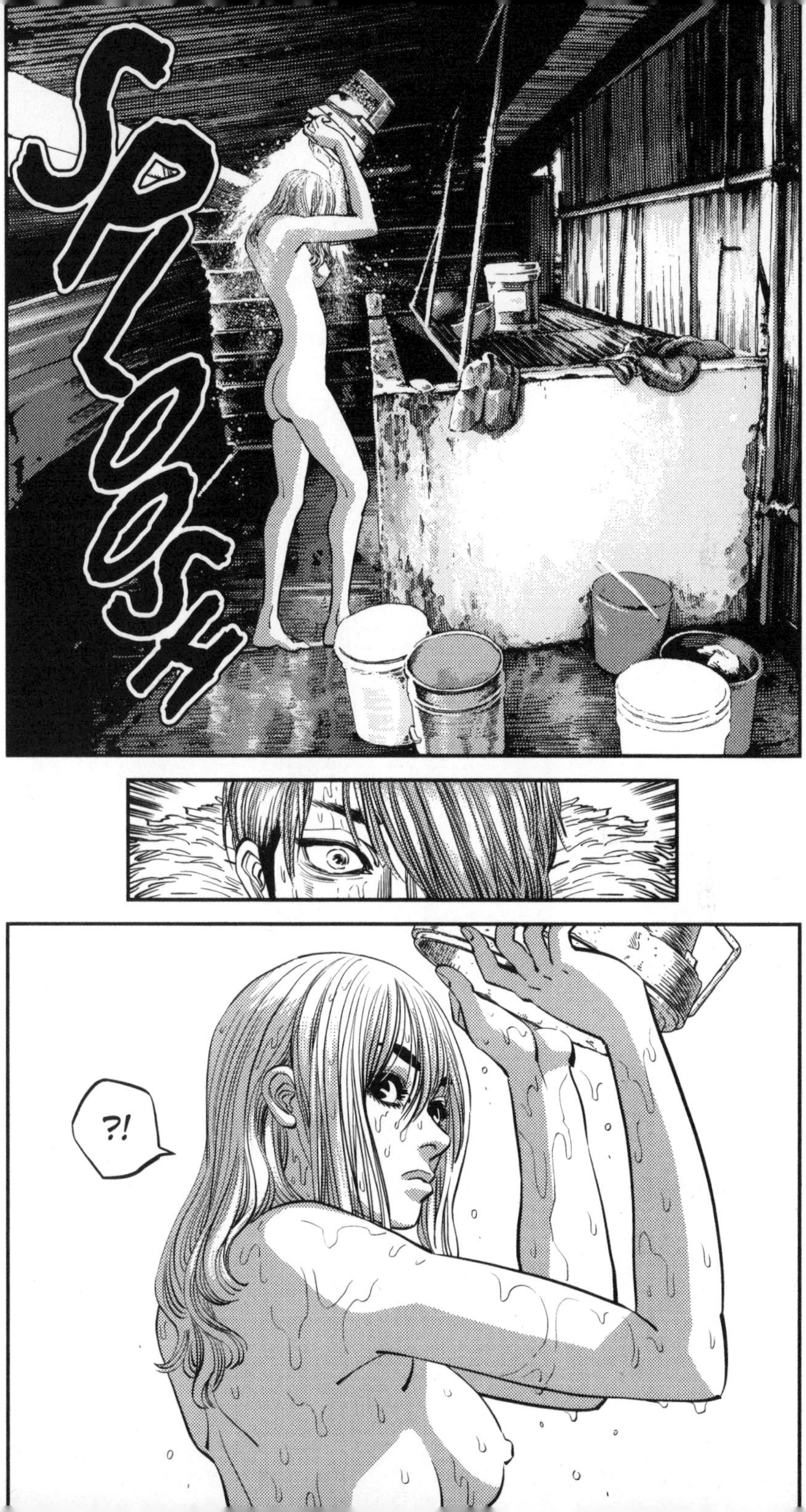
SPLOOSH
?!

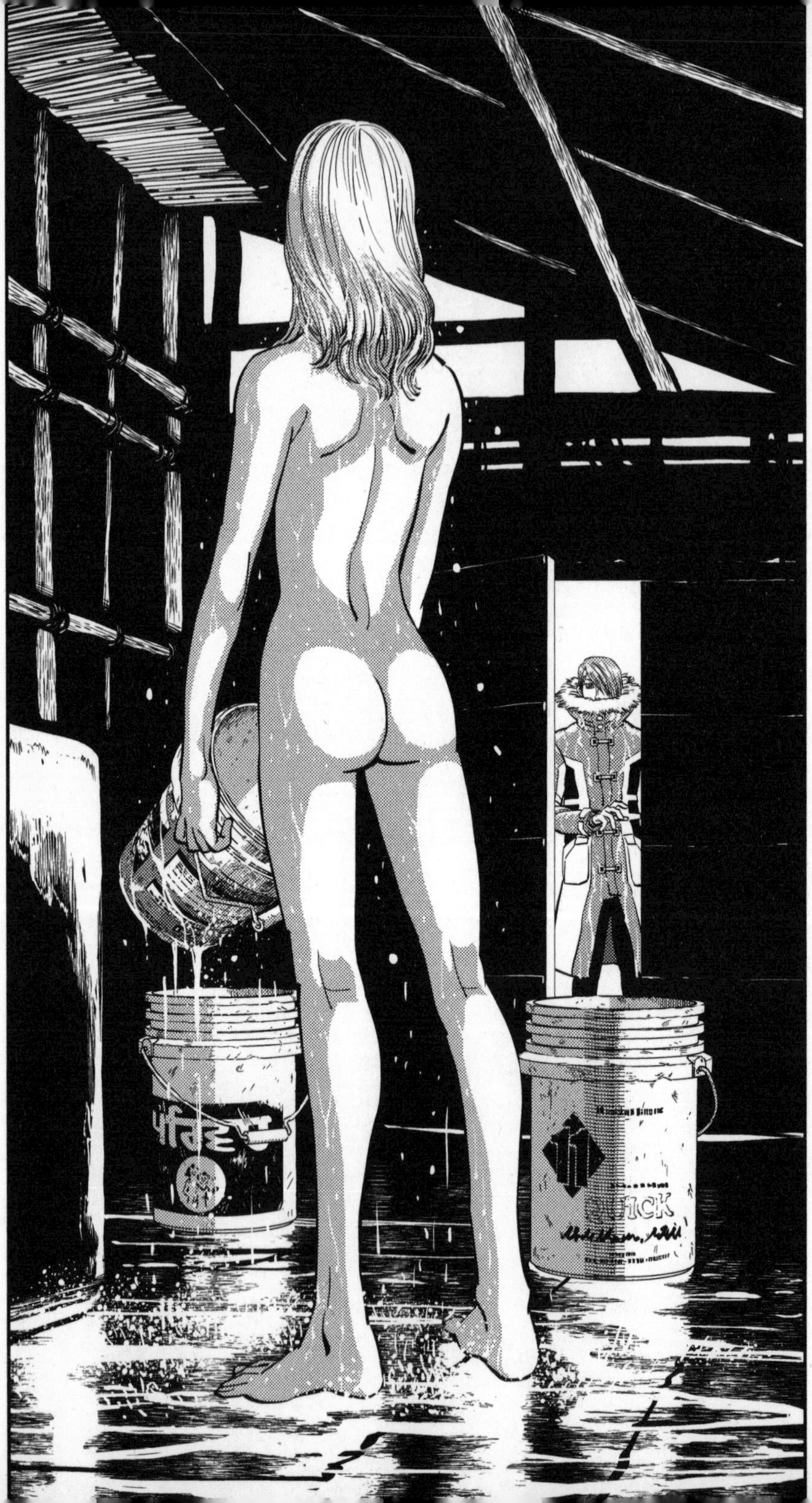

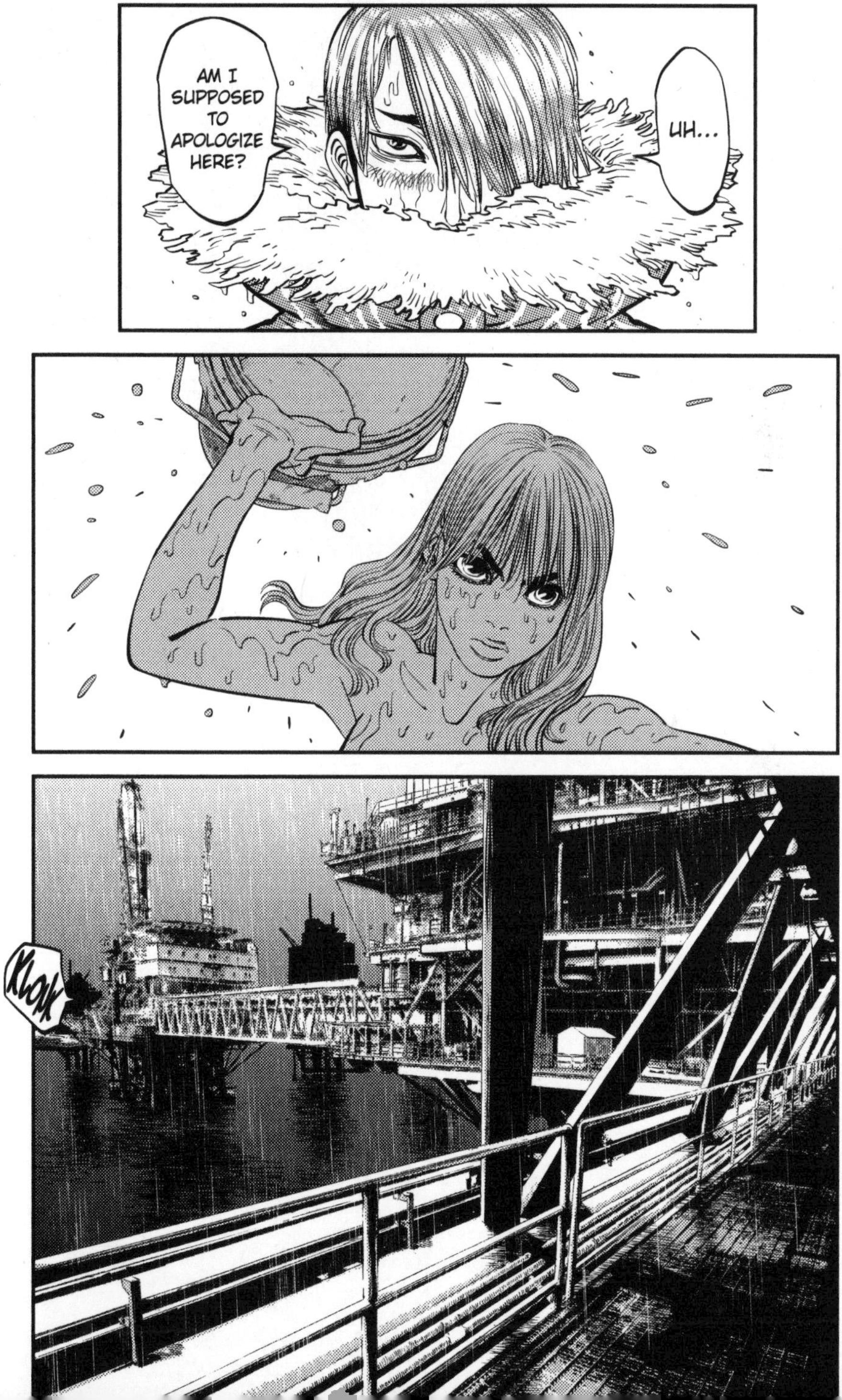
UH...
AM I SUPPOSED TO APOLOGIZE HERE?
KLONK

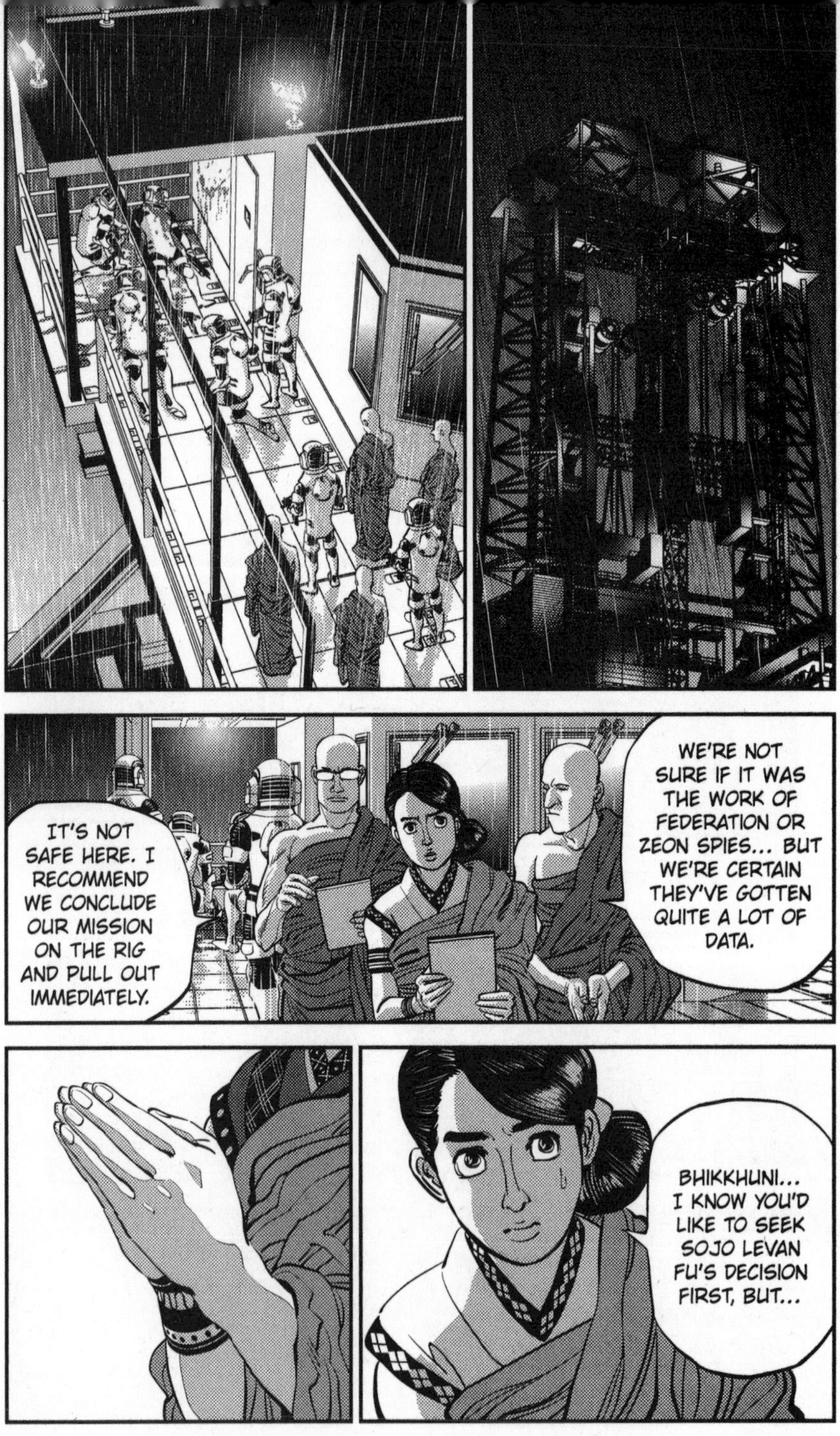
WE'RE NOT SURE IF IT WAS THE WORK OF FEDERATION OR ZEON SPIES... BUT WE'RE CERTAIN THEY'VE GOTTEN QUITE A LOT OF DATA.
IT'S NOT SAFE HERE. I RECOMMEND WE CONCLUDE OUR MISSION ON THE RIG AND PULL OUT IMMEDIATELY.
BHIKKHUNI... I KNOW YOU'D LIKE TO SEEK SOJO LEVAN FU'S DECISION FIRST, BUT...

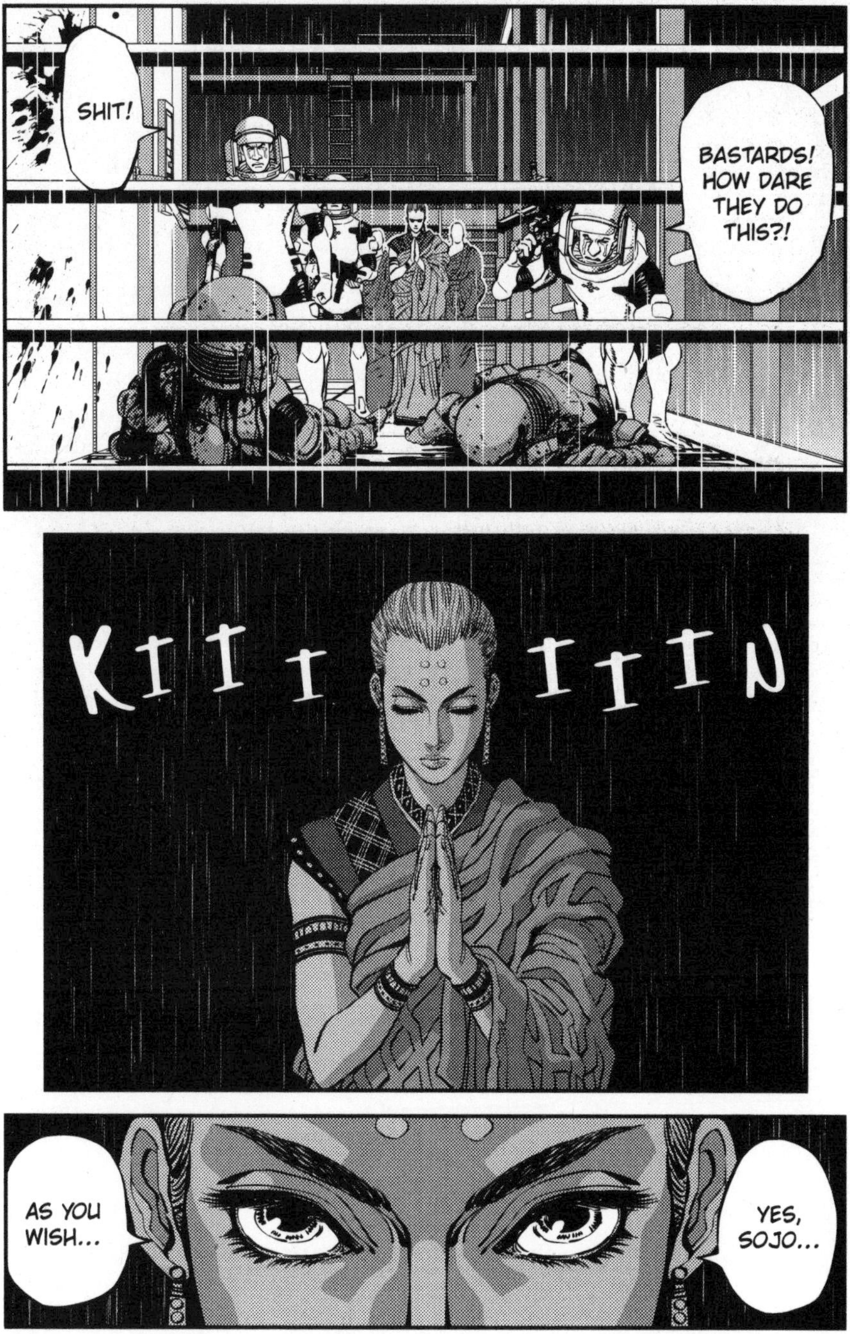
BASTARDS! HOW DARE THEY DO THIS?!
SHIT!
KIIIIIIIN
YES, SOJO...
AS YOU WISH...

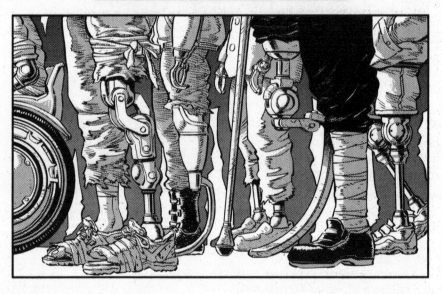

MOBILE SUIT GUNDAM THUNDERBOLT | CHAPTER 68

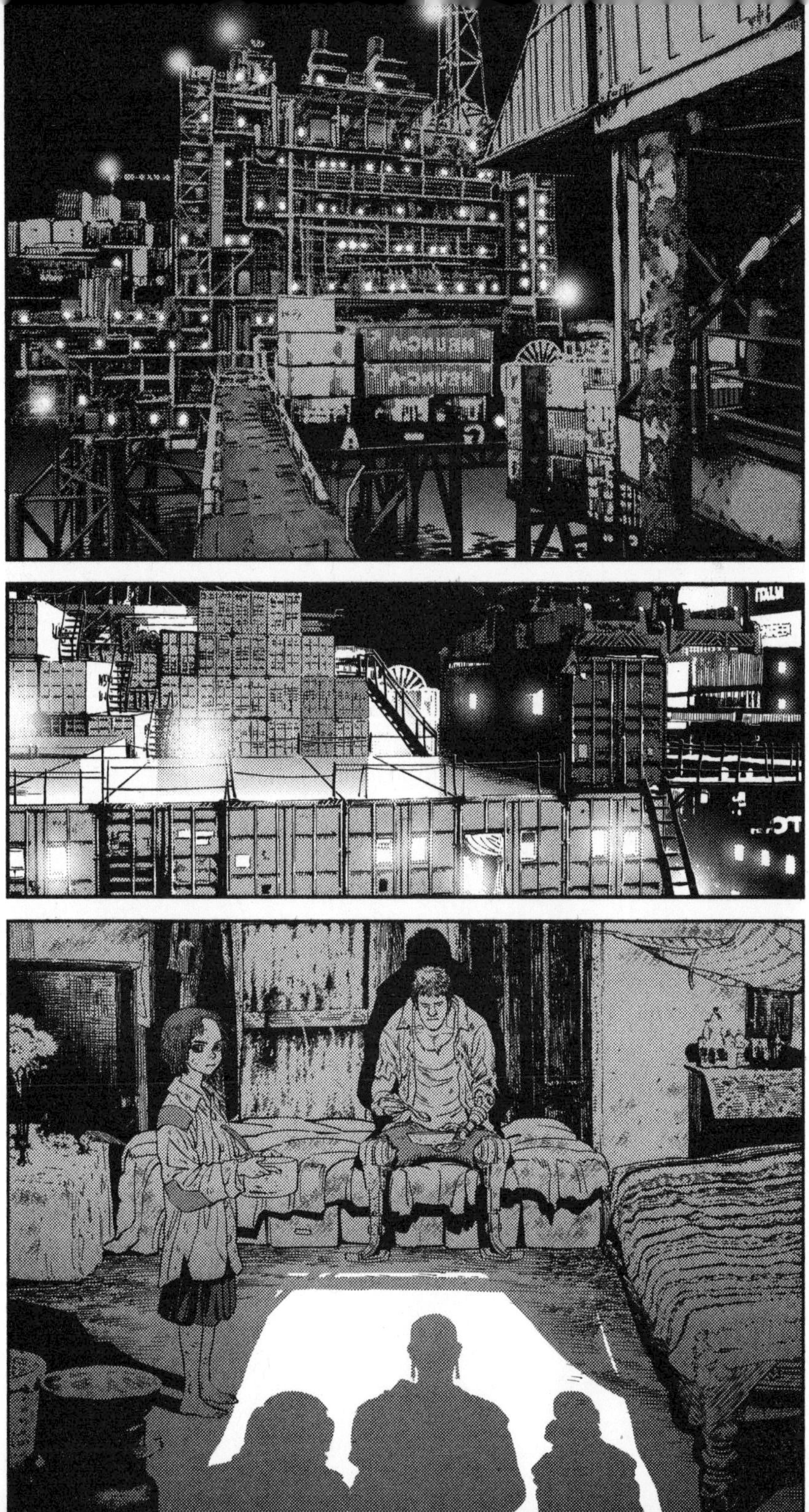

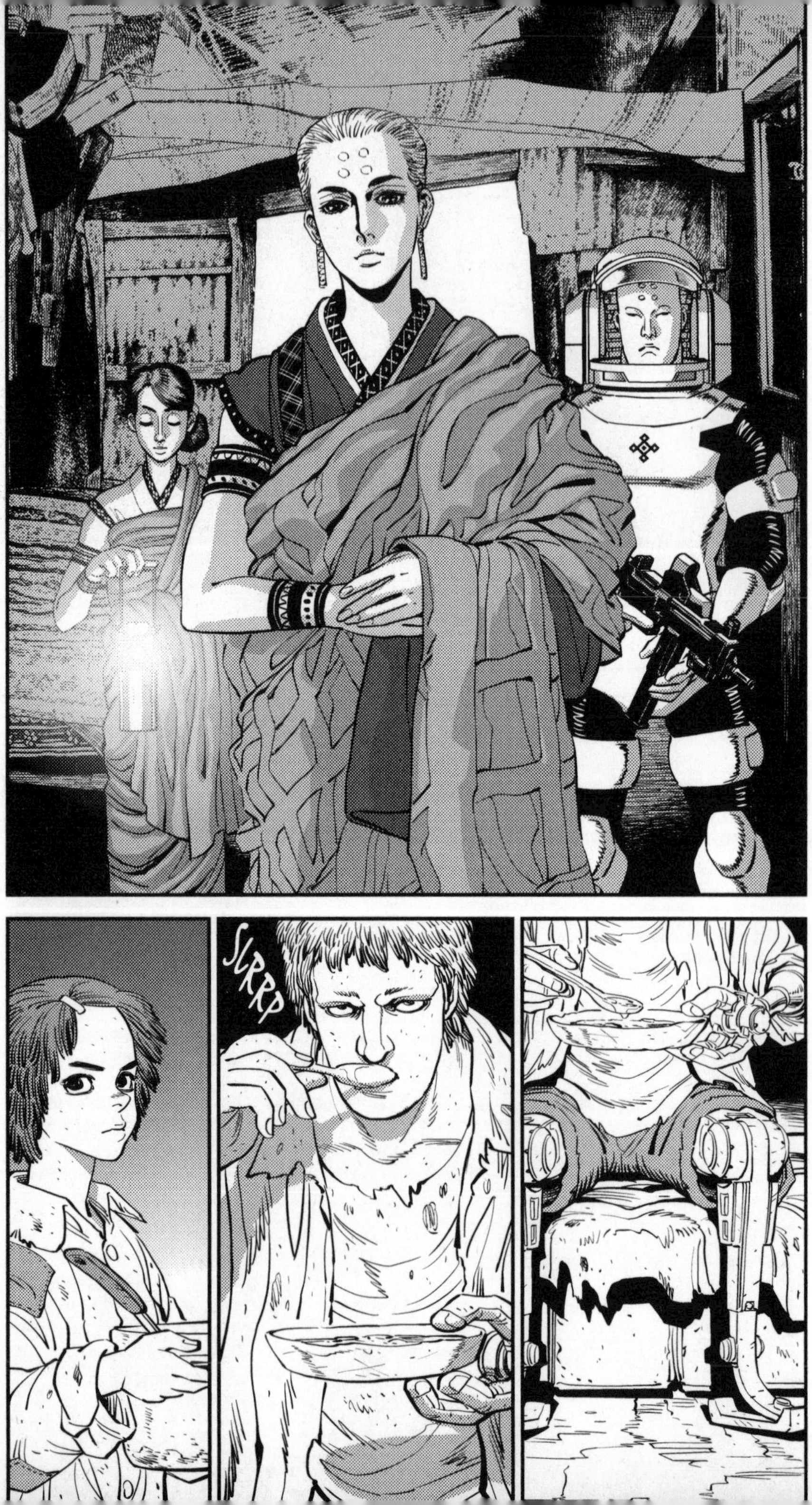
SLRRP

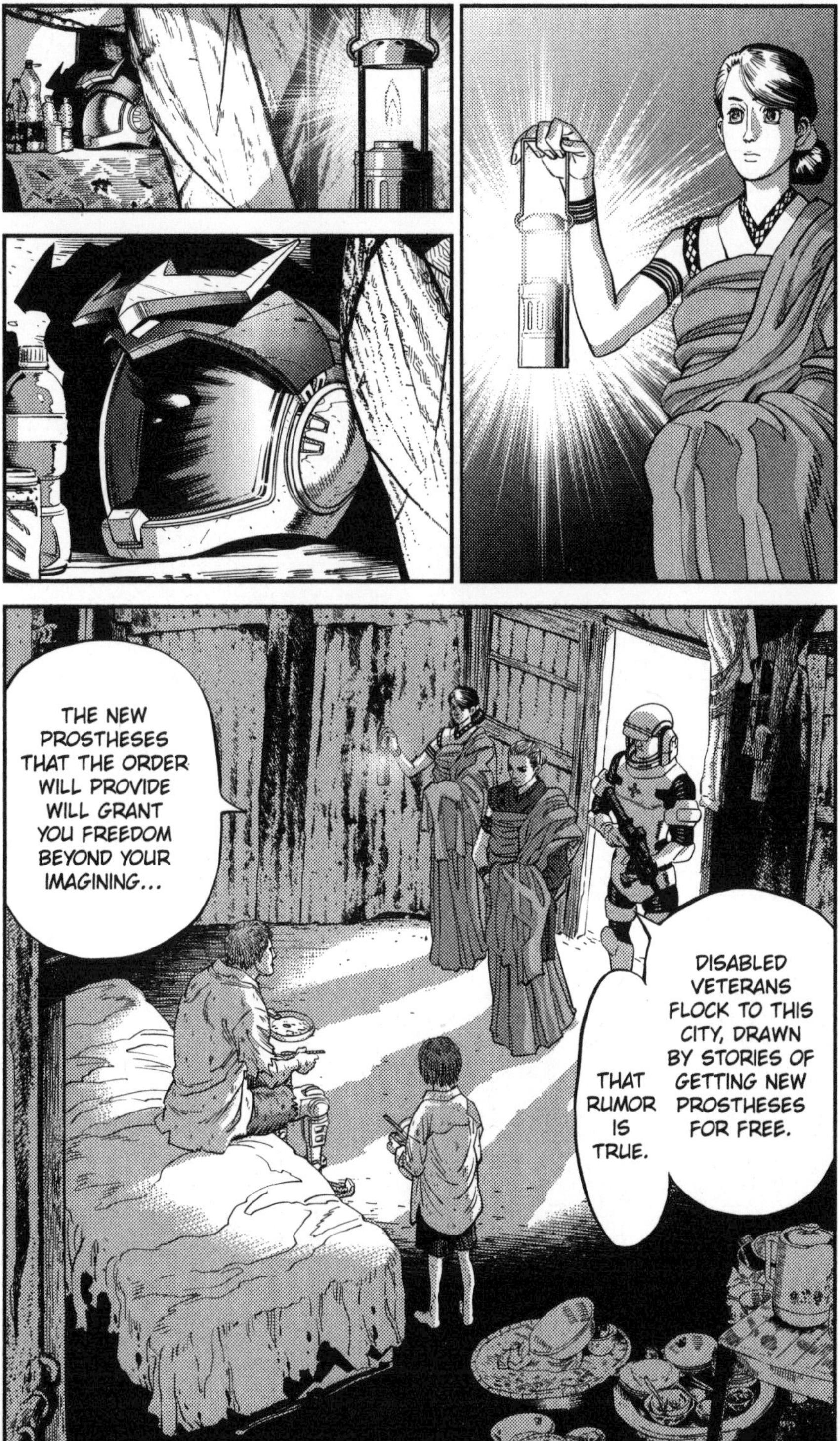
DISABLED VETERANS FLOCK TO THIS CITY, DRAWN BY STORIES OF GETTING NEW PROSTHESES FOR FREE.
THAT RUMOR IS TRUE.
THE NEW PROSTHESES THAT THE ORDER WILL PROVIDE WILL GRANT YOU FREEDOM BEYOND YOUR IMAGINING...

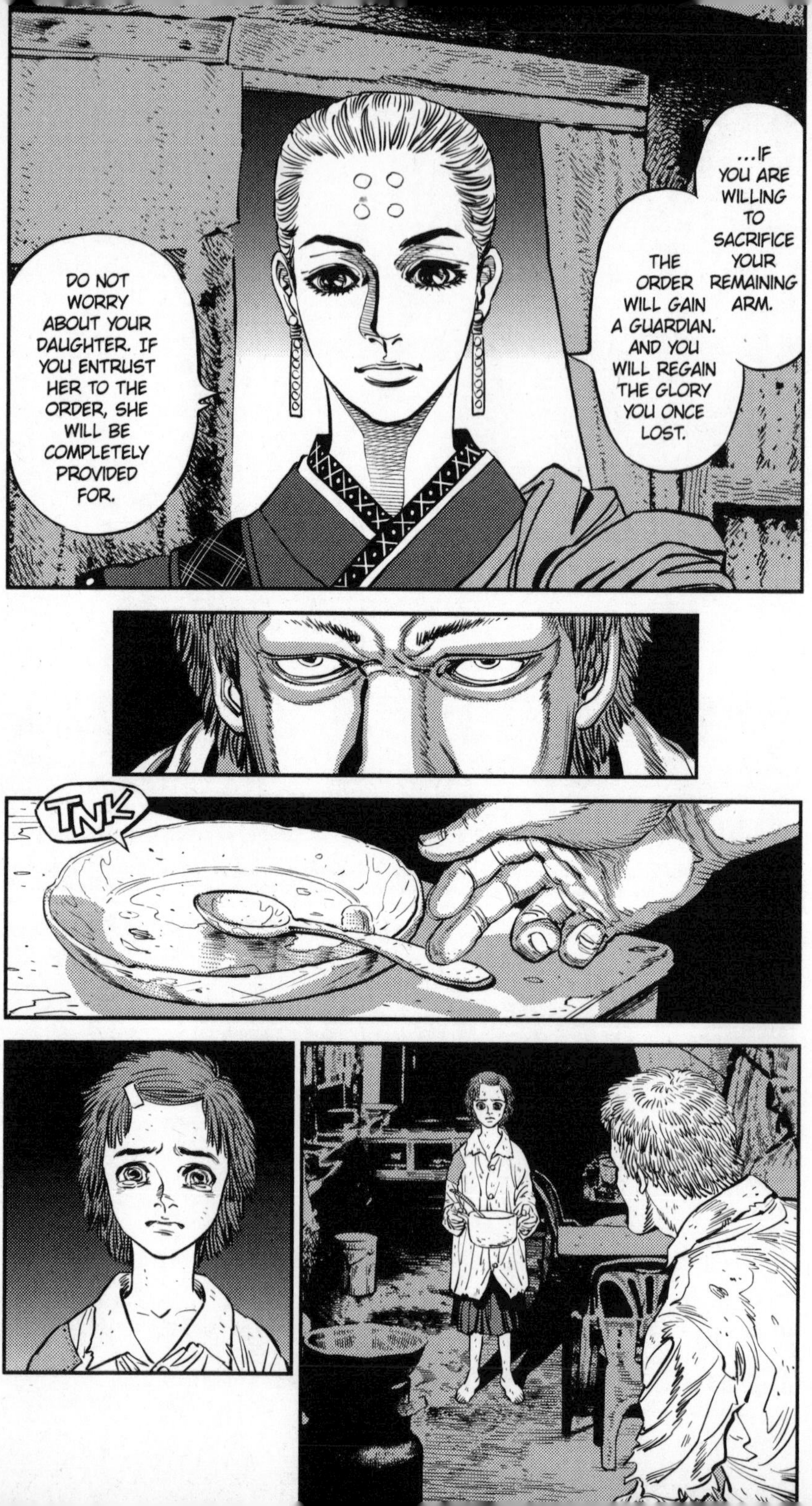
...IF YOU ARE WILLING TO SACRIFICE YOUR REMAINING ARM.
THE ORDER WILL GAIN A GUARDIAN. AND YOU WILL REGAIN THE GLORY YOU ONCE LOST.
DO NOT WORRY ABOUT YOUR DAUGHTER. IF YOU ENTRUST HER TO THE ORDER, SHE WILL BE COMPLETELY PROVIDED FOR.
TNK

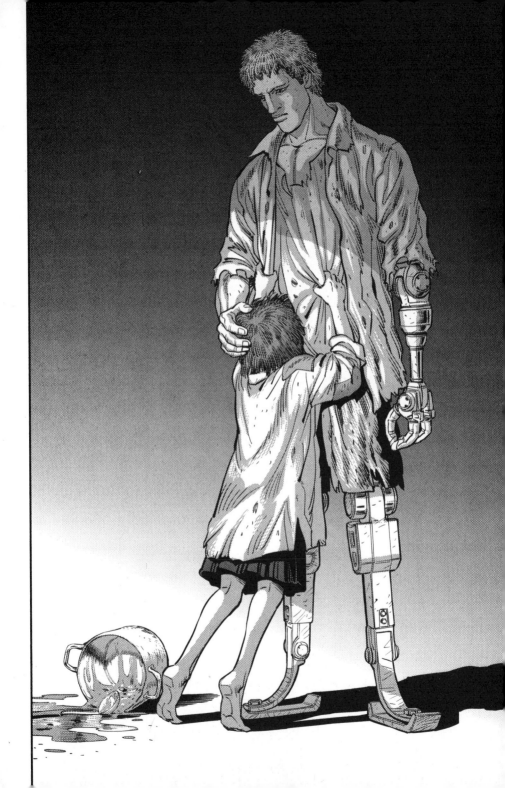

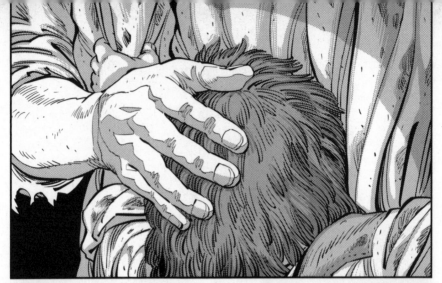

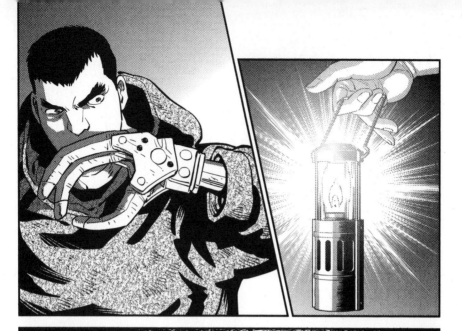

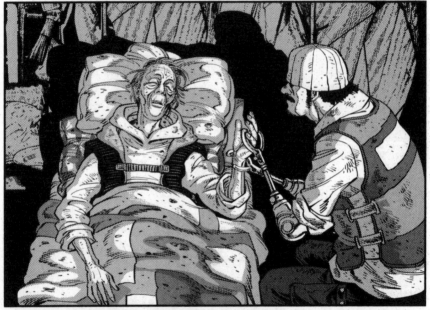

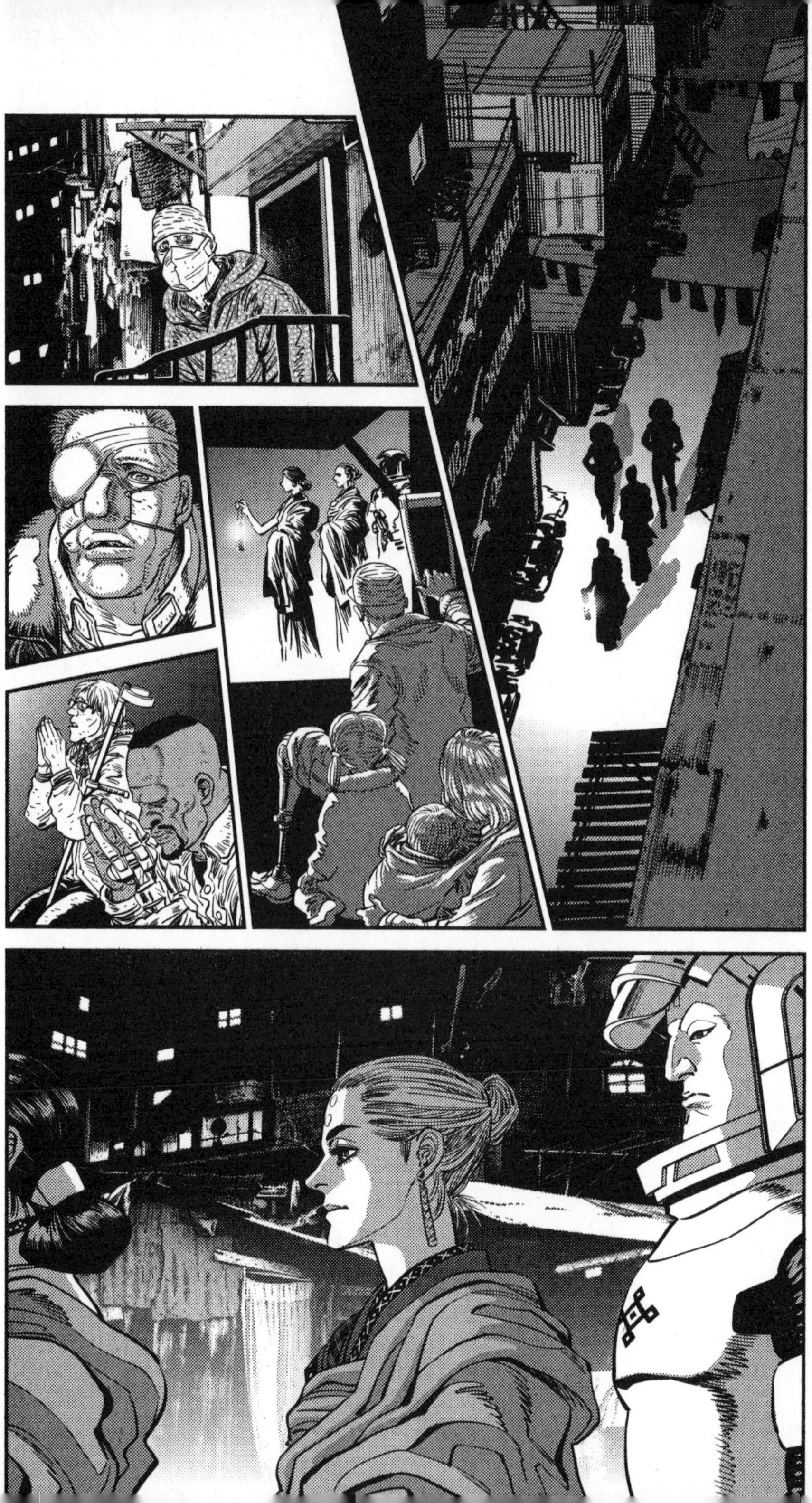

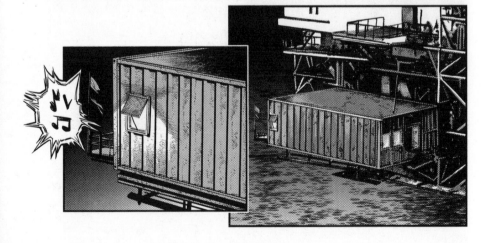

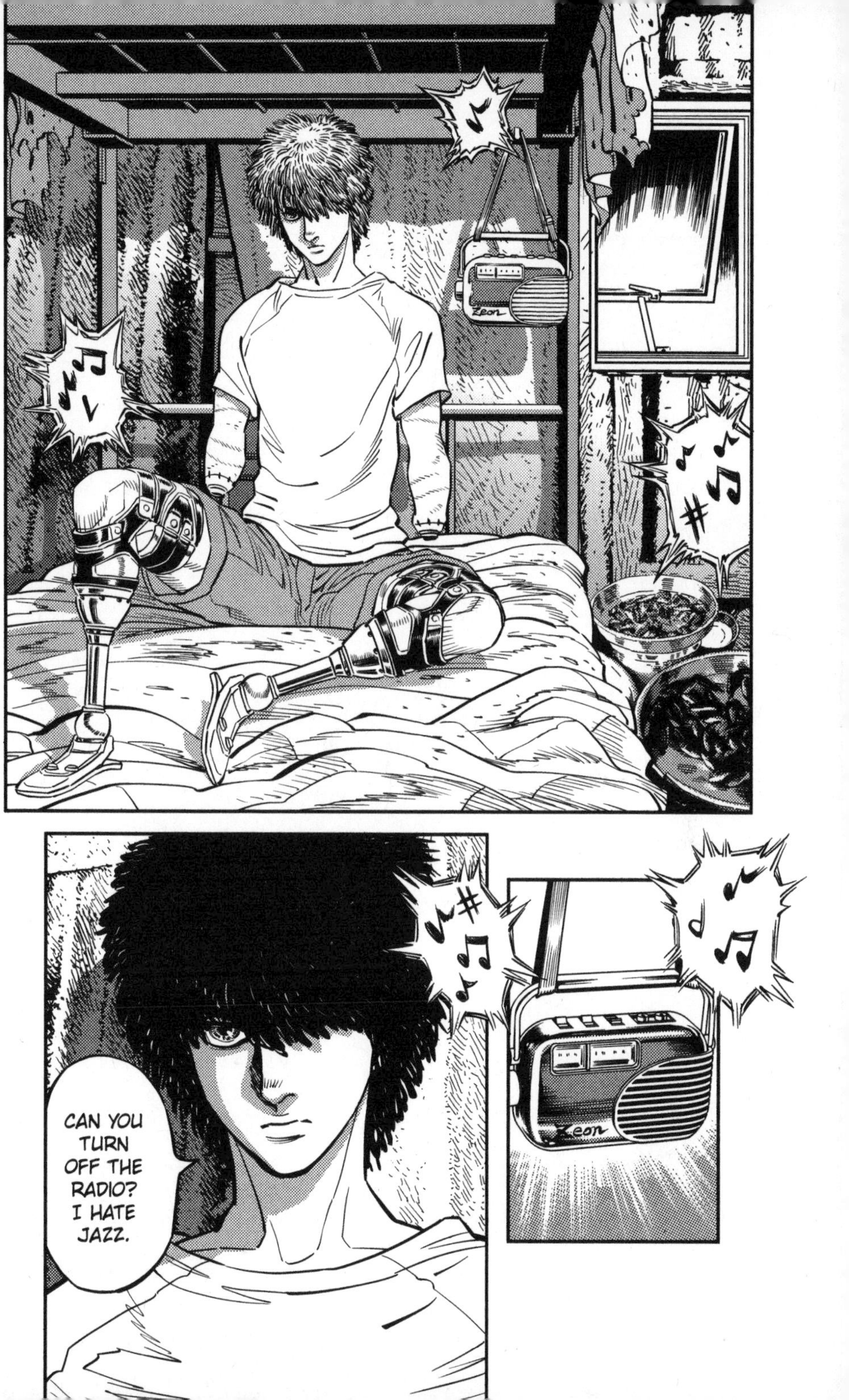
Zeon
CAN YOU TURN OFF THE RADIO? I HATE JAZZ.
Zeon

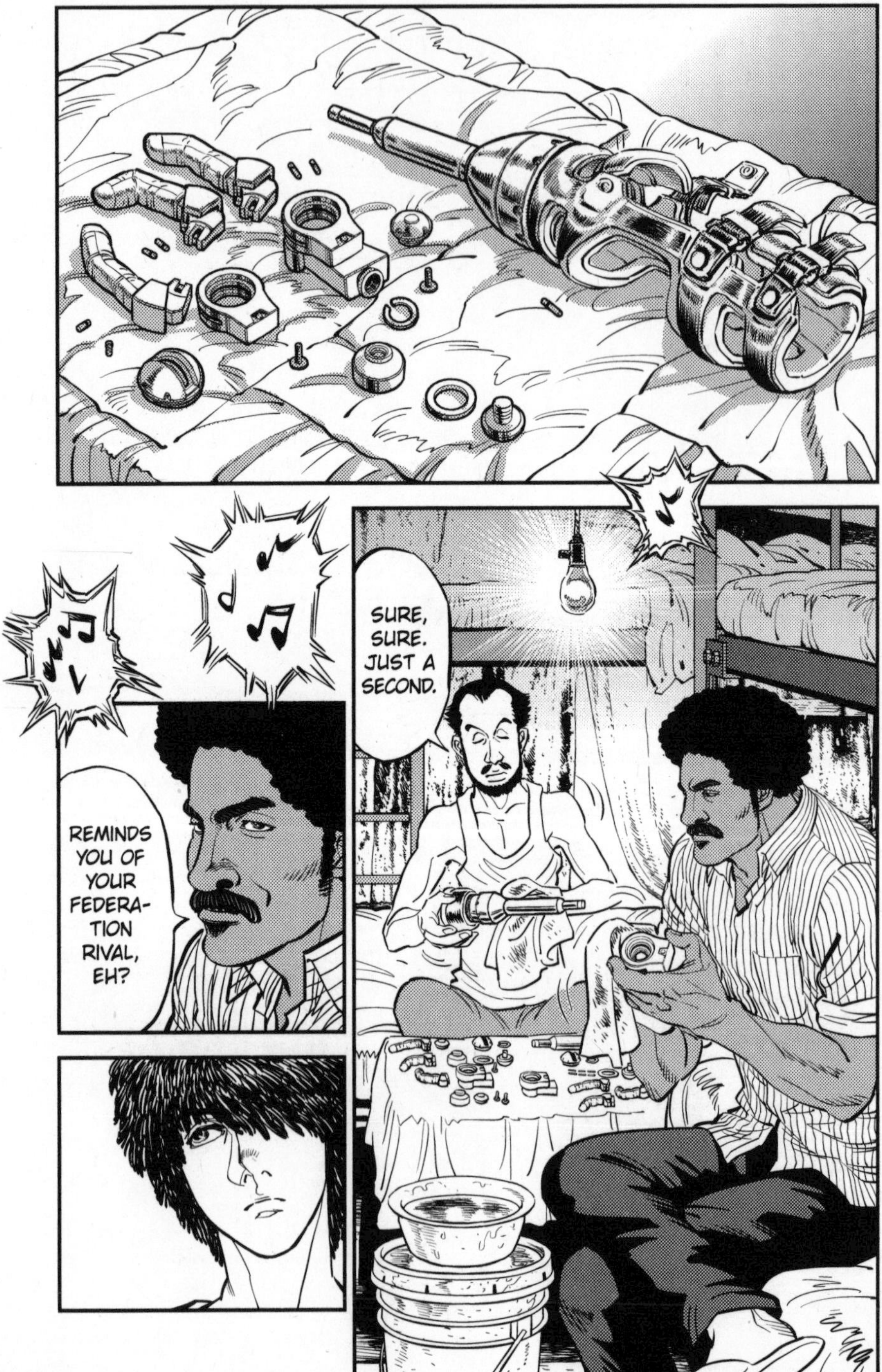
SURE, SURE. JUST A SECOND.
REMINDS YOU OF YOUR FEDERATION RIVAL, EH?

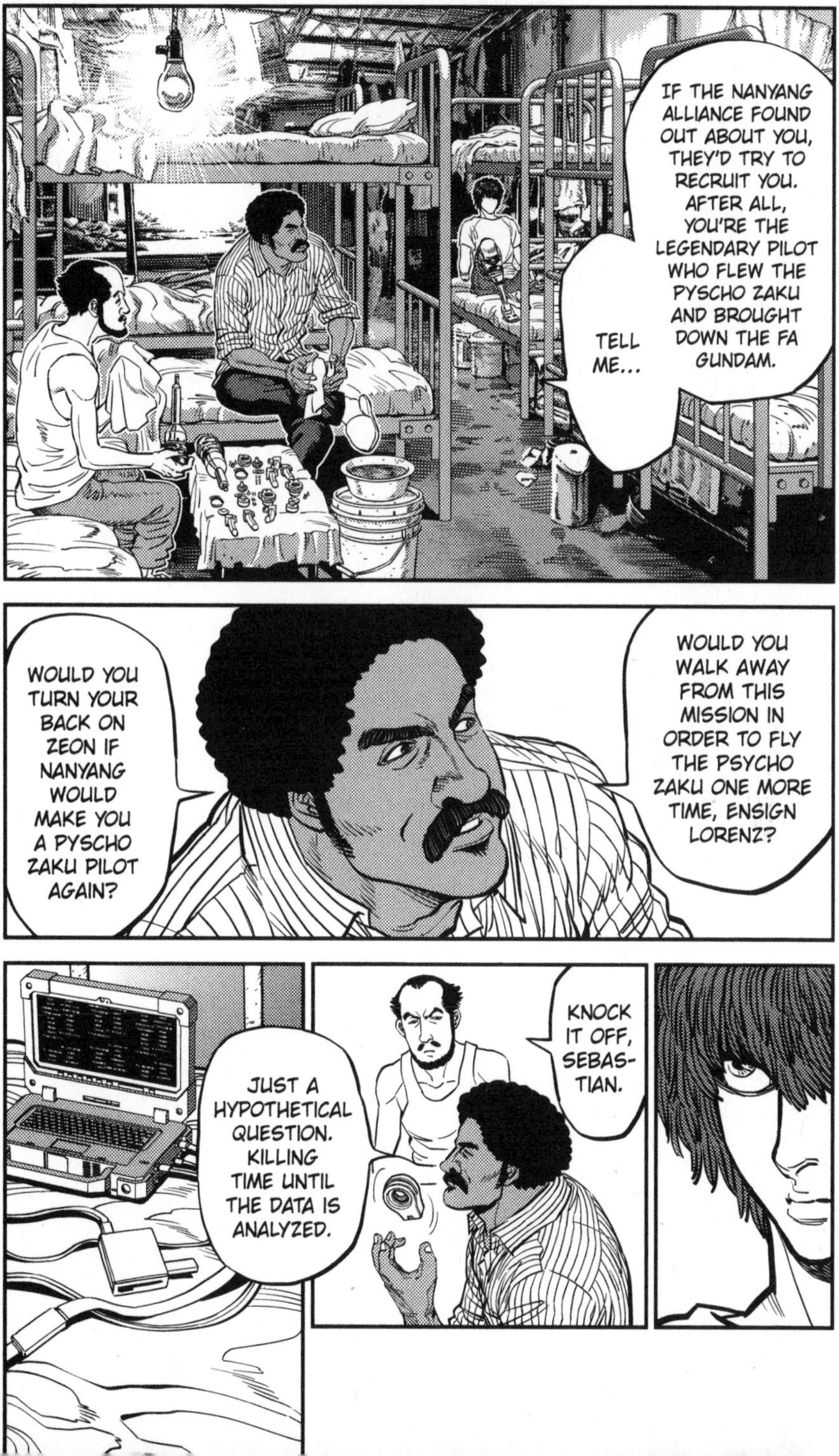
IF THE NANYANG ALLIANCE FOUND OUT ABOUT YOU, THEY'D TRY TO RECRUIT YOU. AFTER ALL, YOU'RE THE LEGENDARY PILOT WHO FLEW THE PYSCHO ZAKU AND BROUGHT DOWN THE FA GUNDAM.
TELL ME...
WOULD YOU WALK AWAY FROM THIS MISSION IN ORDER TO FLY THE PSYCHO ZAKU ONE MORE TIME, ENSIGN LORENZ?
WOULD YOU TURN YOUR BACK ON ZEON IF NANYANG WOULD MAKE YOU A PYSCHO ZAKU PILOT AGAIN?
KNOCK IT OFF, SEBASTIAN.
JUST A HYPOTHETICAL QUESTION. KILLING TIME UNTIL THE DATA IS ANALYZED.

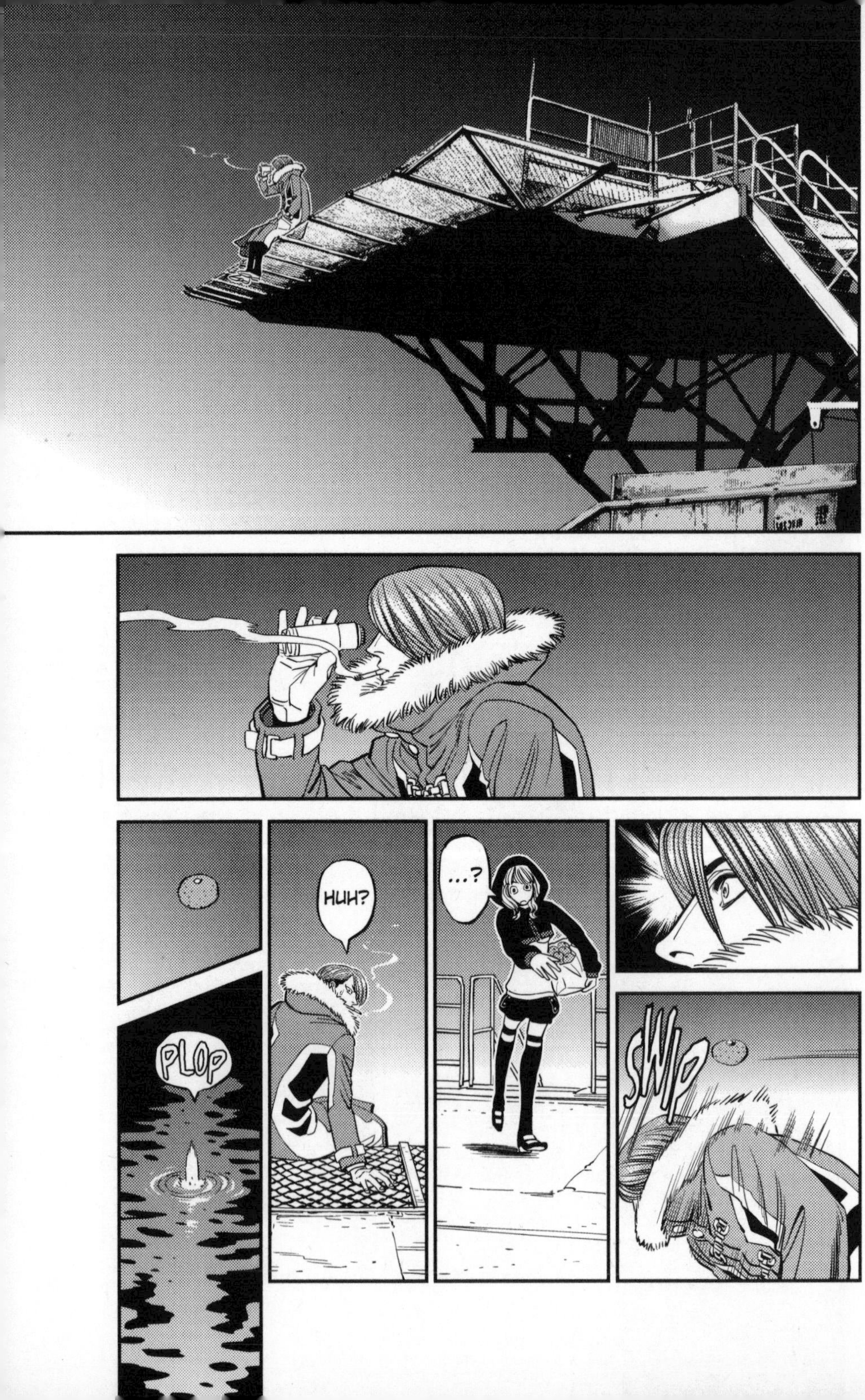
SWIP
...?
HUH?
PLOP

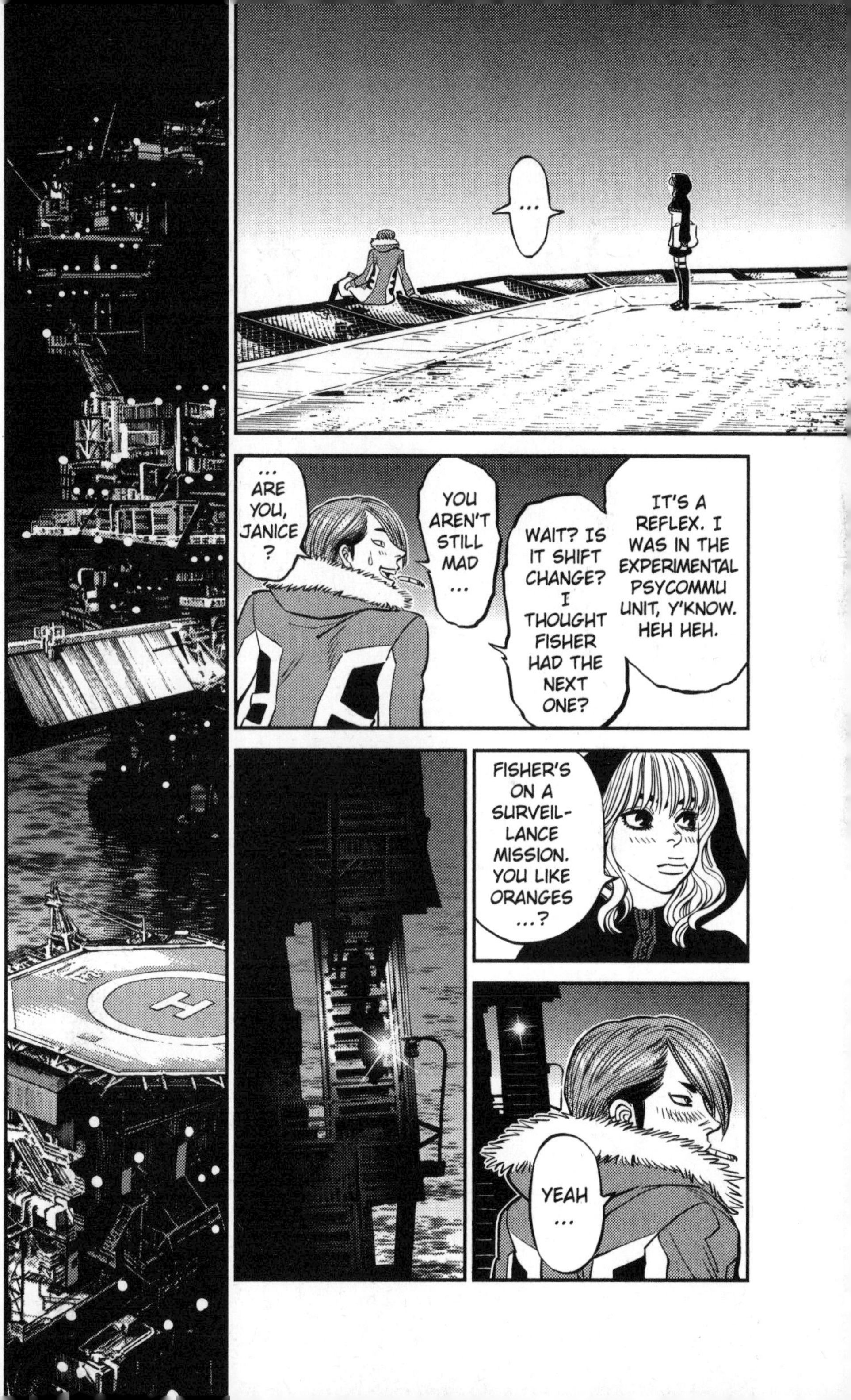
...
IT'S A REFLEX. I WAS IN THE EXPERIMENTAL PSYCOMMU UNIT, Y'KNOW. HEH HEH.
WAIT? IS IT SHIFT CHANGE? I THOUGHT FISHER HAD THE NEXT ONE?
YOU AREN'T STILL MAD ...
... ARE YOU, JANICE ?
FISHER'S ON A SURVEIL-LANCE MISSION. YOU LIKE ORANGES ...?
YEAH ...

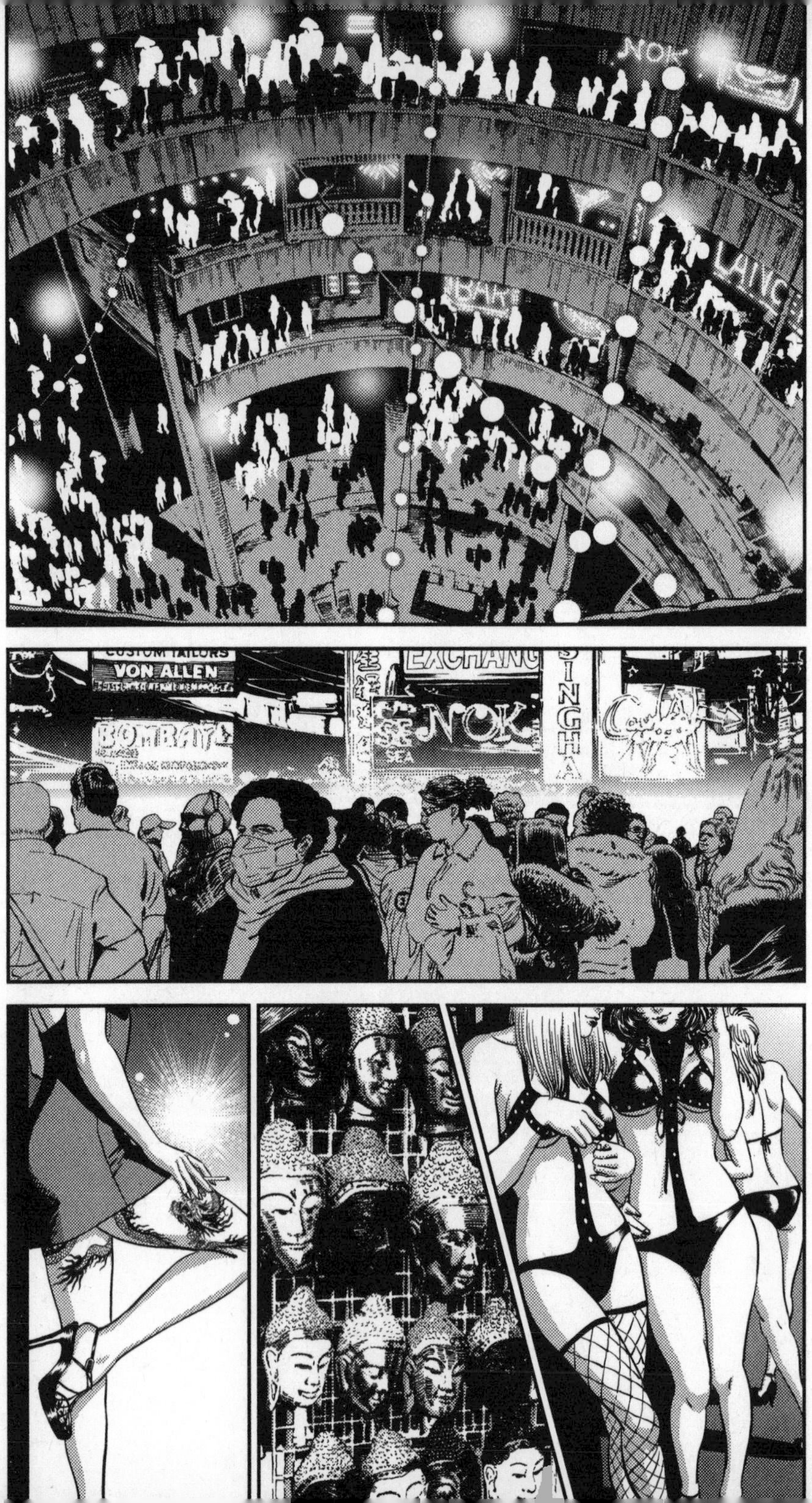
NOK
BAR
SINGHA
EXCHANG
NOK
SEA
CUSTOM TAILORS
VON ALLEN
BOMBAY

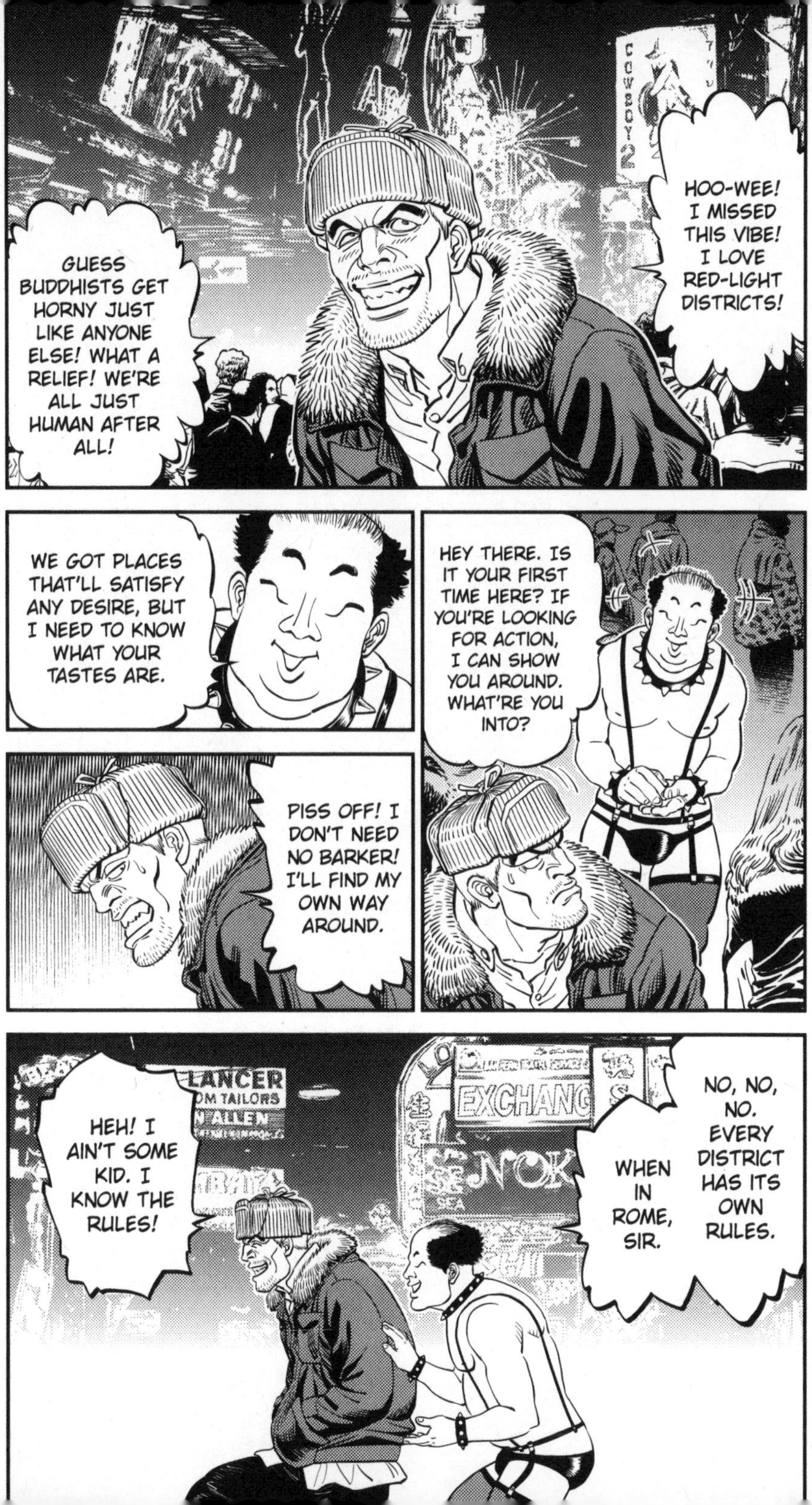
COWBOY 2
HOO-WEE! I MISSED THIS VIBE! I LOVE RED-LIGHT DISTRICTS!
GUESS BUDDHISTS GET HORNY JUST LIKE ANYONE ELSE! WHAT A RELIEF! WE'RE ALL JUST HUMAN AFTER ALL!
HEY THERE. IS IT YOUR FIRST TIME HERE? IF YOU'RE LOOKING FOR ACTION, I CAN SHOW YOU AROUND. WHAT'RE YOU INTO?
WE GOT PLACES THAT'LL SATISFY ANY DESIRE, BUT I NEED TO KNOW WHAT YOUR TASTES ARE.
PISS OFF! I DON'T NEED NO BARKER! I'LL FIND MY OWN WAY AROUND.
EXCHANG
LANCER
NO, NO, NO. EVERY DISTRICT HAS ITS OWN RULES.
WHEN IN ROME, SIR.
HEH! I AIN'T SOME KID. I KNOW THE RULES!

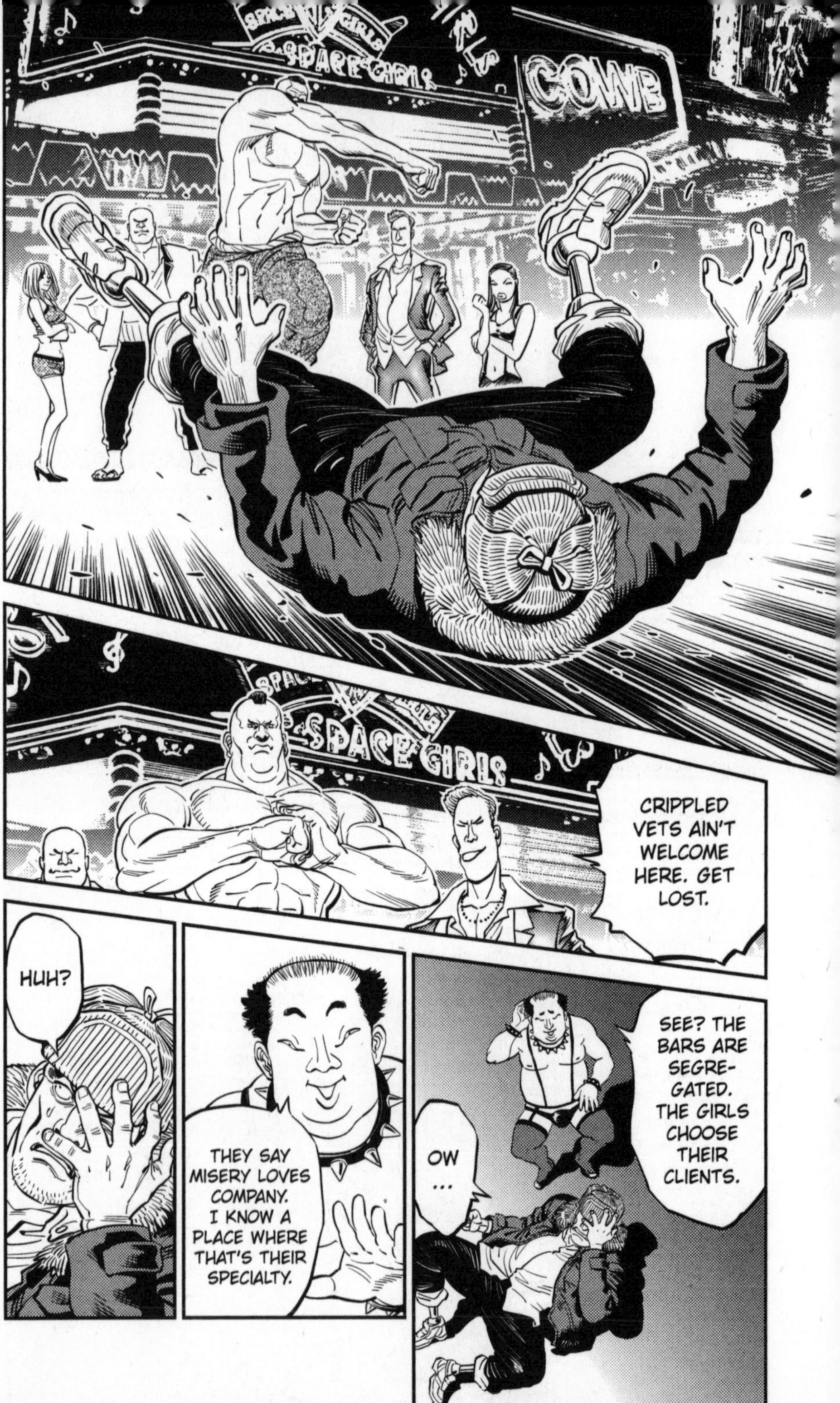
SPACE GIRLS
SPACE GIRLS
CRIPPLED VETS AIN'T WELCOME HERE. GET LOST.
SEE? THE BARS ARE SEGREGATED. THE GIRLS CHOOSE THEIR CLIENTS.
OW ...
THEY SAY MISERY LOVES COMPANY. I KNOW A PLACE WHERE THAT'S THEIR SPECIALTY.
HUH?

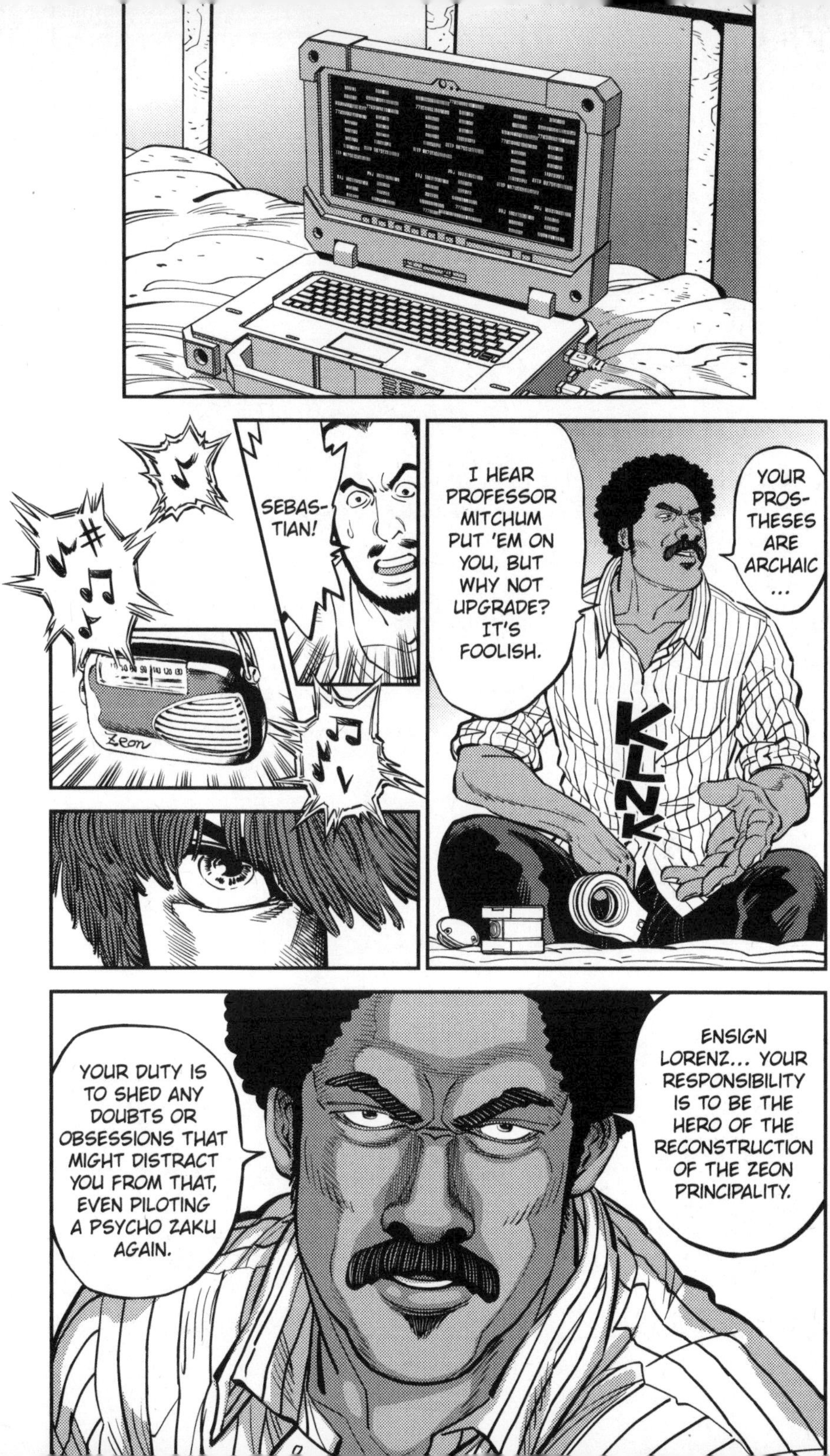
YOUR PROS-THESES ARE ARCHAIC ...
I HEAR PROFESSOR MITCHUM PUT 'EM ON YOU, BUT WHY NOT UPGRADE? IT'S FOOLISH.
KLNK
SEBAS-TIAN!
Zeon
ENSIGN LORENZ... YOUR RESPONSIBILITY IS TO BE THE HERO OF THE RECONSTRUCTION OF THE ZEON PRINCIPALITY.
YOUR DUTY IS TO SHED ANY DOUBTS OR OBSESSIONS THAT MIGHT DISTRACT YOU FROM THAT, EVEN PILOTING A PSYCHO ZAKU AGAIN.

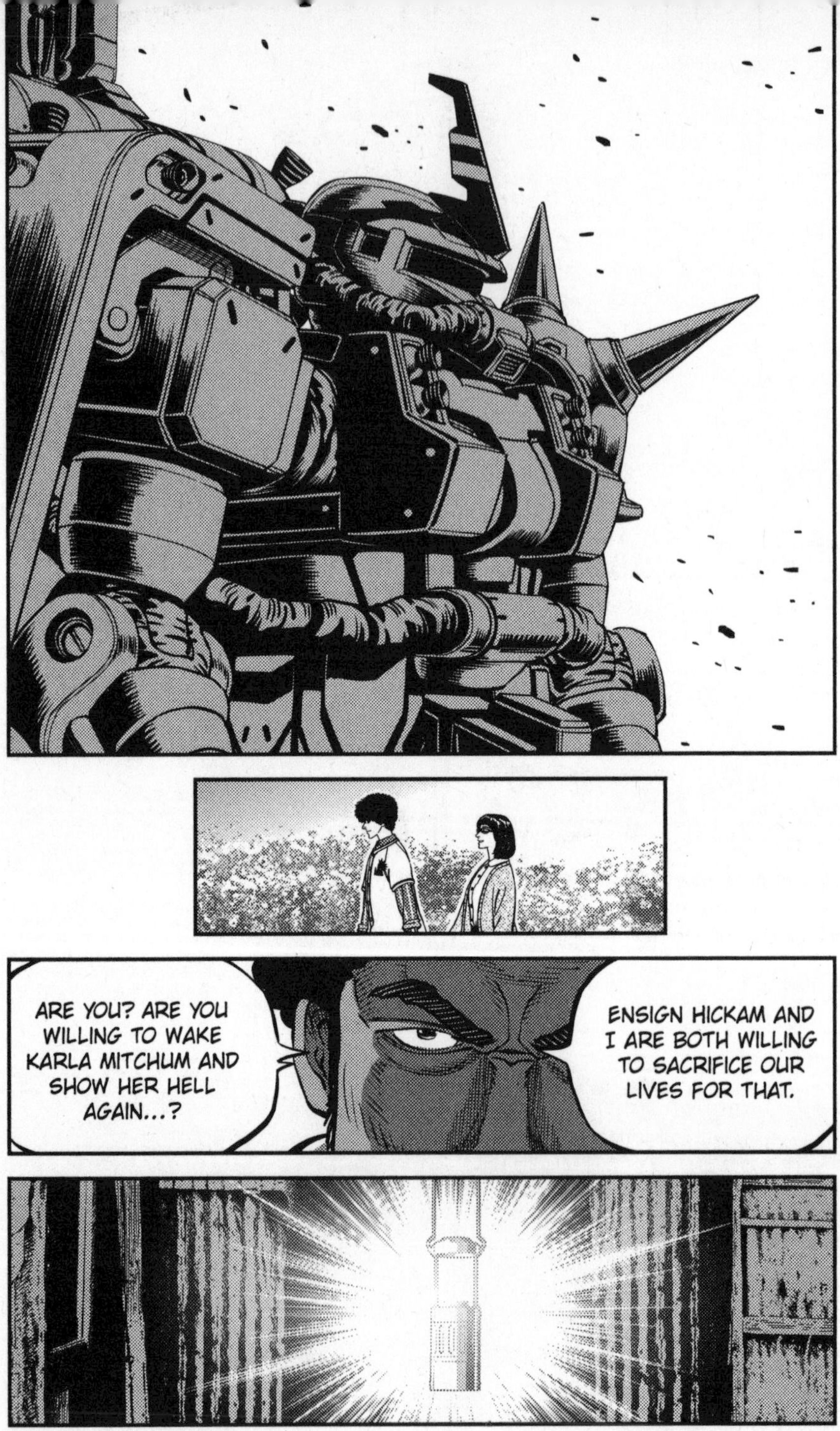
ENSIGN HICKAM AND I ARE BOTH WILLING TO SACRIFICE OUR LIVES FOR THAT.
ARE YOU? ARE YOU WILLING TO WAKE KARLA MITCHUM AND SHOW HER HELL AGAIN...?

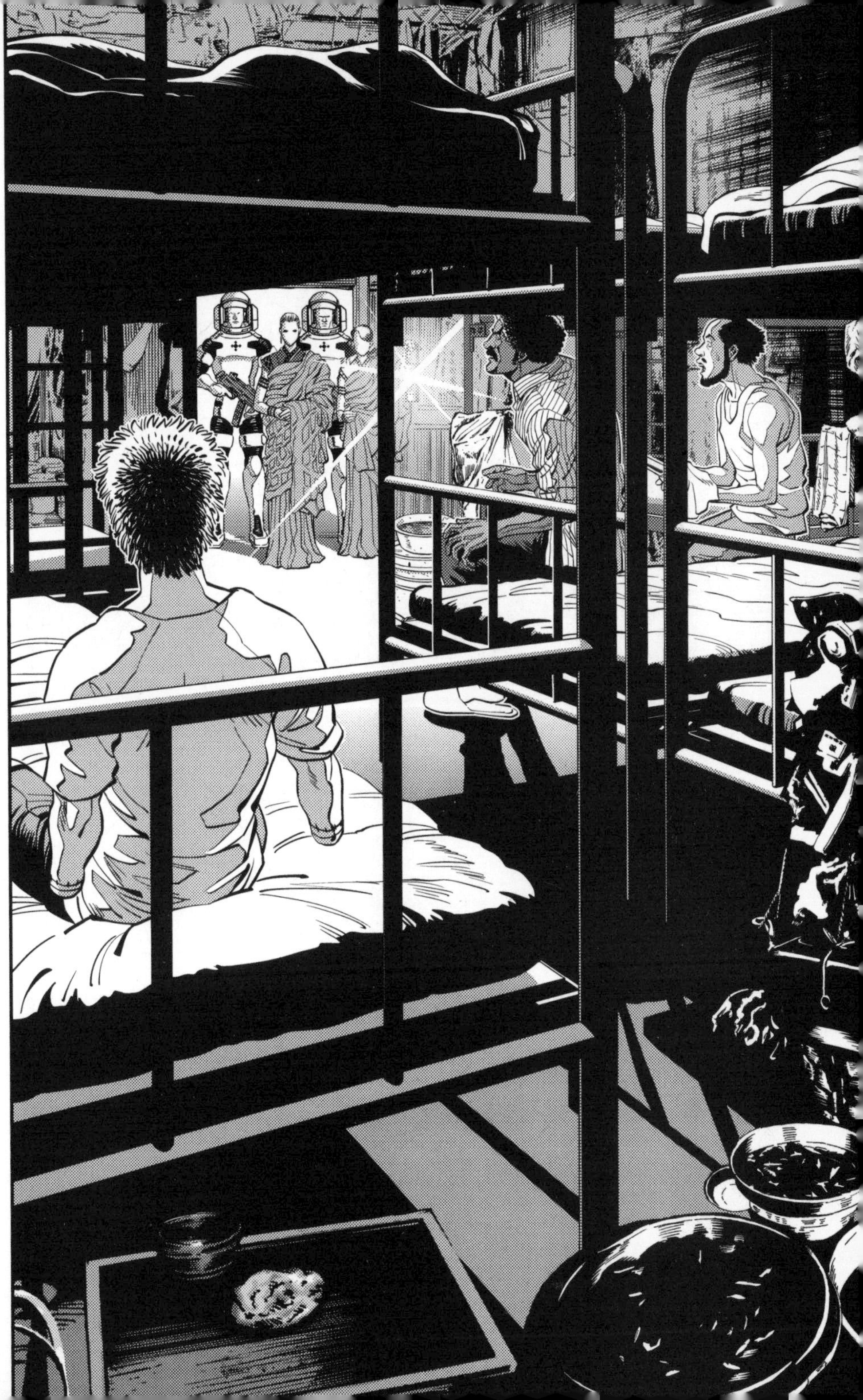

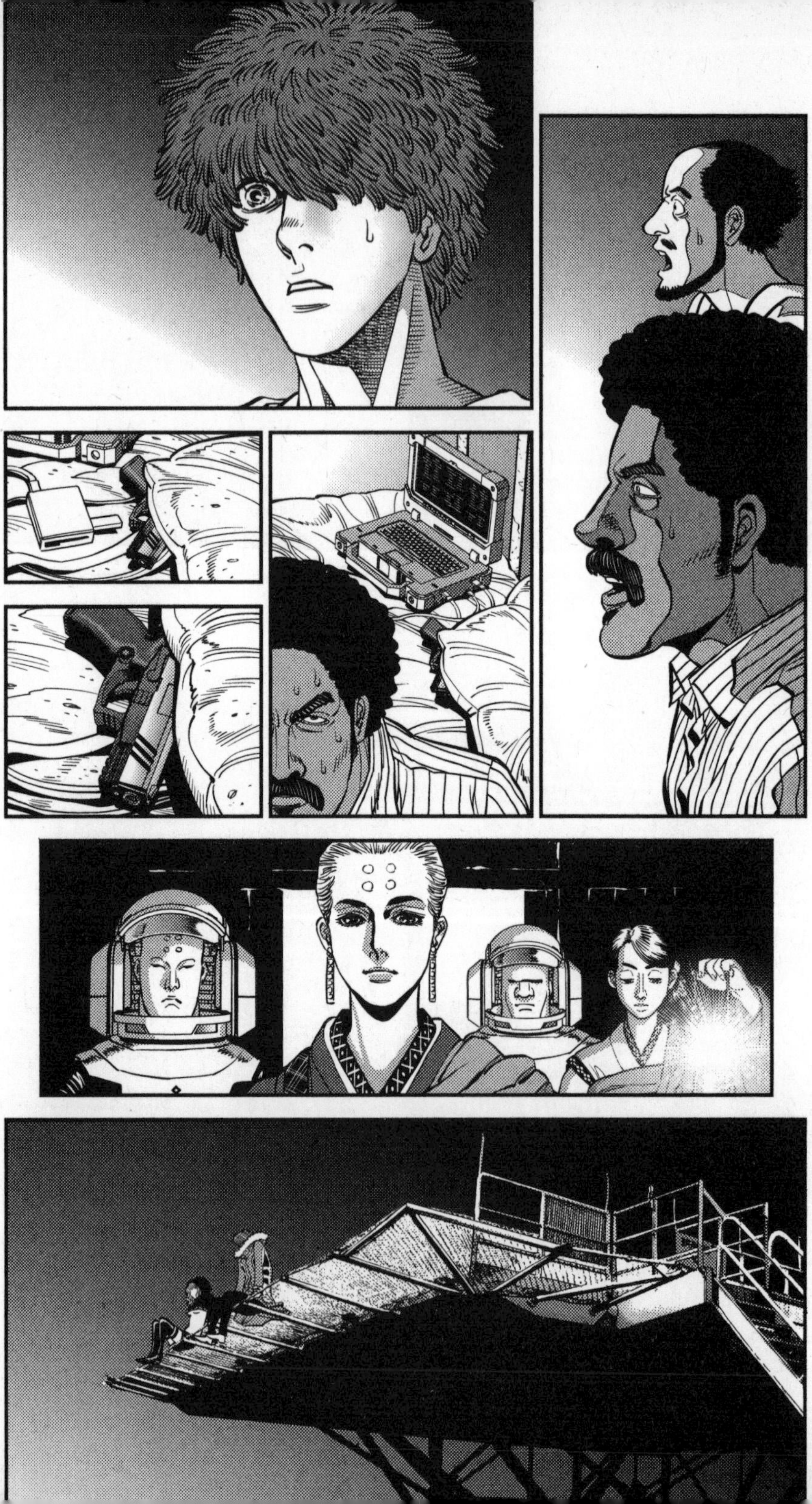

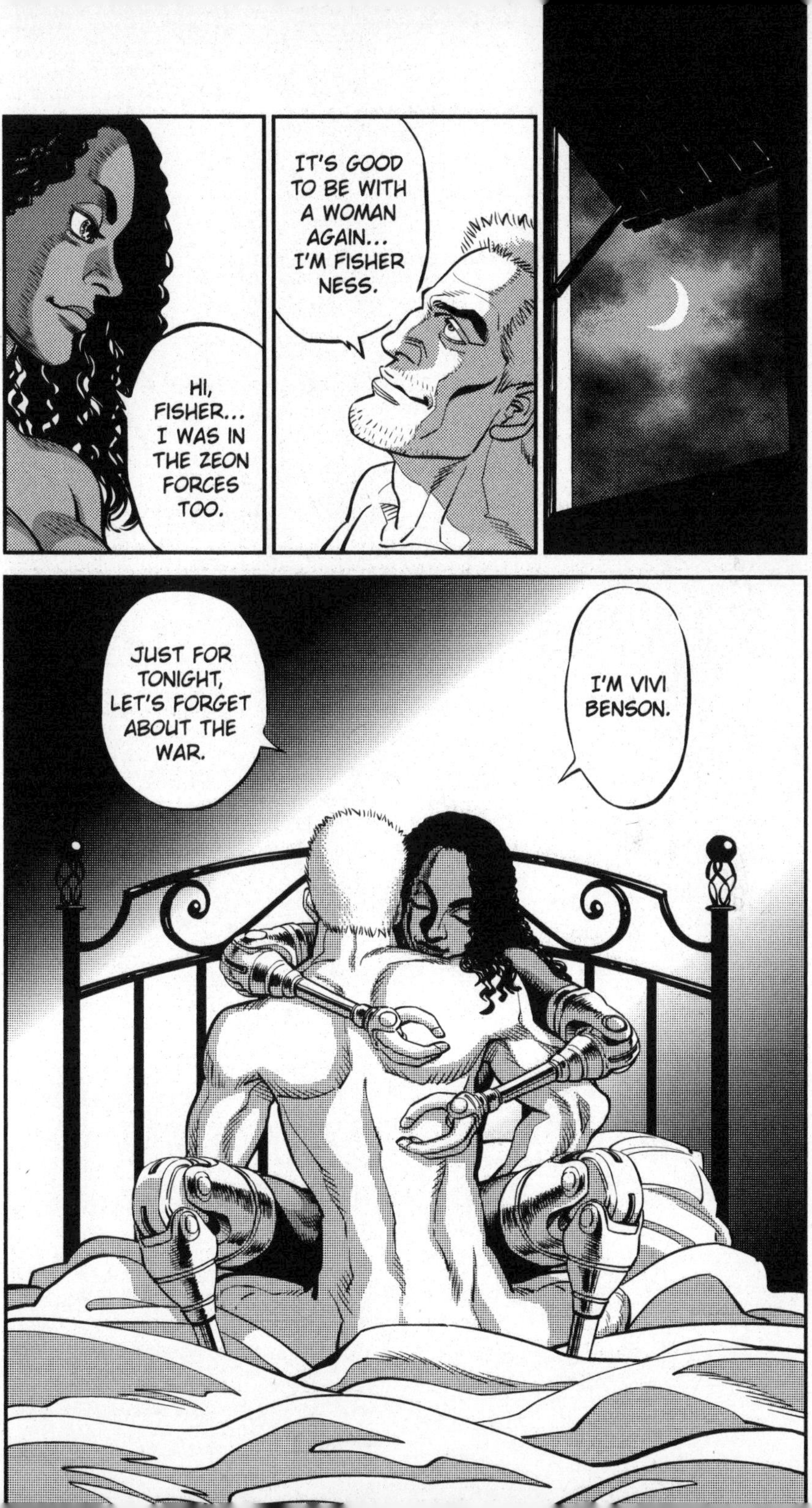
IT'S GOOD TO BE WITH A WOMAN AGAIN... I'M FISHER NESS.
HI, FISHER... I WAS IN THE ZEON FORCES TOO.
I'M VIVI BENSON.
JUST FOR TONIGHT, LET'S FORGET ABOUT THE WAR.

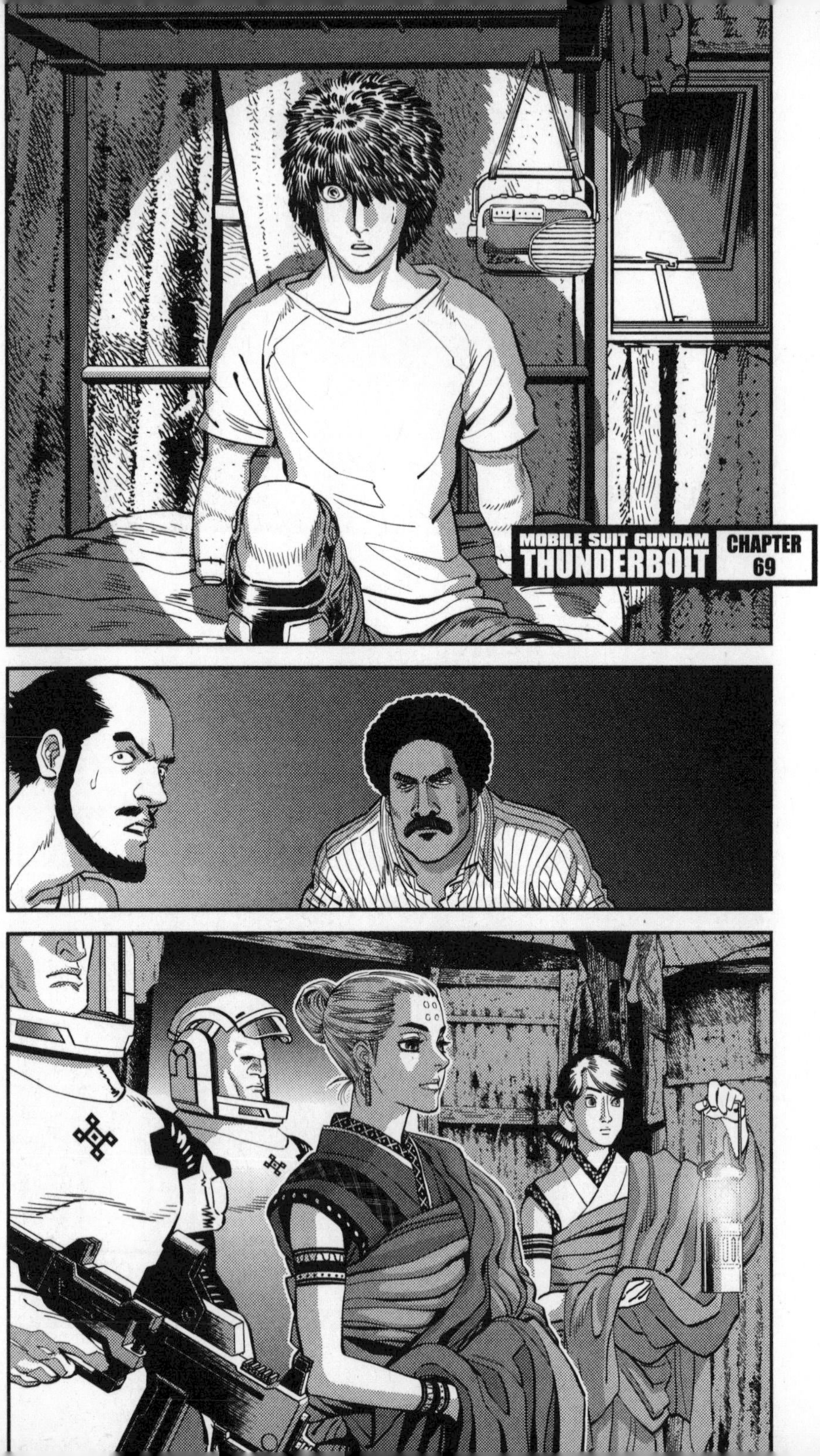
MOBILE SUIT GUNDAM
THUNDERBOLT
CHAPTER
69

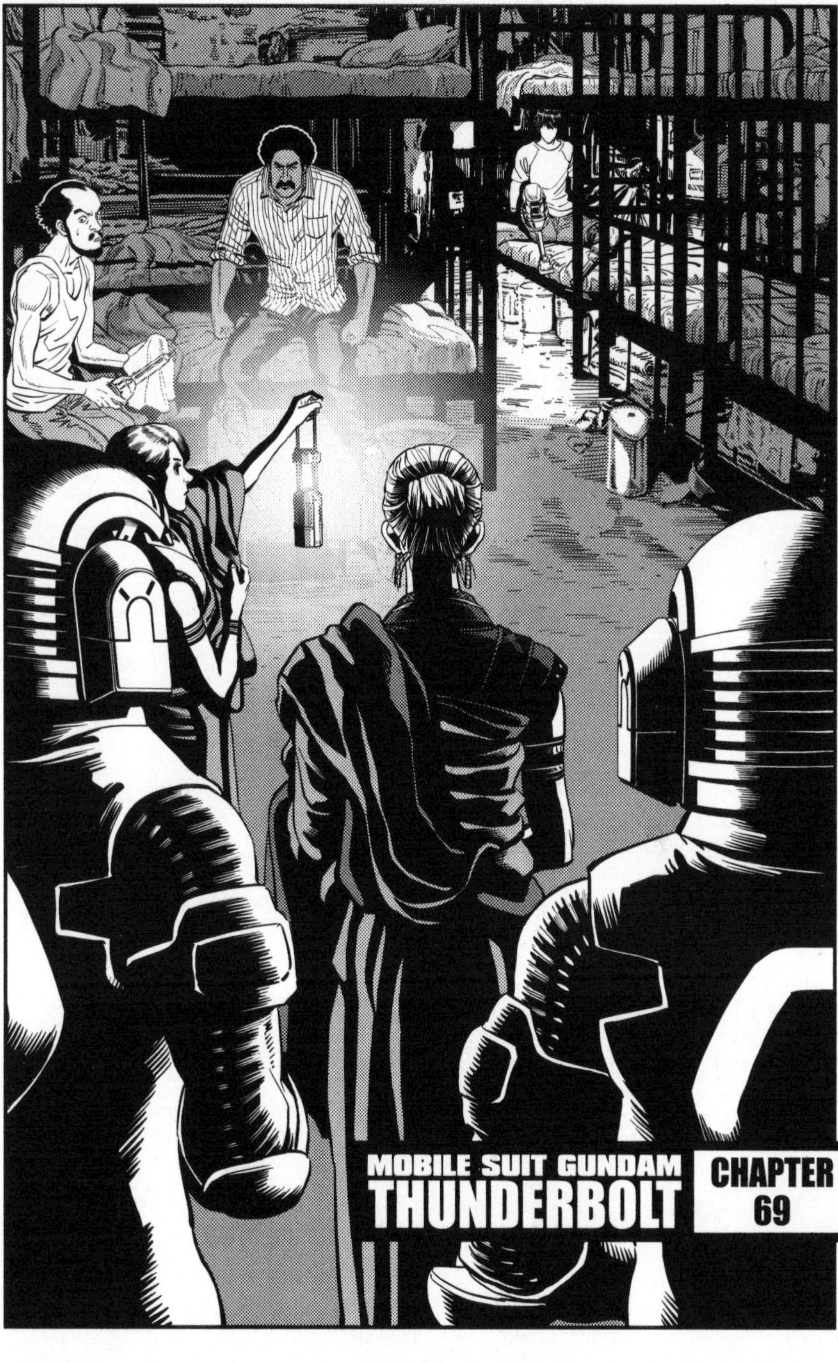
MOBILE SUIT GUNDAM
THUNDERBOLT
CHAPTER
69

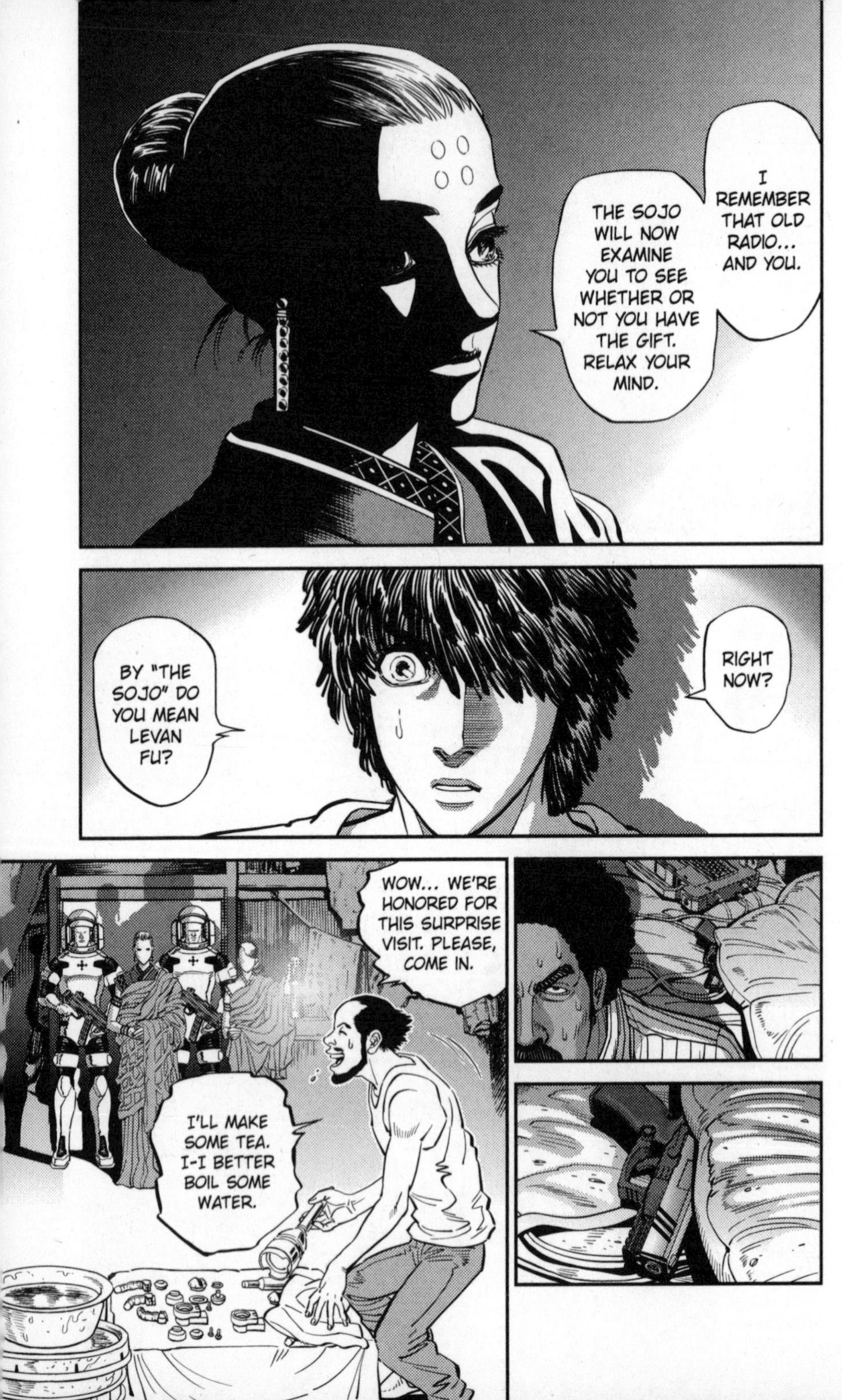
I REMEMBER THAT OLD RADIO... AND YOU.
THE SOJO WILL NOW EXAMINE YOU TO SEE WHETHER OR NOT YOU HAVE THE GIFT. RELAX YOUR MIND.
RIGHT NOW?
BY "THE SOJO" DO YOU MEAN LEVAN FU?
WOW... WE'RE HONORED FOR THIS SURPRISE VISIT. PLEASE, COME IN.
I'LL MAKE SOME TEA. I-I BETTER BOIL SOME WATER.

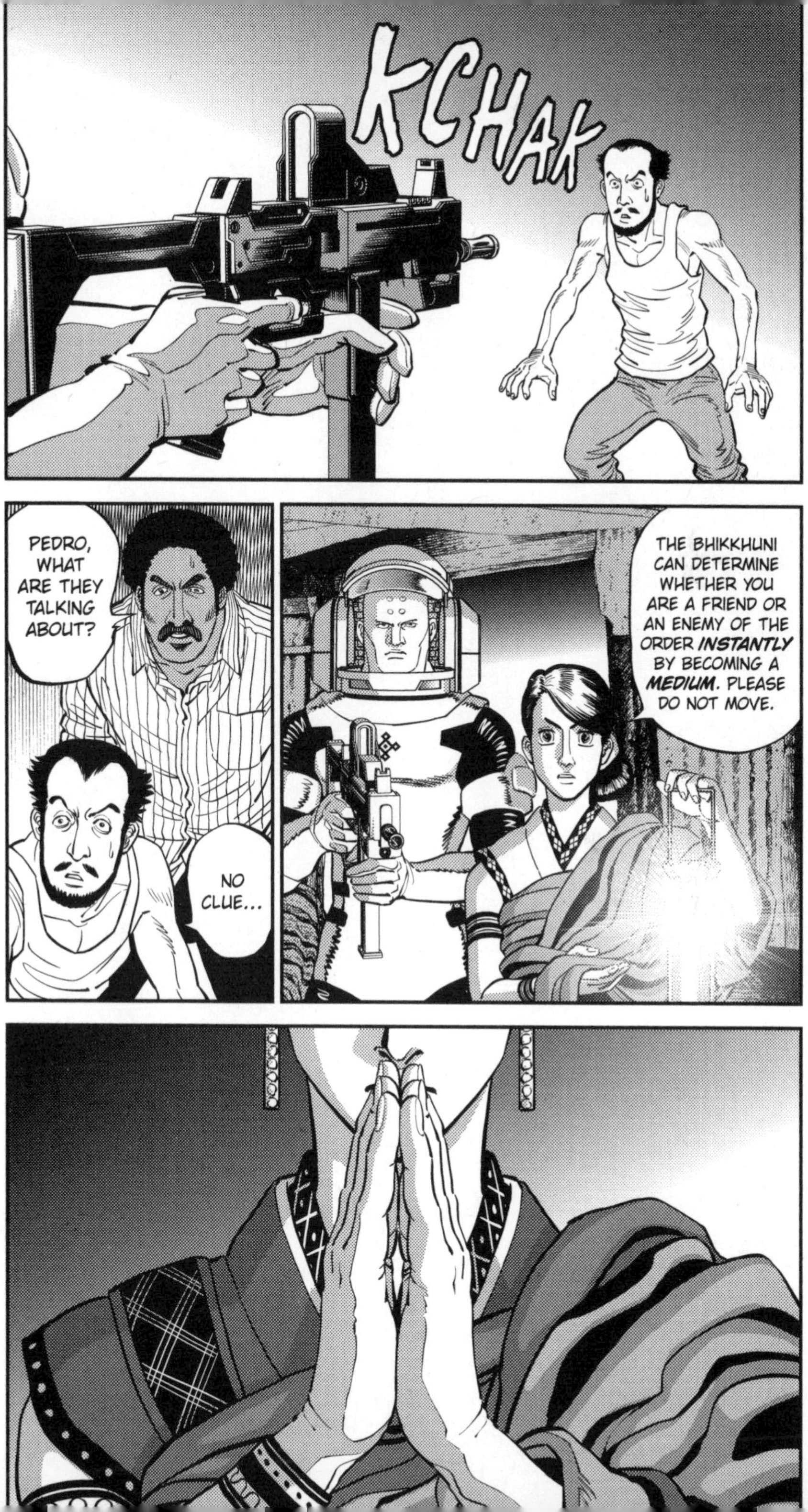
KCHAK
THE BHIKKHUNI CAN DETERMINE WHETHER YOU ARE A FRIEND OR AN ENEMY OF THE ORDER ***INSTANTLY*** BY BECOMING A ***MEDIUM***. PLEASE DO NOT MOVE.
PEDRO, WHAT ARE THEY TALKING ABOUT?
NO CLUE...

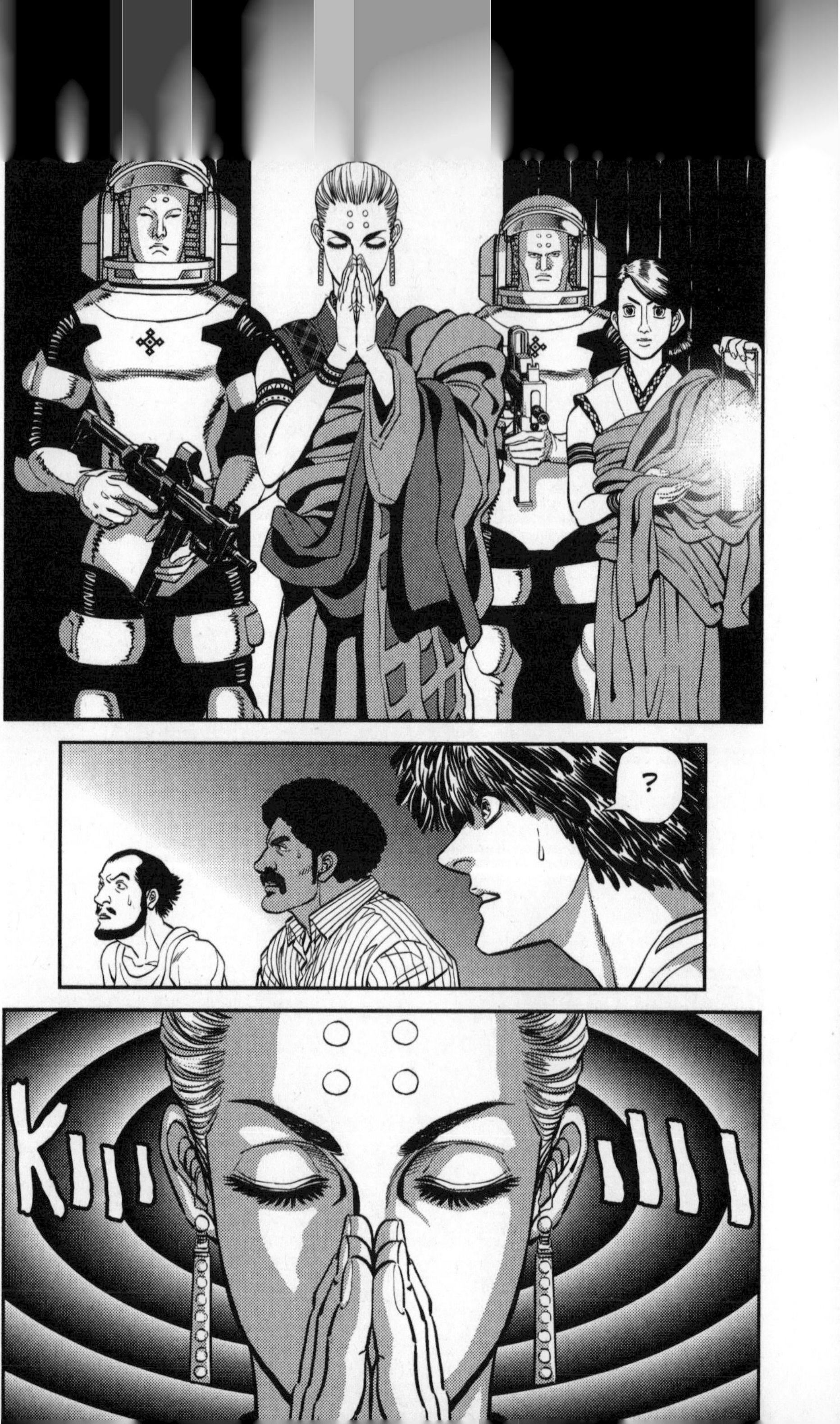
?
Kiiiiii

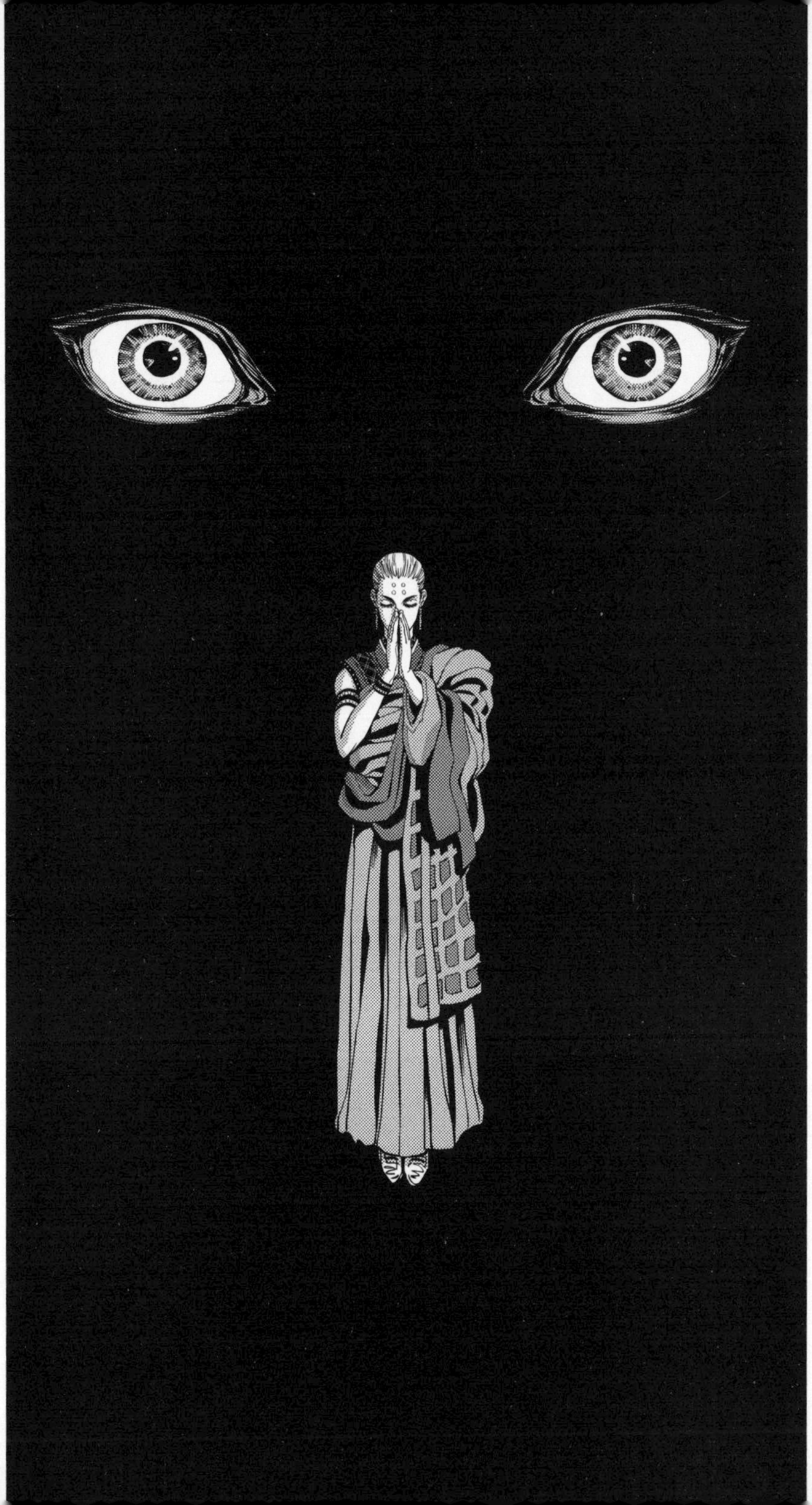

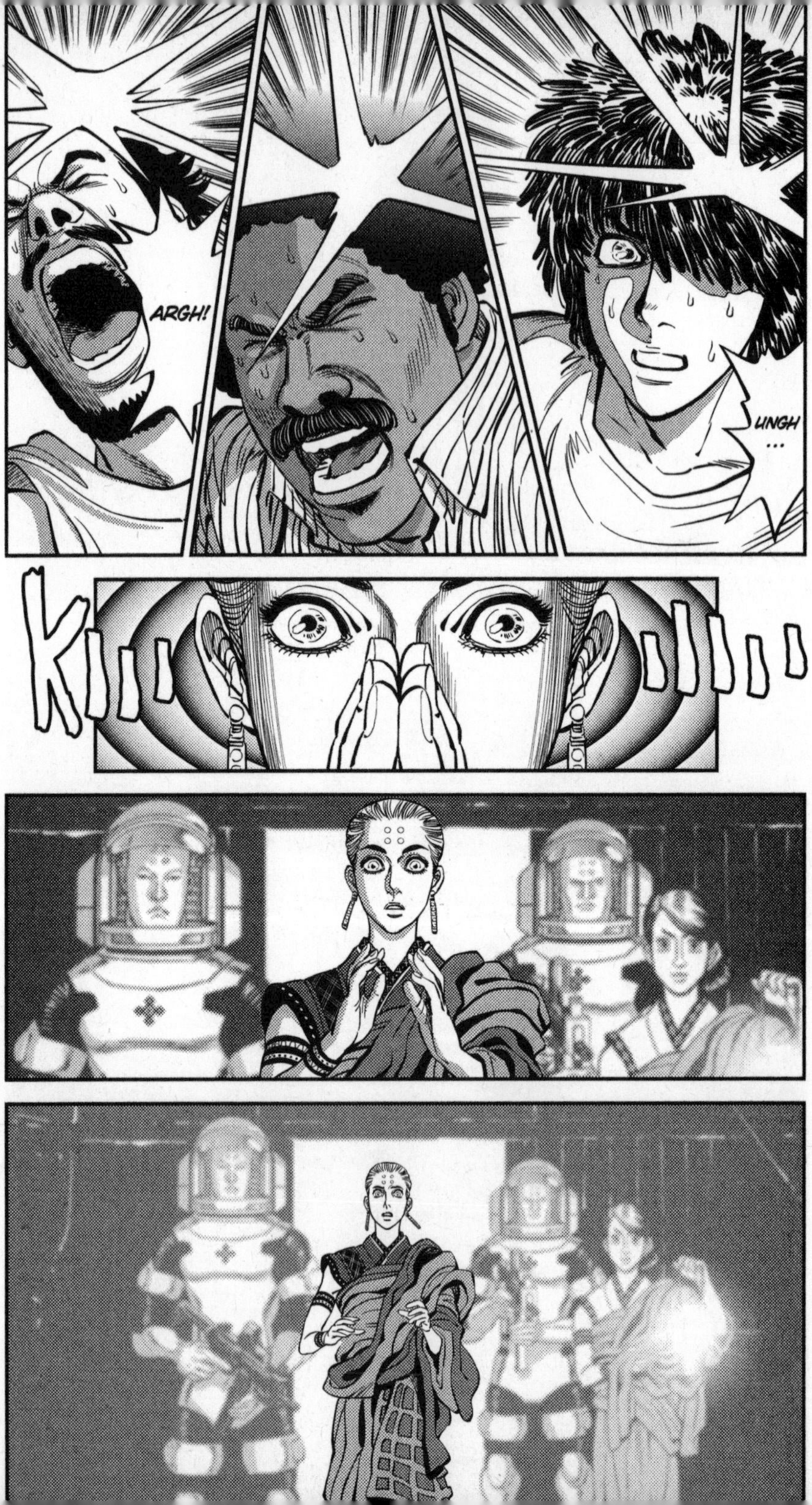
UNGH ...
ARGH!
KIIIIIIIIII

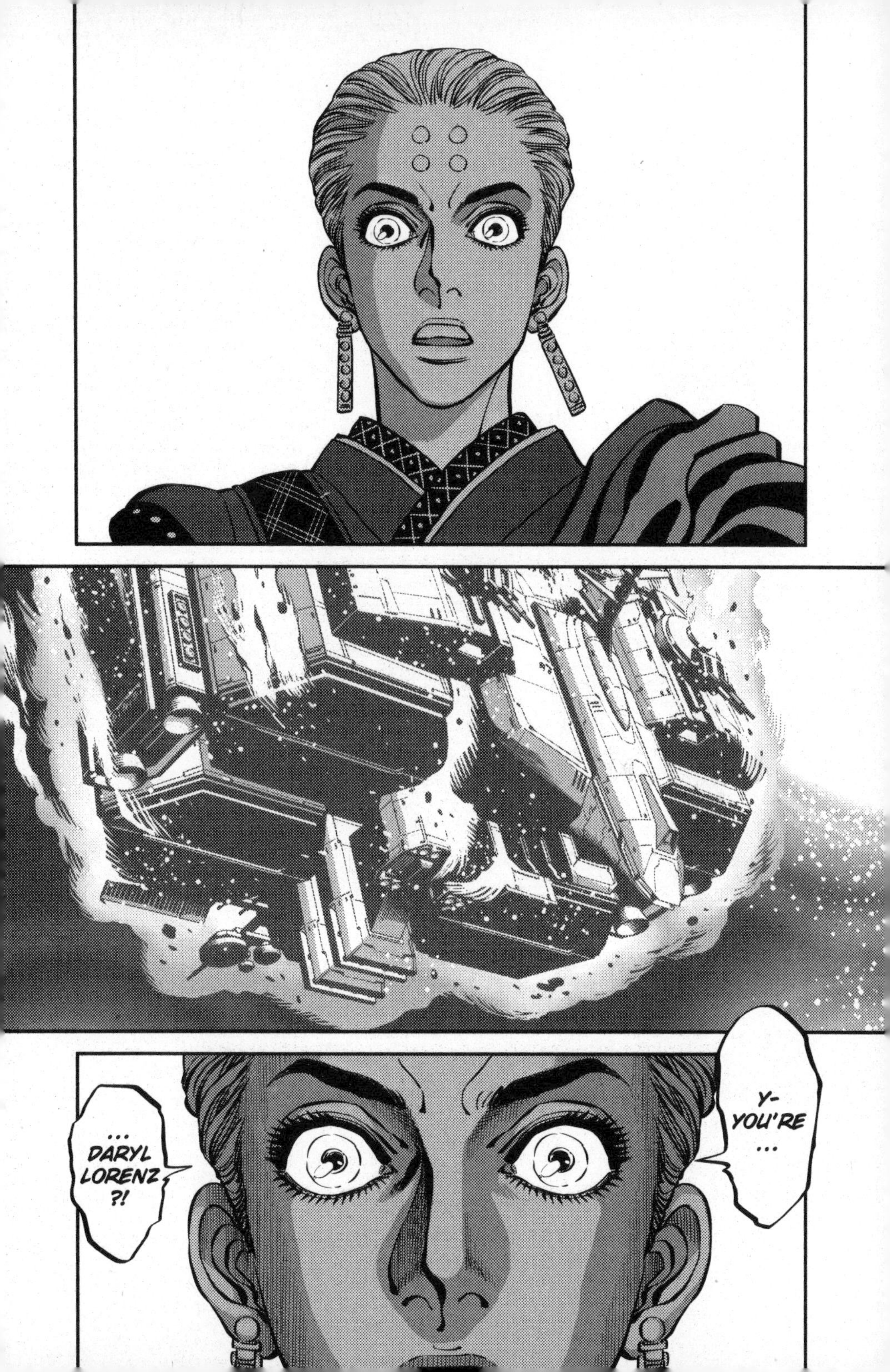
Y-YOU'RE ...
... DARYL LORENZ?!

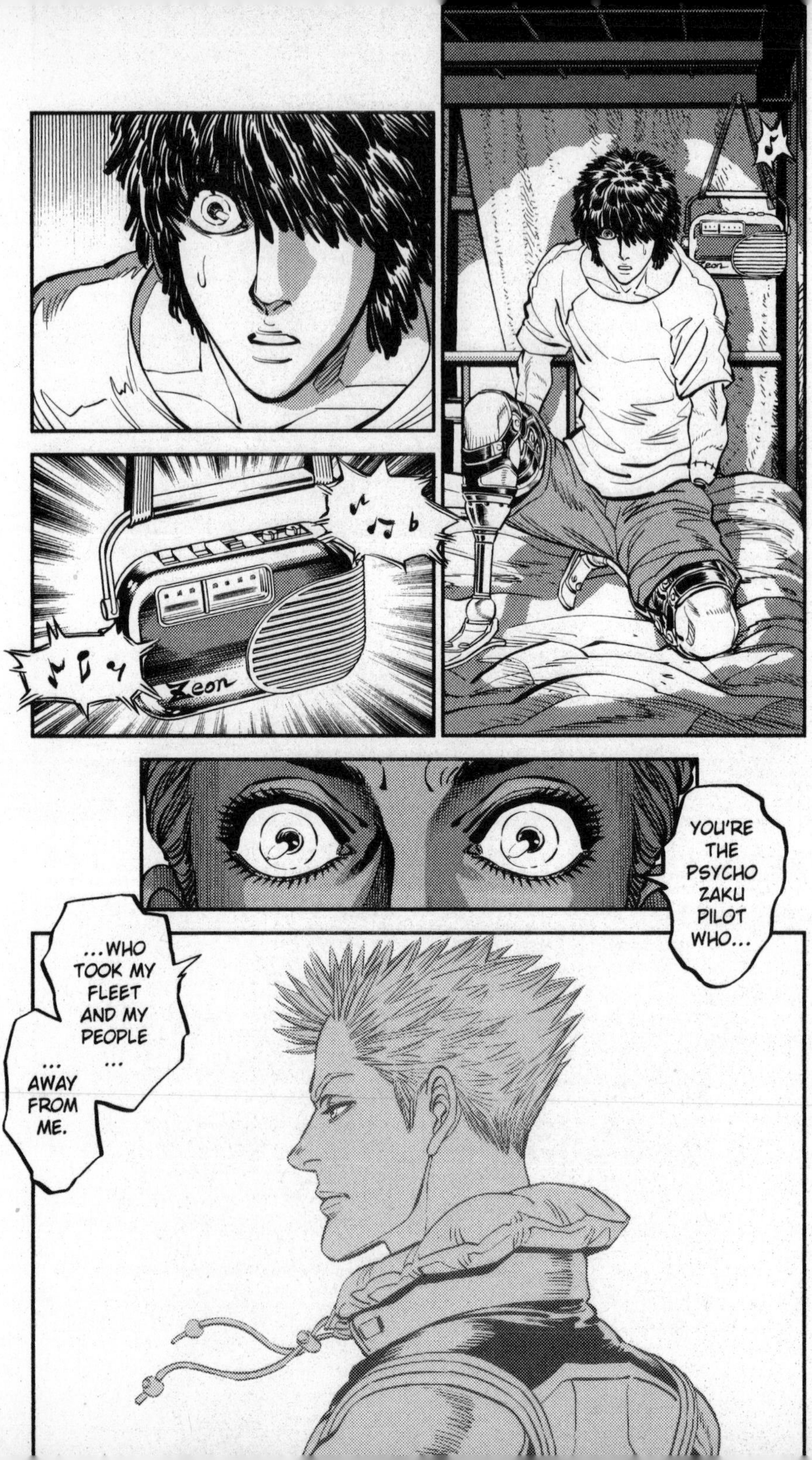
YOU'RE THE PSYCHO ZAKU PILOT WHO...
...WHO TOOK MY FLEET AND MY PEOPLE ... ... AWAY FROM ME.

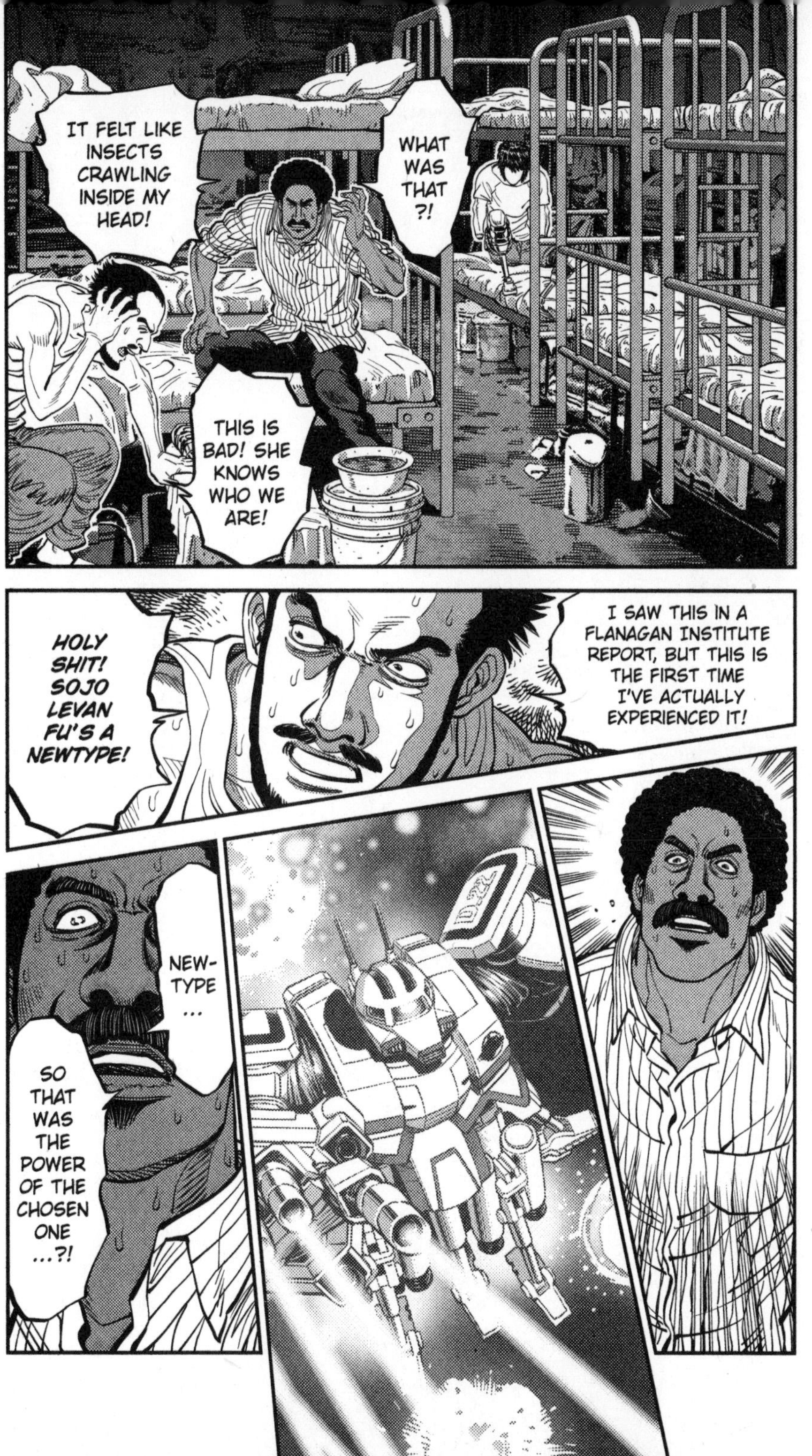
WHAT WAS THAT?!
IT FELT LIKE INSECTS CRAWLING INSIDE MY HEAD!
THIS IS BAD! SHE KNOWS WHO WE ARE!
I SAW THIS IN A FLANAGAN INSTITUTE REPORT, BUT THIS IS THE FIRST TIME I'VE ACTUALLY EXPERIENCED IT!
HOLY SHIT! SOJO LEVAN FU'S A NEWTYPE!
NEW-TYPE...
SO THAT WAS THE POWER OF THE CHOSEN ONE...?!

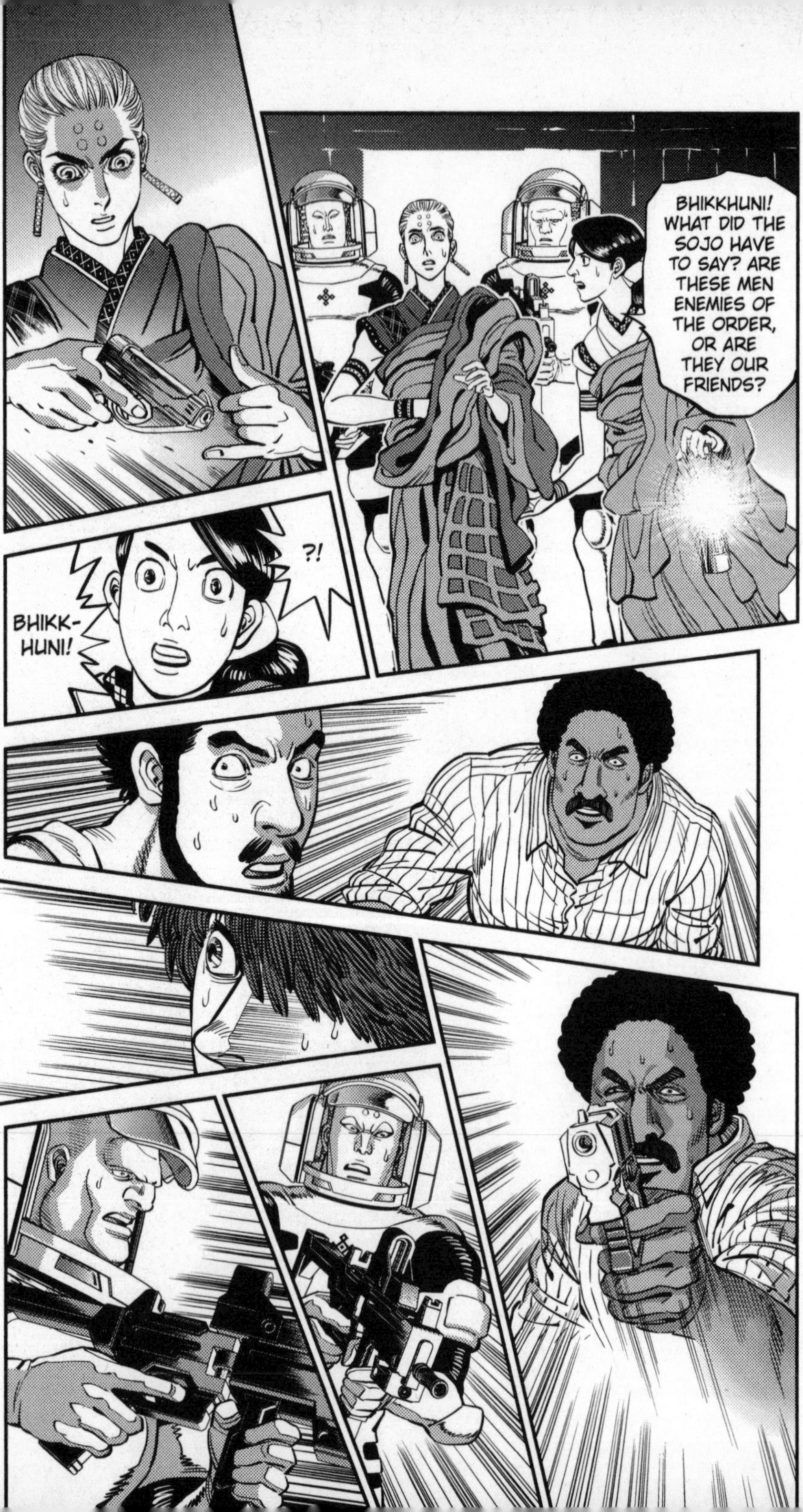
BHIKKHUNI! WHAT DID THE SOJO HAVE TO SAY? ARE THESE MEN ENEMIES OF THE ORDER, OR ARE THEY OUR FRIENDS?
?!
BHIKK-HUNI!

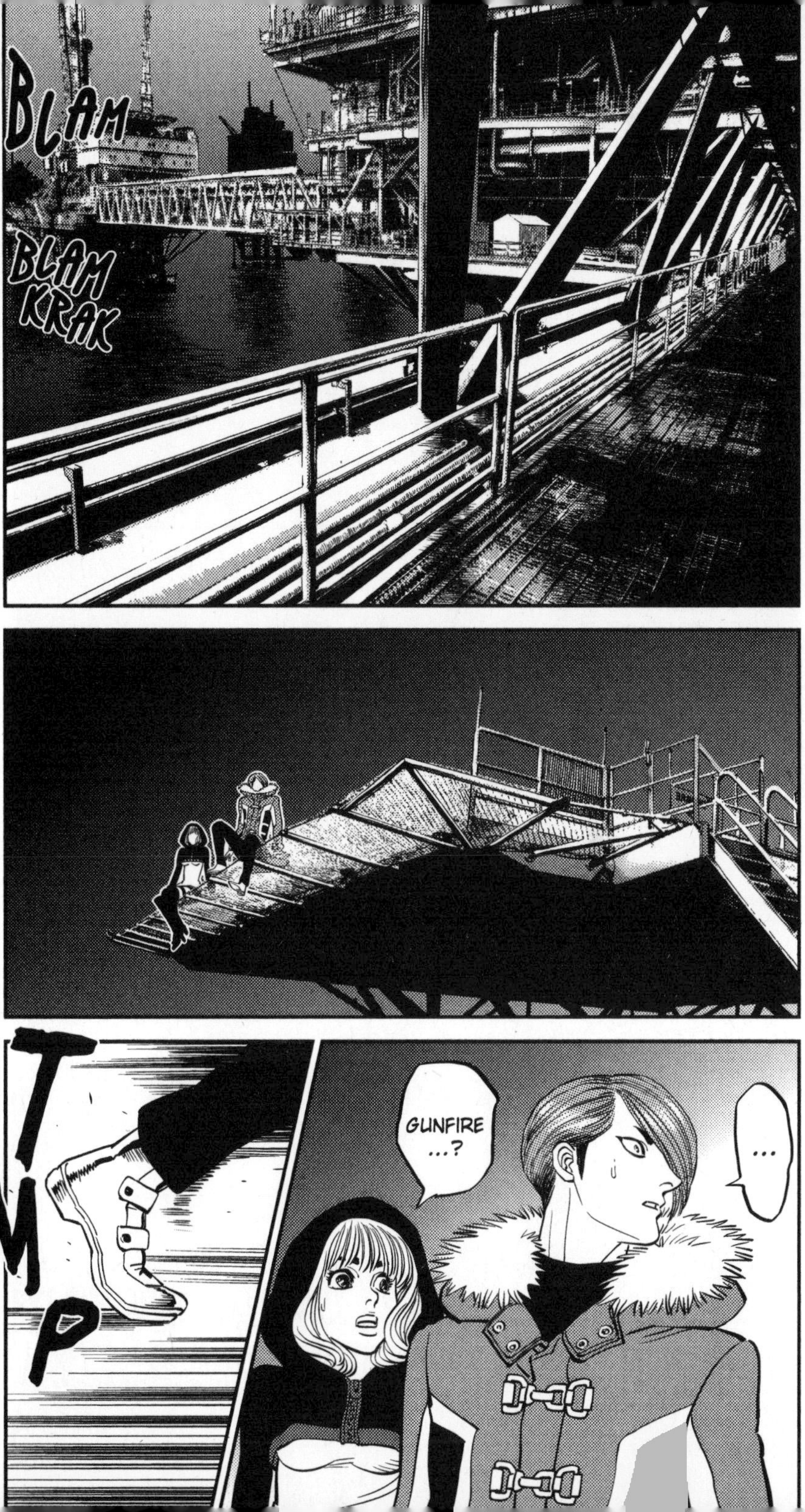
BLAM
BLAM
KRAK
...
GUNFIRE ...?
TMP

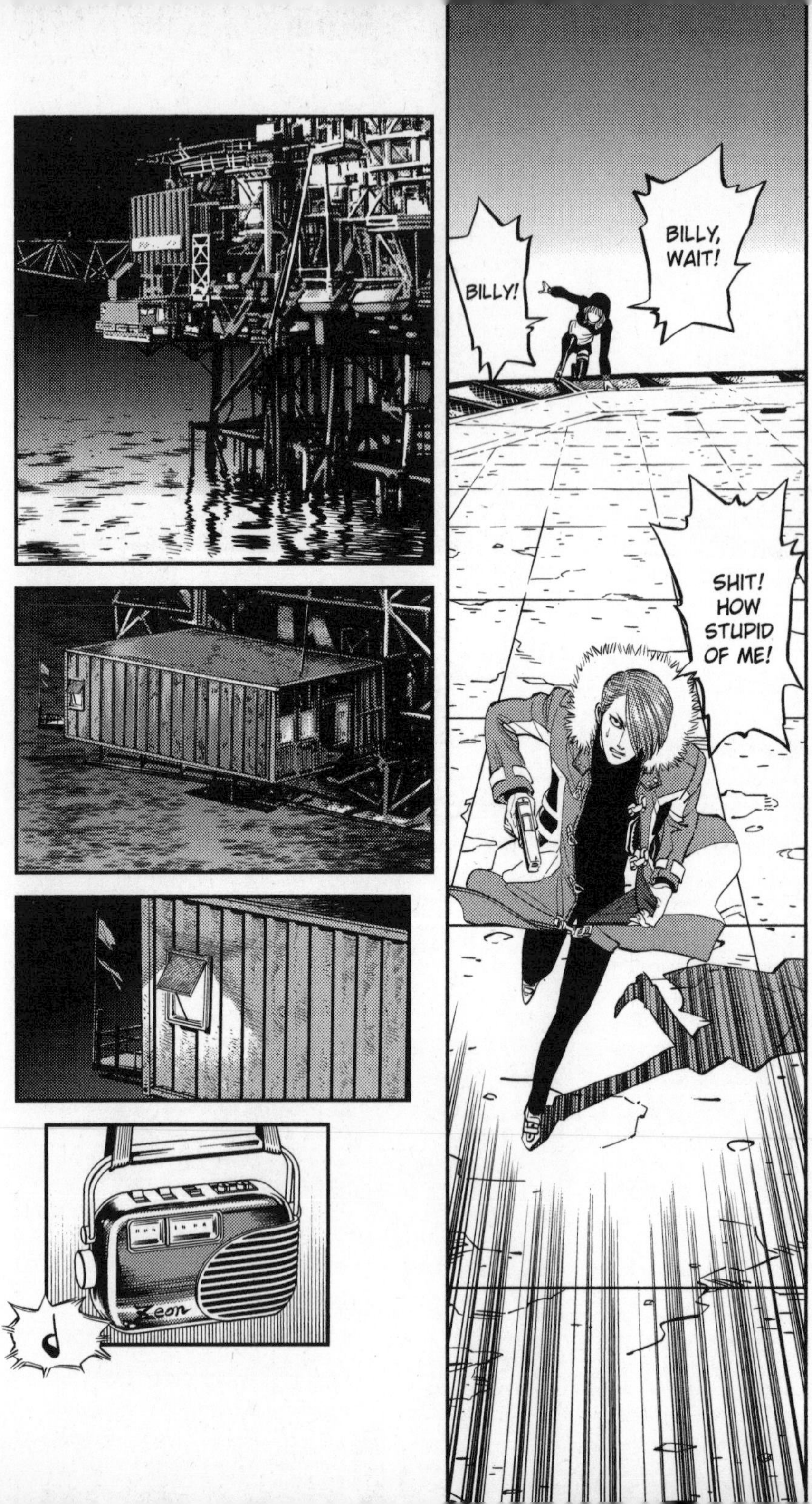
BILLY, WAIT!
BILLY!
SHIT! HOW STUPID OF ME!
Zeon

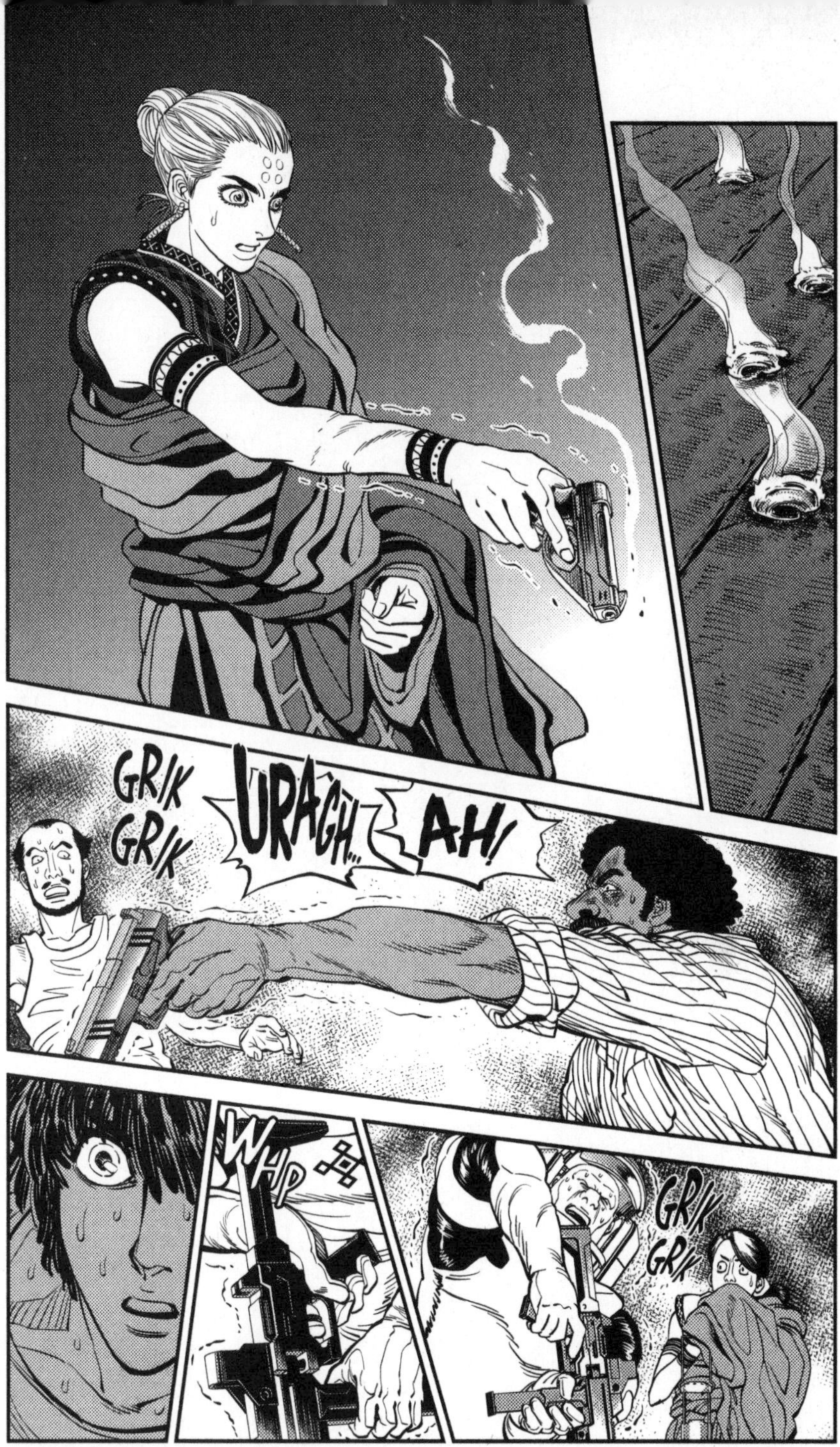
URAGH...
AH!
GRIK GRIK
GRIK GRIK
WHP

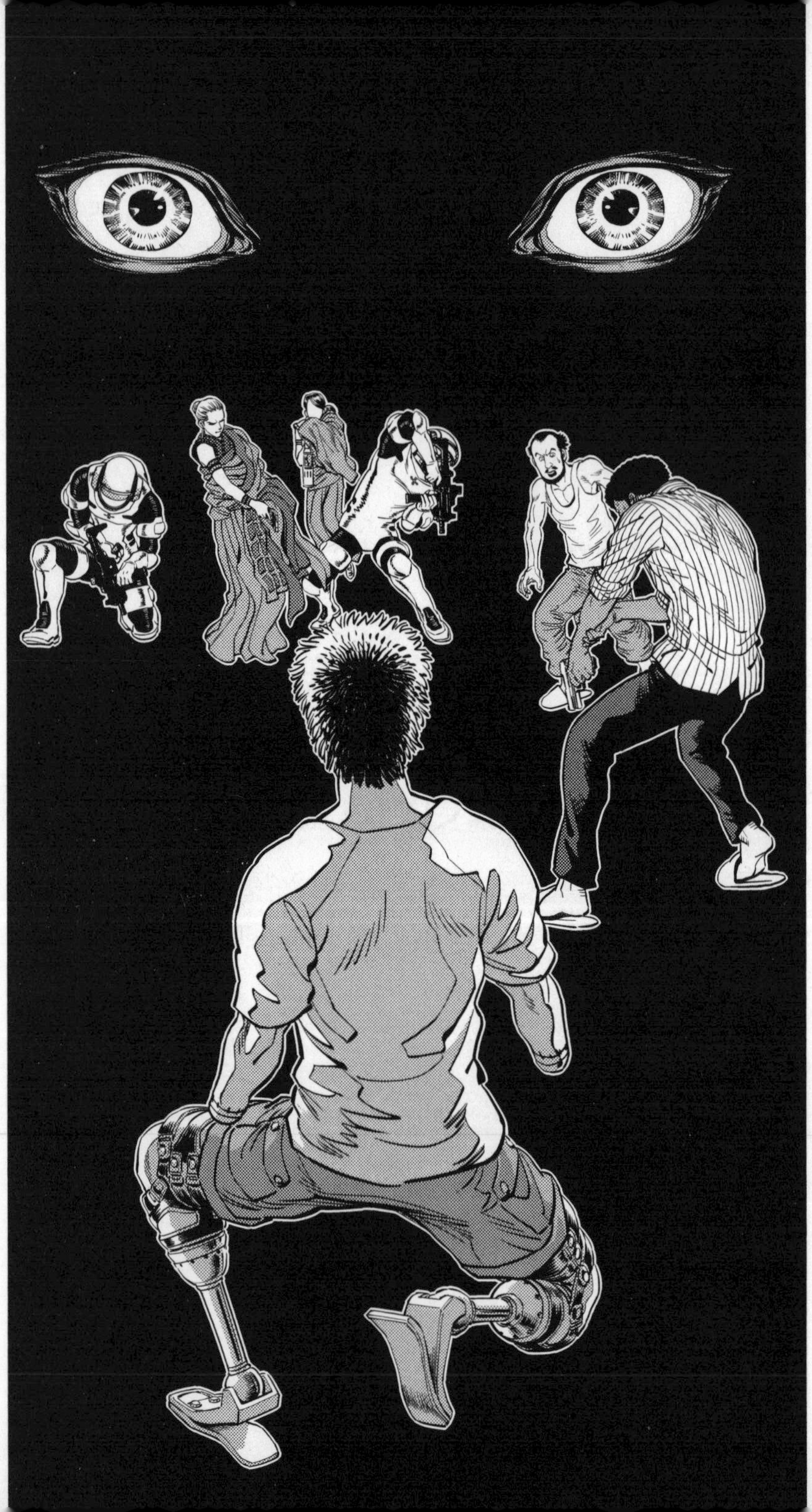

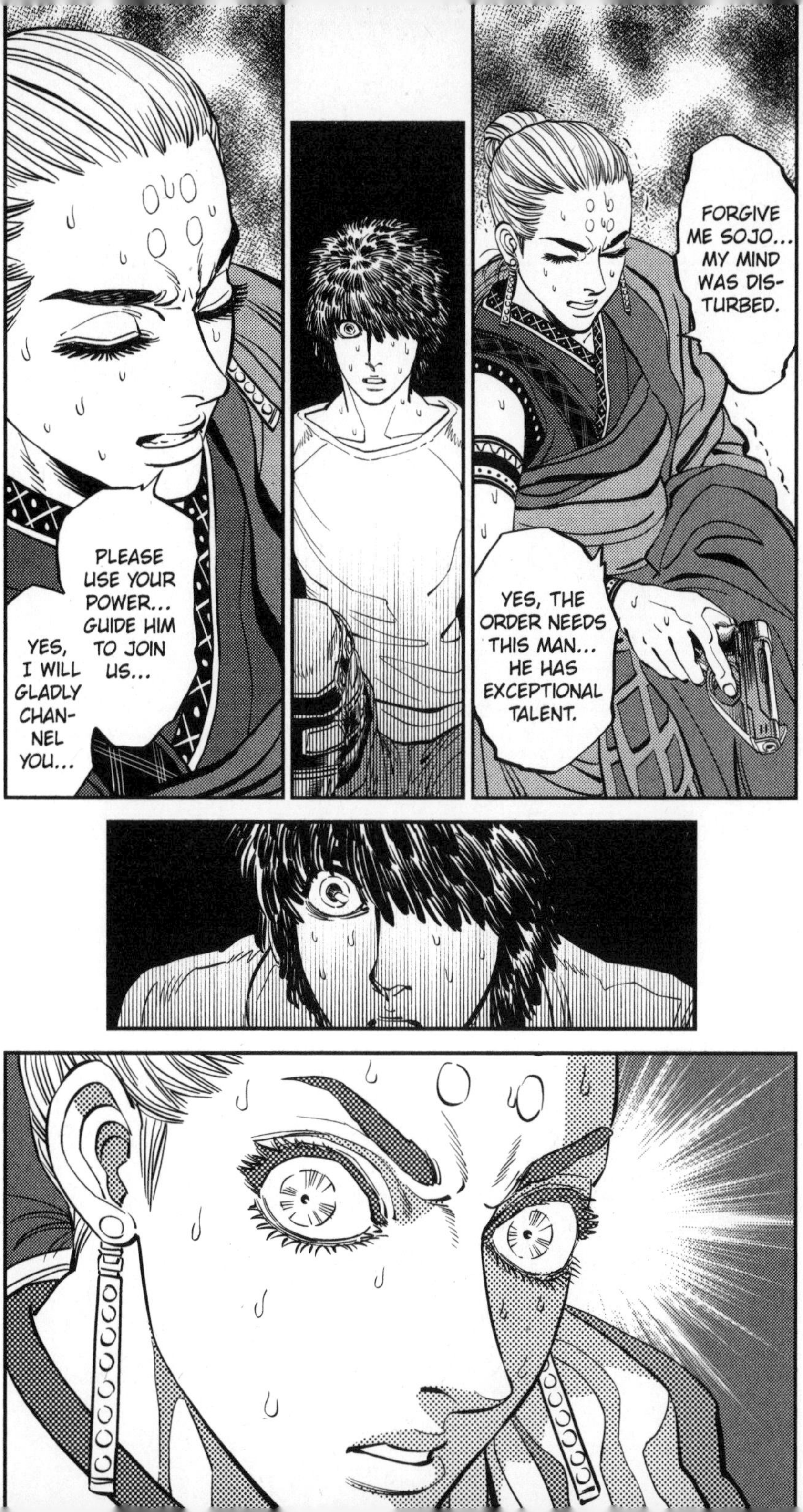
FORGIVE ME SOJO... MY MIND WAS DIS-TURBED.
YES, THE ORDER NEEDS THIS MAN... HE HAS EXCEPTIONAL TALENT.
PLEASE USE YOUR POWER... GUIDE HIM TO JOIN US...
YES, I WILL GLADLY CHAN-NEL YOU...

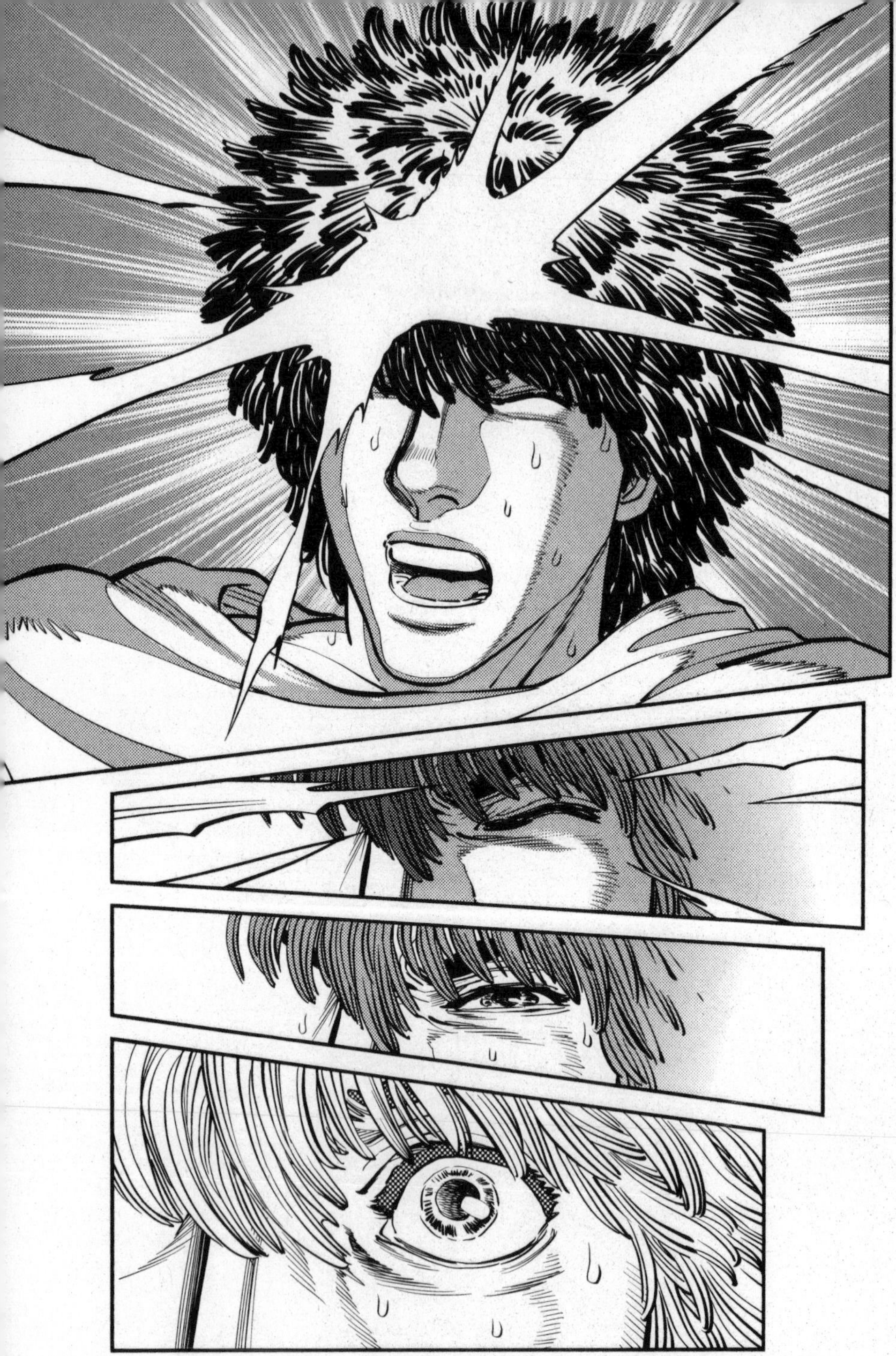

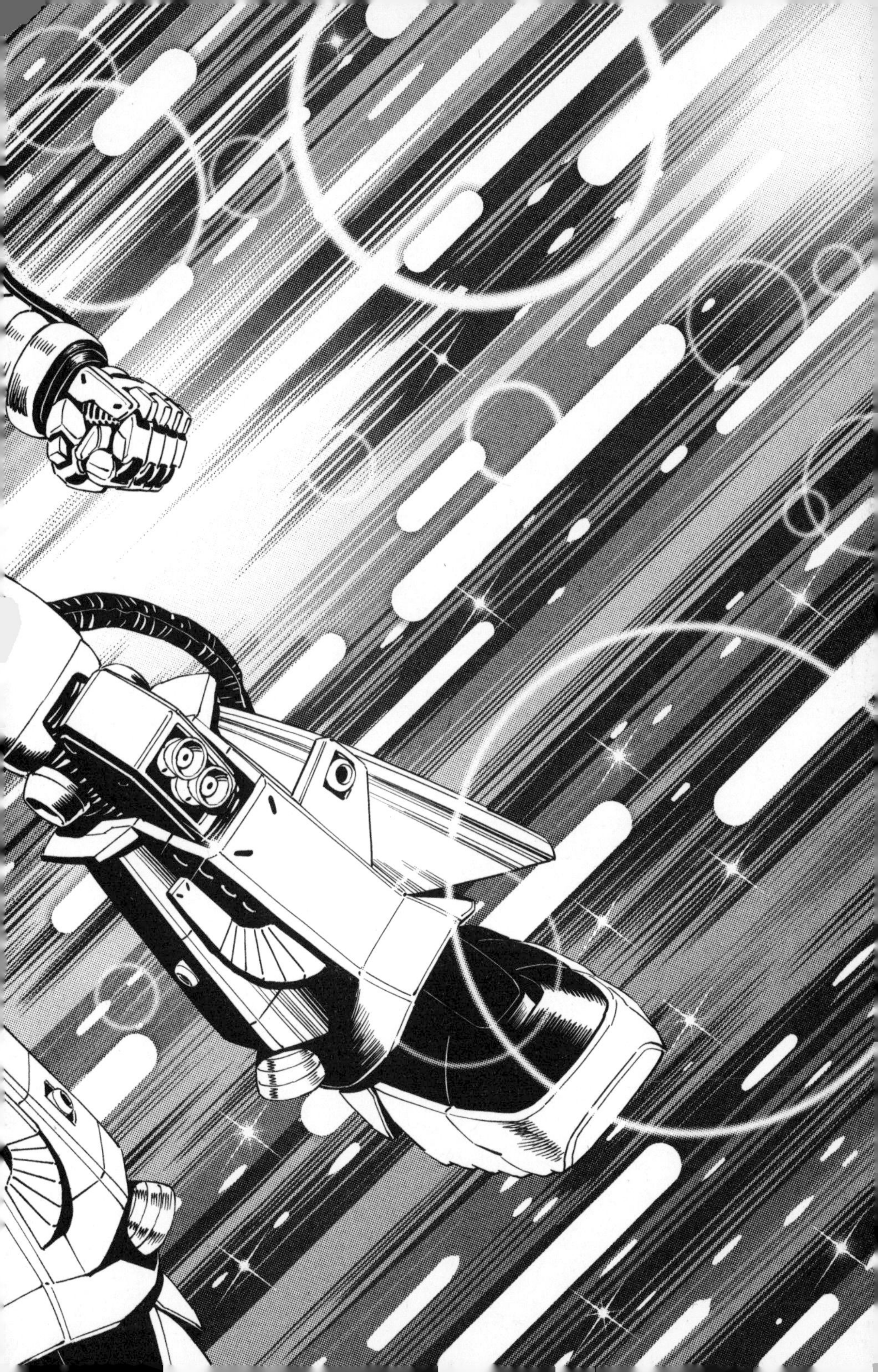

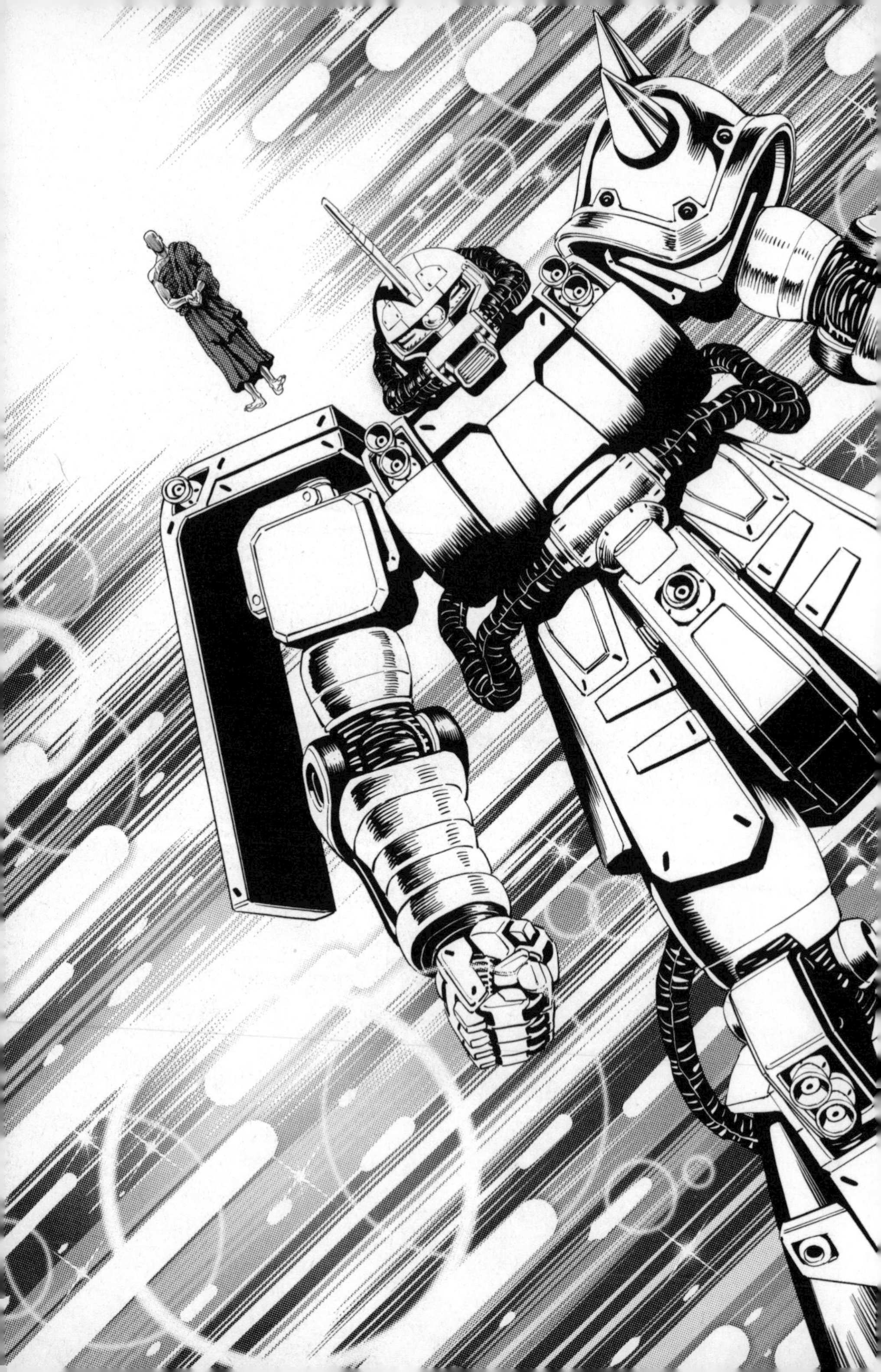

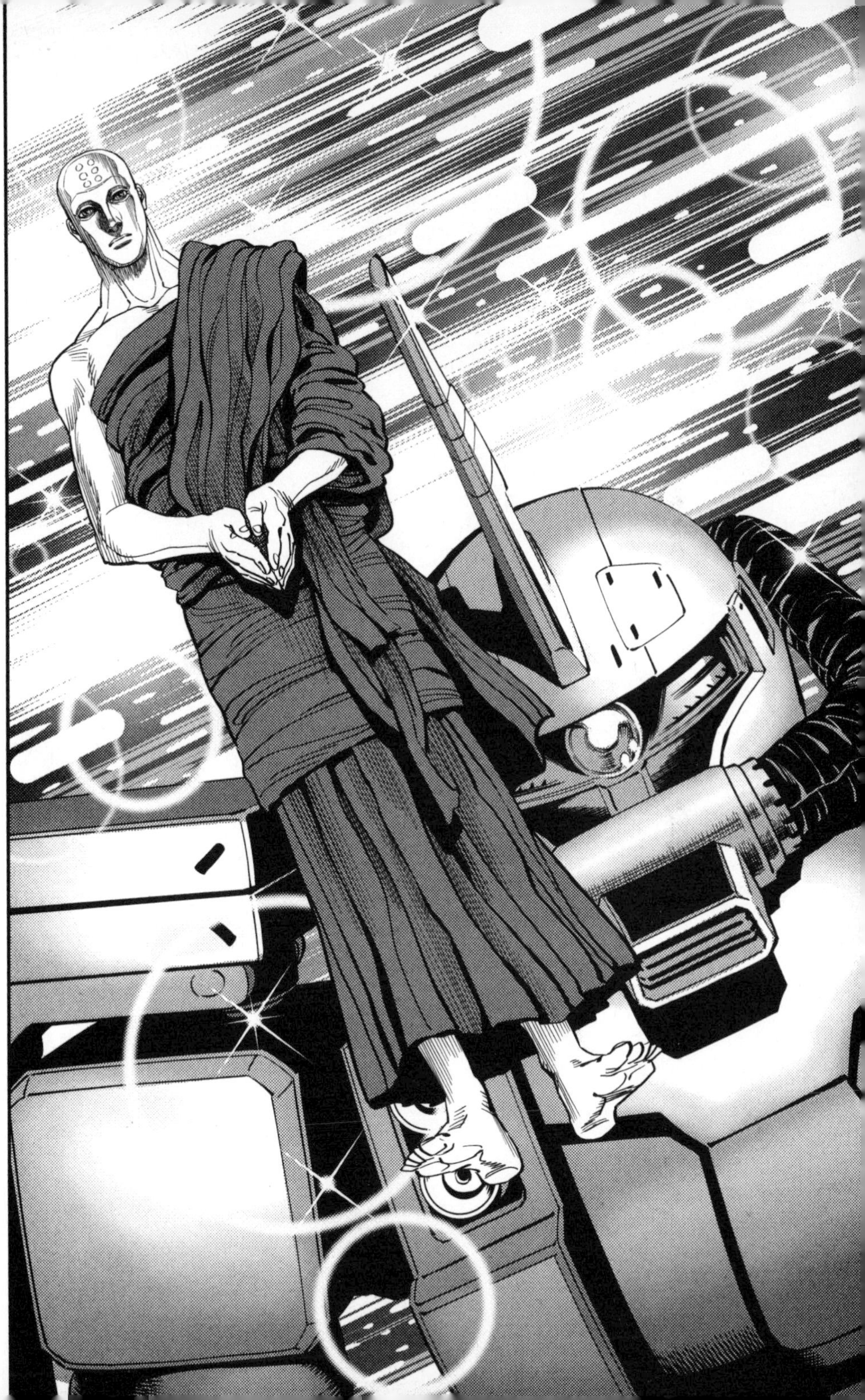

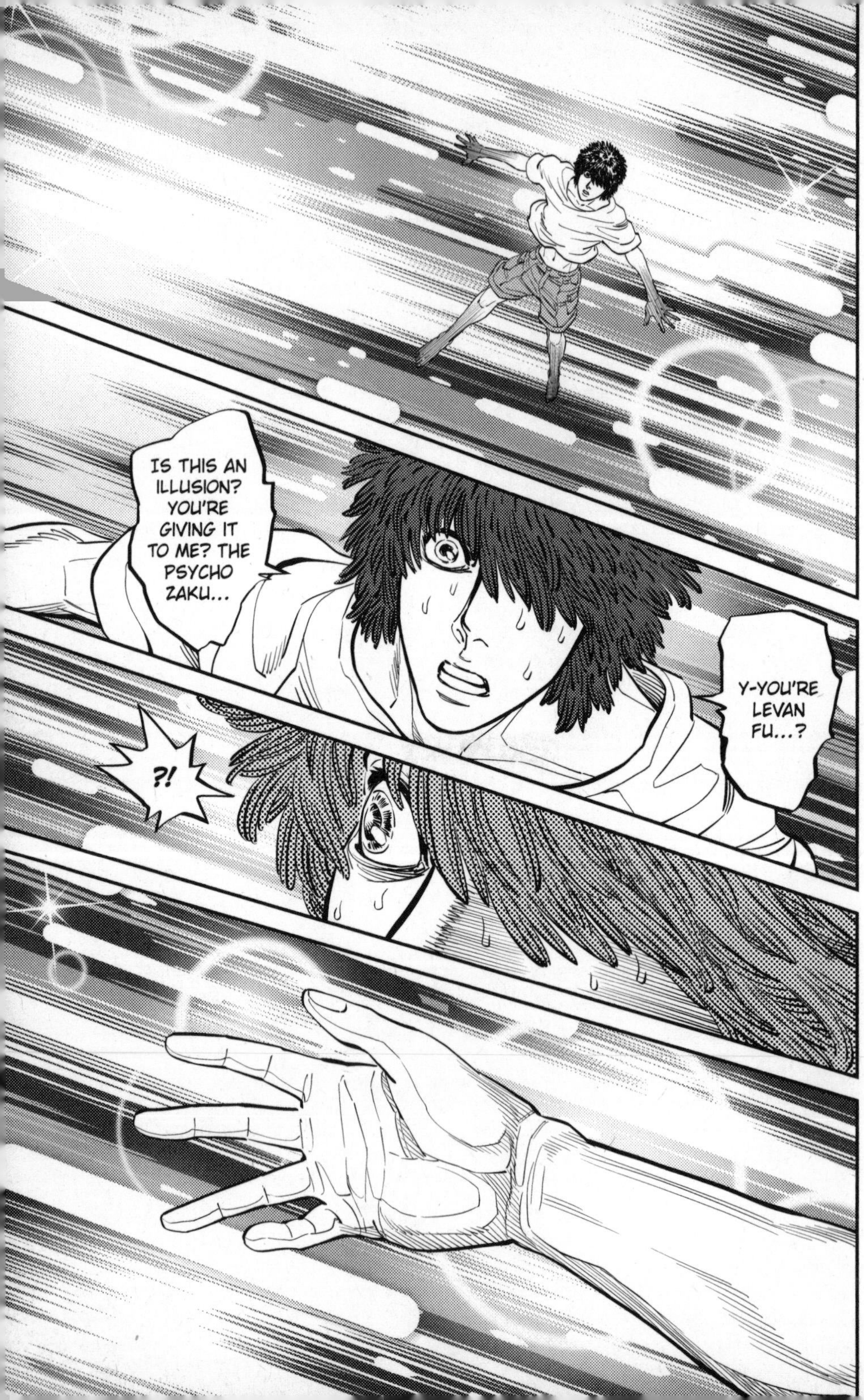
IS THIS AN ILLUSION? YOU'RE GIVING IT TO ME? THE PSYCHO ZAKU...
Y-YOU'RE LEVAN FU...?
?!

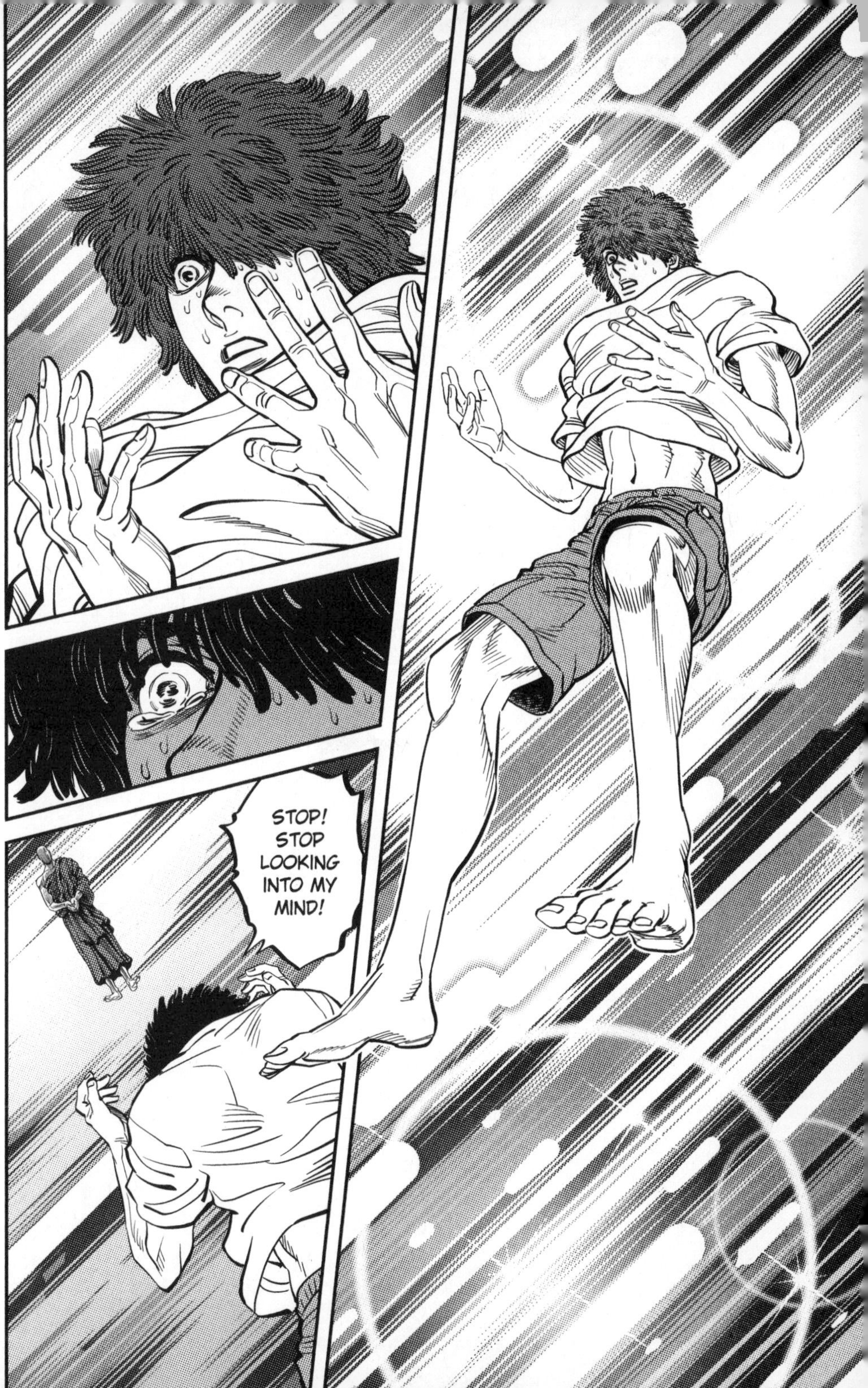
STOP! STOP LOOKING INTO MY MIND!

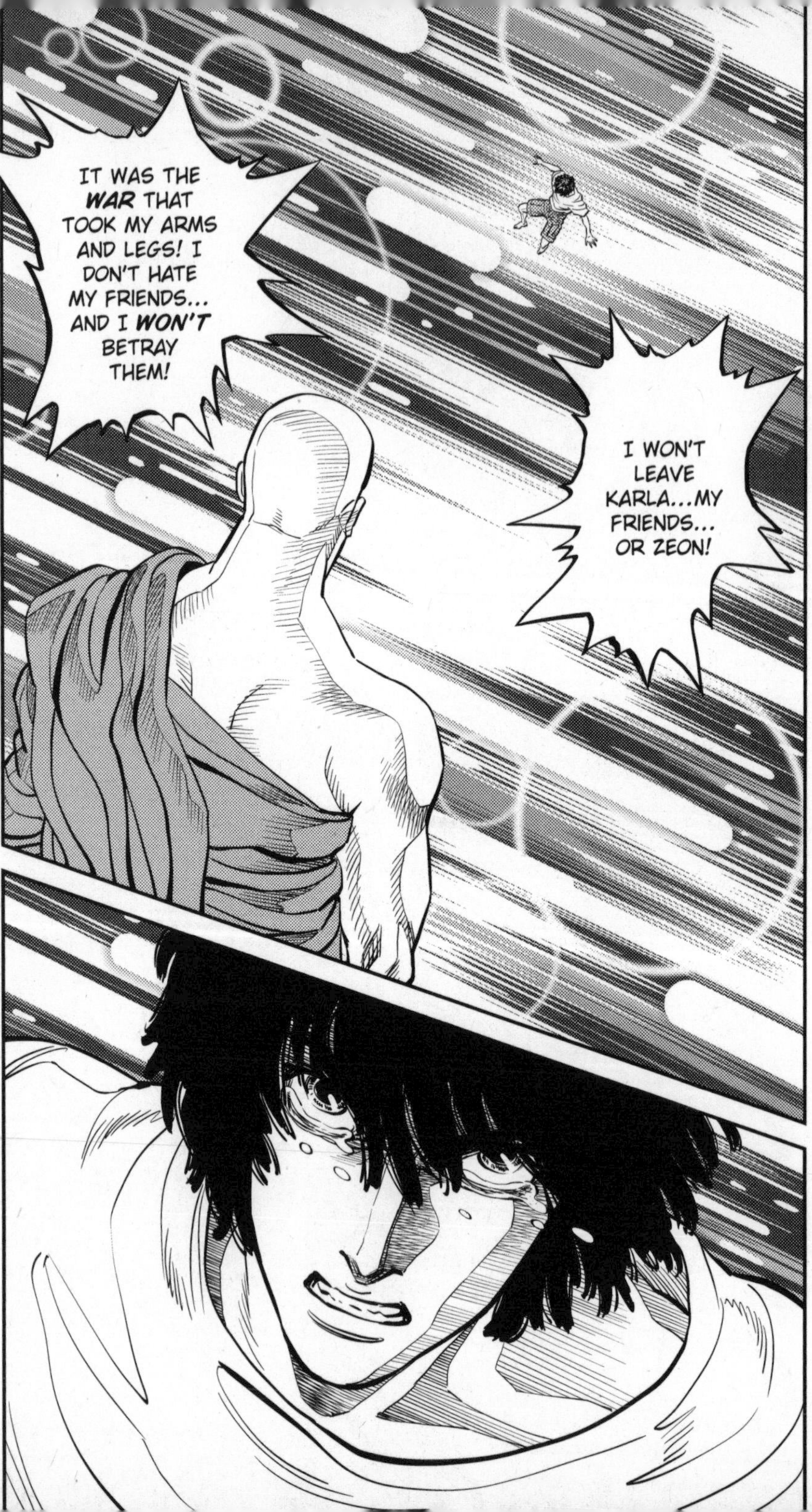
IT WAS THE **WAR** THAT TOOK MY ARMS AND LEGS! I DON'T HATE MY FRIENDS... AND I **WON'T** BETRAY THEM!
I WON'T LEAVE KARLA...MY FRIENDS... OR ZEON!

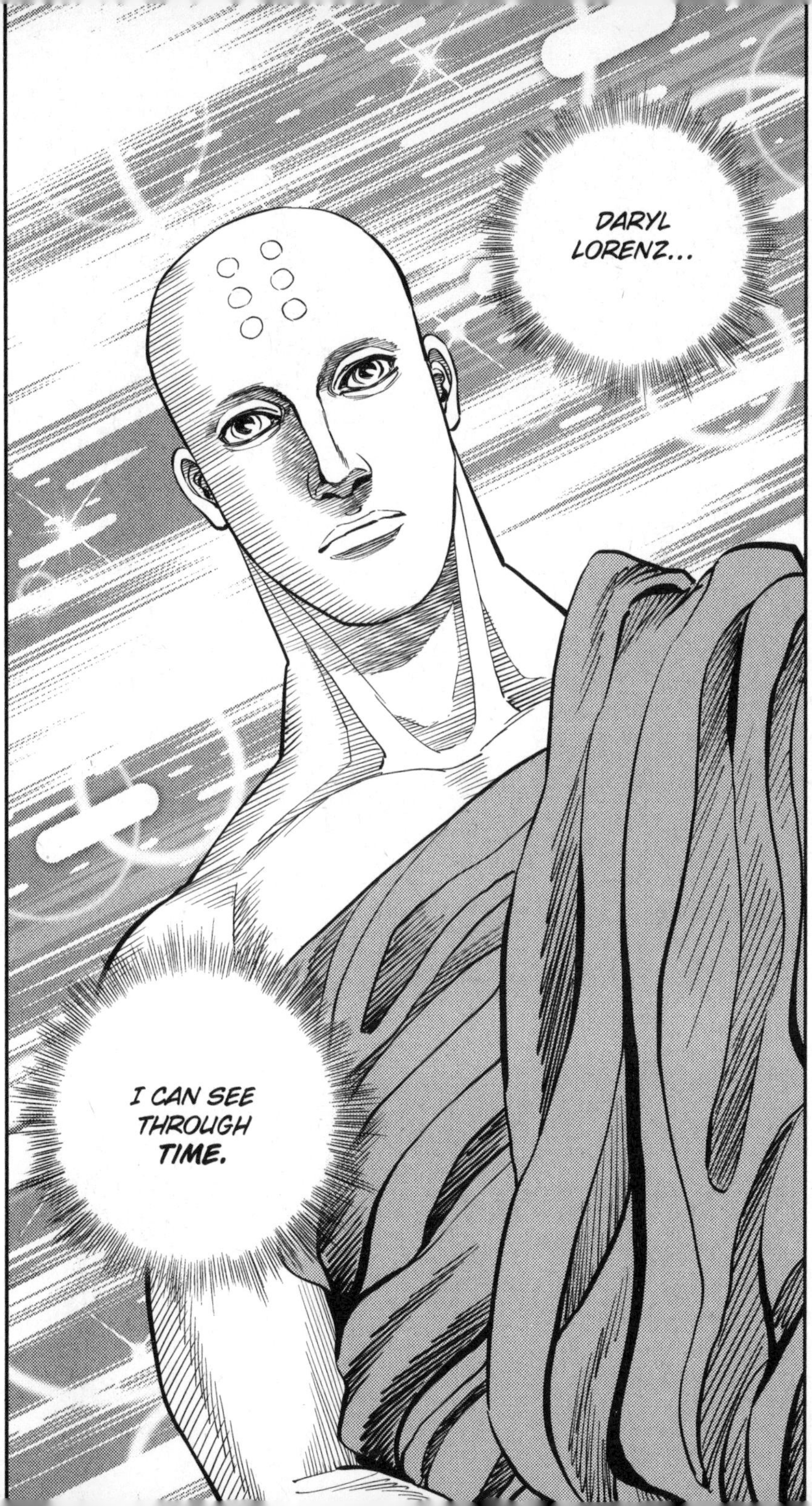
DARYL LORENZ...
I CAN SEE THROUGH TIME.

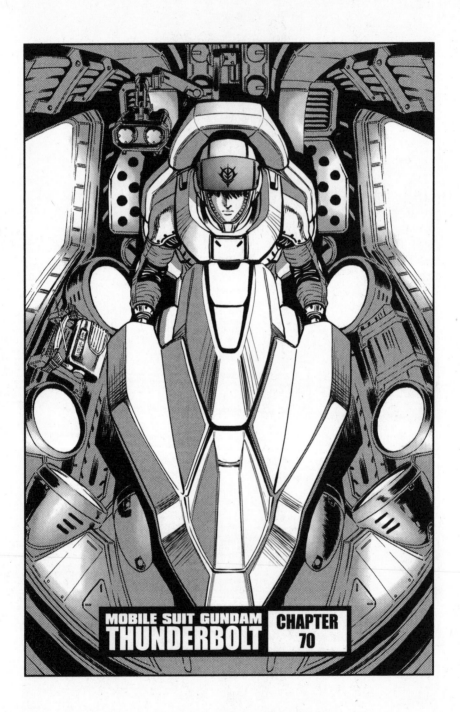

MOBILE SUIT GUNDAM
THUNDERBOLT

CHAPTER
70

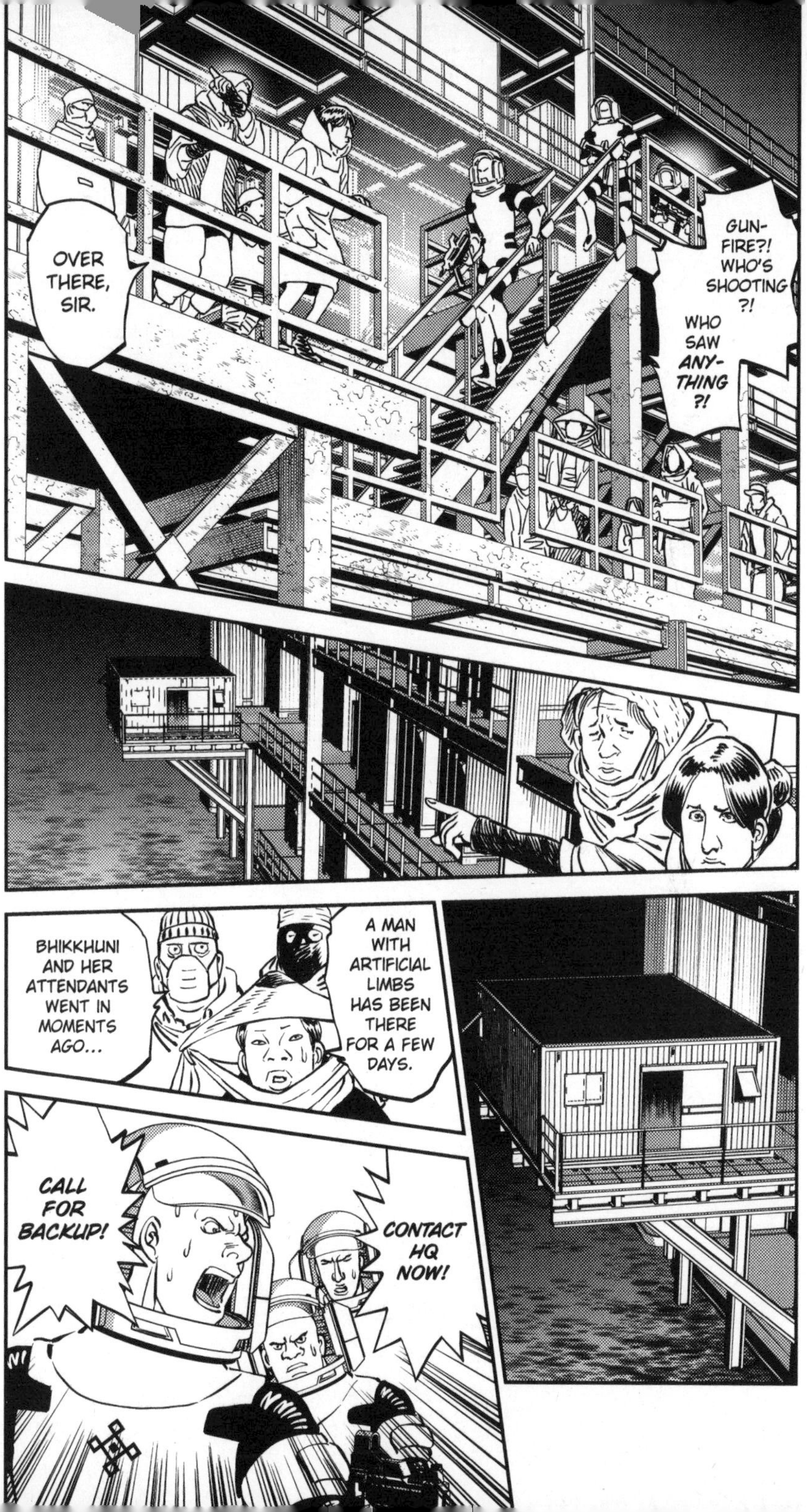
GUN-FIRE?! WHO'S SHOOTING?!
WHO SAW ANY-THING?!
OVER THERE, SIR.
A MAN WITH ARTIFICIAL LIMBS HAS BEEN THERE FOR A FEW DAYS.
BHIKKHUNI AND HER ATTENDANTS WENT IN MOMENTS AGO...
CONTACT HQ NOW!
CALL FOR BACKUP!

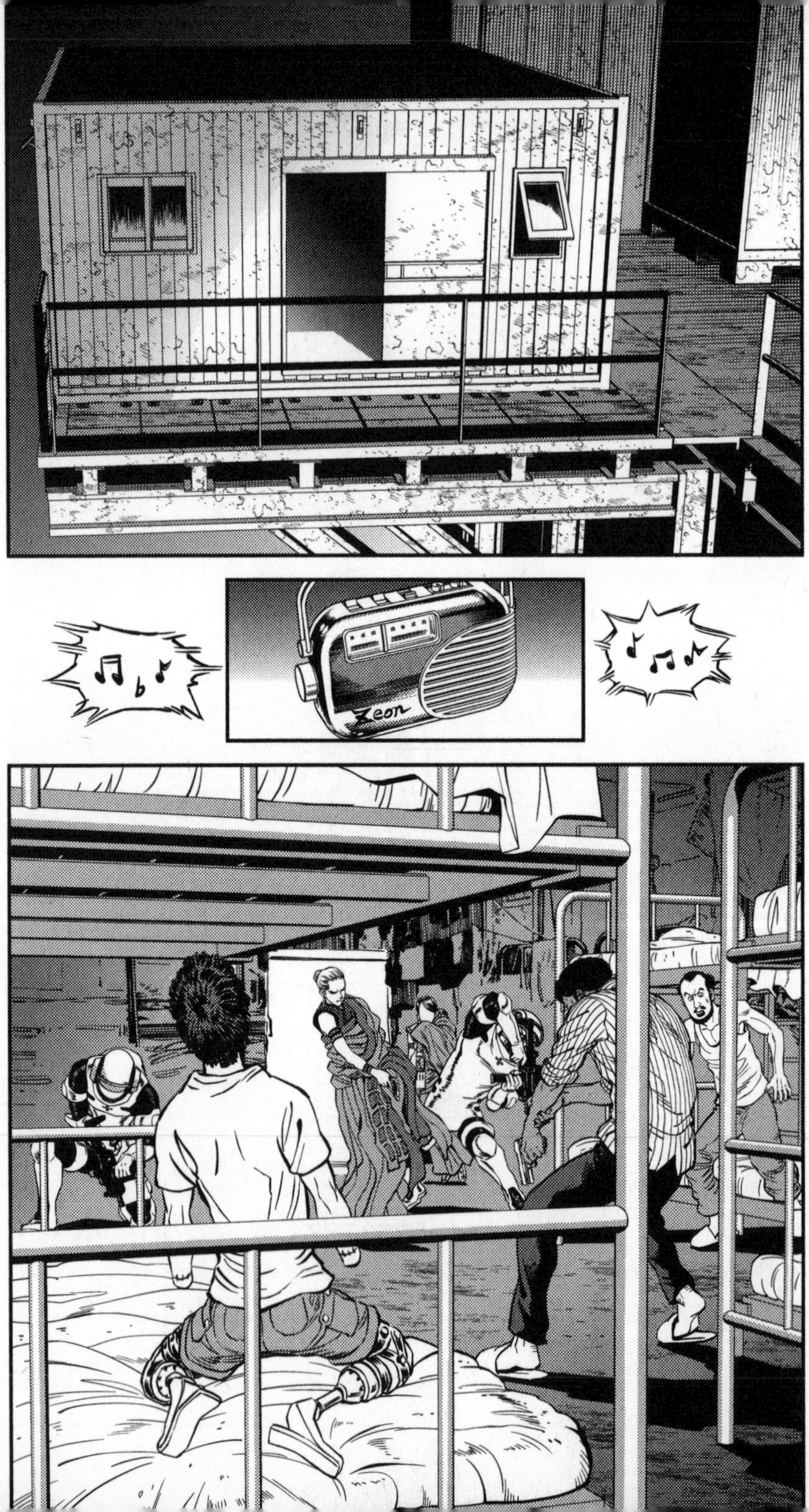
Zeon

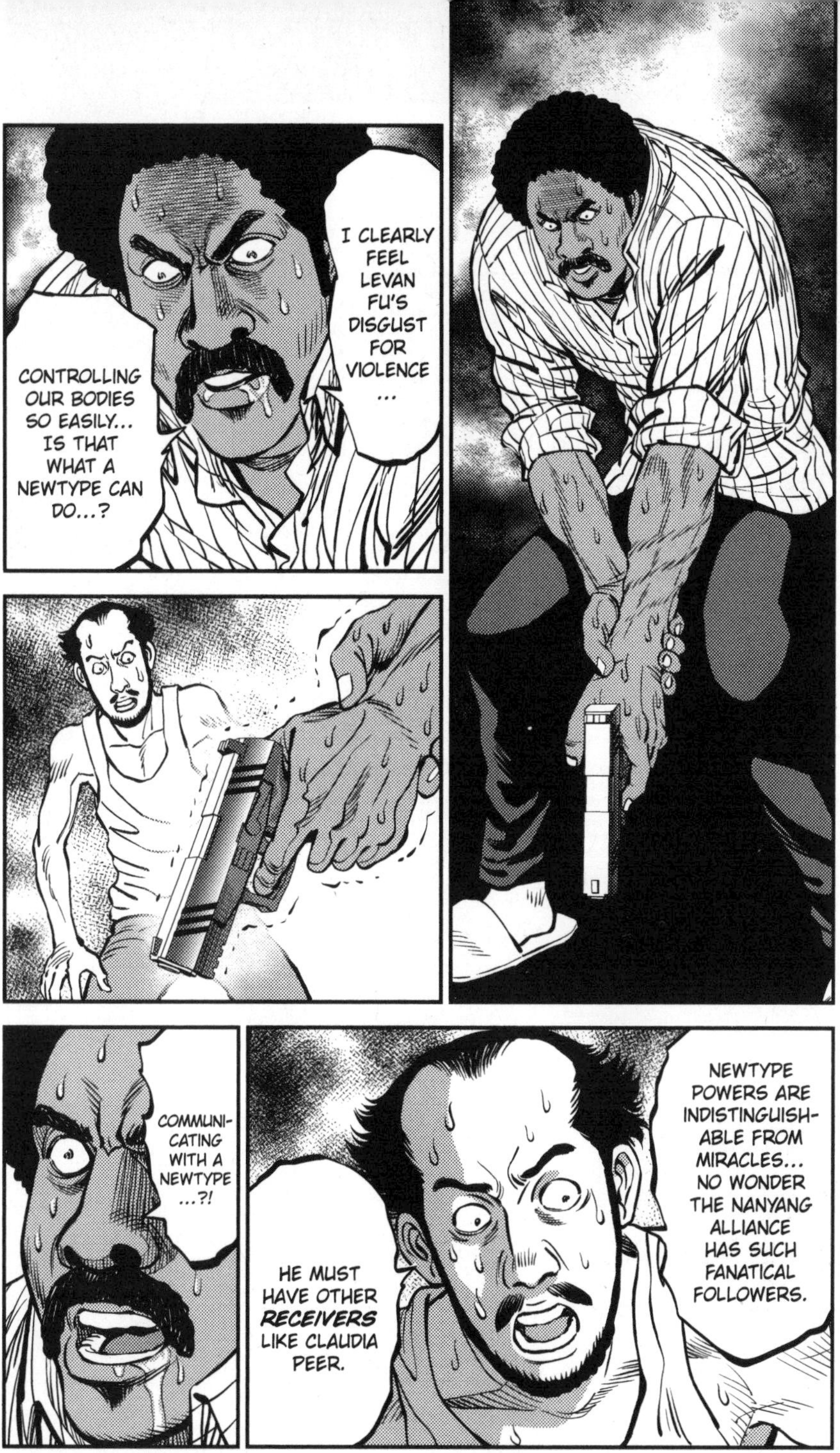

I CLEARLY FEEL LEVAN FU'S DISGUST FOR VIOLENCE ...
CONTROLLING OUR BODIES SO EASILY... IS THAT WHAT A NEWTYPE CAN DO...?
NEWTYPE POWERS ARE INDISTINGUISHABLE FROM MIRACLES... NO WONDER THE NANYANG ALLIANCE HAS SUCH FANATICAL FOLLOWERS.
HE MUST HAVE OTHER ***RECEIVERS*** LIKE CLAUDIA PEER.
COMMUNICATING WITH A NEWTYPE ...?!

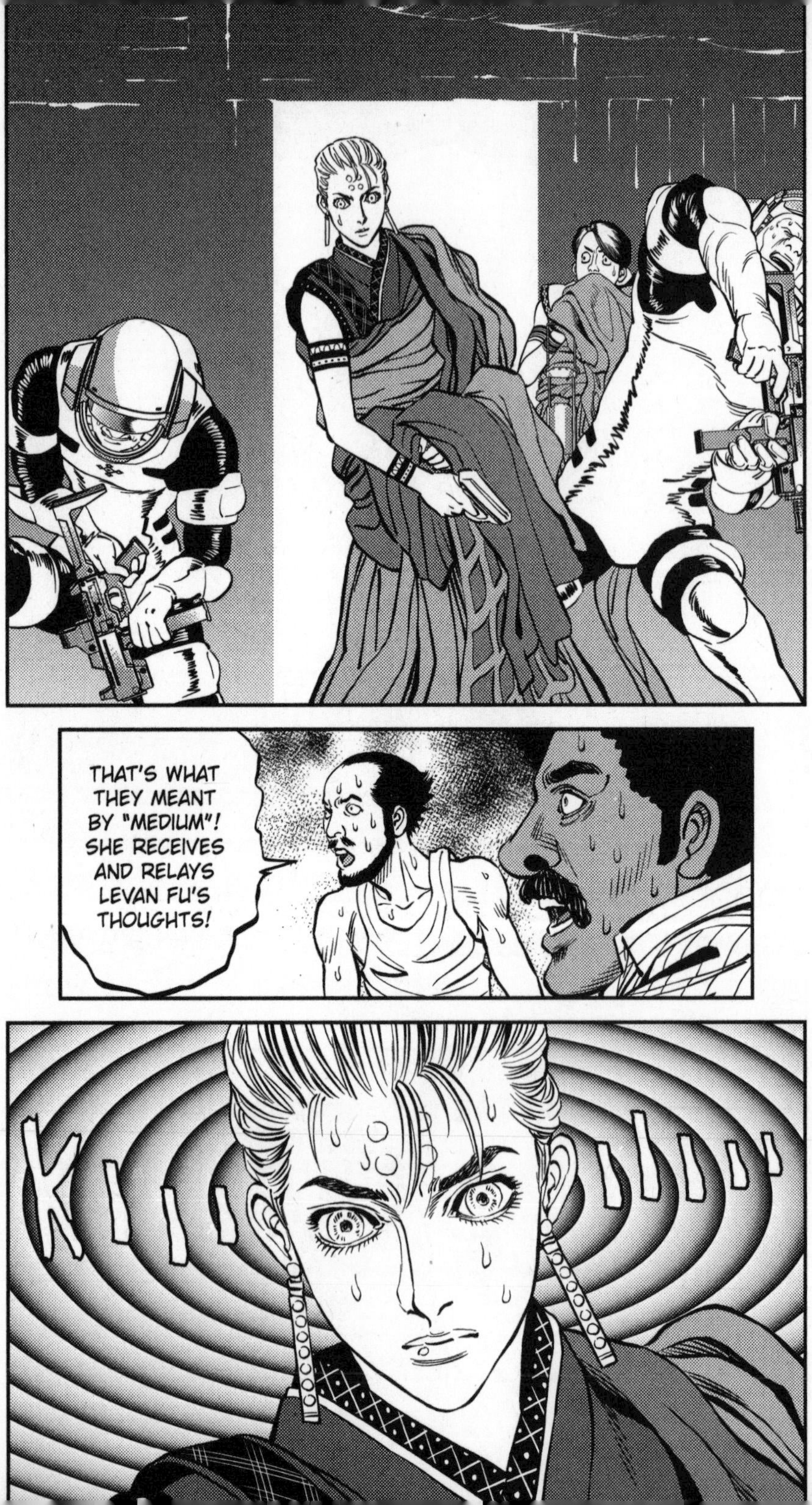
THAT'S WHAT THEY MEANT BY "MEDIUM"! SHE RECEIVES AND RELAYS LEVAN FU'S THOUGHTS!
KIIIIIIIIII

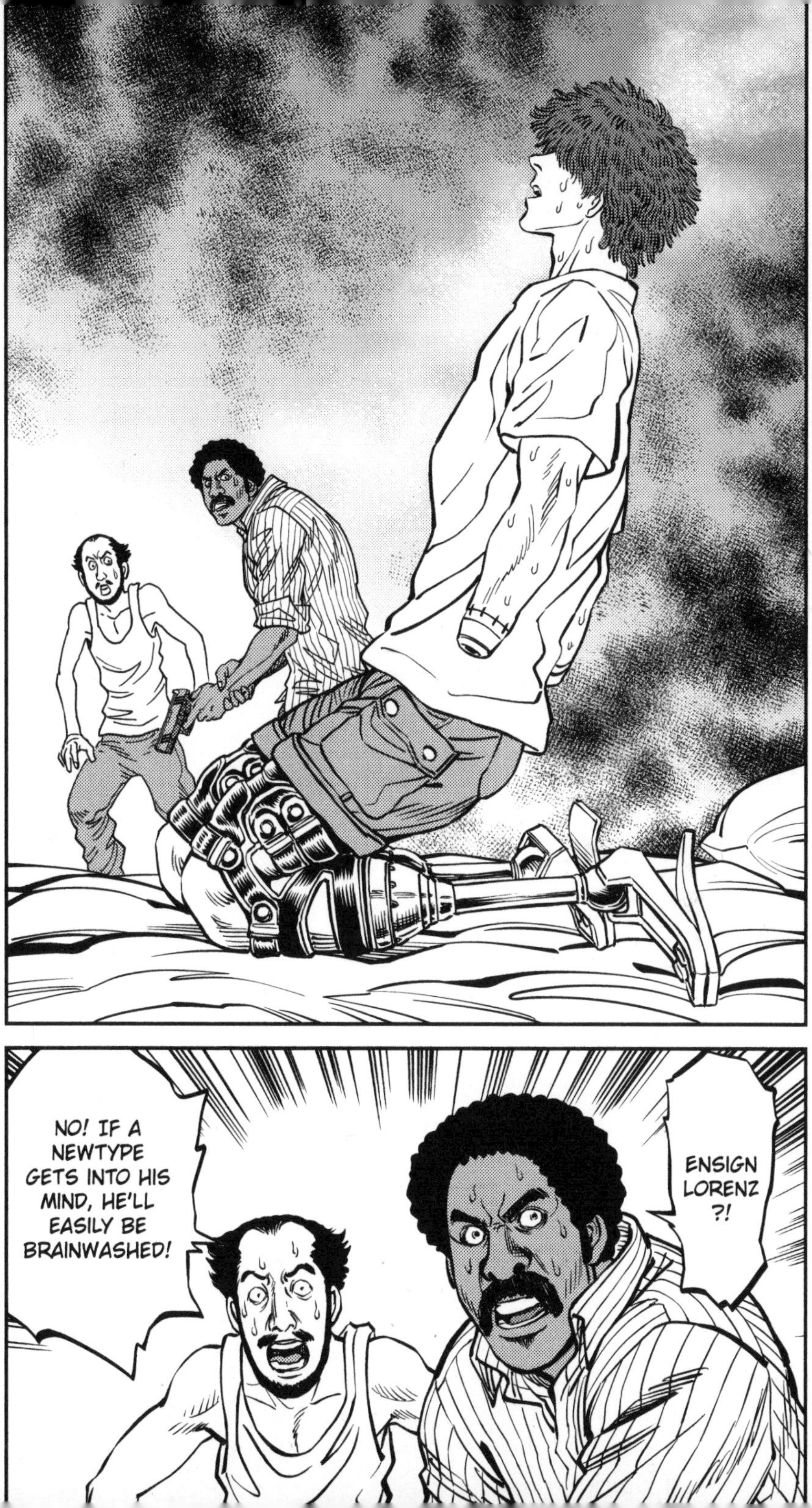
ENSIGN LORENZ ?!
NO! IF A NEWTYPE GETS INTO HIS MIND, HE'LL EASILY BE BRAINWASHED!

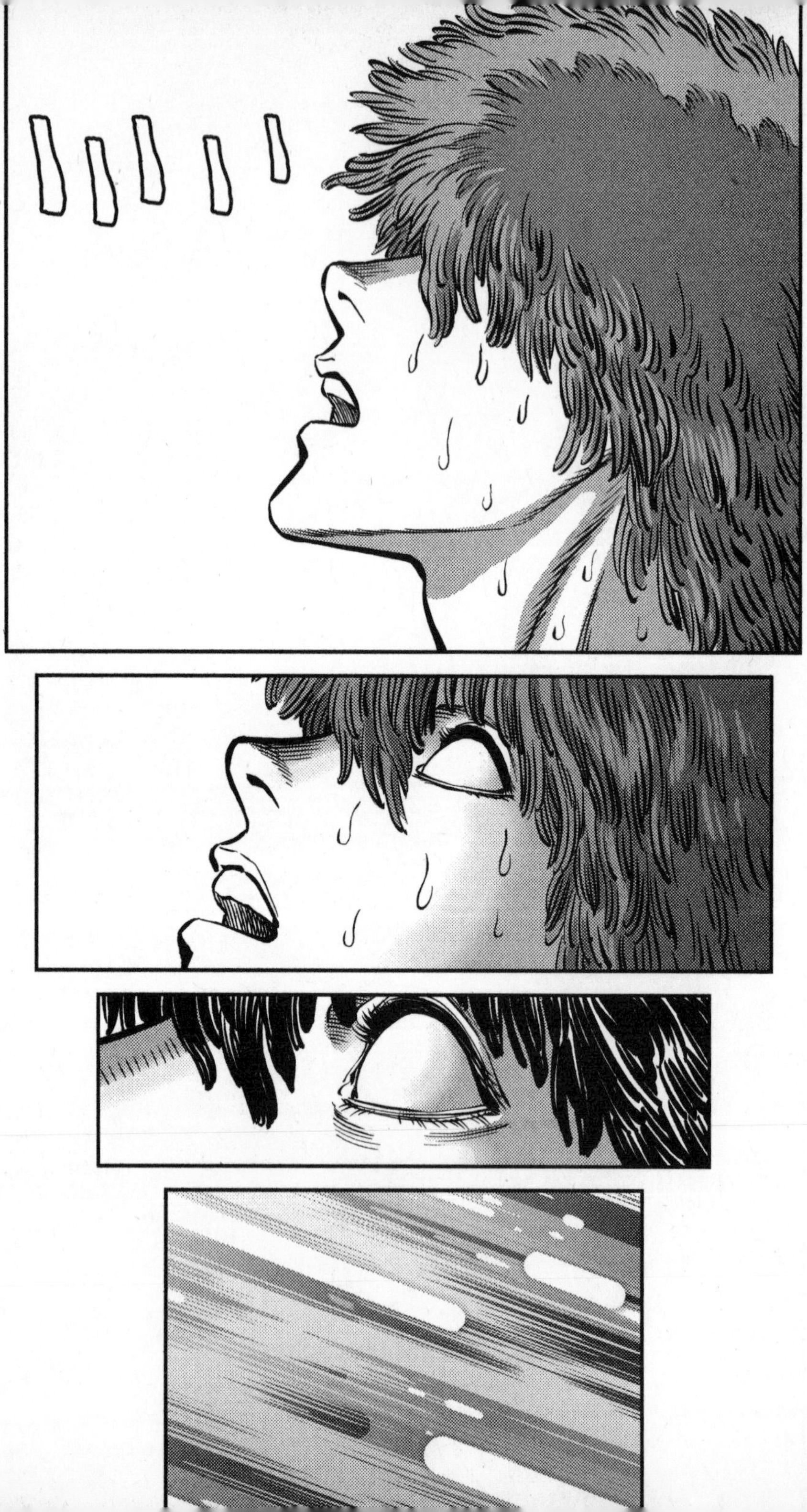

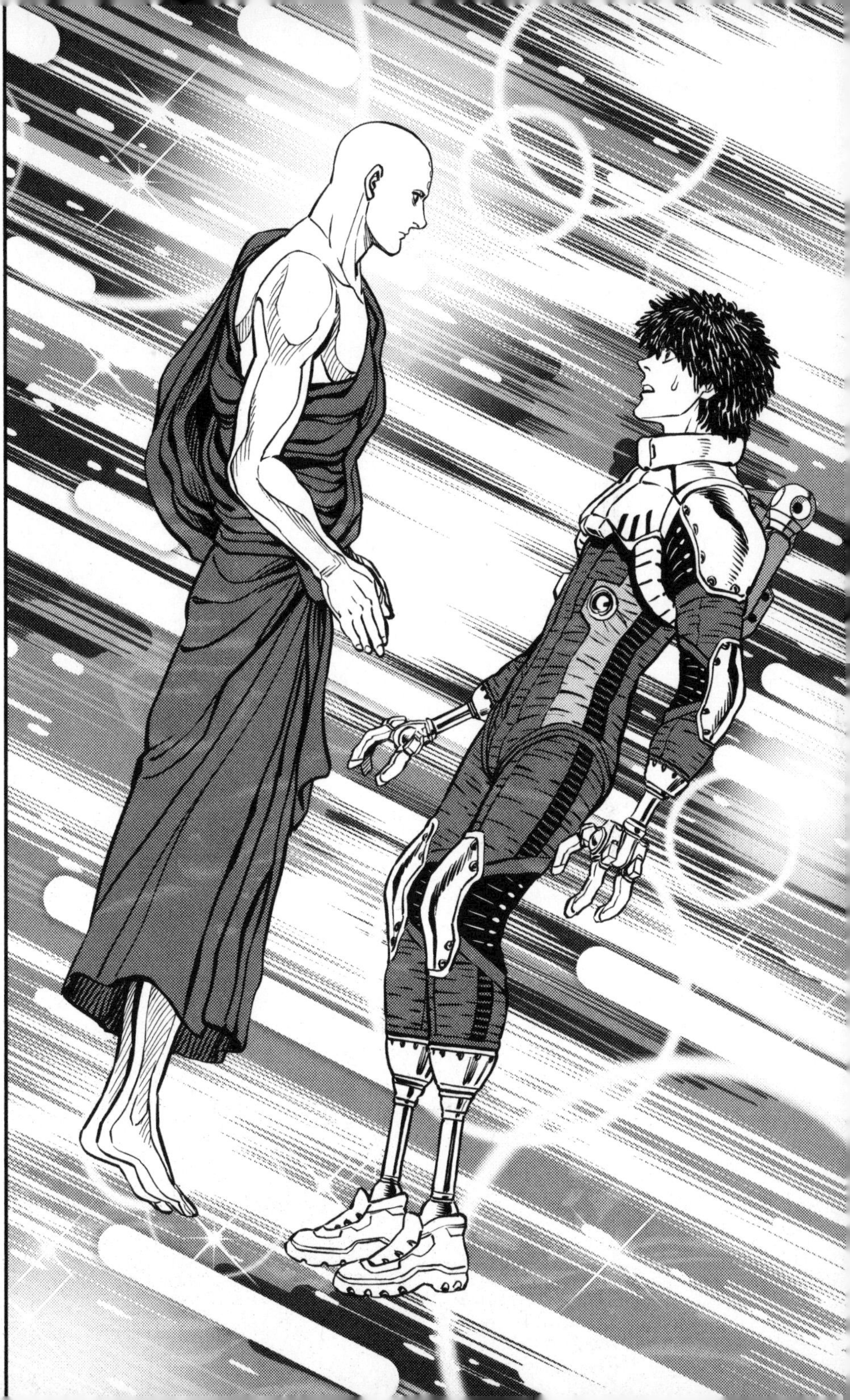

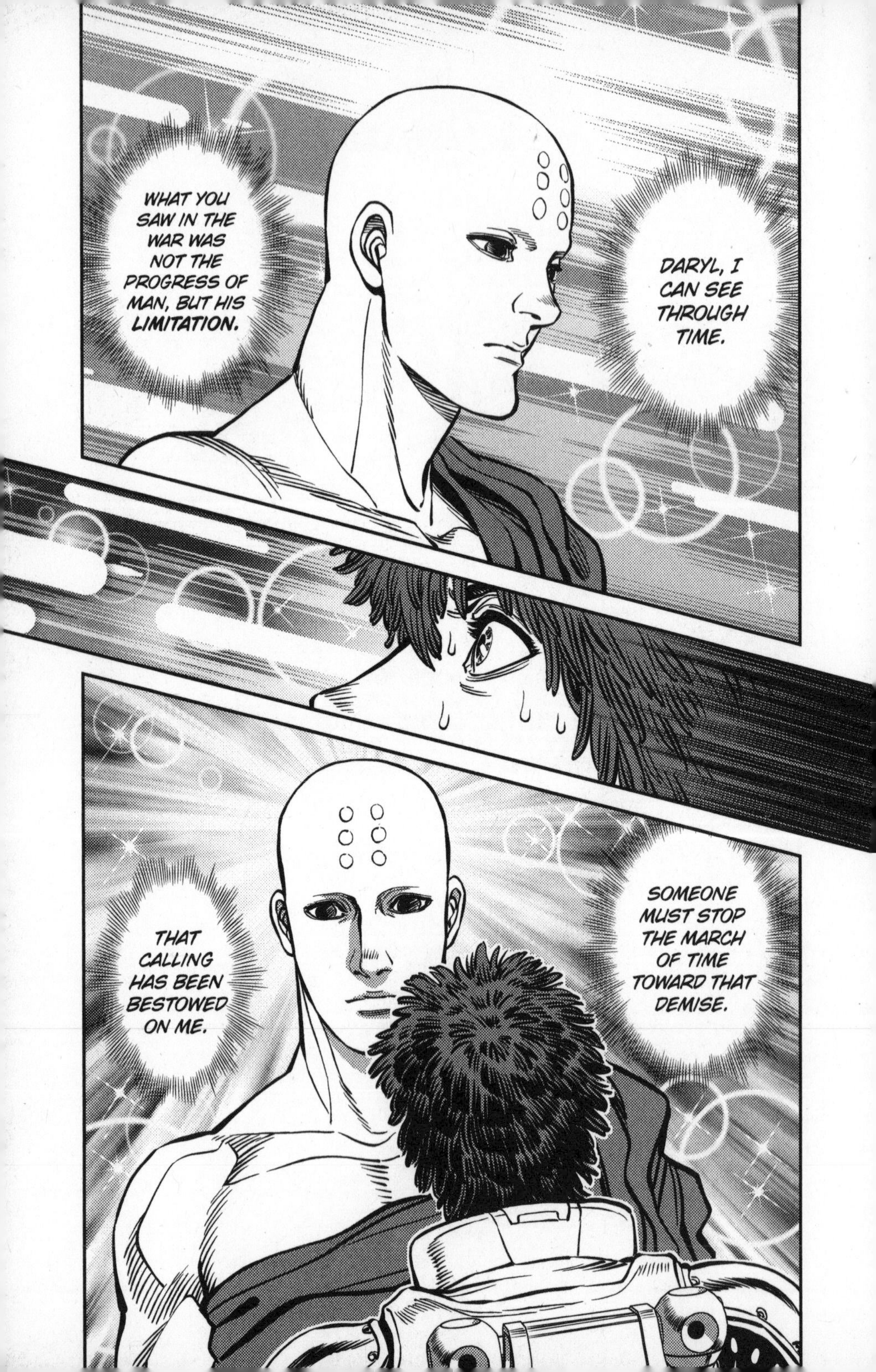
DARYL, I CAN SEE THROUGH TIME.
WHAT YOU SAW IN THE WAR WAS NOT THE PROGRESS OF MAN, BUT HIS **LIMITATION.**
SOMEONE MUST STOP THE MARCH OF TIME TOWARD THAT DEMISE.
THAT CALLING HAS BEEN BESTOWED ON ME.

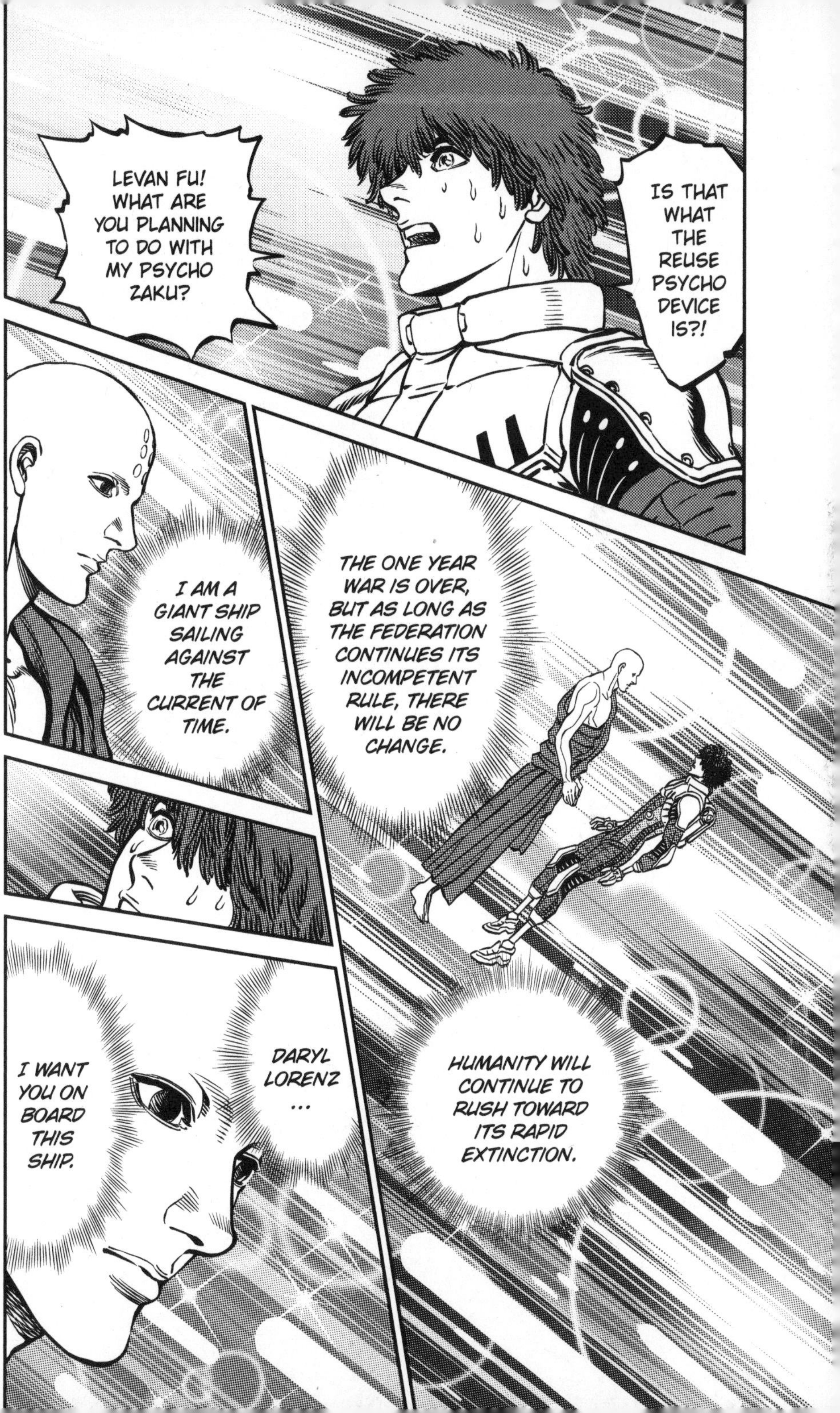
IS THAT WHAT THE REUSE PSYCHO DEVICE IS?!
LEVAN FU! WHAT ARE YOU PLANNING TO DO WITH MY PSYCHO ZAKU?
THE ONE YEAR WAR IS OVER, BUT AS LONG AS THE FEDERATION CONTINUES ITS INCOMPETENT RULE, THERE WILL BE NO CHANGE.
HUMANITY WILL CONTINUE TO RUSH TOWARD ITS RAPID EXTINCTION.
I AM A GIANT SHIP SAILING AGAINST THE CURRENT OF TIME.
DARYL LORENZ ...
I WANT YOU ON BOARD THIS SHIP.

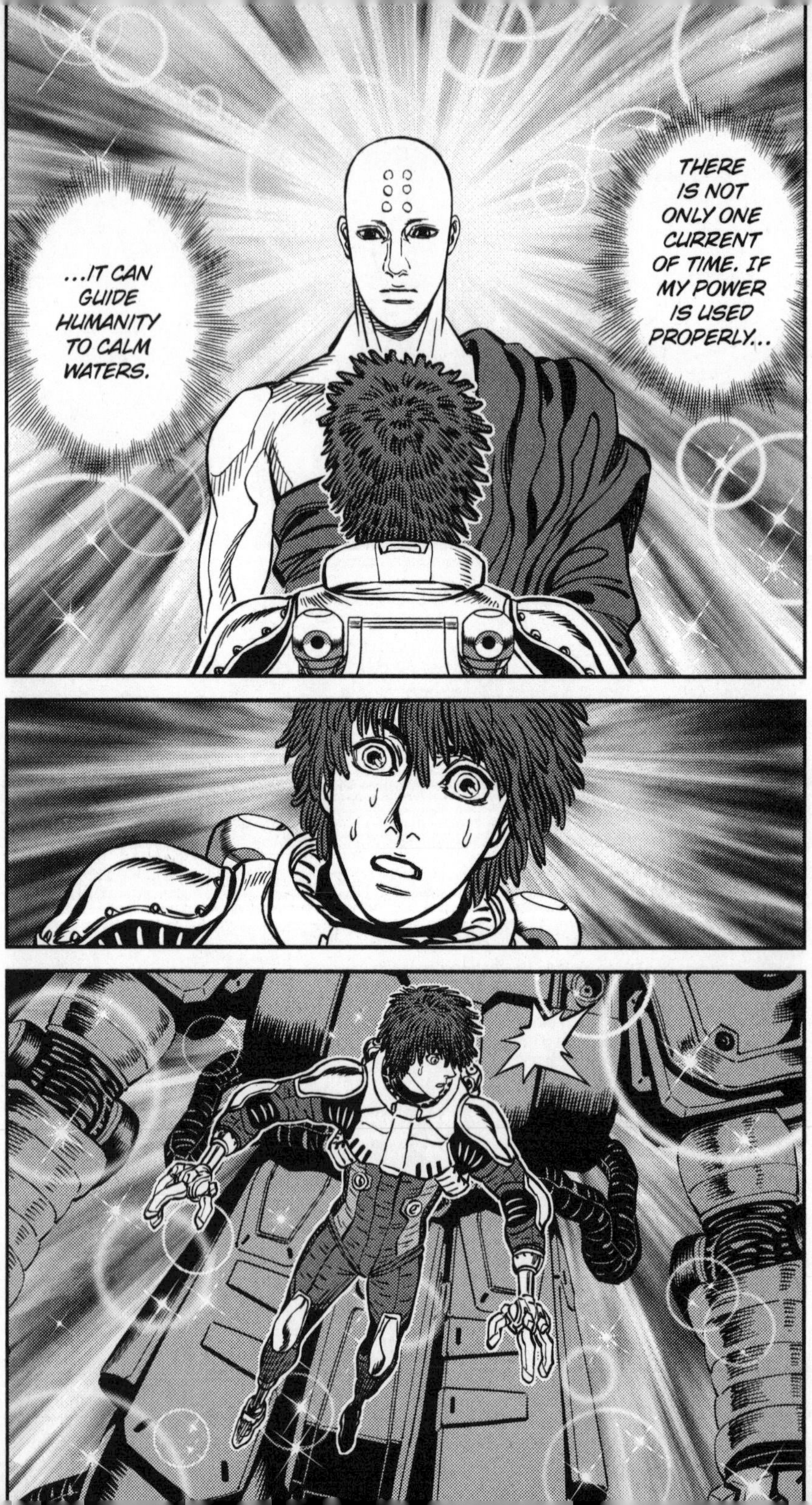
THERE IS NOT ONLY ONE CURRENT OF TIME. IF MY POWER IS USED PROPERLY...
...IT CAN GUIDE HUMANITY TO CALM WATERS.

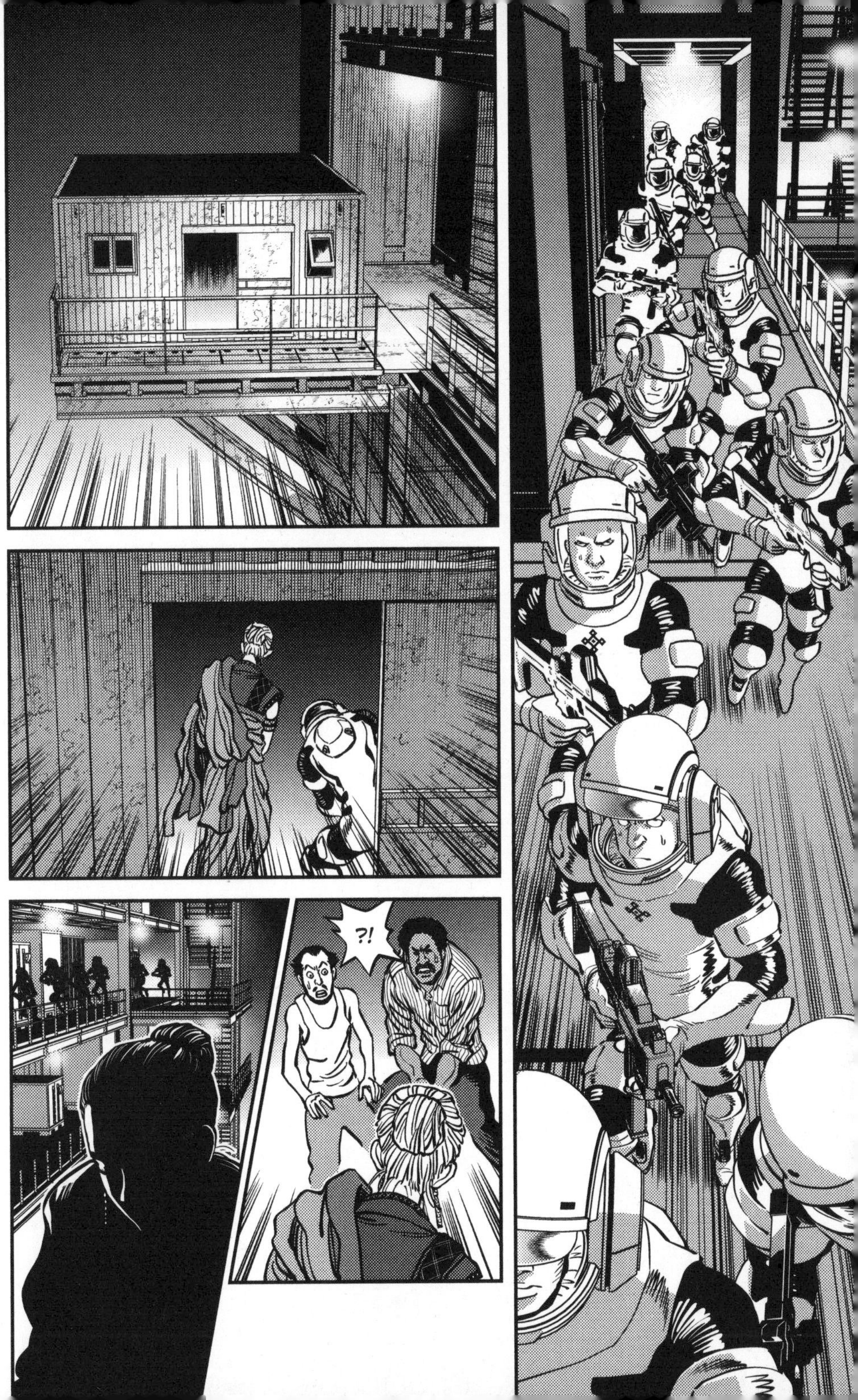
?!

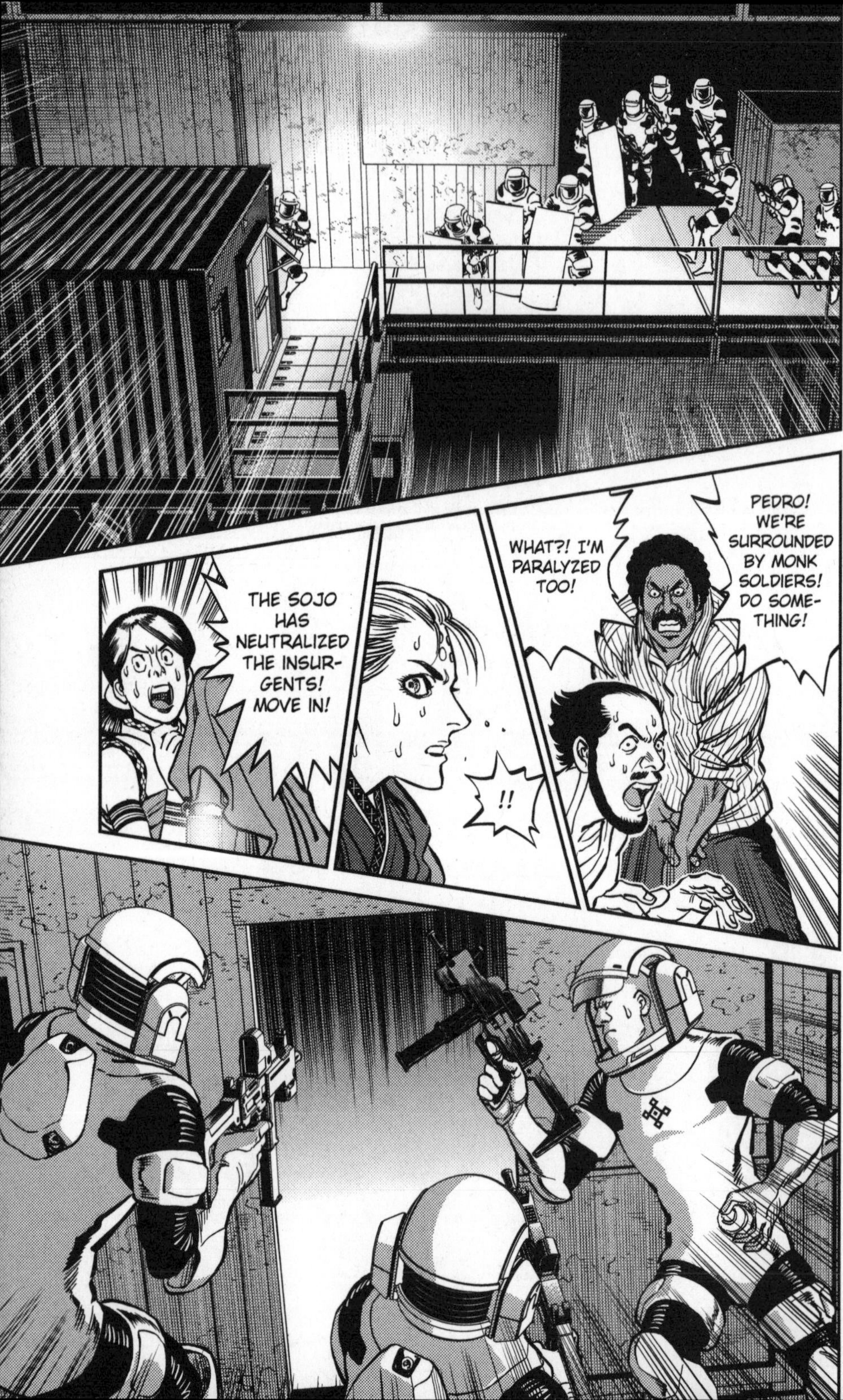
PEDRO! WE'RE SURROUNDED BY MONK SOLDIERS! DO SOME-THING!
WHAT?! I'M PARALYZED TOO!
!!
THE SOJO HAS NEUTRALIZED THE INSUR-GENTS! MOVE IN!

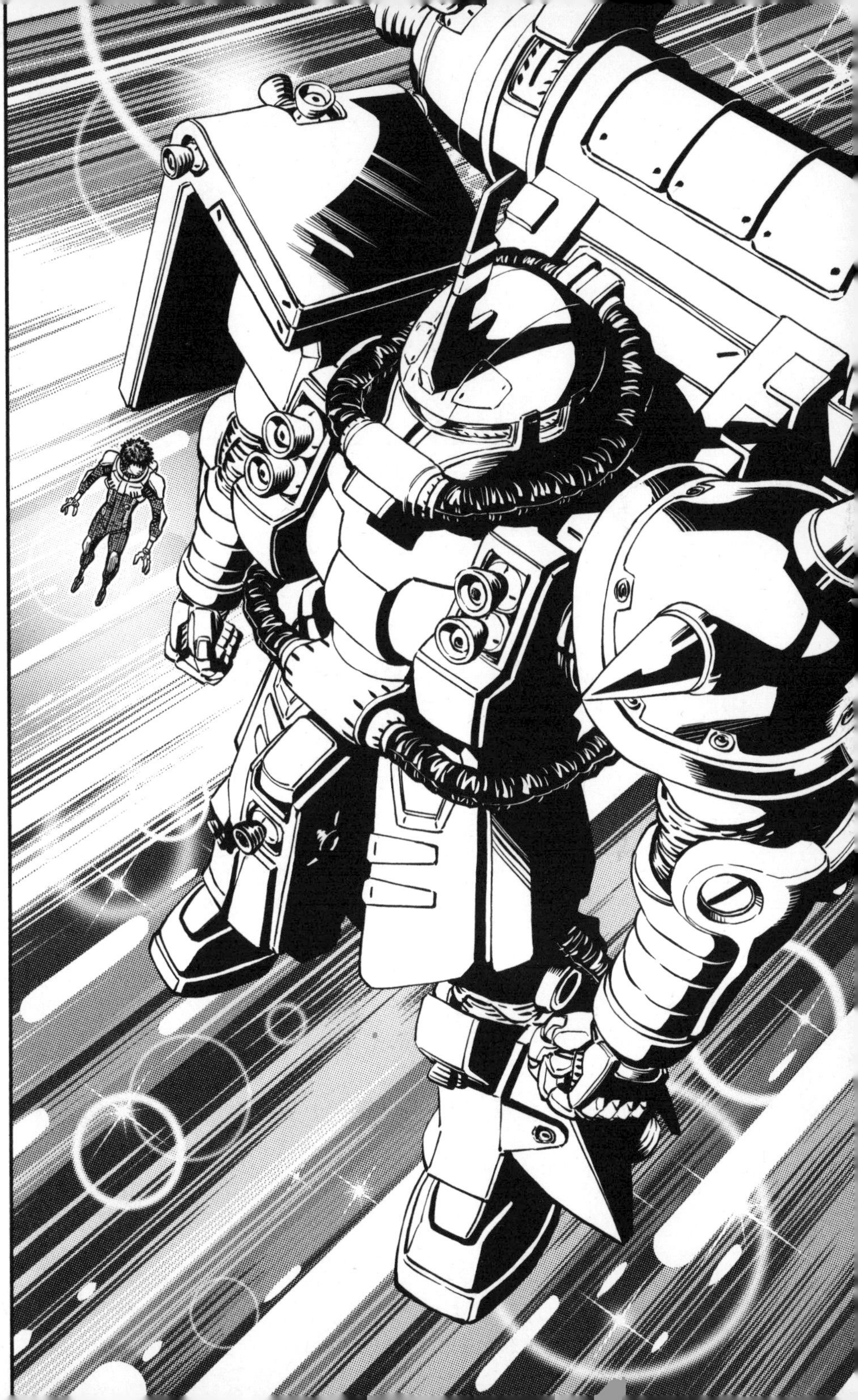

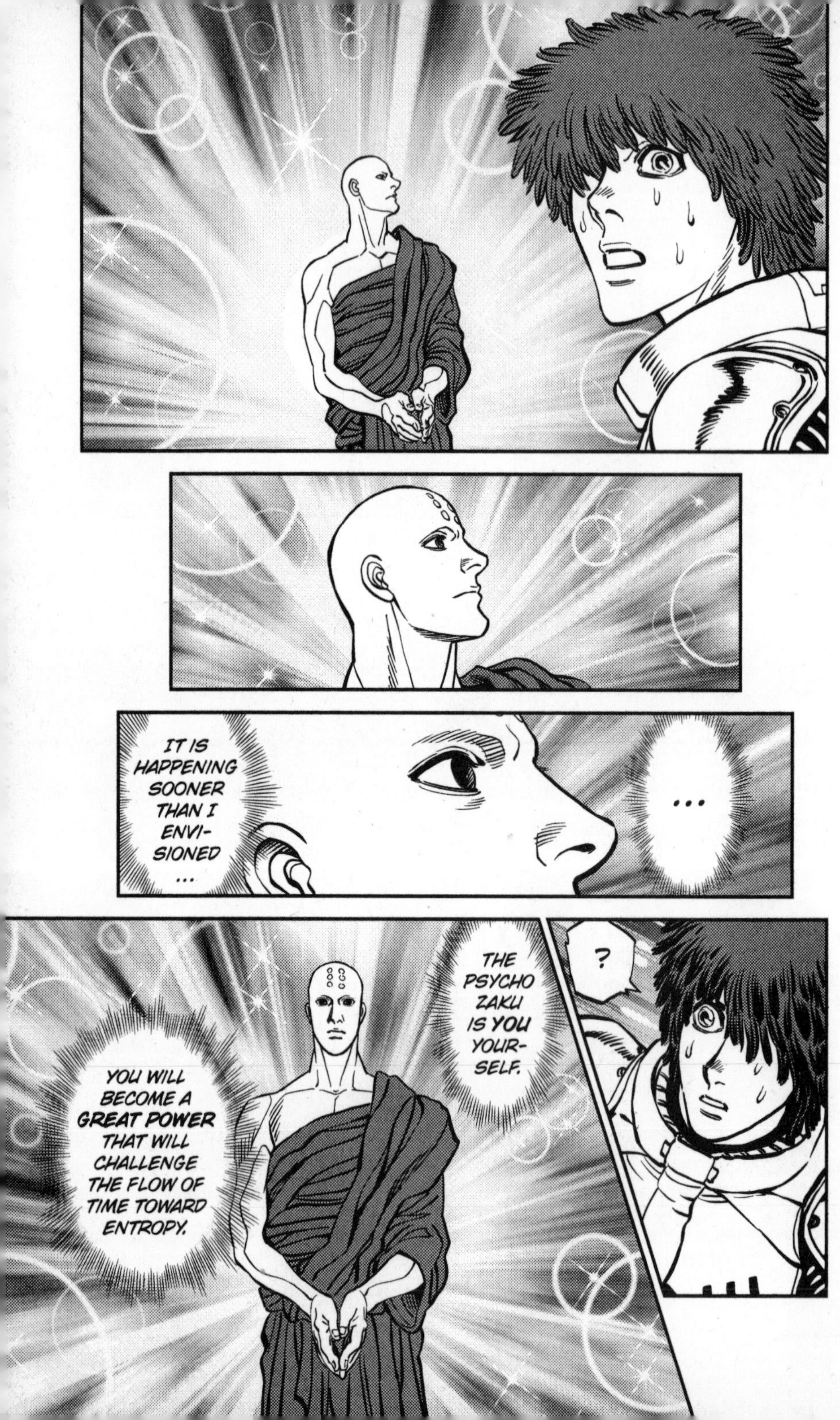
...
IT IS HAPPENING SOONER THAN I ENVI-SIONED ...
?
THE PSYCHO ZAKU IS YOU YOUR-SELF.
YOU WILL BECOME A **GREAT POWER** THAT WILL CHALLENGE THE FLOW OF TIME TOWARD ENTROPY.

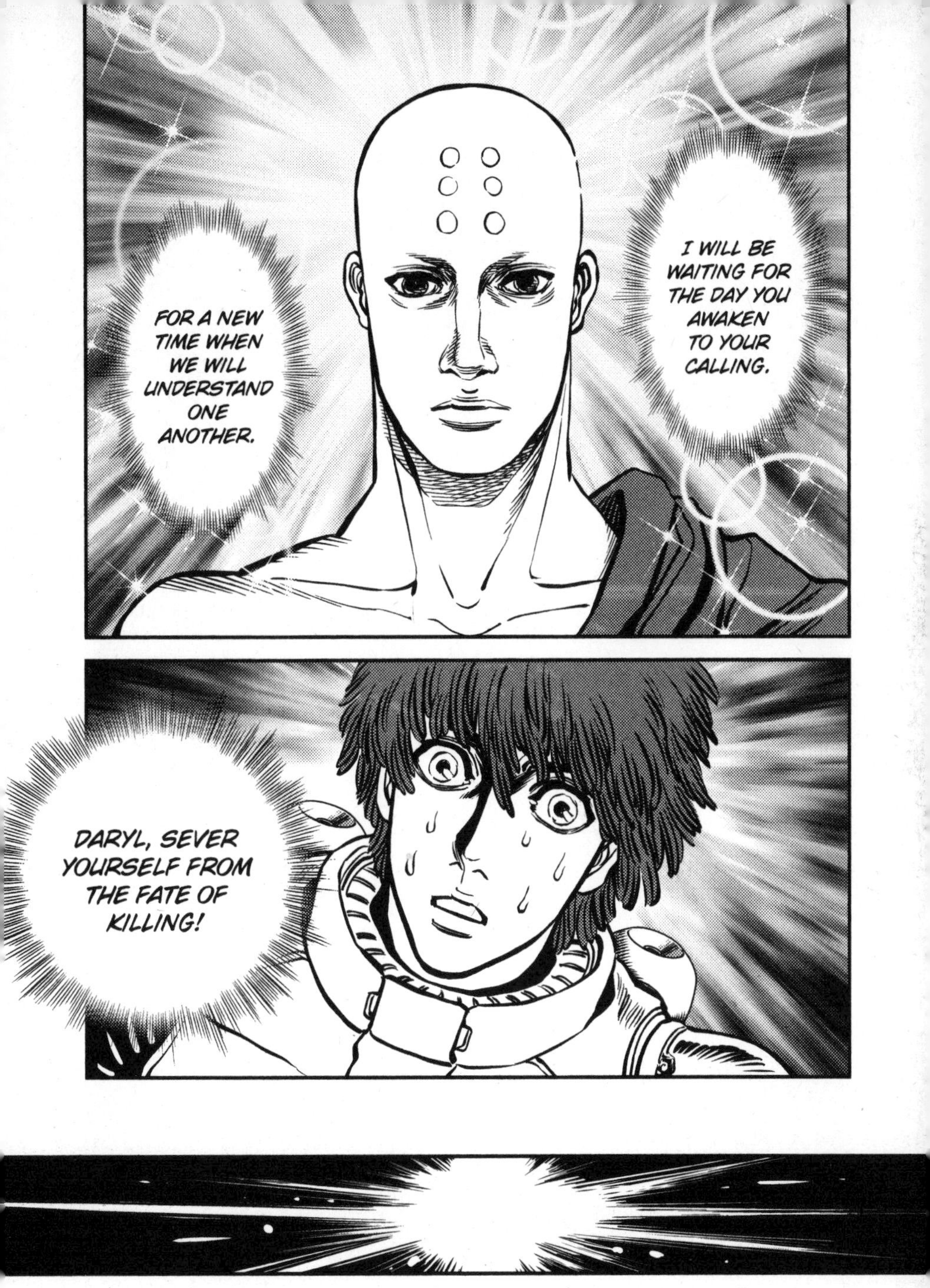
I WILL BE WAITING FOR THE DAY YOU AWAKEN TO YOUR CALLING.
FOR A NEW TIME WHEN WE WILL UNDERSTAND ONE ANOTHER.
DARYL, SEVER YOURSELF FROM THE FATE OF KILLING!

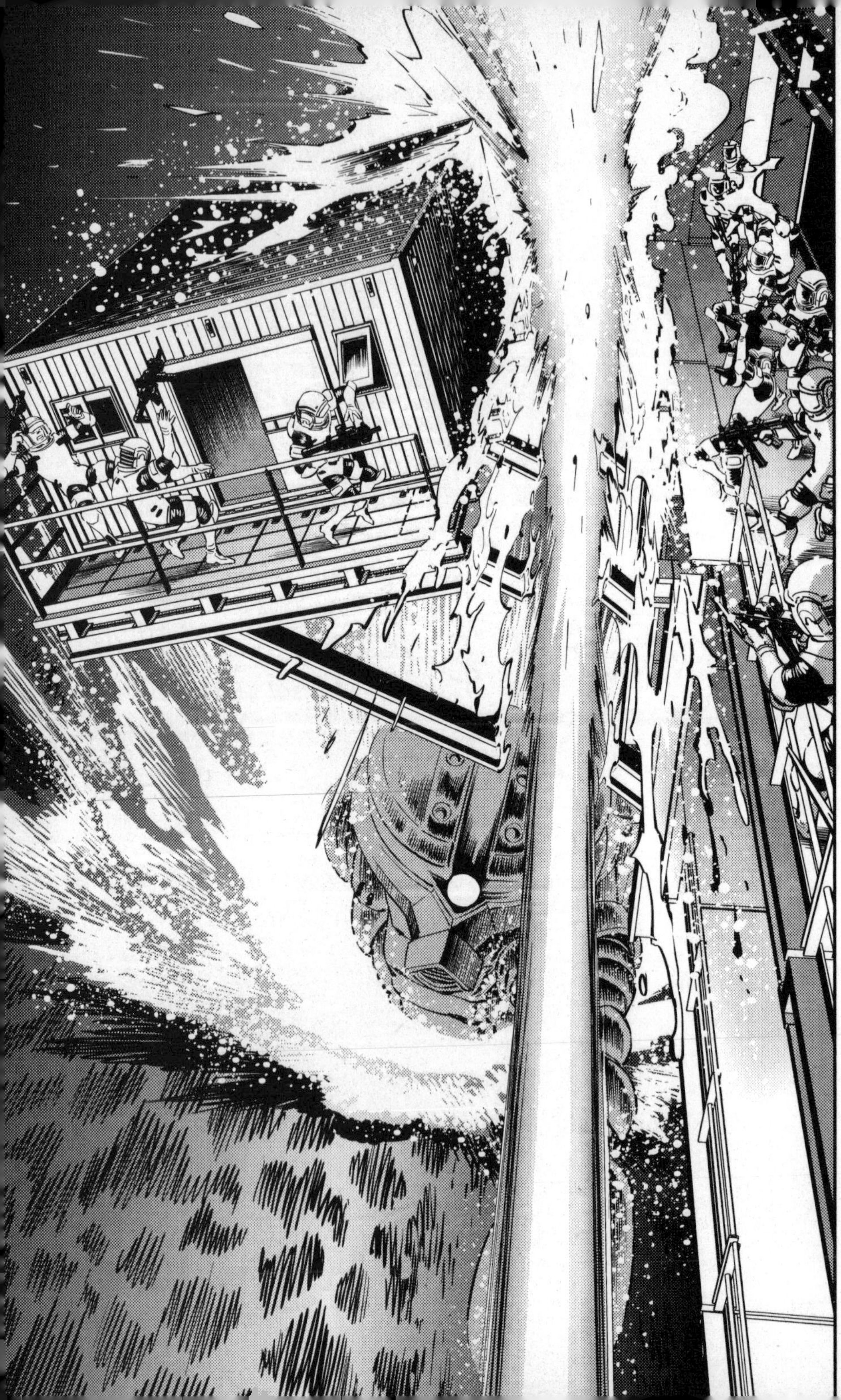

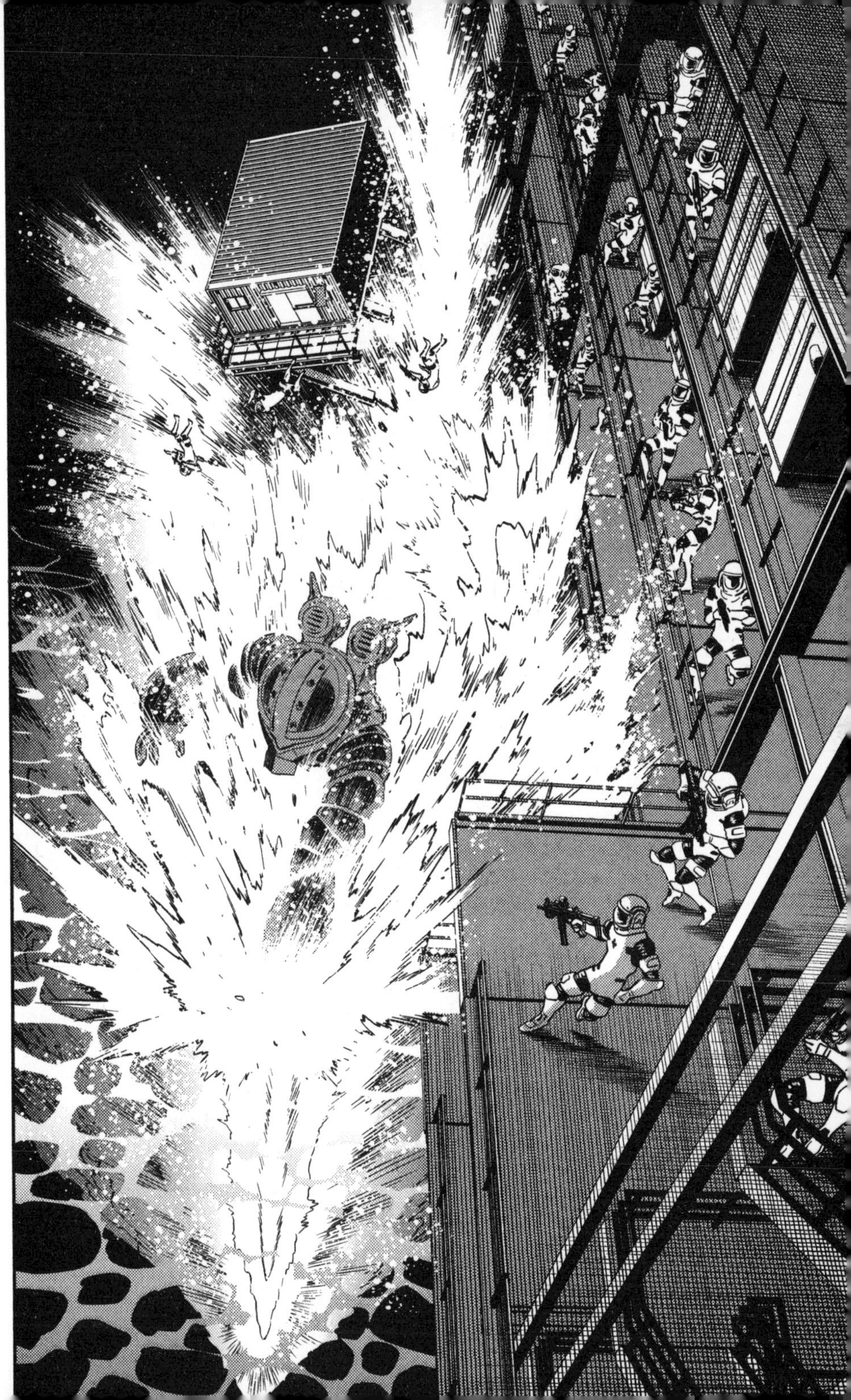

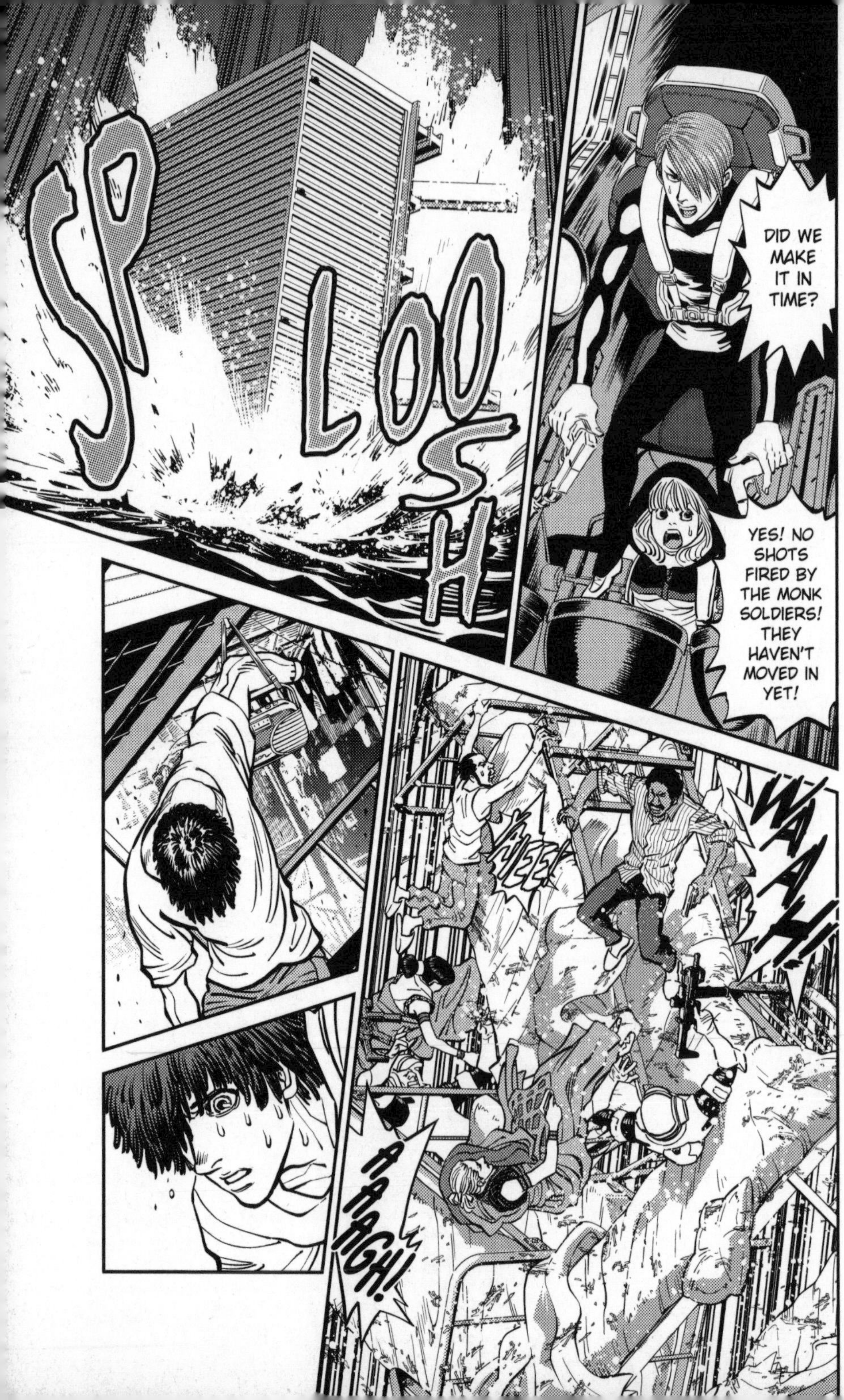
DID WE MAKE IT IN TIME?
YES! NO SHOTS FIRED BY THE MONK SOLDIERS! THEY HAVEN'T MOVED IN YET!
SPLOOSH
WAAAH!
WHEEE!
AAAAGH!

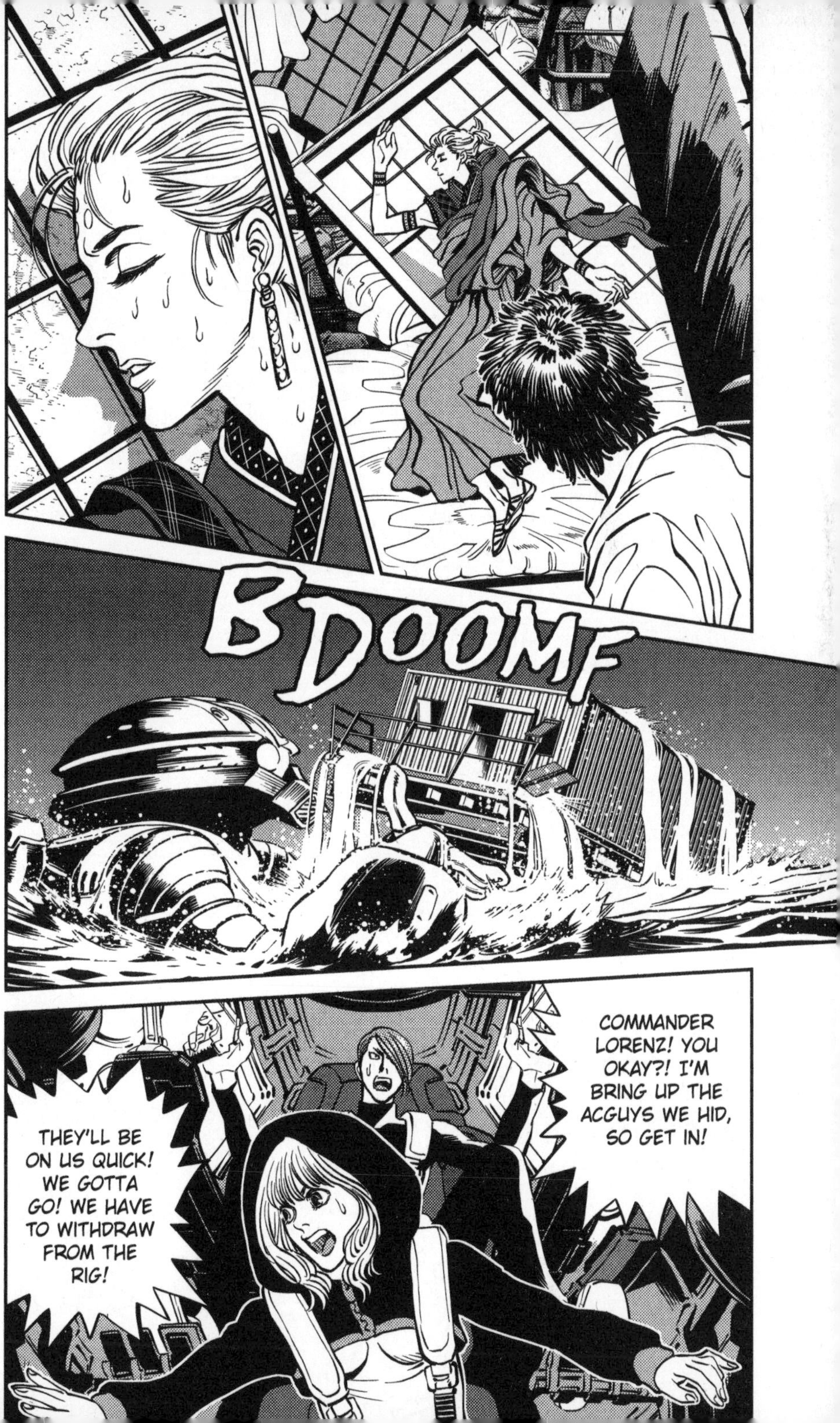
BDOOMF
COMMANDER LORENZ! YOU OKAY?! I'M BRING UP THE ACGUYS WE HID, SO GET IN!
THEY'LL BE ON US QUICK! WE GOTTA GO! WE HAVE TO WITHDRAW FROM THE RIG!

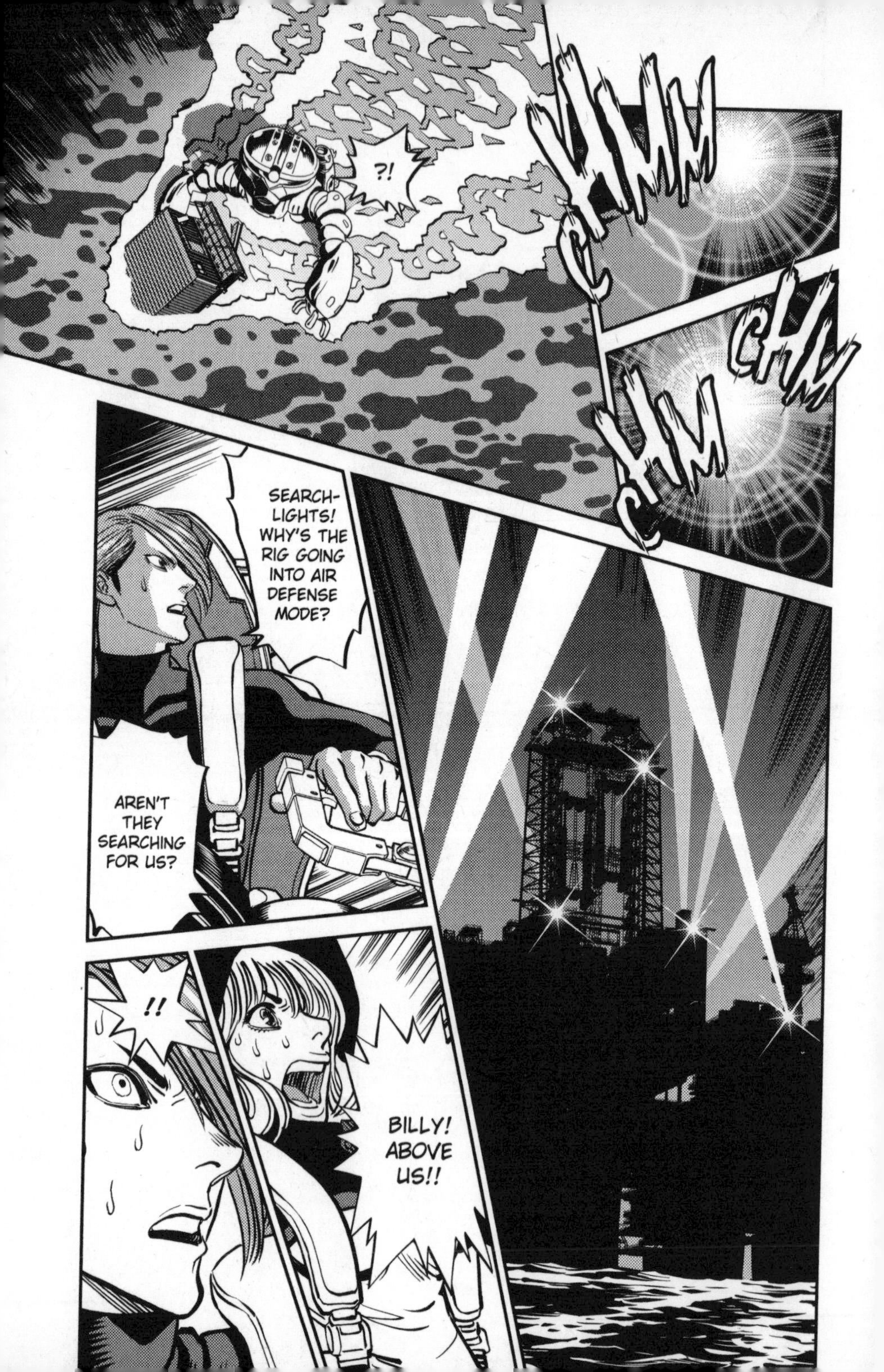
CHMM
CHM
CHM
?!
SEARCH-LIGHTS! WHY'S THE RIG GOING INTO AIR DEFENSE MODE?
AREN'T THEY SEARCHING FOR US?
BILLY! ABOVE US!!
!!

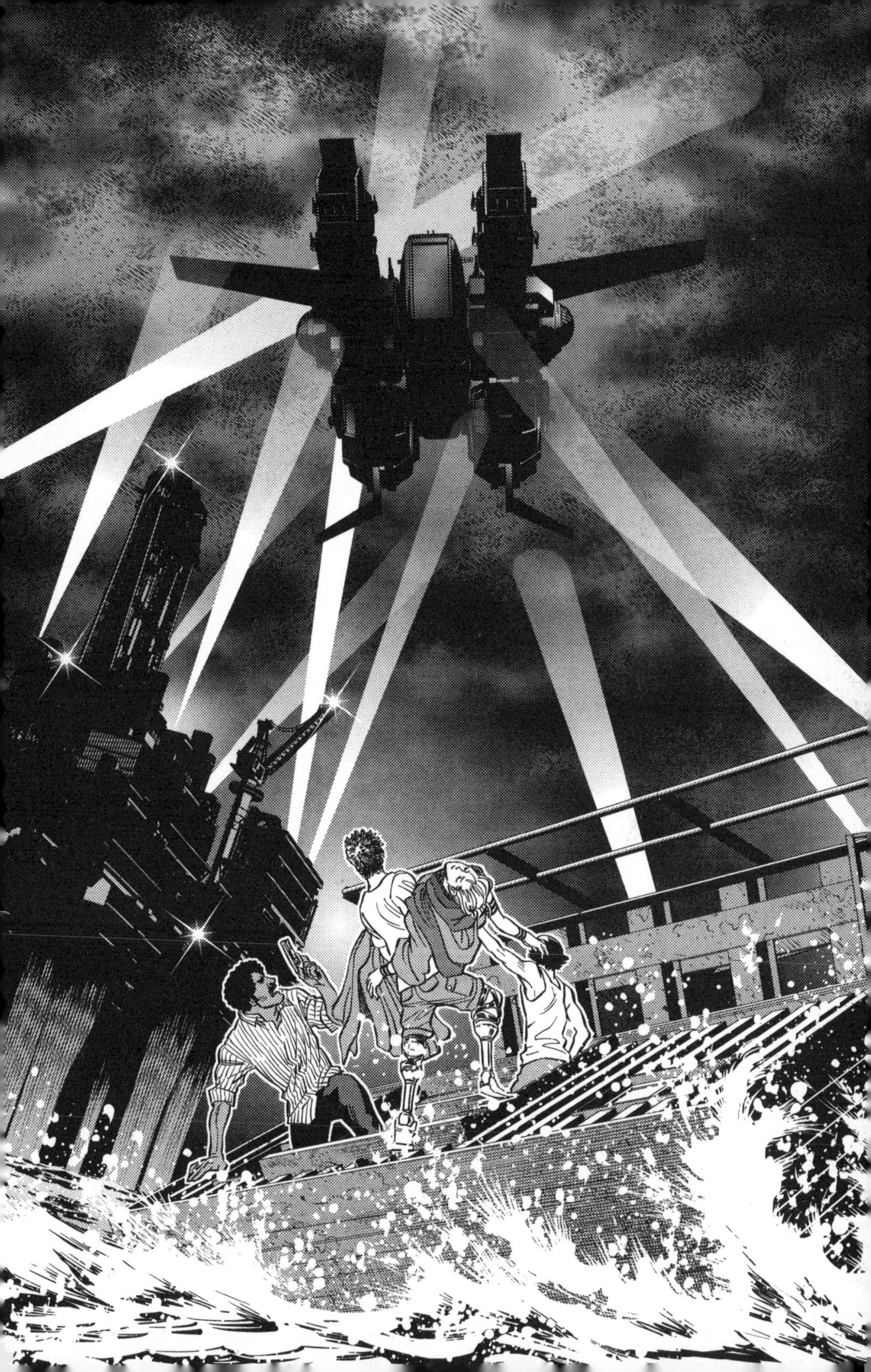

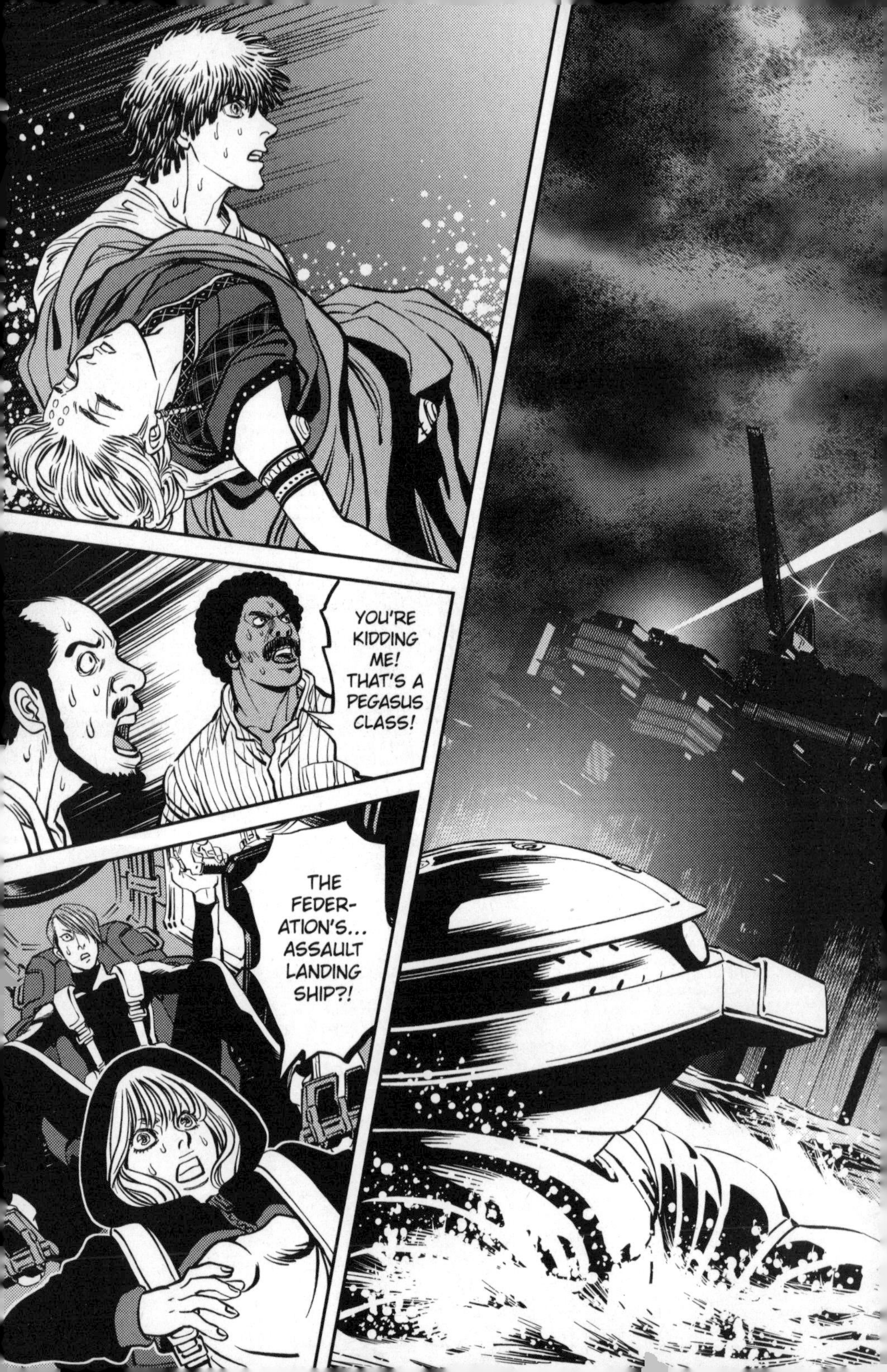
YOU'RE KIDDING ME! THAT'S A PEGASUS CLASS!
THE FEDERATION'S... ASSAULT LANDING SHIP?!

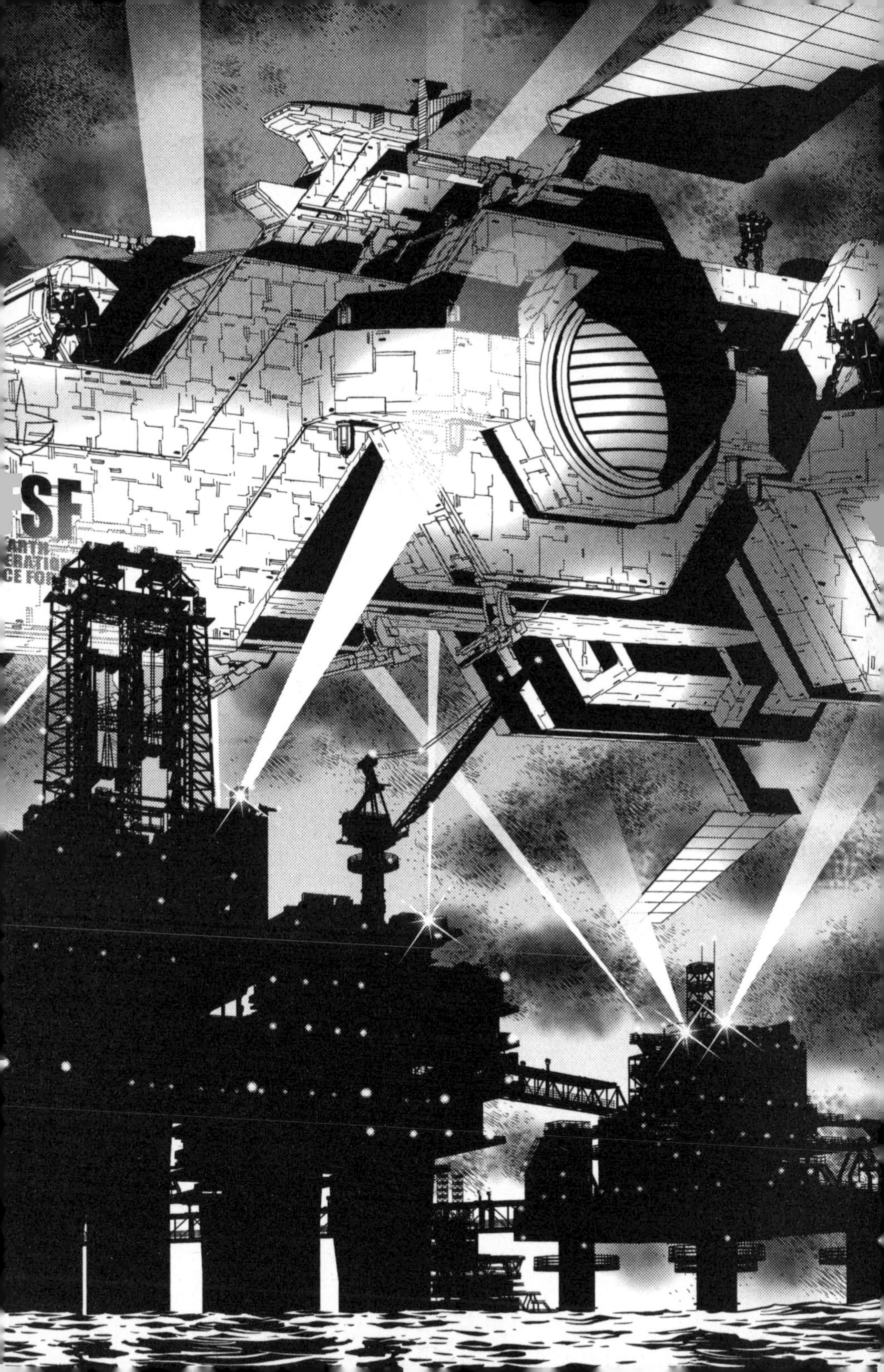
SF

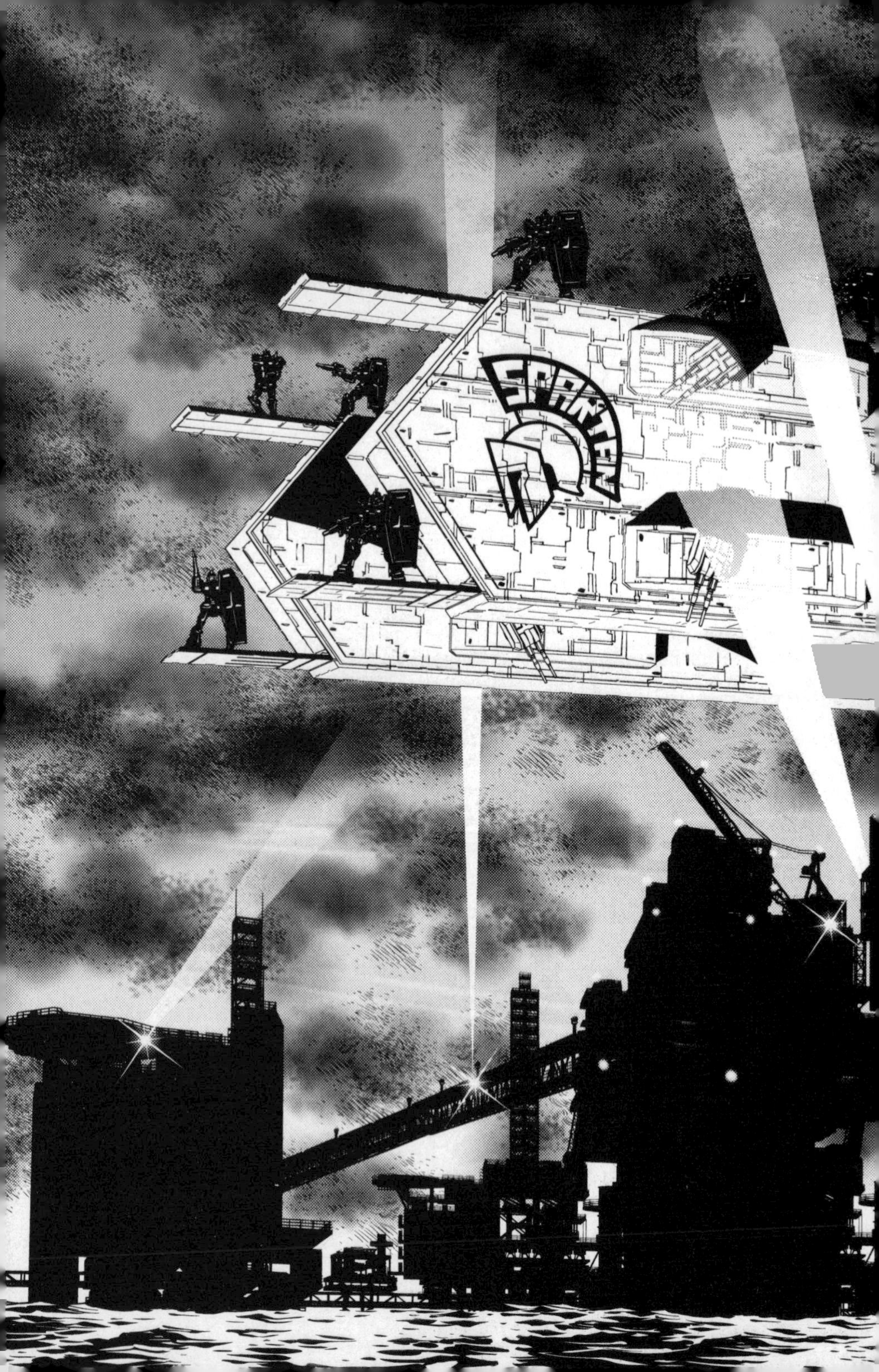
SPARTAN

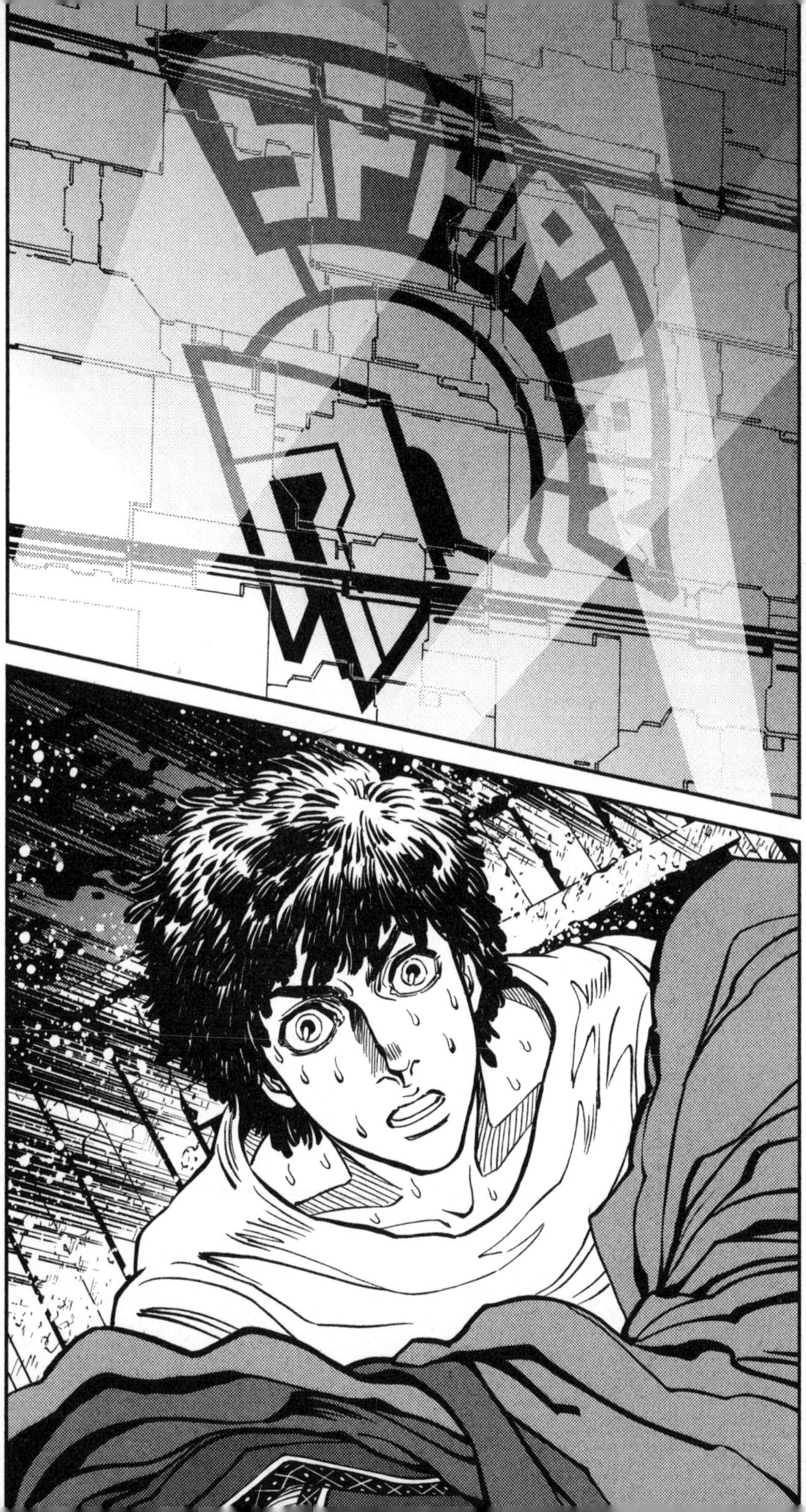

MOBILE SUIT GUNDAM - THUNDERBOLT - VOL. 8 - END

TO BE CONTINUED

STUDIO TOA S.P.A

Executive Director	**Yasuo Ohtagaki**
Chief	**Sayaka Ohtagaki**
Production Manager	**Hideki Yamamoto**
Drawing Staff	**Ryosuke Sugiyama**
	Izumi Yamada
	Shota Sugawa
	Rikuka Kawahara
	Chisato Kawahara
	Tomomi Sawada
Guest Designers	**Ju Ishiguchi**
	Takuya Io
Special Thanks	**Digital Noise Ltd.**